INTERETHNIC
RELATIONS

INTERETHNIC RELATIONS

An Essay in Sociological Theory

E. K. Francis

ELSEVIER

New York / Oxford / Amsterdam

ELSEVIER SCIENTIFIC PUBLISHING COMPANY, INC.
52 Vanderbilt Avenue, New York, N.Y. 10017

ELSEVIER SCIENTIFIC PUBLISHING COMPANY
335 Jan Van Galenstraat, P.O. Box 211
Amsterdam, The Netherlands

Library of Congress Cataloging in Publication Data

Francis, Emerich K   1906-
 ` Interethnic relations.

    Bibliography: p.
    Includes index.
    1. Ethnic groups. 2. Race problems. 3. Nationalism. I. Title.
GN496.F7   301.45'1   75-8271
ISBN O-444-99011-9

Manufactured in the United States of America

Designed by Loretta Li

*This book is dedicated to
the memory of my mother
and to all the women
who formed my life.*

Contents

Contents

Preface

This book covers a wide range of human interest. The period of history which, in the West is drawing to its close, has been called the Age of Nationalism (Kohn, 1962). The emergence of modern nations has engendered the minority problems that have kindled two world wars. After the latest eruption, Europe, like a burned-out vulcano, seemed to have come to rest, at least temporarily. A new sense of international solidarity—nourished by fear and the subconscious wish to repress recent memories—was reflected in a waning interest in national problems. Yet Ireland, Belgium, and Spain are reminders that the unresolved residues of nation-building are still very much with us.

The nations that the white man established in other continents have created ethnic and racial problems of their own. Here, too, minority groups—once a preoccupation of American sociology—disappeared momentarily from the agenda of learned societies. Yet black unrest is again drawing public attention to interethnic relations. As more and more colonial peoples have emancipated themselves politically, the story of Europe seems to repeat itself: Katanga, Biafra, Bangladesh, to name but a few. At the same time, the influx of Commonwealth immigrants to England, of foreign laborers to West Germany, have generated, or foreshadow, problems that parallel those in the United States at the height of industrialization. No wonder that since the mid-sixties scores of publications in our field are once more accumulating.

I

Despite the ubiquity of ethnic problems, there really exists no generally accepted designation for the subject matter of the present study. Particular aspects, it is true, have been treated under different labels by several learned disciplines, such as ethnology and anthropology, history, political science and law, social psychology and sociology, but the essential underlying unity has been recognized by few. Lack of a standardized nomenclature made the choice of a telling title difficult. A title that enumerated suggestive terms, such as *Nations, Peoples, Races, Minorities,* was one alternative. Descriptive book titles of this kind had been popular in Central Europe (e.g., Neumann, 1888;

Seipel, 1916; Renner, 1918; Salomon, 1927) but are now out of fashion. One knowledgeable reader thought *Ethnicity and the State* more appropriate. However, this would not have properly reflected the range of my argument. Eventually the present title was adopted, which had been my original working title. It seems to be reasonably suited to indicate the general topic. The reader, however, must not relate it exlusively to "ethnic groups" as commonly understood, but must consider ethnicity as a universal dimension of human relations, even if its relevance in social-action orientation and its actual virulence depend on the historical situation.

The subtitle signals my intention to make a contribution to social theory rather than to describe and analyze a variety of ethnic phenomena. Although all science is "theoretical," proceeds by abstraction, and aims at generalization, there are different degrees to which a scientific statement may be "theoretical." My original ambition was indeed to formulate a deductive theory of the ethnic group. When I told this to Morris Janowitz, who was then still a graduate student at Chicago, he shot back: "Why don't you write a theory of the group?" More than I realized at the time, he was right in suggesting that theory construction in some sociological specialty was not possible, except within the framework of a general sociological theory. More recently, the same insight was expressed by van den Berghe: ". . . the failure to arrive at a theory of race relations may simply reflect the fact that the subject has no theoretical leg to stand on (1967, p. 6)." Traces of my initial idea are still reflected in the last part of this book, which I have presumptuously labeled "Outline of a Theory." Even if I had to relinquish the attempt to present a general explanatory theory of interethnic relations, I still believe my approach to be genuinely "theoretical." What I had hoped to accomplish was a consistent conceptual scheme that would consolidate the terminologies of several relevant social sciences, and thus make it possible to utilize their accumulated knowledge. My second, and more important, aim was to arrive at a comprehensive set of interlocking empirical generalizations on the basis of evidence supplied by four social sciences, and selected from three continents and different historical periods. The subtitle, therefore, signifies that this was meant to be an essay in inductive theory as a stepping-stone "toward a theory" in the stricter sense of the word.

II

The general design suggested the mode of exposition I have chosen. A quarter of a century ago, I was inspired by Homans' *The Human Group (1950)* to adopt the case method. What he wrote of its nature, merits, and drawbacks also applies to my own procedure. Since a general knowledge of this classic can be presumed, a brief reminder should suffice. The case method appears to be appropriate, Homans seems to say, because "general theories . . . arise out of, and [are] supported by, specific, detailed matters of observation" (p.18). The statement is two-faceted: it implies that in an empirical science, generalizations are not only extracted from, but are also proven by, factual evidence. It is not easy to reconstruct the actual course of scholarly production, which rarely follows the precepts of methodologists who are more interested in the logical structure of science than in the psychology of scientists. In his book, Homans gave the deliberate impression that his findings had been essentially the result of inductive reasoning, although a closer inspection shows that he had probably arrived at his generalizations by both inductive and deductive methods, which in all likelihood is the more common procedure of theory construction in the social sciences.

Quite another question is the mode of exposition through which discoveries, by whatever devious means they may have been made, are presented to a scientific community and (if all goes well) eventually incorporated in the body of a science. This rhetorical aspect of the case method was obviously not the least reason for Homans' advocacy of it. "A case method," he explains, "does not deal with isolated facts" but gives "a connected body of information" (p. 18); it is "concerned with the total situation" as well as "the nature of the totalness." He concludes: "We must not, in the classical manner, use isolated facts to back up our theory, but related facts" (p. 19). Thus, the method of presentation is a matter of both verification and rhetoric.

When we review the long line of textbooks, general compendiums, as well as specialized theoretical monographs in the field of interethnic relations, we find that most of them exhibit an abstract, topical structure of discourse. Frequently, the facts and data consist of fragments culled from a variety of sources, often torn out of context, which are used to illustrate some theoretical statement or to demonstrate its validity without, however, amounting to logically conclusive proof—which is not to say that the method of using isolated facts to support a theory is always bound to fail. As Homans remarks, "many good theories have been established in this way" (p. 18). It goes without saying that there are scores of monographs reporting on field studies of isolated cases that have made significant contributions toward a general theory: I have drawn heavily on some of them for both their descriptions and generalizations. Moreover, a number of authors dealing with interethnic relations in a more general, theoretical manner have adopted a method of exposition similar to my own, although perhaps not as consistently or extensively.

In summing up, these are the reasons for my heavy reliance on the case method for presentation: (1) factual evidence can be properly evaluated, by the author as much as by his peers, if presented in the context of a total situation; (2) the method is most appropriate for empirical generalizations and inductive theory; (3) the reader is able to judge for himself whether the author has succeeded in proving his point; (4) the method is not only apt to demonstrate to a more general public a typical mode of theory construction in the social sciences, but also to structure the process of understanding psychologically rather than logically, which adds the flesh and blood of experience and intuition to the skeleton of abstraction and generalization; and (5) it is also easier to keep the mind alert by analyzing reports of actual field research than by discussing learned arguments.

At this point, a major objection comes to the mind: Is it legitimate to generalize upon so few instances even if they are entire case studies? The inductive method does not necessarily require to repeat attempts at falsification, which are as likely to succeed the first as the nth time. Moreover, I have not relied on the one type case, which I eventually selected for presentation because of its paradigmatic qualities. Many more case studies not included in this book have been analyzed over the years by myself or by assistants and students. In addition, fairly broad studies of the literature and some field research, which was carried out too casually to be suitable for publication, as well as the manifold personal experiences in many lands and walks of life, have supplied me with sufficient relevant knowledge to handle empirical materials judiciously.

The strategic role that the case studies occupy in the present context made their selection all the more crucial. In addition to my own limited field work, I had to rely on the secondary analysis of published reports. Success depended heavily on the quality and completeness of the information. In many instances I found classical monographs in sociology and cultural anthropology best suited for my purpose. This had one drawback: the serious student was acquainted with them, whereas the same could not be assumed of other prospective readers. Even at the risk of repetition I was compelled to recapitulate their accounts rather naïvely and in detail so as to present all the information necessary for an understanding of my own interpretation of the evidence. Furthermore, for each theoretical argument I had to find a telling type case. At the same time I had to keep many relevant factors as constant as possible to utilize the comparative method. Finally, although it was not feasible to duplicate the research and check the findings of my informants, I took care to have at least some firsthand experience of, or a "general feel" for, the situations described. This narrowed down the choice of empirical material geographically to Central and Western Europe, North America and sub-Saharan Africa.

The conditions with which I had to cope explain but do not excuse some serious gaps. The entire orbit of socialist countries had to be excluded; for apart from my own ignorance, sufficiently reliable field studies are as yet not available; studies that would allow a really responsible analysis of how Marxist theory and practice actually affect interethnic relations, and how, *in their real consequences,* they differ from Western nationalism. I equally regret my inability to study Arab nationalism and the impact of Mohammedanism on ethnic problems. In fact, no high civilization other than our own has been taken into consideration.

I consider it a lesser drawback that few of the case studies have a high degree of actuality. Lack of actuality is no argument against using a particular case for theoretical purposes. Sociological theory, after all, cannot be based on other than accomplished fact and on processes that have run their course. The "actuality" of the theory presented in this book is not to be found in the empirical material, which has been collected many years ago, but in its applicability to future research and to the solution of current practical problems. Theory is valid only for the assemblage of the variables that it takes into account. If marginal conditions change, the theory may still account for the disturbance. The "laws" that govern interethnic relations in modern societies need not "determine" our fate. Their recognition can serve as a means to better it. If we want to forestall the ethnic and racial conflicts that are bound to arise in nation-states, one should perhaps put those "laws" out of action by changing political doctrine and practice; that is by abandoning the principles and legal fictions on which nation-states are built.

III

If a more personal remark may be allowed in an author's preface, then this is the place to explain how I came to write what I did. To me science is a human device to aid man in his endeavor to solve his practical and intellectual problems with a higher degree of reliability than other sources of knowledge seem to guarantee. As for sociology, I am convinced that it must be firmly rooted in the facts of social life in order to be at all distinguishable from philosophy. I have never considered sociological theory as an end in itself, but rather as a guide to, and instrument of, empirical research. Nor did I consider the theory of interethnic relations merely for the sake of cerebral satisfaction. It was rather the other way around.

As an Austrian I was confronted with national and nationality problems from early youth, and I have had to cope with them throughout most of my life. The upsurge of nationalism after World War I put its stamp on my intellectual development. While training as a philosopher and historian, I became intensely interested in the principles with which the national movement, then spreading like wildfire, tried to legitimize its claim to power. During the nearly twenty years that I spent in Canada and the United States, I had the opportunity to experience race problems in a different setting. It was there that I turned to sociology as the discipline which, in America, was leading in ethnic research. There I also became associated with some of the top scholars in the field, such as Everett Hughes, Robert Redfield, Louis Wirth, and Herbert Blumer, all of whom offered me much personal encouragement. Teaching appointments in America, Europe, and Africa not only enabled me to try out earlier versions of the present book, but also brought me into close contact with students belonging to a variety of "minorities" and "new nations"; to them no less than to colleagues I owe important information and lasting stimulation.

My practical concern with interethnic relations was also the initial reason for engaging in field studies, first in Central Europe and later in America. Soon, however, I realized that good empirical research depended on good theory which was difficult to obtain at the time. Thus, to solve the problems that occupied me, I was forced to take up theoretical research of a quite general and interdisciplinary kind.

This book has taken several decades to write and rewrite. It is based on earlier essays, most of which have been collected in a German publication under the title of *Ethnos und Demos* (1965). Even before its publication, I began to prepare for an elaboration of the same general theme in a much more systematic manner, which took me many years to complete. The central theme of my work concerns the contradictions between the principles on which the modern nation-state is based and its inability to solve the ethnic problems that these inconsistencies have engendered. Although nationalism is still with us, it seems to me that the nation-state has run its course. I have little hope that, within its own framework, more promising methods of solving its innate conflicts will be discovered. Human ingenuity will have to invent novel designs of social and political organization to avoid repeating past mistakes and disasters. In this, the knowledge of an age, which I have tried to sum up and consolidate—without, however, venturing to suggest recipes for improvement or practical advice—should provide the kind of aid to social action that an empirical, nonnormative science has to offer.

IV

Two strands of thought, which I have symbolized by the Greek words *ethnos* and *demos,* are at the bottom of this dissertation, although they are not presented precisely in the sequence they had taken shape. My initial professional interest was in "minority groups," and Part III, dealing with this aspect of social structure, remains the heartpiece also of this book. At an early stage of my field studies, however, I realized that, no matter how such obviously related terms as "minority," "ethnic group," or "nationality" had been defined, they were bound to lead to absurd conclusions, except in the context of the modern nation. Yet the common-sense meaning of this word, as much as innumerable attempts made by various scientists and sciences to define it, proved no less inconsistent and confusing. Eventually, I realized that "nation" was not a scientific but a political concept, which became intelligible only in its relationship to the nation-state.

In studying the antecedents and nature of this particular species of political power structure I discovered that the nation, which the nation-state subsists, was a "historical type" in the sense of Max Weber, and a product of Europe, whence it has spread to other parts of the world. The crucial problem of nation-building appeared to be the integration of preexisting societies into superordinate political power structures. Although the components of large-scale political structures are bound to be ethnically heterogeneous, the idea of the nation-state requires that its entire population form a unity of purpose arising from a common culture. An inspection of the facts showed that the heterogeneous population of a modern state is integrated into its structure by dint of specifically "national" institutions, which link the individuals directly to the central authority without the mediation of subsocietal, including ethnic, units. When further studies revealed that such mechanisms were not confined to the nation-state, the term *demos* suggested itself to indicate that the nation was but a variety of a more general type of global society. Such considerations constitute the bulk of Part II, which relies heavily on evidence supplied by history and political science.

This left me with the task of clarifying the general role of the ethnic factor in society. To this end I turned to ethnology, whose very name indicated that the *ethnos* is its central concern. In Part I, ethnological evidence reveals not only ethnicity to be a human "universal," but also the demotic devices by which ethnically heterogeneous components may be articulated with the polity. The findings presented in Parts I and II enabled me to analyze with greater confidence the ethnic problems of modern society, which are generally created on the one hand by national ideology and policy, and on the other by industrial economy, especially the migrations brought about by it. Accordingly, Part III is, in a stricter sense, more sociological than the first two. In Part IV an attempt has been made to apply the insights gained in the preceding sections to the interpretation of ethnic phenomena in colonial and postcolonial situations typical of the so-called Third World.

V

The manner in which the book has grown makes it extremely difficult to specify its sources. The mode of exposition is not suited to argue with the teachings of other authors. Such information is contained in *Ethnos und Demos,* to which I must refer the reader. He may, however, rest assured that I am acutely aware to what extent I am standing on the shoulders of many others, too many to list here. Yet I must confess that at times I have been more confused than enlightened by ever-new and contradictory opinions and arguments as they came to my attention. In such moments I often felt that I had to stop reading and concentrate on my own thinking. Moreover, individual portions were written at different times, and not necessarily in the sequence in which they are now presented. Although I have endeavored to keep abreast of new publications, once the over-all structure of the discourse had been established, it was not always possible to bring earlier parts in line with recent literature without substantial rewriting. At one stage it became mandatory to close the account and strike a balance.

While I was plodding along, frequently interrupted by the demands of my academic duties, the student revolt, and personal adversities, books anticipating some of my own findings were published. The question of priority is besides the point. But I could not very well cite sources not yet known to me when I made my discoveries. However parallel inventions are not unusual. On the contrary, new insights are supported by the fact that they have been gained independently and along separate ways. Whatever merit my book might have should be looked for not so much in the details but in their totality. Ultimately, the design as a whole will have to stand on its own feet.

VI

Junior staff members and advanced students of the Sociological Institute in Munich have assisted me in sifting the wealth of literature that has been published on the general subject matter of this book. Some of them were specialized in ethnology, history, economics, and philosophy. They prepared abstracts of research reports and submitted position papers on a variety of topics. Drafts of the manuscript were discussed and criticized in regular team sessions. Mr. Cord Culemann, Dr. Bernd Zimmermann, and particularly Dr. Dominic Kofi Agyeman have done more than their share in preparing Chapters 24 and 25 of Part IV. Since I have closely edited and, in large part, rewritten their drafts, I take the final responsibility for these portions, just as I do for the rest of the work.

Frequent changes in personnel make it impossible to express my deep gratitude for their invaluable cooperation except by listing their names alphabetically (although nature, volume, and significance of individual contributions have varied greatly): Dominic K. Agyeman, Denise M. Baur, Kristine Binder-Krauthoff, Geneviéve Bonieux, Alfons Buchdrucker, Walter L. Bühl, Cord Culemann, Ingrid Drexel, Ulrich Fleischmann, Stefan Gaitanides, Gabriele Gerngroß, Margit Grubmüller, Michael Hall, Paul Kellermann, Horst Krähe, Gilbert Kutscher, Christoph Lau, Helmut Loiskandl, Josef Lukatsch, James L. Morrison, Franz U. Pappi, Luis M. Pujana, Conrad Schuhler, Horst Schusser, Gerlinde Schwappach, Irmgard von Stedman, Sieglinde Tömmel, Yasuada Yawata, Bernd Zimmermann. Several of my former associates have done significant research of their own. Their published works are mentioned in the bibliographies. The remainder, especially drafts of case studies not included in this volume, are deposited at the Sociological Institute of the University of Munich.

I am particularly indebted to Mrs. Denise Baur and her gracious mother, Mrs. Monica Sherwood-Smith, as well as to Mr. Michael Hall for their effort and skill in editing the manuscript and in improving upon its language and presentation. I am also thankful for the loyal services of the Institute's secretaries, especially the sisters Annemarie und Inge Kröner, Mrs. Inge Pethram, and Mrs. Monika Hoff.

The greatest debt, however, is owed to Herbert Blumer, upon whose suggestion I embarked upon this venture. He has lavished encouragement and advice upon its progress ever since. Last not least, I wish to thank Mr. William L. Gum, Elsevier's Editorial Director, whose enterprise and generosity I have come to appreciate greatly during the time of our cooperation.

A theoretical treatise of this kind is probably not suited for class use as a regular textbook in ethnic relations, but should prove useful as a reference and source book in upper-level college and graduate courses. Beyond sociology, I hope that it will also appeal to scholars in the fields of history, political science, and anthropology. It should tap the current interest in "new nations," and it is my hope that it will be read also in the Third World. There are still other possible uses. I have never been entirely satisfied with the general text books (including my own paperback) that introduce beginners to sociology. Would it not be more effective, I kept thinking, if basic concepts and theories were explicated by demonstrating their use in analyzing one particular dimension of social life? In fact, what I have tried to do all along was nothing more than to unravel the skein of social relations by following one particular thread through all its interweavings with other strands. Thus the book could also have its place in interdisciplinary studies in the history of modern civilization, in social evolution, or quite generally, in the humanities.

Innsbruck, in the Spring of 1975

E.K. FRANCIS

R E F E R E N C E S [1]

Francis, Emerich, *Ethnos und Demos: Soziologische Beiträge zur Volkstheorie*. Berlin: Duncker und Humblot, 1965.
Homans, George C., *The Human Group*. New York: Harcourt, Brace & Co., 1950.
Kohn, Hans, *The Idea of Nationalism*. New York: The Macmillan Company, 1961.
———— *The Age of Nationalism: The First Era of Global History*. New York: Harper & Bros., 1962.
Neumann, F. J., *Volk und Nation*. Leipzig: Duncker & Humblot, 1888.

[1] For copies of Munich doctoral dissertations, write to Universitäts bibliothek, Dissertations stelle, Geschwister-Scholl-Platz 1, 800 München 22.

Renner, Karl, *Das Selbstbestimmungsrecht der Nationen in besonderer Anwendung auf Österreich*, Teil I: Nation und Staat (2nd ed.) Leipzig: Franz Deuticke, 1918.

Salomon, Gottfried (ed.), *Nation and Nationalität*. Jahrbuch für Soziologie, Erster Ergänzungsband. Karlsruhe: Verlag G. Braun, 1927.

Seipel, Ignaz, *Nation und Staat*. Vienna: Braumüller, 1916.

Van den Berghe, Pierre L., *Race and Racism: A Comparative Perspective*. New York: John Wiley & Sons, 1967.

INTERETHNIC RELATIONS

THE ETHNIC FACTOR IN SOCIAL INTERACTION

I

INTRODUCTION

The subject matter of this book does not have a definite place in the social sciences, nor has the designation "interethnic relations" a generally accepted meaning. In the past, particular aspects of it have been treated by various specialists, but traditions have differed from country to country. The essential unity and homogeneity of the problems involved have as yet been recognized only vaguely. Worse still, no standardized terminology exists to verbalize our intentions in a readily intelligible manner. Several approaches are available for a general introduction.

DIALECTICAL APPROACH

A critical discussion of the relevant literature is widely used as a springboard. If some aspect of a mature science is concerned, a historical survey seems well suited to sensitize the reader to a particular problem emerging from the present state of the science. In our case this would hardly be successful; it would certainly be much too cumbersome. A more traditional method of exposition consists in arguing the merits or failures of past attempts made by prominent scholars to cope with the problem under scrutiny. This approach may properly be called dialectical in one of the several meanings of the word (cf. Gurvitch, 1962). More recently it has been used by Schermerhorn (1970, pp. 3–85) in the extended introduction to his book on ethnic relations, and more succinctly also by van den Berghe (1967, pp. 2–11) for the limited field of race relations. It is hardly necessary to repeat the attempt.

1

Neither Schermerhorn nor other authors writing on the subject have defined it as broadly as will be done in this book. Lack of a definite scholarly tradition makes it necessary to search for some other method of introducing the reader to the entire range of our endeavor. Depending on the nature of the problem and the state of the science, it is often quite sufficient to point at commonplace experiences and common-sense concepts. Yet the elements of everyday speech pertaining to the subject matter of the social sciences are, as a rule, meant to serve a practical rather than a theoretical purpose. Since they are apt to be loaded, it is dangerous to rely on them. Even a list of more technical terms that have been used by different sciences to designate some aspect of the general problem would be inadequate to outline its perimeter.

Whenever several academic disciplines are involved, as in the present case, an added difficulty arises, because the different sciences have their own traditions, perspectives, idiosyncrasies, and idioms. One cannot introduce technical terms that have been developed within the framework of one science without translating them into the language of the other relevant sciences, or at least relating to each other different terms that apparently have a similar meaning. It is therefore difficult to make widely scattered ethnic research cumulative and productive of theoretical insight without first consolidating several scientific languages. Yet, overexpansion and duplication of terms tend to obstruct the standardization of terminology and the tightening of definitions. Connotations of words that have been coined to cope with definite historical phenomena, which have a precise meaning only in a particular historical and cultural context, such as "nation" or "race," are bound to lead to unwarranted inferences and conclusions if applied to different phenomena in other settings. Equally misleading is the use of terms originating in different frames of scientific discourse for essentially homologous phenomena, such as "tribe" and "people" or "nationality," "minority," "cultural" and "ethnic group"—duplications that frequently occur as a result of the separate development of different sciences and the relative lack of communication between them. In any event, it is hazardous to make a selection from the available range of terms simply according to one's personal preference.

Semantic Approach

Instead of following the historical or dialectical method, some authors prefer to begin with the semantic analysis of key terms to arrive at a common understanding of their meanings and the general problem these are meant to cover. When settling on one definition two alternatives are open: either we stipulate the denotation of a word or we consider all the instances that are conventionally designated by it and try to find an element common to them. Yet, as A. D. Smith remarks: "Both procedures have their disadvantages. . . . The first tends to narrow down the field in a highly arbitrary manner, while the second usually fails to come up with a sufficiently distinctive common denominator which can mark off the phenomena from other related ones" (1971, p. 166). Smith sees a solution to the dilemma in the construction of ideal types. Since his theme happens to be theories of nationalism, he sets out by using the term "nationalism" in its broadest meaning of "collective resistance to foreign rule," and goes on "to ask if there are additional common elements." On occasion, this method has been adopted also in the present volume, for instance, when dealing with political concepts related to nationalism and racism. Otherwise, we have found it unsatisfactory to use words in their broadest meaning. The concepts we need for our present purpose are, as a rule, defined in so many different ways that the attempt to come up with the least common denominator is apt to yield definitions on so high a level of abstraction that they are nearly meaningless.[1]

The semantic approach raises still other problems. Numerous attempts, including our own (Francis, 1965), to critically analyze the words that at one time or another have been employed in connection with our subject matter, have revealed not only a profusion of terms but also a confusion of concepts. It has been repeatedly shown that whichever conventional definitions are chosen, they are bound to lead to inconsistencies in their application to comparative research, and that the traditional taxonomy does not adequately cover all the empirical facts in question. Moreover, the signification of words is frequently changing, either in answer to changing social conditions or political interests, or without apparent scientific reason under the influence of some current fashion. Occasionally, different words, originally coined to make an important distinction, are used interchangeably or their meaning is even reversed. This has happened more than once, for instance, with regard to the pair "nation" and "people" and their equivalents in other languages (cf. Hertz, 1927; Francis, 1965, pp. 60–87).

---

[1]This is also true of Smith's suggestion because absence of foreign rule, or resistance if threatened, is implied in the concept of a politically organized society. It would seem redundant to introduce a term that has assumed a rather specific meaning for such a common phenomenon. Moreover, nationalism need not find its actual expression in the struggle to remain or become independent, nor is such behavior confined to it. It often concerns intrasocietal rather than intersocietal relations.   An earlier attempt by MacIver (1948), which follows a similar line of reasoning, shows more clearly the kinds of questions such definitions are apt to raise. He defined "nation" as "a community so coherent by sentiment that it possesses or at least strives to possess political autonomy." When he describes "nationality" as "a type of community sentiment . . . so strong that those who feel it desire to have a common government peculiarly or exclusively their own" (p. 155), he follows Max Weber, who defined the nation as "a common bond ot sentiment whose adequate expression would be a state of its own, and which therefore normally tends to give birth to such a state" (1946, p. 176). Does this imply that every strongly coherent community (e.g., a religious sect) strives for political autonomy? Would it not be necessary to specify the kind and size of communities which, if they have political aspirations, may be considered a nation? Would an isolated and politically independent tribal village also be a nation? Could this concept be applied to prenationalistic India, medieval Burgundy, or a Greek city-state? Should we consider the French-Canadians a nation just because they have a great deal of political autonomy in the Province of Quebec?

Process Approach

The method we intend to adopt can be called "process approach." Apart from the remarks included in the Preface, we shall make no further attempt to outline the scope of this treatise, but simply invite the reader to follow our argument patiently from the beginning to the end.[2] This, however, does not answer the need of a common means of communication since, as we have seen, everyday English will not suffice. We propose to develop our special language as we go along. Our preoccupation with conceptualization calls for an explanation. The philosopher Yves Simon (1952) once wrote: "Since human knowledge normally approaches perfection by moving up from vagueness to precision, there is nothing shameful about being vague, although it is a shame to do nothing about it. But is is much worse to counterfeit precision when vagueness is the real state of affairs." Now, the perfection to which sociology aspires is the standing of an exact science. This cannot be achieved without that precision of concepts which the nature of its subject matter permits. Theoreticians, of course, have always been aware, as one of them insisted, that "without 'good' . . . concepts it is impossible to develop confirmable theories, and without the development of confirmable theories the fruitfulness of concepts cannot be determined" (Levy, 1952, pp. 236f.).

Terminological Problems

There is no compelling reason for adopting any particular frame of discourse, nor is there any limit to the formation of concepts except our imagination. Within a scientific theory the choice of concepts is, nevertheless, anything but arbitrary. Although concepts cannot be said to be either true or false, their "goodness" depends on their expected utility in the process of improving upon, or adding to, human knowledge. Obviously, no science can rely entirely on carefully defined technical terms: it must start with everyday language. Moreover, in our much-discussed field of study, there are also many scientific concepts ready for use. Yet, not all available concepts are adequate for our purpose.

Our principal aim, as stated in the Preface, is the attempt to arrive at empirical generalizations concerning a class of social phenomena (which so far have been dealt with by several sciences under different perspectives) in order to make comparative ethnic research cumulative and productive of new theoretical insights. Ultimately, a cluster of interlocking generalizations will be synthetized into a consistent, though by no means complete, "narrow-gauge theory" of interethnic relations.[3] In this way, it should become possible to

---

[2]The impatient may be referred to the Outline of a Theory in Part V.

[3]Easton's "narrow-gauge theories" are remindful of Merton's "theories of the middle range." For the present purpose we prefer the former term. Merton's definition (1949, p. 5) puts the emphasis, with an undertone of regret, on a self-imposed limitation reflecting the actual state of sociological

understand not only the phenomena to which these generalizations are originally related, but also other phenomena which had hitherto been shrouded in doubt (Easton, 1953, p. 56).

In keeping with this aim, we propose to follow the inductive method. Induction begins with the inspection of directly presented data in order to find "by trial and error the postulated entities and relations which are the epistemic correlates of the inspected data" (Northrop, 1947, p. 119). The data upon which we intend to generalize are included in the case studies. However, the presentation of their contents poses a terminological problem. Since their authors have been motivated by different interests and follow different scientific traditions, it becomes necessary to establish one language for all of them. But this can only be done gradually. As a first step, we will have to settle on one designation for a familiar concept even if the authors themselves have used different words.

Additional problems arise in interpreting and comparing the results of individual case studies. Certain phenomena, which have been viewed under different aspects and named differently, must be demonstrated to constitute one homogeneous type, while other phenomena, which so far have been assumed to belong to one class and have been conceptualized accordingly, must be shown to represent in actuality different types. Any important reclassification also requires redefinition. Sometimes, the meaning of traditional terms has to be narrowed, at other times, broadened. Moreover, when hitherto unnoticed relationships between classes of phenomena are discovered, this has to find its expression also in the definition of the relevant concepts. The procedure of reclassification and redefinition, however, is difficult to explain in the abstract; it will be better understood by inspecting its actual application.

Another consideration is of more immediate interest. In sociological textbooks one finds the tendency to introduce sets of synonyms and to define them differently for no better reason than the widespread use of different words. It does not appear to be particularly fruitful to adopt a word first and then to ask what it "really" means. We have tried to observe parsimony in our terminology, and have introduced new terms only when they were indispensible in coping with a particular problem or situation. In this way the reader is able to follow the thought process that has led to the adoption of terms.

---

theory. Easton, on the other hand, points at the logical structure of inductive theory. Empirical generalizations simply state that experience shows that all the phenomena classified under some significant category possess certain common characteristics; that—as far as our experience goes—certain variables have always been associated with each other in a certain way, but not why it is so. "A necessary generalization asserts not only that the proposition has always been verified in fact but that it is necessarily always true at all times and in all places" (Furfey, 1953, p. 76). For this purpose, a deductively formulated theory is required. But generalized descriptions are not simply substitutes for a "real" theory that is not yet available. On the contrary, narrow-gauge theories are not only indispensible stepping stones toward an all-embracing, explanatory theory which may never materialize (many respectable sciences have to go without such a theoretical system), but they have their own value because they promote a better understanding of human affairs and even permit predictions with a greater or lesser degree of probability.

But our procedure has its disadvantages. Occasionally, the concepts that we have adopted after much trial and error do not exactly fit in any scientific tradition. Thus, scholars may feel that we have defined familiar terms in an unorthodox manner. It might be better if we had introduced artificial symbols for designations. Although this might have eliminated irksome connotations, the discourse would have become unnecessarily clumsy and difficult to follow. We have therefore tried to strike a middle road. As a rule, we have adopted terms whose common meaning came nearest to the one intended by us; at the same time, giving them precise denotations by way of careful definitions, and then invariably sticking to one meaning even if this did not exactly add to the elegance of diction.

ETHNICITY

With all these qualifications and mental reservations, however, we cannot do entirely without at least a minimal vocabulary as a starting point for the ensuing discussion. Our key term will be *ethnicity*. By it we shall understand the ethnic aspect in social behavior. It generally expresses the fact that certain people are socially defined as belonging together by virtue of common descent. Ethnicity may be said to be dominant if it is salient in the orientation of social action, especially in determining the personnel of a social unit as well as the rights and obligations of the people involved.

A global society in which the ethnic principle of action orientation is dominant, that is, in which social action is primarily defined in ethnic terms, we shall call an *ethnic society*. Because in common parlance as well as in professional language, *society* has at least seven or eight possible meanings (cf. Francis, 1963, pp. 418f.), we shall use the term *global society* to indicate the most comprehensive type of social collectivities with which people actually identify themselves at a given place and time, and within which solidarity may be activated. Not only global societies but also their components may be dominated by ethnicity. In this sense we shall speak of *ethnic communities, ethnic subsocieties, ethnic groups,* and so on.

We shall occasionally find it difficult to determine from the outset under which class of social phenomena a particular unit of observation should logically be classified; for this reason, until the point has been clarified, we need a more general term. We shall call an *ethnic unit* any major collectivity that is socially defined in terms of common descent. Our discussion will furthermore reveal that societal units that are ethnically quite heterogeneous and actually based on territorial, economic, or political principles of social organization may be reinterpreted and socially redefined as if they were based on shared ethnicity. We shall call such units *secondary ethnic societies*. More precise definitions for each of these terms will be supplied as we go along.

Global societies are rarely completely self-sufficient and isolated. Together with other global societies, they operate within a wider social context with somewhat vague boundaries. Insofar as such a context is defined in ethnic terms, we shall speak of an *ethnie*. Obviously, the ethnic factor differentiates people as much as it identifies them. We therefore shall use the phrase *shared ethnicity* to indicate that an aggregate of people are considered as belonging together because of the belief that they are descended from one, however distant, ancestor, ancestral pair, or ancestral group.

Genealogical Relationships. Before we can attempt to give a more precise meaning to the notion of ethnicity, we must pay attention to two more basic and ubiquitous dimensions of social organization: genealogical and spatial relationships. A genealogical relationship exists when people are socially defined as forming a social unit or category, as "belonging together," because they are considered related to each other through consanguinity ("blood") or affinity (by marriage). Groups based on the genealogical principle of social action orientation include the family and various other kinds of kinship groups, such as the lineage and the clan.

Wherever the rule of exogamy prevails, members of one family naturally belong to different lineages and clans. Yet marriage and family bonds are the principal mechanisms by which several kinship groups are joined together into larger structures. Thus, in a given population intermarriage between members of many different kinship groups often produces an intricate web of consanguinal and affinal relationships. Even if interaction between the components of a social web primarily based on genealogies is infrequent and intermittent; even if social ties are rather loose; and if the cohesion of the whole remains so rudimentary that it can hardly be described as one "global society"—such a unit nevertheless lends itself to the social interpretation that underlies the notion of what we have called *shared ethnicity*.

Spatial Relationships. The second fundamental dimension of social organization is spatial relationship. It is based on the fact that people are commonly defined as forming a social unit because they live together in one place, and because they collectively make their living there, usually by exploiting its natural resources. (Spatial proximity is not only one precondition for establishing social relations, but where technology is less developed, it is the most important precondition.) Spatial relationship can also reinforce genealogical relationships. Not only do larger kinship groups tend to reside in one place and to occupy and exploit the same territory, but living in the same locality increases the chance of intermarriage, thus multiplying kinship ties. Accordingly, there is a tendency to extend the notion of shared ethnicity to the population of a definite place or territory, even if actual genealogical relationship between all its component family and kinship groups cannot be established nor clearly remembered.

Consciousness of Ethnicity. We must not imagine that the people forming an ethnic unit are constantly aware of being a definite aggregate of related persons occupying a territory with definite geographical boundaries beyond which lie the lands of different ethnic units; or that their shared ethnicity is constantly evident in their thoughts and actions. Whereas the family or the local community are matters of immediate daily experience, the ethnic unit—vaguely conceived as a complex web of kinship ties (often more symbolic than real) covering a wider territory—more often than not is of latent significance but only rarely activated. A fact it is, nevertheless, and it has its definite consequences for actual behavior under certain circumstances. Moreover, it cannot be taken for granted that populations having a common language and culture, being subject to one political power structure, or exhibiting similar racial (or subracial) characteristics are necessarily identical with those real societal units which we have described as ethnic. For these can only be identified by determining how far actual social behavior is guided by the principle of ethnicity.

There are yet other circumstances that complicate the task of discovering real ethnic units. Although these latter belong to the largest order of societal units in which traces of identification and solidarity may be ascertained, there are still other units that may be activated in different situations. Thus, shared territory may serve a function similar to that of shared ethnicity in establishing a societal unit and in legitimizing it. The phrase "shared territory" refers to the fact that people are defined socially as belonging together because they occupy a circumscribed area of land and exploit its resources cooperatively. Then again, political unity may be symbolized and legitimized by reference to territorial jurisdiction. The total web of processes that makes up a societal unit may be likened to an assemblage of magnetic fields, each affecting different populations and becoming activated in different situations. Two such fields are of primary interest to us: the ethnic field, the attraction of which is exerted through the dimension of kinship in the widest sense; and the demotic field, the attraction of which is felt in the political dimension.

A further distinction will help bring order to the wealth of available ethnographic materials. Ordinarily, social scientists are dealing with politically organized societies. Yet the study of social systems having no distinct and separate political institutions is apt to throw considerable light on the nature of ethnicity. Whilst among some of them, like the Mandari, societal identity and solidarity is derived from legitimate and religiously sanctioned ownership of, and jurisdiction over, a definite territory; others, like the Nuer, stress genealogical and ethnic bonds to set themselves off from all others who do not belong. Societies in which the exercise of political power is diffused among a variety of subsocietal structures performing many other functions as well have been called "segmented political systems," "tribes without rulers," or "acephalous societies," a term coined by Max Weber.

More common, however, is the type of societal unit with differentiated political institutions where political functions and authority are vested in special agencies acting for the whole. When found in primitive societies, this type conforms frequently to the modern notion of a global society. There is no great difficulty in defining a politically organized tribal society in terms of identity and solidarity. As far as the first criterion is concerned, we should distinguish between synchronic identity, which answers the question of who belongs to a given society at a given time, and diachronic identity, which answers the question of how the collective identity of a society is maintained through time. In some of the cases to be discussed below, synchronic identity is based on the allegiance of individuals and groups to one definite ruler. By *allegiance* we understand the recognition of a binding obligation to support a ruler and to submit to his political authority. In such instances, the identity of the tribal society through time may be derived from the continuity through descent within the dynasty, clan, or lineage to which successive rulers belong. Although solidarity is expressed mainly through participation in some subtribal unit, sentiments of loyalty and devoted attachment to the ruler, and thereby to the tribe as such, can be readily activated in emergencies such as war or other situations involving the tribe's existence and well-being.

PLAN OF PART I

In the following analysis of type cases we propose to progress from simpler to increasingly complex social structures; from tribes without rulers to politically organized societies; and in Part II, from tribal societies to empires and nation–states. Our primary concern is always the meaning of ethnicity and its specific role in various social interaction patterns, and the integration of ethnically diverse groups in existing societal units. We are, however, interested neither in the origin of human society nor in the goal towards which mankind is progressing. Man, in his attempt to solve the problems of his existence, to make social life possible, tolerable, and productive of higher values, has gone many different ways in the course of the ages, and has invented many different devices of social organization only to discard them again and to start out in another direction. The particular arrangement of our case studies was determined with a view towards discovering fundamental elements of social organization and of social change wherever we were able to ascertain them empirically. Thus, the logical sequence of presentation was chosen because it seemed best to serve our stated purpose not to indicate a necessary sequence from the simple to the complex.

Our first concern will be with tribes without rulers. The Nuer case serves as a paradigm of a fairly large ethnie. In proceeding to politically organized tribal societies, we are mainly interested in the manner in which ethnically diverse elements become integrated into a politically organized society. This may be achieved in several ways: (1) by establishing genealogical relationships between a paramount ruler and the chiefs of the component units (type case: the

Tswana); (2) by superimposing upon the component tribal units a superstructure linking the paramount ruler directly to his subjects (type case: the Zulu); and finally (3) by progressively substituting demotic bonds for genealogical relationships, thus transforming an ethnically heterogeneous population into a politically organized society (type case: the Ganda).

A last, more technical note: in each of the following case studies an attempt is made to reconstruct the situation as it existed just before strong and direct European influences made themselves felt. For their presentation, however, it seemed convenient to use the present rather than the past tense.

REFERENCES

Easton, David, *The Political System: An Inquiry into the State of Political Science*. New York: Alfred A. Knopf, 1953.

Francis, E. K., "Soziologie," in *Staatslexikon: Recht, Wirtschaft, Gesellschaft,* vol.IV (6th ed.). Freiburg i.B.: Verlag Herder, 1963.

———, *Ethnos und Demos. Soziologische Beiträge zur Volkstheorie*. Berlin: Duncker and Humblot, 1965.

Furfey, Paul H., *The Scope and Method of Sociology: A Metasociological Treatise*.

Gurvitch, Georges, *Dialectique et Sociologie*. Paris, Flammarion, 1962.

Levy, Marion J., Jr., *The Structure of Society*. Princeton, N.J.: Princeton University Press, 1952.

Merton, Robert K., *Social Theory and Social Structure: Toward the Codification of Theory and Research*. Glencoe, Ill.: The Free Press, 1949.

MacIver, Robert M., *The More Perfect Union: A Program for the Control of Inter-group Discrimination in the United States*. New York: Macmillan Co., 1948.

Northrop, F. S. C., *The Logic of the Sciences and the Humanities*. New York: Macmillan Co., 1947.

Schermerhorn, R. A., *Comparative Ethnic Relations: A Framework for Theory and Research*. New York: Random House, 1970.

Simon, Yves, "From the Science of Nature to the Science of Society," *The Owl*, June 1952.

Smith, Anthony D., *Theories of Nationalism*. London: Gerald Duckworth and Co., 1971.

Van den Berghe, Pierre L., *Race and Racism: A Comparative Perspective*. New York: John Wiley & Sons, 1967.

Weber, Max, *Wirtschaft und Gesellschaft: Grundriss der Verstehenden Soziologie*, translation in *From Max Weber: Essays in Sociology*, ed. by H. M. Gerth and C. Wright Mills, New York: Oxford University Press, 1946.

Ethnicity in Acephalous Societies

1

The ethnic factor in social organization stands out most clearly in tribes without rulers where cohesion is established essentially by genealogical relationships. An impressive example is provided by the Nuer, among whom the genealogical basis of identification and solidarity is gradually extended from the lineage and the clan to the tribe and, finally, to the largest social unit based on the notion of common descent, the ethnie.

THE NUER

The Nuer, numbering about 200,000, are a Nilotic people of the Southern Sudan with a rather primitive technology.[1] Their main source of livelihood is stock breeding. During the rainy season they also cultivate small patches of land around their villages, which are built on sandy ridges that are from five to twenty miles apart. Most of the year the Nuer live in the villages, but during the dry season they gather with their cattle in camps. Thus, when we wish to study the role of shared territory among them, we must consider both village and camp as elementary social units.

SPATIAL RELATIONSHIPS

The local community consists of an interlocking web, not only of spatial but also of genealogical and economic relationships. A Nuer village is composed of homesteads, each occupied by a nuclear family in which ownership of cattle,

---

[1]Abstracts of empirical materials included in this section are adapted with the permission of the publishers from E. E. Evans-Pritchard, *The Nuer: A Description of the Modes of Livelihood and Political Institutions of a Nilotic People*. Oxford: Clarendon Press, 1940a.

land, wells, as well as stores of home produce and tools is vested. A household is thus defined in terms of family ties, place, material possessions, and everyday activities, mainly of an economic nature. The village is conceived of as an extended household whose members not only live in spatial proximity, but actually maintain close contacts, are personally known to each other, and interact frequently and regularly. Many activities in village and camp are undertaken collectively by members of several households, nearly always kinsmen to whom mutual aid is both a right and obligation. Even when there is no active cooperation, the whole community passively participates in all economic enterprises. Although food is provided by and for individual households, it is actually shared by all villagers.

This simple and clear-cut structure of the local community is somewhat blurred by the institution of cattle camps to which the families move during the summer, leaving the village site deserted. Scarcity of forage and water force them into a seminomadic existence; camps are set up and left again. They vary in size, regularly increase at the peak of the dry season, but are abandoned as soon as the rains threaten to flood the open savannah. In the camps cooperation and intimate association between members of different families are, if anything, still more intensive. Yet, not all the people of a village gather in the same camps, and families from other villages are also admitted on occasion. Nevertheless, the total area utilized for farming and grazing is considered to belong to one definite village. Although its permanent site may be shifted and the boundaries of the grazing lands may undergo change, the local community always maintains its identity. The reason becomes clearer once it is realized that common habitat and the economic exploitation of a given territory are not the sole foundation of the local community.

Social relationships in a Nuer community are established in many other ways: members of a village support each other in feuds and fight side by side in wars. Social bonds are furthermore initiated and strengthened through gifts of artifacts, food, or cattle. Even kinship relations are sanctioned through the exchange of cattle and symbolized in these terms. This is particularly true of the bride-wealth; that is, the cattle to be supplied by the groom in entering a marriage. Finally, visiting and feasting reinforce the economic and kinship ties within the local community so that a sense of identity, sentiments of solidarity, and a lasting attachment to the place result.

Similar relations are also established between people living in adjacent villages through group visits, common festivities, intermarriage, joint raiding parties, or feuds between lineages. The cattle camps offer added opportunities for people belonging to neighboring villages to associate even more closely. The Nuer word for an aggregate of intensively interacting village communities is the same as for a single village; it signifies a community based on spatial proximity.

In addition, there are larger combinations of local communities. Such subtribal divisions are superimposed upon each other like geological layers for special purposes only. Fighting—either with each other or together against a larger

division of equal rank—provides the most conspicuous activity and the principal social bond between the subtribal divisions. Yet the alliances for raiding
and fighting come to an end at an important point: the tribe. Within its territory
the institutions of blood-feud and blood-wealth are operative, of which more
will be said below. Beyond it, warfare is unrestricted and no compensation for
homicide is either called for or acceptable.

Nevertheless, social relations do not stop at the boundaries of the tribe. Not
only may Nuer tribes form temporary federations, particularly for warlike purposes, but members of one tribe may also be permitted to graze their cattle or
even to settle permanently on the territory of another tribe. Contacts between
border settlements belonging to different tribes may be more frequent and
intimate than those among distant settlements of the same tribe. Moreover, if
strangers from different tribal sections of Nuerland meet, friendly relations can
be established without difficulty.

GENEALOGICAL RELATIONSHIPS

So far we have dealt with territorial units which, under certain circumstances, become activated so that real groups emerge which cooperate for
specific purposes or are linked together through regular patterns of conflict.
The situation cannot be properly understood, however, without taking into
consideration the kinship relations that not only constitute territorial units but
also cut across them and bind them together. Social order in Nuerland is always
expressed in kinship terms. Thus, everyone with whom one has any actual
dealings can be approached through a kinship relationship, real or fictious,
which—in the last analysis—is determined by the relative genealogical status of
the parties concerned. "Ultimately and potentially everybody is kin or can be
made appear so if circumstances demand" (Evans-Pritchard, 1940b, p. 290).

All rights and duties within any social unit are ascribed on the basis of one's
position in the kinship structure. No patterned interaction can take place unless
one knows the kinship relations between the actors involved. Social position in
kinship terms is the criterion for the provision of blood-wealth and bride-
wealth.

Sentiments of solidarity end beyond the intricate web of kinship relations;
those who cannot in some way be fitted into this pattern of consanguinal and
affinal relations are aliens. Feuds, marriages, and ritual observances are the
most important occasions on which the social categories by which kinship is
determined become activated. They determine by whom and to whom blood-
wealth and bride-wealth are to be paid and in what proportion; and also which
sexual relations are incestuous and whether marriage is forbidden or advised.

There are indications that, at one time, spatial and genealogical units coincided; the local community, for instance, with a minimal lineage, the tribe with
a clan. Although Nuer lineages are widely dispersed today, members of
lineages that are dominant in a particular place, because they are assumed to be

the original and true owners of the land, still have a somewhat higher prestige in their territory of origin, and are given a special name: "dil." In contrast, a person belonging to a Nuer lineage other than that claiming priority in a given place is called a "rul." The designation, "jaang," is used for foreigners who have become integrated into a local community and, consequently, into the tribe.

The Jural Community

The tribe is not only based on a network of genealogical relationships and on shared territory, it represents also a jural community. Among the Nuer, as we have already indicated, conflict is as important a factor as cooperation in strengthening social bonds and in giving rise to social units. Fighting and violence are perfectly acceptable forms of social interaction. There are regular patterns of armed conflict between various divisions of Nuer tribes. From time to time bands of young men raid the herds of their neighbors, take away their land, women, and children, and inflict all sorts of harm upon them. Robbery, depredation, and conquest, no doubt, are means of exploitation. Yet the economic rewards are not the sole reason for such raids. For among Nuer youth, fighting is socially encouraged as an opportunity to prove oneself a real man. Social recognition, prestige, and power, for both collectivities and individuals, depend on prowess in fighting.

Violence of this kind is bound to result in bodily injuries and homicides. In the Nuer culture any homicide, whether resulting from a dispute between individuals or from collective fighting between social units, activates at once the solidarity of the close agnatic kin of both slayer and slain; for it is the duty of the lineage to exact vengeance. The chain of mutual killings, which is the inevitable outcome, is called a *blood-feud*. There exists, however, a social device for curtailing blood-feuds before they end in mutual extermination. Its main feature consists in the payment of a considerable number of cattle (*blood-wealth*) by the kinsmen of the slayer to the kinsmen of the slain, whereupon the latter agree to refrain from taking revenge. The accepted way of settling blood-feuds is by arbitration. Eventually, the parties are expected to submit their case to the so-called leopard-skin chief who is neither a ruler having the authority to restore peace in the community nor a judge entitled to pronounce a verdict on the merit of the case. His office is rather that of a qualified arbitrator. Although he may threaten to curse the recalcitrant party, he cannot determine the amount of compensation due to the injured party nor can he force them to accept the blood-wealth offered.

Ethnic Units

Compared with the local community, in which the greatest variety of social dimensions is vested, other social units (including the tribe) appear segmental.

Even if we would hesitate to call a Nuer tribe an ethnic society in the strict sense of the word, its ethnic character is beyond doubt. For the boundaries of a Nuer tribe extend as far as solidarity, by virtue of common descent, is recognized. It is this ethnic solidarity that makes the operation of the jural community possible. The tribe represents the widest web of kinship relations within which incest taboos and rules of exogamy are recognized: within it, rights and obligations are differentiated according to genealogical status. Thus, the framework of social action among the Nuer is inextricably oriented to the notion that ethnicity is a valid ground for social identification and solidarity.

The tribe, however, is neither the most comprehensive nor the most inclusive societylike unit. Although the specific bonds of the jural community are absent, and specific kinship obligations and taboos are no longer operative, all Nuer tribes taken together form a still wider, though vaguer, unit in that they are assumed to be descended from one common ancestor, named Nuer. As Evans-Pritchard puts it:

> The different local communities of a whole tribe could be presented on a single genealogical chart. Given unlimited time and patience, the entire population of Nuerland could be so presented (Evans-Pritchard, 1951, p. 29).

This is a highly impressive concretization of the basic meaning of ethnie, as the term is used in this book. Because every *rul* has a place somewhere in Nuer genealogy, he also has a definite genealogical status from which proper conduct, rights, and obligations can be inferred without difficulty. This does not mean that the relationships thus established are exclusively friendly or peaceful. We recall that Nuer habitually fight Nuer, and that regular wars are carried out between Nuer tribes in the same way as between Nuer and non-Nuer tribes. Still, under ordinary circumstances a member of any Nuer tribe may roam about freely and safely throughout Nuerland; he may visit relatives and remain there for any length of time; he may even settle permanently in another Nuer community regardless of whether it is part of his own or of a different tribe.

A Nuer is recognizable not so much by his racial appearance, which he shares with neighboring peoples, but mainly by the tattoo marks he receives during initiation. Among people who wear no clothes such marks have, besides their ritual significance, a function similar to folk costumes, badges, beards or headgear elsewhere. They serve as readily perceptible signs which make it possible to place an unknown person correctly and to interact with him properly. The Nuer are also distinguishable by a common language and culture, although in this respect, too, they bear many similarities to neighboring tribes. Although common characteristics facilitate communication and mutual understanding, they are not the reason why all Nuer conceive of themselves as belonging together and as being tied to each other through bonds of solidarity; bonds similar to those that can be activated between the members of a tribe or subtribal division. But they are weaker and vaguer; they serve rather as symbols and as a confirmation of their belief in the shared ethnicity of all Nuer.

INTERETHNIC RELATIONSHIPS

The full meaning of shared ethnicity becomes clear, however, only when one also considers its contrast effect. Foreign peoples are primarily those of different ethnic origin. Social contact may be established either with foreigners who remain united in collectivities entirely separate from one's own group or with individuals who enter it from the outside. In the first case we find that between the Nuer and non-Nuer social units the most common form of social relationship is hostility and war. Yet, as we have seen, fighting is also normal between different collectivities of Nuer tribesmen. The Nuer use different words for armed conflict: one for intratribal feuds which involve settlement by arbitration and payment of blood-wealth, the other for "international" wars in which no claim for compensation would be recognized. Although wars between Nuer tribes are rare, both intratribal feuds and wars against Dinkas are taken for granted.

Among all non-Nuer peoples the most frequent and closest relations are maintained with the Dinka. They are, as it were, the most intimate enemies of the Nuer. The frequent wars with the Dinka have far-reaching consequences for interethnic relations. Nuer war parties not only tend to linger in Dinkaland and to exploit its natural resources and its defeated population, but they also take with them captives when they return to their own territory. At times, the Nuer occupy adjacent Dinka territories permanently. Although in that case, the original owners are often forced to abandon their land, it sometimes happens that considerable numbers of Dinka stay behind or return to live among the Nuer conquerors. In peacetime Dinka also enter Nuer territory to visit relatives, to trade and, especially during famine, to take refuge with their traditional enemies. By and large, Dinka who, either as captives, as a conquered population, or of their own free will, have come to live among the Nuer, are fully integrated so that a very large proportion of the Nuer population, in some tribes as much as fifty percent, are actually of Dinka origin.

This situation provides us with an instructive example of how, under primitive conditions, foreigners may be assimilated and finally absorbed. The process is facilitated by the fact that Dinka culture resembles that of the Nuer in many respects. This cultural affinity is interpreted as an affinity through common descent. According to the myth, the founders of the Nuer people and the Dinka people were brothers, two sons of a common deity. Although they migrated in different directions and now constitute separate and distinct ethnic units, and although they have made war since time immemorial, a remote and indefinite kinship and a vague ethnic identity are still recognized, so that the Dinka are more socially acceptable than other foreign peoples. As regards their social position very definite differences exist between a Nuer *rul* and a Dinka *jaang*. Yet the methods by which they become integrated in a Nuer local community are basically the same.

There are three ways in which a *rul* or *jaang* can be transformed into a *dil*: (1) he may be adopted, and thereby assigned a definite position in a dominant lineage on equal terms with those born into it, (2) he may marry into such a lineage and thus become a cognatic kin able to establish a colateral or satellite lineage, which is then grafted on to the principal agnatic stem, and (3) by way of mythological reinterpretation of cognatic kinship ties, a female ancestor may be treated as if she were male, and thereby a lineage sister transformed into the ancestral father of a new minimal lineage. Such kinship fictions may also serve to establish relations between entire *rul* or *jaang* groups and the dominant lineage in a given territory.

CONCLUSIONS

In this chapter we have established the general meaning of ethnicity as the term will be understood throughout this book. It refers to the fact that (1) a relatively large number of people are socially defined as belonging together because of the belief in their being descended from common ancestors, (2) on account of this belief they have a sense of identity, and (3) they share sentiments of solidarity. Shared ethnicity extends genealogical relationships to a wider population whose precise genealogical nexus is unknown or disregarded. Three basic propositions may be added:

1. Shared ethnicity becomes salient in social action orientation (a) if there is a contrast effect between two or more groups of people interacting in a given social context, and (b) if the contrast can be interpreted in ethnic terms.
2. The saliency of shared ethnicity as a principle of societal organization differs with the general type of society. Shared territory may serve a similar function in organizing and legitimizing a societal unit.
3. Where the genealogical principle of social organization is dominant, there is a tendency to socially define a population sharing a common territory in terms of shared ethnicity.

Because the general theme of this book is the role of ethnicity in different types of society, we have first investigated ethnicity in acephalous societies. When the genealogical principle of social organization is dominant, there is a tendency to conceive of a tribe as an ethnic unit by basing identification and solidarity on the belief in common descent from one mythological ancestor. Several tribes may be combined into an ethnie by the belief that they have a more distant ancestor in common. Anybody who cannot be fitted into the prevailing pattern of genealogical and ethnic relationships is considered an alien. Individual aliens may be integrated into the ethnic structure by adoption, marriage or mythological reinterpretation of kinship ties. A functioning group of aliens may be integrated by attaching it as a satellite subunit to a charter kinship unit.

The remainder of this book deals with ethnicity in politically organized societies. We turn first to tribal societies. Chapter 2 will be concerned with a tribal society with an ethnically heterogeneous population in which genealogical relationships serve as the dominant principle of social organization. Our problem here is the role of ethnicity in legitimizing the political power structure.

REFERENCES

Evans-Pritchard, E. E., *The Nuer: A Description of the Modes of Livelihood and Political Institutions of a Nilotic People*. Oxford: Clarendon Press, 1940a.

———, "The Nuer of Southern Sudan," in *African Political Systems*, eds. Meyer Fortes and E. E. Evans-Pritchard. London: Oxford University Press, 1940b.

———, *Kinship and Marriage among the Nuer*. Oxford: Clarendon Press, 1951.

Multiethnic Politically Organized Tribes

2

THE TSWANA

The Tswana, numbering about 850,000, belong to the Sotho division of the Southern Bantu.[1] In the course of long drawn-out migrations, which in many respects resembled the migrations of the Indo-Europeans, Bantu tribes reached the southern portion of Africa in many successive waves, starting in the thirteenth century. This veritable African *"Völkerwanderung"* was partly checked when it encountered the Boer Voortrekkers, and was finally brought to a complete halt when the British consolidated their colonial order under the Pax Britannica. Before the arrival of the Bantu the country was inhabited by Khoisan-speaking peoples, such as the Bushmen, who are of an entirely different race and culture. The advancing Bantu either pushed the aboriginees into more remote and less desirable regions, or absorbed them into their own stock.

The Nguni proceeded mainly along the coastal areas of the Indian Ocean until, in the last century, their vanguard was stopped near the Fish River by the Europeans advancing in a broad front from the Cape. In the course of time they hived off into a great number of tribes; among these were the Swazi and Zulu (to be discussed in the next chapter). The Sotho separated from the main body of the Bantu somewhere near the Great Lakes and migrated south over inland routes. One Sotho people reached Botswana during the thirteenth or fourteenth century; the first Tswana began to move south one or two centuries later. Today the Tswana occupy a region along the eastern edge of the Kalahari desert. The bulk of them live in Botswana, the remainder in the Republic of South Africa. Other Sotho peoples are the Transvaal Sotho and the Basutu of Lesotho. The Sotho taken together may be described in our terms as a wider

---

[1]Abstracts of empirical materials included in this section are adapted with the permission of the publishers from I. Schapera,The Tswana. *Ethnographical Survey of Africa: Southern Africa,* **Part** III. London: International African Institute, 1953.

19

ethnie. They differ from their African neighbors in speech and culture; they also believe themselves to be closely interrelated and of common descent.

ETHNIC COMPOSITION

Present-day Tswana are ethnically quite heterogeneous. Fully five-sixths of their largest tribe, with a population of about 100,000, are of alien origin. The composition of other tribes is similar. Most of these alien elements—Bushmen, Sotho, and other Bantu—have become fully integrated into the Tswana people; they speak the same language, have the same culture, and are considered true Tswana. Nevertheless, differences in ethnic origin are still reflected in the social structure. Other members of Tswana tribes however—mostly later immigrants—speak non-Tswana languages, have different cultures, and sometimes form separate ethnic communities and subsocieties. It is fully recognized that they are of non-Tswana stock.

It is this situation that makes the case of the Tswana so interesting for the study of interethnic relations. The primary identification of the Tswana is with the tribe, which represents a politically organized society with a definite territory and central authority. Although ethnically heterogeneous, all Tswana tribes are considered to belong together as one people, quite distinct from other Sotho peoples. In the following analysis, an attempt will be made to uncover the social mechanisms by which such an identification in ethnic terms may be achieved among preliterates.

A clue to our problem may be provided by the fact that the history of the Sotho in general, as told by themselves, is usually related in terms of chiefs and their kinship groups, just as earlier European history is handed down in stories of kings and dynasties. Thus, most of the Tswana tribal chiefs claim descent from one ancestral ruler who had four sons, the founders of tribes still in existence. Other tribes are said to have originated in a series of fissions and fusions. The reasons given for tribal secessions are disputes over dynastic succession, jealousies and quarrels among the ruling families, insubordination and banishment of some junior member—human motives found also in the myths and heroic sagas of the European past.

LOCAL COMMUNITIES

Tswana tribes vary in size from two thousand to a hundred thousand. A major part of the tribe, sometimes all of it, is concentrated in one large settlement, the capital, which is the residence of the chief. In addition there are scattered villages ranging in size from less than one hundred to more than two thousand inhabitants. Cattle posts are occasionally located at a distance of a hundred and more miles from the permanent settlements. Herdsmen and owners of distant fields are often absent from their communities for the major part of the year. In earlier days it was customary for a Tswana tribe to reside in one place around the homestead of their chief while the attached foreigners would live in villages of their own, some distance from the capital. The present situation is far more complicated. Local communities, except for the smallest, are divided into hamlets which consist of clusters of huts arranged on a circular plan. Such a subdivision may be called a *ward*. The ward is the basic administrative unit in any Tswana tribe and is of utmost importance for its social structure.

It is probable that each ward was originally the settlement of one agnatic kinship group. Later on, some of its members moved to other communities, while strangers attached themselves to the charter lineage. The later wards are not uniform in their composition. They consist typically of about three extended family groups, each comprising several households whose heads have a common male ancestor. Such family groups are described by Schapera as kinship groups, which "may however, also include relatives of other categories, such as affines and uterine nephews, and perhaps even one or more families of unrelated dependents" (Schapera, 1953, p. 40). The family groups forming the nucleus of the wards may sometimes claim common descent or may be related through repeated intermarriage. Wards also originate in other ways; some of them are even composed of foreigners who were accepted into the tribe and placed in a particular location by the tribal chief.

TRIBAL ORGANIZATION

The entire tribe is welded together by a pyramidal system of delegated authorities. The lowest administrative unit is the ward whose headman is usually the elder of the senior family group. Several wards form a village whose headman is the head of the senior ward. Clusters of villages are organized into districts. The district head is chosen from among the village headman. The administrative officers of subtribal divisions report to the tribal chief who himself is the head of the royal ward in the capital. All subdivisions function more-or-less independently without much interference by the tribal chief; they regulate their own affairs under the supervision of their respective headman. General authority over a major division is always accompanied by special authority over a minor division. For example, a village headman is also the head of his ward, of his own family group, and of his personal household. The chief is the hereditary ruler of the tribe. He

> is the central figure round whom the tribal life revolves, and through whom the activities of the tribe are ordered and controlled. He is at once its ruler and judge, maker and guardian of its law, and director of its economic life . . . leader in war and its principal priest and magician. It is primarily through allegiance to him that the members of the tribe express their unity (Schapera, 1940a, p. 64).

If the chief has no son, the order of succession follows by seniority of descent. Only a senior member of the ruling family can succeed the chief.

KINSHIP RELATIONS

Although all members of a ward regard themselves as a body of kindred people, they are quite aware that they belong to different lineages. Also beyond the wards, "the ill-defined body of kindred, embracing all the people genealogically connected by consanguinity and marriage" (Schapera, 1940b, p. 62), binds the Tswana together in complex systems of reciprocal rights and duties. Yet kinship relations are much less pervasive here than among the Nuer. In some respects they are rather divisive, for they cut right across the administrative divisions of which we have spoken. Spatial and political relationships are far more important than kinship ties in establishing social identity and solidarity. It would seem that in a population in which kinship plays a minor role in the orientation of social action, societal unity and solidarity cannot be legitimized directly by reference to shared ethnicity (which, after all, is an extended kinship). Yet ethnic heterogeneity cannot be a major obstacle to establishing common bonds, even if heterogeneity is clearly reflected in social stratification and political organization.

CONCLUSIONS

The Tswana nucleus, like the Nuer, do interpret their identity in terms of common origin. Nevertheless, the Tswana are unable (or do not bother) to conceive and rationalize their societal unity as a web of genealogical relationships in the same way as the Nuer, partly because they do not have the same habit of expressing all their social relations in kinship terms. Political relationships are the primary data of Tswana unity; genealogical relationships are much more limited in scope, exerting their influence primarily on the level of extended family groups. The fundamental local units, the wards, are formed around the nucleus of a dominant lineage, it is true; but the wards also encompass strangers who belong, not because they are perceived as kinsmen, but on the basis of spatial, economic, and administrative solidarities.

The Tswana are vaguely conscious of the fact that a large part of their population is of alien origin. Indeed, many of the more recently absorbed foreign groups retain sufficient corporate life to be regarded as separate communities. This situation once more raises the question: How does a multiethnic society uphold its sense of diachronic and synchronic identity? How is it possible for this identity to be expressed in ethnic terms? In point of fact, two kinds of identity are under scrutiny: one concerns the identity of a politically organized tribal society; the other concerns the identity of the true Tswana belonging to different tribes.

The problem of what makes the true Tswana one ethnie is not so difficult to solve. For the alien peoples who have been incorporated into Tswana tribes at early stages of their formation have become fully acculturated, and their precise origin has been forgotten. Through a wide accessory web of affinal relationships, many kinship ties have been established between them and the Tswana ethnic core. The fact that kinship among them is not exclusively or predominantly agnatic has made it possible to eventually accept these aliens on equal terms. This does not explain, however, how the identification has been achieved in the first place when memories of alien descent were still vivid and intermarriages were as yet few.

A comparison with English history may provide a clue. In all instances we find a basic division between aristocracy and commoners, which corresponds to an early differentiation between a variety of aboriginal tribes and their conquerors. When they established their rule over conquered peoples, the Tswana might have accepted—as the Normans are known to have done—some of the native rulers and their families into their ranks. In order to strengthen solidarity they then established genealogical relationships among the upper stratum in much the same way as the Nuer do with strangers: by intermarriage and adoption.

It must be admitted that these are unverifiable conjectures. It would, nevertheless, be difficult to deny a frequent tendency to transform indentification and solidarity based on political organization and allegiance into identification and solidarity symbolically expressed in terms of kinship relations and shared ethnicity. There are indications that the Tswana of alien origin, once the distinguishing marks of alien speech and culture were overcome, tended to identify with the chief and his kinsmen, and thus with the ethnic nucleus of the tribe. The intrinsic dynamism of kinship also guaranteed the diachronic identity of the tribe as a politically organized society embracing the whole population including aliens. Our conjectures help to explain (1) why even those Tswana, who are genealogically unrelated, identify and recognize solidarity, not only with the political system of the tribe but with its ethnic base as well; (2) why the story of the Tswana is told in terms of what happened within the families of chiefs; and (3) why the relationships between the local communities within the tribe as well as those between tribes are defined in terms of genealogies of their heads and charter lineages while all other, sometimes substantial, components of their population are disregarded.

REFERENCES

Schapera, I., "The Political Organization of the Ngwato of Bechuanaland Protectorate," in *African Political Systems*. eds. Meyer Fortes and E. E. Evans-Pritchard. London: Oxford University Press, 1940a.
——, *Handbook of Tswana Law and Custom*. London: Oxford University Press, 1940b.
——, The Tswana. *Ethnographical Survey of Africa: Southern Africa*, Part III. London: International African Institute, 1953.

Rudimentary Nations

3

Available studies on the Swazi and the Zulu shed considerable light on the relationship between ethnic composition, social stratification and political organization. Moreover, the analysis of these cases reveals a new principle of political organization—the demotic—which transcends both ethnic and spatial relationships. The Swazi and Zulu live in close proximity in Southern Africa. Both belong to the Nguni division of the Southern Bantu, but have also absorbed some Sotho peoples.

THE NGUNI

When the Nguni reached their present locations, they were divided into a great number of tribes, each comprising only a few thousand people. Once again, the story of Nguni tribal origins is told in terms of rulers and their clans. The Swazi trace their descent some thirty generations back to an ancestral founder from whom the dominant, and by far the largest, Swazi clan takes its name. Only some thirty clans are of genuine Swazi stock. From the true Swazi are to be distinguished the descendants of Nguni tribes who arrived prior to the Swazi tribal nucleus but were subsequently absorbed into it; they are still known as "Those Ahead," and are divided into some ten clans. Still later additions include as many as twenty-three clans of more distant Nguni extraction, five Sotho clans and eight Tonga clans.

By the end of the eighteenth century three Nguni chiefs exercized considerable power in the northern part of present-day Natal: Sobhuza I of the Ngwane, Dingiswayo of the Mtsetfwa, and Zidze of the Ndwandwe. The manner in which these ruled over their tribes and managed to extend power over neighboring peoples is comparable to the political and military activities of European kings during the Middle Ages. The formation of strong kingdoms embracing a considerable multiethnic population, in which political organization replaced kinship relations as the dominant integrative factor, emerged as a result of profound changes in the methods of warfare, which may possibly have been influenced by European example.

The Nguni kings pursued a policy of deliberate expansion by conducting a long series of military campaigns against neighboring tribes, which involved ever larger armies and more drastic and cruel modes of warfare. In time the big military powers themselves were bound to clash. First, Zidze defeated Sobhuza, who retreated with the remnants of his tribe into Swaziland where he and his successor continued to wage war against the Nguni and Sotho tribes residing there. Later, Zidze fought with Dingiswayo whose successor, Shaka, finally won a decisive victory which left the Zulu under his leadership in un-challenged possession of northern Natal.

THE SWAZI

The Swazi kingdom was consolidated under its rulers in a manner that sheds considerable light on our problem.[1] Some of the original Swazi tribes submitted to Sobhuza and were allowed, upon payment of tribute, to retain their heredi-tary chiefs, their land, and a limited political autonomy. Those who resisted were defeated and plundered; the men were usually killed, the women and children absorbed by marriage and adoption. Some of the aboriginal families became serfs to members of the royal house who had taken over the conquered territory in the name of the king. A similar policy was pursued as the Swazi kings expanded their rule over other territories. A defeated tribe that acknowl-edged allegiance to the king was integrated into the political system as a rela-tively autonomous administrative unit under a governor responsible to the king.

As a rule, the hereditary chief of the conquered retained his office; alterna-tively, a new chief was appointed by the king from among his own kinsmen. Political bonds were often strengthened by establishing kinship relationships between the ruling lineage of a subject tribe and the royal clan. Conquest, however, was not the only way by which the Swazi kingdom expanded. Occa-sionally, small groups—generally weak and insignificant, some leaderless, others distant relatives of subject peoples—voluntarily put themselves under the protection of the mighty Swazi king. To this day their descendants are distinguished from the true Swazi by a term signifying "immigrants."

The ethnic composition of the Swazi is reflected in their social structure. Status in Swazi society is primarily ascribed according to the origin of the strictly exogamous clans and lineages. Highest in rank is the clan to which the king and the royal lineage belong. In addition, Swazi nobility includes the lineages that have provided queen mothers, collateral lineages, and the lineages of chiefs who once ruled independently over tribes now incorporated in the political superstructure. Other lineages and clans form the bulk of the popula-tion. Commoners may improve their status by marrying into the nobility, or may be granted noble rank as a reward for particular services and achieve-ments.

---

[1]Abstracts of empirical materials included in this section are adapted with the permission of the publishers from H. Kuper, *An African Aristocracy: Rank Among the Swazi.* London: Oxford University Press, 1947.

Tribal unity is not based primarily on kinship but on political relationships·
Nevertheless

> Swazi maintain the concept of the nation as a kinship group with the aristocracy as the
> core of the wider kin. The nation can . . . be described as the 'family writ
> large'. . . . for it stresses the fiction of kinship and the personal bond extended to
> political leaders along patterns of kinship behavior (H. Kuper, 1947, p. 115).

The division of tribes into clans does not prevent the spinning of a web of
kinship throughout the tribe. On the contrary, clan exogamy requires the establishment of affinal kinship, thus bringing about a complex network of economic
and social obligations. The sense of caste and ethnic antagonism are weakly
developed among the Swazi, and definite mechanisms exist to adopt people of
inferior status and strangers into the families and clans of the nobility. Even
Europeans—English adventurers and Boer settlers—were accepted in this
manner.

The Royal Family

The backbone of the political power structure as it emerged under the military kings, is the royal family and the army. Ordinarily, a Swazi settlement is
composed of the separate households of one family. The households of the
royal family, on the contrary, are scattered over the whole country, each serving as an army base and a link with the central authority. Rulership is divided
between the king and his mother. The royal mansion in the capital of Swaziland
is the residence of the queen mother and the repository of the national shrine.
The king has his mansion in the king's village, which is the administrative and
ceremonial center of the country. While some of his wives maintain their own
households within the royal compound, others occupy separate mansions that
are located in different royal villages; here they live together with their children
and servants under the supervision of the most senior queen in each place.

Each of the royal villages serves as the garrison for a military district, where
recruits are trained, supplies stored, maneuvers held, and the full regiments
assembled in time of war. The garrison's commanding officer and the civil
governor of the administrative district also reside in the royal village, which
serves as the administrative center for several tribal subdivisions. Some of the
tribal subdivisions are formed by vanquished tribes who have been incorporated under their own hereditary chiefs. Sometimes, however, subdivisional
chiefs are princes of the royal house (almost half belong to the royal clan).
Other important offices are not usually held by members of the nobility, but are
entrusted to commoners with whom kinship ties to the royal house are often
established through intermarriage.

THE ARMY

The army is organized on the basis of age-sets. This institution, which is widely known among African tribes, requires a few words of explanation. When a youth reaches puberty, he has to undergo certain initiation rites together with others of approximately the same age. The intervals between one initiation and the next lasts several years. All those who have taken part in these rites during the same initiation period belong to one age-set. Different age-sets convey to their members a definite status of seniority, equality, and juniority. Age-mates associate in work, war, and leisure; share each other's possessions; and offer each other hospitality. Similar to the kinship system, age-sets function as a means of social categorization and status differentiation. Among the Swazi, unlike the Nuer, age-sets are also drafted into regiments which are kept on active duty for a considerable length of time. Such age-regiments develop an ésprit de corps which binds together all the different ethnic elements in the country. The king is their supreme warlord; their officers are appointed by him and only responsible to him. At the same time, the administrative authorities of the tribal divisions to which the soldiers belong are excluded from all influence upon them while they are serving in the army.

THE ROLE OF ETHNICITY

To sum up our findings: Swazi societal cohesion results primarily from political relationships. A Swazi is a man who owes allegiance to the Swazi king. The diachronic identity of Swazi society is maintained not through the assumed common descent of all its people, but through the continuity of the royal lineage and clan. The diversity of origin and the ethnic heterogeneity are recognized, and are, in part, preserved in civil administration and social stratification. Tribal identity is closely allied to their conception of territory. As Kuper writes: "In Swazi ideology the land and the people are interlocked, and the political bond between rulers and subjects is based largely on the power that the rulers wield over the soil on which people live" (H. Kuper, 1947, p. 44). The land belongs to the chiefs. But it is the responsibility of the king and the subdivisional chiefs to see that every family has the use of sufficient land for its needs.

Nevertheless, kinship affinity, real or (more often) fictitious, and sentiments of solidarity based on the assumption of shared ethnicity extending to all Swazi, are still in evidence. Strict clan exogamy promotes the establishment of affinal relationships among all sections of the population, so that in time they are or appear to be linked together by one intricate web of genealogical relationships. Identification with the royal house and ruling clans symbolically suggests common descent. Serfs, servants, retainers, vassals, and clients, even if they were aliens, are treated like other family members and eventually adopted into clan and lineage.

But the most important single device for integrating the Swazi and for establishing bonds of unity across ethnic or territorial divisions is the army. For the age-regiments provide a powerful focus of identification and lifelong, intimate solidarity.

THE ZULU

Although the political and military organization of the Zulu kingdom closely resembles that of the Swazi, certain salient features appear significant.[2] As has already been said, in the early nineteenth century three rival superpowers emerged in northern Natal. One of the minor dependent tribes was the Zulu. Through a series of tribal intrigues and feuds, Shaka, a son of the Zulu chief, usurped the chieftainship of his tribe, and finally combined several tribal societies into one power structure. Through brute force and cunning in addition to military genius and political acumen, he succeeded in expanding his kingdom over a large area, forcing such of his enemies who survived to pay him allegiance. While the Zulu clan and tribe remained the ethnic core of the kingdom named after it, all its manifold components were quickly welded into a cohesive political superstructure which outlasted Shaka's assassination in 1828.

THE KING

The Zulu call themselves "people of the land of Zulu" and not "descendants of Zulu." (Zulu, who lived at the turn of the eighteenth century, was the founder of the royal clan.) Even the fiction of common descent as the focal point of self-identification for some hundreds of clans is abandoned in favor of common allegiance to a ruler and the occupation of a territory subject to his rule. The king, we read, was addressed as *the* nation.

> What tradition and history was common to all the Zulu had to be told in the names of the Zulu kings, and it was largely their common sentiment about the king and his predecessors which united all Zulu as members of the nation (Gluckman, 1940, p. 30).

Despite this personification, the Zulu's sense of identity implied, even though it remained vague, the notion of a particular historical power structure, an institution that remains intact even after a king has died. The national territory was not only defined by the reach of the king's effective power and jurisdiction, it also represented the essential means of production; namely, land, of which

---

[2]Abstracts of empirical materials included in this section are adapted with the permission of the publishers from E. J. Krige, *The Social System of the Zulus* (3rd ed.). Pietermaritzburg: Shuter & Shooter, 1965. See also References: Gluckman, 1940; Omer-Cooper, 1966.

only he could dispose, while each of his subjects was entitled to a portion necessary for his support. In addition to his political functions the king also had religious and magical duties. In the national ritual he assured the land and the people of the protection and help of his own ancestral spirits.

CIVIL AND MILITARY ADMINISTRATION

The civil administration of Zululand hardly departs from the general pattern we have observed in previous case studies, except that the chiefs had greatly reduced powers. As we pointed out, so-called subtribal divisions occasionally coincided with formerly independent tribes, each centered round a hereditary ruling clan. The incorporation of a new tribe into the Zulu kingdom was achieved when its chief submitted to the overlordship of the Zulu king. Frequently new tribes came into existence through the splitting up of a parent tribe; in this case the king gave the new tribe land to settle, and recognized the clan head as its chief. The autonomy that these tribes originally enjoyed slowly diminished, while the power of the central government grew. The authority that the chiefs traditionally enjoyed among their own people was replaced by authority delegated to them by the king, thus transforming them from vassals into administrative officers. This was clearly demonstrated by the king's policy of replacing recalcitrant chiefs with his own appointees. Princes of the royal house were frequently imposed as rulers on tribes throughout the country.

But the social and political significance of even the administrative divisions was eroded by a military organization that was strictly centralized and exempted from civil authority. Its core was the system of age-regiments. Among the Zulu these occasionally numbered up to eight thousand warriors. They belonged to the king alone, the divisional chiefs having no control over men from their own territory during the period of their military service, which could last a decade or more. The warrior's duties also included personal service to the king and his house; this entailed caring for his immense herds of cattle. As among the Swazi, the regiments were stationed in royal villages which were centers of military districts, each covering the territories of several tribes.

A man remained attached to his military district even if in later life he moved to a territory that was subject to a different chief. His descendants reported to the same barracks as he had. In this way the military structure of the Zulu kingdom cut across territorial units of civil administration. Relationships based on military service became permanent through succeeding generations as were kinship relationships, which thereby lost much of their importance. Every garrison included men from each of the different age-regiments that were organized on a national basis. Female age-regiments followed a similar pattern. Young people, male and female, were compelled to remain single until the king released them from active duty. Then the men might be ordered to take wives from the corresponding female regiment.

THE ZULU NATION

The problem that interests us most is this: Does our evidence about the Zulu and Swazi justify the application of a term we have not yet used in our discussions—the term "nation"? A good reason for introducing this concept at this point is the rhetorical dilemma of using the same word "tribe" both for politically organized tribal societies that are subordinated to and integrated into a wider political power structure, and for this superstructure itself. Yet the difficulties and ambiguities are still more subtle. Consider the terms with which we have become familiar so far in the Zulu case study. The king is not only the head of his family and agnatic lineage but also of his clan, which is the nucleus of his own tribe. Each tribe is organized in a similar manner. Yet the erstwhile tribes, subtribal divisions, and so on, become administrative divisions and subdivisions of the kingdom, a political power structure superimposed upon many tribes. What name shall we give to this overall system?

In order to avoid equivocation Kuper suggests the following terminology:

> I use the word "nation" for a number of tribes owing allegiance to a central authority, "tribe" for a group composed predominantly of kin and under the leadership of a dominant kinship group; "clan" for the furthest extension of kinsmen traced either through the father or the mother; "lineage" for a subdivision of a clan, the lineage members being able to trace genealogical relationship with each other (H. Kuper, 1947, p. 11).

Similarly Gluckman:

> The inhabitants of the largest divisions of a nation I call "tribes," and their heads I call "chiefs" (in distinction to the "king," the ruler of the nation). The tribes were divided into smaller groups ("wards") under relatives of the chief or men of other clans . . . responsible to the chiefs (Gluckman, 1940, p. 30).

There may be valid reasons for reservations about the use of the term "nation" without regard to a specific time or place. In Part II we shall deal with the factors that contributed to the rise of nation-states in Europe. There we will find marked similarities to what we have just described. Were it merely a question of the semantic confusion, we might profitably make use of such an expression as "supertribe." In some respects, indeed, this term is particularly suggestive. For, purely from the point of view of expansion of forms and absorption of new elements, "supertribe" conveys the message that the tribe has been surpassed, just as the clan and the lineage had been superseded by the politically organized tribal society, thus forming a higher societal unit.

But there is more to the problem than this. The Swazi and Zulu political systems were no mere federation of tribes. They formed new societal entities over and above the various tribal components—entities of a different type, bringing into dominance a new unifying scheme which, when present at the tribal level, was subservient and not fully developed. The various tribal societies, whether politically independent or subject to the king, were effectively defined in territorial terms, and were integrated primarily through kinship relationships, real or symbolic. The Zulu nation, on the other hand, was united through political and military relationships, without significant attempt to symbolize these relationships in kinship or ethnic terms. In fact, in their relation to the nation, the tribes were largely reduced to territorial and administrative subunits even if vestiges of the kinship structure survived. Through the assistance of an army that was oriented entirely towards the king, and which represented the core of the nation incarnated in him, a new pattern of social relationships was created and superimposed upon the underlying tribal pattern. Although an ethnic unit may persist without any definite power structure, a nation is unthinkable without reference to a politically organized society. Indeed, it is just such a society whose salient features may be summed up in the following section.

INTERLOCKING LEVELS OF SOCIAL RELATIONSHIPS

A Zulu is linked to Zulu society through a variety of societal units, each of which is predominantly oriented to a particular species of social relationships. Some of these seem to be of primary significance for our central topic: kinship relationships and ethnic units, political relationships and administrative units.

Such social systems may be conceived as different levels of social relationships, superimposed and interlocking. Some relationships pertaining to the lower levels form the nucleus of social units at a higher level. At the bottom of a Zulu-type society we find units mainly based on kinship relationships—local communities built around a nuclear lineage, tribal divisions built around a nuclear clan, and the tribal society built around a nuclear ethnie. The term "nuclear" is here used to indicate that communities and subtribal divisions always contain, in addition to members of the dominant lineage or clan, members of other lineages and clans as well as aliens and collectivities of aliens. The nucleus of the tribe is made up of the dominant clan from which the rulers come, in addition to some other clans supposedly related to each other through more remote kinship ties. Together, these clans and the lineages of which they are composed form an ethnic unit. This arrangement is strengthened by the establishment of actual kinship ties between the clans that are dominant in the alien subunits and the dominant clan of the ruling tribe, or else by providing the alien elements with chiefs belonging to the dominant clan.

On the second level, people are identified with the tribal society, not necessarily because of kinship ties—real or symbolic—but because of common residence in a territory over which the tribal chief exercises paramount control. To make this relationship more clearly understood, we should recall that the Zulu people are defined by their rights in the land of the ruling king's ancestor, Zulu, and implicitly by their obligations to, or their dependence on, his successors. The lower level of societal organization interlocks with a higher level in that the nucleus of the nation, the Zulu tribe, is still based on shared ethnicity. Moreover, the chiefs of all other tribes included in the Zulu kingdom are linked through kinship to the Zulu clan, which is the nucleus of the Zulu tribe. All other elements of Zulu society, though they may not have entirely lost their separate ethnic identity, "belong" by virtue of the occupation of a common territory and of the rights and duties that go with it.

The third level is political in character. The effective administration of a large and heterogeneous territorial population requires a system of delegated authority and a corresponding system of loyalties. This political authority emanates from the king, through tribal chiefs and divisional subchiefs, down to the heads of local communities. It is complemented by a system of obedience and allegiance "emanating" from the local community through its headman, through subchiefs and tribal chiefs, up to the Zulu king. Such a system has been classified as pyramidal. Yet the political power structure is but one dimension of society. Other dimensions based on shared ethnicity or shared territory need not follow the same pattern. Moreover, the model of pyramids piled upon each other takes into consideration only the chiefs, subchiefs, and so on at the top of each pyramid, but not their administrative staffs, which are often referred to as a bureaucracy. We shall approach this problem in the following chapter.

Another point of interest that will further justify our application of the term "nation" to the Zulu system is the following: Social status and authority at the lowest level are assigned almost exclusively on the basis of kinship; functions and offices are hereditary and "ascribed." Although this principle of status assignment is still maintained to a considerable degree at the higher levels, it is increasingly superseded by what Linton calls "status achievement." Political functions are distributed, authority is delegated, officers are appointed less and less by virtue of a fixed position in the kinship structure, more and more in consideration of individual ability, services rendered, proven loyalty, and sometimes just because of the sheer whim of those in power.

By and large, increased spatial and social mobility tend to decrease the saliency of kinship and ethnic ties in favor of spatial and political relationships. In addition to the pyramidal system of descending political authority and ascending obedience, we discover yet another system, a military organization superimposed upon the political system. Membership in hereditary age-regiments is just as ascriptive as genealogical status. Yet the Zulu military system suspends all the warrior's other bonds during the period of his active duty. Neither kinship nor territory, not even the administrative pyramid links him to the global society: he is directly bound to king and nation without reference to intermediary groups and powers. Viewed from this aspect, the Zulu nation is neither a federation of tribes nor a web of kinship ties nor merely a territorial population under common political rule: it consists essentially of the king and his army. The army encompasses the entire society, for every man and woman must serve, and it sets each individual in a direct relationship to the king. The nation may be said to be present wherever the king with the help of his army exercises social control.

CONCLUSIONS

Further on, we shall see how institutions other than the military may also provide the effective core of a nation. The significant point to be stressed here is that the nation is not the sum total of all the collectivities it encompasses, nor is it the product of the various types of social relationships operative within its territory. One finds national institutions and specific relationships that cut across the other social units. When large heterogeneous populations can no longer be controlled by a pyramidal administrative structure nor by an appeal to kinship solidarity, the nation-type of politically organized society appears to be the solution to the problem of maintaining internal unity and solidarity, on the one hand, and collective identity and concentrated power in external relations, on the other. A nation is by no means based on shared ethnicity but on political relationships. Yet the nation, as we shall see later on, may be reinterpreted and legitimized in ethnic terms.

R E F E R E N C E S

Gluckman, Max, "The Kingdom of the Zulu of South Africa," in *African Political Systems*. eds. Meyer Fortes and E. E. Evans-Pritchard. London: Oxford University Press, 1940, pp. 25–55.

Krige, E. J., *The Social System of the Zulus* (3rd ed.). Pietermaritzburg: Shuter & Shooter, 1965.

Kuper, Hilda, *An African Aristocracy: Rank among the Swazi*. London: Oxford University Press, 1947.

Omer-Cooper, I. D., *The Zulu Aftermath: A Nineteenth-Century Revolution in Bantu Africa*. Ibadan History Series. London: Longmans, Green & Co., 1966.

Ethnic and Demotic Structures

4

THE GANDA

We have found that military organization may serve as the principal structural element of a nation. In our study of the Ganda other elements will assume importance, in particular, bureaucratic administration and taxation.[1] L. A. Fallers (1964, p. 99) suggests some striking parallels between the kingdoms of Buganda and Dahomey in tropical Africa and the absolute monarchies in Western Europe which, as will be shown in Part II, played a decisive role in the formation of modern nations. It is in fact our contention that *nation-building always presupposes the unifying and homogenizing influence of a centralized administration in order to create the societal units that provide rallying points for national movements from below.*

Such units, which were preformed by the modern absolute state and which eventually developed into nation-states, we propose to label *demotic.* Although the precise meaning of *demotic,* as distinguished from *ethnic,* structures cannot be elucidated until later, it should be made clear that the "national" structures that concern us at this point are demotic in character without being nation-states in the modern sense. Nevertheless, the analysis of a demotic unit like the kingdom of Buganda in mid-nineteenth century should prove instructive in view of our later discussions on the modern nation-state.

BUGANDA

The Ganda belong to the so-called interlacustrine Bantu who live between the great lakes in Uganda, Tanzania, Ruanda, and Burundi. Shortly before European influences became strongly felt, Mutesa I (1856–1884), claiming to be

---

[1]This section is based on empirical materials adapted with the permission of the publishers from L. A. Fallers, *The King's Men: Leadership and Status in Buganda on the Eve of Independence.* London: Oxford University Press, 1964. See also References: Apter, 1961.

34

the thirtieth kabaka in an uninterrupted line of succession, was by far the most powerful king in the entire area, who ruled despotically but efficiently a fairly homogeneous population of about a million. Economically, the Ganda relied principally on agriculture and horticulture and on the exploitation of neighboring peoples by raiding them or forcing them to pay tribute. Warfare was the main activity of their able-bodied men, while the cultivation of the fertile soil was largely left to women and children.

Despite their simple subsistence economy, the Ganda developed a relatively differentiated social system with a complex political structure. Its genealogical and spatial aspects follow closely the pattern of other Bantu peoples already familiar to us. Political relationships and their pyramidal structure, culminating in the institution of kingship, do not differ substantially from what we have already discussed. The new information pertinent to our central problem is almost entirely concerned with the "national" level of political organization, which appears to have been not only more refined but also more stable and permanent than among the Zulu.

The Administrative System

As in all our previous cases, we find a basic pattern of dominant lineages and clans associated with local communities and ever widening territorial units. Spatial relationships, however, take precedence over genealogical to a much larger extent even than among the Zulu. Economically self-sufficient family homesteads are combined into villages. Each village is not only under the administrative authority of its headman; it is also his estate. There are two kinds of headman: hereditary heads of landowning lineages and appointed officers who have received the land as their principal means of support from the king upon appointment to office. Thus, on the community level, the local lord is also the administrative chief.

Buganda is divided into several layers of subsocietal units in a manner already familiar to us. On the higher levels, the chief is lord of one or several estates, and at the same time administrative head of a wider territorial unit. The Ganda peasant, on the other hand, is not bound forever to the soil, but if he feels oppressed, he may move away and put himself under some other headman in return for land and protection.

A third type of chief is not only the administrative head of a major division but also a household official at the kabakas court; he may be either appointed or hereditary. The most important prerogative of these chiefs is that they have direct access to the kabaka, thus exercising a certain control over all other ranks of appointed officials. Whether appointed or not, however, all the administrative chiefs hold their offices and the estates that go with them at the pleasure of the kabaka. He is empowered to promote, demote, or dismiss them, and also to transfer them from office to office and from place to place.

Administrative offices are combined with judicial functions. Disputes are first brought before the immediate chief of the litigants. The unsuccessful party may appeal to the judge's next superior; the kabaka himself acts as the highest court of appeal. Fallers surmises that

> his authority to adjudicate disputes concerning relations of superiority and subordination among clan and lineage heads must be reckoned among the most important centralizing influences in the Ganda policy (Fallers, 1964, p. 109).

Besides the hierarchical system of executive, administrative, and judicial offices, which are, on principle, open to everybody, taxation is a further institution that binds all Ganda directly to the central authority. Royal tax collectors make their rounds annually to gather set amounts of cattle and products from each homestead. Part of the revenue goes to the tax collectors, administrative chiefs, and palace officials, while the remainder is redistributed by the kabaka to reward his favorites. In addition to taxes, every Ganda is required to render certain services, mainly construction work on national roads and royal buildings.

The most important national institution, however, is once again military service. Besides the territorial militia, recruited and commanded by the divisional chiefs, there is also a national army which is exclusively at the king's disposal and under the command of professional soldiers. The objective of military expeditions is mainly to despoil the enemy of livestock, women and children, and to force them to pay tribute. In this way the wealth of the "nation" is increased, and the officers and men receive their appropriate shares of the spoils; the pick of the cattle and prisoners, however, are reserved to the kabaka.

THE ADMINISTRATIVE CENTER

The center of the country is the capital city built around the royal palace. Although the kabaka has his private estates scattered throughout the country, his wives and concubines together with their families and a host of servants and retainers live in the palace enclosure. Among the regular gifts offered to the kabaka by important people are children. They are sent there in the hope that the daughters will be accepted into the royal harem, and the sons into the corps of royal pages. While rendering every type of service to the king, the pages also receive a thorough training in the affairs of state, and from them the most able are later selected as the kabaka's appointees for office.

All the leading nobles and territorial chiefs have their houses in the capital, whose population comprises some tens of thousands. Most of them, however, maintain a foothold in the country where their estates provide a permanent home for their families. All the important territorial chiefs spend a major part of the year in the capital attending court, always ready to take command of some military or raiding expedition, while the affairs of the administrative units entrusted to them are actually looked after by deputies permanently residing in the outlying districts.

In addition to the territorial chiefs through whom the kabaka rules, there is a second set of officers whom we might call "palace officials." These include the prime minister (who is the ritual head and principal adviser of the king), the head of all the other palace officials (who is the representative of the king in his absence), the senior members of the royal house, the chief of the treasury and tax collectors, the commanders-in-chief of the army and the navy, and many others.

CONCLUSIONS

There is no need to dwell on the Ganda at great length. What we may observe here is simply a more developed and refined expression of the same trend noted among the Zulu—the trend away from the ethnic and towards the demotic. Ganda institutions present an efficiently planned, well-established orderliness and a coolly rational centralization that can compare with European models. Ruthlessly but efficiently, arbitrarily but rationally, Ganda policies have eroded the traditional kinship and ethnic structures, salvaging what is useful, disposing of the rest. A last stronghold of traditional tribalism is preserved in the divisional and subdivisional chiefs, whose authority is ascribed on the basis of descent and hereditary property in land.

The supremacy of the king over these "barons" is achieved in various ways: he and his lineage are supreme among all chiefs and clans; his approval is required for succession to a vacant chieftainship; and he has the power to remove a hereditary chief, or even to take away the hereditary territory of a lineage or clan in exchange for its equivalent in another locality. In this way the original aristocratic power structure has been weakened; the traditional bonds of solidarity between tribe and chief have been eroded. A separate system of bureaucratic institutions has been superimposed upon the traditional social structures, partly replacing them. Through this system, direct channels of communication and chains of command have been established between every single citizen and the paramount overlord who has many of the qualities of an absolute monarch.

Just as Louis XIV explained to the crown prince that the French nation wholly resided in the person of the king, it is no exaggeration to maintain that the Baganda nation is personified by the kabaka. His absolute rule is made possible by a system of nationwide administration and by his control over the allocation of land, revenues, and offices. In addition to rents, taxes, and services rendered by the great mass of peasants to their lords and ultimately to the king, substantial economic support for national institutions is derived from military expeditions and the exploitation of semidependent peoples. Demotic unification under a national government, which was able to maintain itself for a length of time undisturbed by outside interference, promoted—in addition to a sense of common identity and solidarity—the cultural homogenization of the Baganda "nation." As kinship relations were superseded by political relationships, the diversity of descent was forgotten and ethnicity began to lose its social relevance.

REFERENCES

Apter, David E., *The Political Kingdom of Uganda: A Study in Bureaucratic Nationalism.* Princeton, N.J.: Princeton University Press, 1961.
Fallers, Lloyd A., *The King's Men: Leadership and Status in Buganda on the Eve of Independence.* London: Oxford University Press, 1964.

A COMMON FRAME OF REFERENCE

Interethnic relations may be arranged in a multitude of different ways. It would be a gross overstatement if we claimed to have exhausted available ethnological evidence. But we must keep in mind that the purpose of Part I was no more than the development of a common frame of discourse.

Several general concepts needed for our undertaking have been given a more precise meaning, not merely through formal definition but by way of intuition and discovery. By revealing the implications of certain abstract concepts in real-life situations, we are able to distinguish them from each other and at the same time demonstrate their interconnection. Certain facts stand out as ever-present realities of the human condition: the organism, its location in space, its sustenance, its association with other human organisms. Another such factor is the mind through which man works out his destiny, partly by adjustment, partly by manipulation.

KINSHIP AND ETHNICITY

Sex, age, and procreation are biological givens; yet, within limits, man can and does manipulate their consequences. He gives a meaning to each socially relevant period of the life cycle and to processes of mating and procreation. In primitive society it would seem that a man's status is defined primarily through his position in the kinship structure. He is born to a set of parents who themselves are related by consanguinity and affinity to a fixed set of persons. He is also born in a definite place. Yet he can move from one place to another and to some extent he can also manipulate the significance of his kinship relationships through myth and symbol.

Shared ethnicity, seen empirically, appears to be little more than the extension of the kinship principle of status assignment to a wider population whose precise genealogical nexus is unknown or disregarded. An ethnie is, as it were, a manmade unit of kinsfolk. Of course, all kinship relations are "artificial" in the sense that biological genealogy is given significance by social definition. In the case studies examined so far, we have seen that people do not necessarily identify themselves with others or extend sentiments of solidarity to them, simply because they are "objectively" descended from common ancestors. Precisely the reverse may be generally true: because they are somehow associated with each other, they tend to express this relationship in ethnic terms. Myths of common origin, fictitious kinship, or symbolic identification with a descent group serve to legitimize and strengthen already existing solidarities. In our examples we have also seen that ethnicity is not of constant saliency as a principle of societal organization. In tribes without rulers as well as in politically organized tribal societies, it may be more-or-less dominant. It means most to the Nuer, least to the Ganda.

TERRITORY AND COOPERATION

Man is always located somewhere in physical space, and physical distance has a definite bearing upon association. Especially under more primitive conditions, territory is significant in two ways; as a place of permanent residence and as a resource for sustenance. People who live near to each other tend to interact more frequently and develop sentiments of solidarity. They also tend to intermarry, except where rules of exogamy interfere. Sharing the natural resources of a given area leads, as does spatial proximity, to economic cooperation. Intermarriage, association, and cooperation naturally promote the integration of ethnically heterogeneous components, resulting in a common sense of identity and solidarity. A shared territory may become a symbol of identification or an object of sentimental attachment.

Territory is therefore not merely a place where man is incidentally located; in a real sense and with practical consequences, territory may belong to man, and man to it. According to the spatial principle, one people may be differentiated from another by virtue of their respective occupancy of different territories. Here ethnicity would seem to be irrelevant. Yet the fact that people constitute a societal unit by virtue of sharing a common territory may be reinterpreted in terms of shared ethnicity. In other words, because they share a territory, interact, intermarry, and cooperate within its boundaries for a certain length of time, they are assumed to be of common descent. Even if facts to the contrary are known and recognized, they may be purposely disregarded.

A further fundamental requirement of human existence is association. Social relationships consist of regular sequences of actions and reactions. What we have called "societal units" are—in the last analysis—systems of socially defined positions. Social structure consists in the regular distribution of rights and obligations among unequal status categories. Association can be systematized on the basis of various principles of social organization depending on whichever type of values is paramount in the culture.

POLITICAL POWER STRUCTURES

Association between the ethnically heterogeneous components of a major societal unit can apparently be established and maintained for any length of time only through the exercise of political power. *Whenever identification with, or allegiance to, a ruler (or a given political power structure) take on primary importance, a societal superstructure emerges over and above the structures that are based on genealogical or spatial relationships.* Bonds with the ruler may be indirect, so that the common people are politically related only to the head of the lower social units; for instance, a cluster of villages or a clan that may be economically and socially self-sufficient. In this case the unity of the entire society is established through the relationships between the ruler and the local chiefs and clan heads who are his vassals. Because these mediate between the paramount ruler and the people, and because they also link the basic social units to the political superstructure, they may be referred to as the "mediating elite."

If those who are subject to a centralized political rule are directly linked to it, we speak of a demotic type of political organization. In this case, political power is exercised not through the traditional heads of subtribal units but through territorial administrators appointed by the ruler or in his name. In a demotically organized society ethnicity is not a constitutive element but rather a potentially disturbing factor. It may be neutralized through the homogenizing effect of demotic institutions such as military service.

ABSORPTION OF ALIENS

The absorption of ethnically diverse components takes place in various ways. Individual strangers may be adopted by a charter kinship group or marry into it, and are thereby assigned a status in the existing social structure. In primitive societies the members of a household share in the public status of its head, regardless of whether they are related to him by kinship or are attached to his household as clients, servants, or serfs. Within the household, however, the various members are clearly differentiated as to their relative status. The allotment of land is another device for integrating aliens; that is, for providing them with a status. What is commonly meant when aliens are said to become integrated into a community or society is that they have effectively been assigned to a recognizable social category. A man without a known status within a local community or global society remains an outsider and at the mercy of those who do have status, that is, who belong.

The integration of functioning groups of aliens as such requires other methods. On the kinship level they may be attached as satellite lineages to a charter clan, on the spatial level they may be allotted a contiguous parcel of land and be treated as a new division among the existing territorial subunits of the charter population. In politically organized societies two mechanisms seem to be most common: either the native leaders of the alien group are bound to the paramount ruler under some form of vassalage, or else the ruler assumes direct political control through appointed administrators to replace the native leaders.

Our list is far from exhaustive but does indicate some typical methods by which strangers and alien groups may become integrated into a given society. This should prove helpful when, in the following chapters, we shall concentrate more specifically on the relation between ethnie and polity using data supplied by European history.

One last remark: While the ethnic heterogeneity of the components of a societal unit does pose certain problems of identification and solidarity, *none of the ethnological cases analyzed here support the idea that people should be united in one collectivity solely on account of shared ethnicity; or that the people included in a politically organized society should necessarily be ethnically homogeneous.* We are not aware of any instance, where these twin principles (which are at the bottom of nationalism) are found in what we call "primitive" societies. Nationalism, which has emerged in the course of modern European history and has since spread to most parts of the world, would appear to be an entirely new factor in interethnic relations. This problem will be of central concern in Part II.

ETHNIE
AND
POLITY
II

INTRODUCTION

In the preceding chapters we have endeavored to clarify the general meaning of ethnicity by relating it to other dimensions of social action orientation, notably, genealogy and shared territory. The analysis of ethnological materials has also indicated the possible role of political processes in interethnic relations, a role that appears to be of such strategic importance that the entire Part II will be devoted to it. Before we continue, however, another preliminary agreement about the terminology seems to be called for.

By "power" we mean the capacity of persons or groups to make others obey orders even against their will. Since social processes involving the exercise of power are present in any collectivity, the qualifying adjective "political" has two meanings: (1) political power implies the establishment and maintenance of a more-or-less stable order among a variety of coexisting social units (kinship groups, locality groups, special-interest groups, status groups, and so on); and (2) political power is exercised by special agents who assume the appropriate role of authority either permanently or intermittently. The function of political power structures is not only the maintenance of internal "peace and order," but also the safeguarding of collective interests in the face of the outside world. This includes, among other things, protection against external influences threatening the internal order. Ultimately, political power relies on violence or threat of violence. Yet violence alone does not suffice to maintain a societal order for any length of time. Accordingly, those exercising political power tend to mobilize moral forces so as to induce submission without recourse to violence. The most effective moral support of a given power structure is recognition of its legitimacy. Among other factors, shared ethnicity may serve to legitimize a political power structure.

In Part I we have discovered two different methods by which political power structures may be superimposed upon ethnically diverse societal units so as to combine them into larger and more complex tribal societies.

1. People belonging to traditional subunits of the political power structure are linked directly to a paramount ruler and his staff through a system of separate institutions. We have called this the *demotic type*, which may be considered a primitive form of the modern nation-state.
2. Existing tribal units are linked collectively to the paramount ruler through the mediating elite of clan-heads and local chiefs. An elaboration of this second type, to be discussed presently, we have chosen to call the *empire type* of political power structure.

The bulk of our treatise deals with interethnic relations in modern society. We propose to demonstrate that the problems arising from interethnic relations in modern society are closely related to its prevailing type of political organization, the nation-state. In the course of our investigation, ethnicity will be found to have no immediate relevance for the functioning of imperial power structures, not even as a disturbing factor, yet we have nevertheless good reasons for devoting considerable time to the discussion of this point. First, the state, especially the nation-state, is so preponderant and pervasive in the political organization of modern societies that today it is difficult for many people even to imagine any other possible arrangement in which ethnicity does not pose the same problems. Furthermore, as a rule, misconceptions about the sociological nature of empires are widespread, and a precise knowledge of their internal structure is limited. Therefore, a detailed analysis of the empire type of political power structure, insofar as it represents the antithesis to the modern nation-state, should prove helpful in enabling us to discern all the more clearly the relationship between ethnic and political structures in modern society as well as the role of political factors in interethnic relations.

We would have had little difficulty in presenting suggestive cases by simply expanding the ethnological studies of Part I. We shall, nevertheless, concentrate on European history. For it is here that the modern nation-state has gradually emerged from imperial power structures whence it has spread over most of the globe, so that it is now considered the fundamental unit of international politics and law. European history from the early Middle Ages to the threshold of the most recent times will provide us with the empirical evidence needed to fully understand contemporary interethnic relations. As we said before, ethnicity had practically no relevance for imperial power structures. The modern state, on the other hand, initiated the transformation of its ethnically heterogeneous population into a culturally homogenized nation. The process, which we propose to call *nationalization,* continued under the auspices of the nation-state. Resistance to it and demands for cultural autonomy and even political emancipation were—and still are—usually legitimized on grounds of ethnic diversity.

In Chapter 4 we intend to outline briefly the transitional period between antiquity and the Middle Ages, a period during which the conditions in Europe were in more than one respect similar to those in precolonial Africa. This will provide a proper background for the analysis of medieval empires, their historical development, as well as their typical characteristics. In Chapter 5 we shall study the emergence of the modern state, the nation-state being one variety. Chapter 6 deals with the genesis of nationalism, its basic principles, and its effects upon social organization. It also deals with the main types of nationalism and the social forces supporting them. In Chapter 7 typical problems that arise from the practical application of the principles of nationalism to concrete situations will be discussed, together with some of the political and legal attempts that have been made to solve these problems.

REFERENCE

Deutsch, Karl W., *Nationalism and its Alternatives*. New York: Alfred A. Knopf, 1969.

Interethnic Relations in Empires

5

The following analysis of historical cases focuses attention upon (1) the emergence of medieval empires, and (2) ethnic phenomena in such power structures.[1] Our first task will be aided by what we have learned in Part I. To overcome the drawback of having ethnologists and historians speak different languages, we shall, contrary to established conventions, use ethnological terms when discussing the so-called Dark Ages.

THE MIGRATION OF PEOPLES

What we have learned about Bantu migrations into eastern and southern Africa also throws some light upon the so-called migrations of peoples in Europe. More often than not these were raiding expeditions organized on a voluntary basis by warlords who usually belonged to the lineage of some tribal chief. Occasionally, bands of adventurers were recruited from different tribes. When they settled in foreign lands and were joined by some of those they had left behind, they did not really restore the original tribal units. Common experiences, common sufferings, common victories—all tended to overshadow the memories of a more remote tribal past; the general unsettled conditions also tended to weaken traditional kinship and ethnic ties. These were replaced by the warrior's allegiance to his military leader and by a new sense of historical continuity.

If it is true that ethnicity implies awareness of a common history, obversely a common history may be expected to suggest an interpretation of existing groupings in ethnic terms. The more effective and stable a new political and social structure proves to be, the more common interests, cooperation, and senti-

---

[1]In the present context the terms "empire" and "imperial power structure" will be used in the specific sense that corresponds more with the German word *"Reich"* than with the meaning given to "empire" and "imperialism" in political writing since the nineteenth century, frequently in connection with modern colonialism. See also References: Eisenstadt, 1963; Emerson, 1960.

46

ments of solidarity will be created, and in time, the political structure will acquire the legitimacy of tradition. The common identity of heterogeneous components will be strengthened through the establishment of kinship ties, real, fictitious, or symbolic, and will be supported by epics and social myths. In this way we may picture the social and political structures that emerged in conquered countries, gradually assuming the character of secondary ethnic units, often under a new name.

THE DUALITY OF TRIBAL STRUCTURES

The *Grosskönige* (big chiefs) of medieval Europe bear an obvious resemblance to the paramount rulers of composite Bantu tribes. Their kingdoms were characterized by a superimposition of interlocking social structures similar to that among the Tswana and Zulu. On a lower level there was a multitude of tribal units that had been joined to the king's tribe by conquest or through military alliance. Their traditional chiefs were bound to the paramount ruler, whose tribe constituted the dominant nucleus of the kingdom, not only through contract and personal allegiance but also through the magic of blood transfusion and through affinal kinship relations. On a higher level, however, the king directly controlled the military, administrative, and judiciary institutions that molded the whole kingdom into a sociopolitical superstructure.

This structural duality was the cause of much competition and conflict, for which there were two possible solutions: (1) whenever the king succeeded in destroying the power and relative independence of divisional chiefs, the stage was set for the emergence of demotic units; and (2) if, however, the king's claim to sovereign rule was successfully checked by territorial lords and barons, and a balance was struck between the lower divisions and the superstructure, a political organization of the empire type emerged.

When we turn to the internal organization of a medieval empire we find a political superstructure embracing a variety of political units while leaving their social structure and ethnic traditions largely undisturbed. The links between the superstructure and its components were forged by personal relationships between the chiefs of the component units and the paramount ruler of the superstructure. The pivotal institutions regulating these relationships were vassalage and feudalism.

FEUDALISM

The German social historian, Otto Brunner (1959), has pointed out that the popular concept of feudalism is heavily influenced by the writings of the nineteenth-century political philosophers (including Hegel and Marx), reacting against a social order in which the upper classes maintained tyrannical positions by virtue of their possession of land and wealth acquired through violence and injustice. In a more precise and objective sense, however, the term *feudalism* refers to social relations based on the legal institutions of vassalage and feud. These developed in the Frankish empire and spread from its original center between the Rhine and the Loire; they matured between 900 and 1250 A.D. but did not reach the marginal regions of Europe till much later, if at all. By the time the modern territorial state began to displace the imperial power structures of the Middle Ages, feudal society, for all practical purposes, had already been replaced by another type which can hardly be termed feudal.

Originally the term *vassal* was applied to a freeman who, while maintaining his legal status, placed himself under the protection and at the service of another freeman who thereby became his lord. A lord was obliged to provide for the maintenance of his vassals, usually by giving them land as a "loan" (in German *"Lehen,"* equivalent to the French *"fefier"* or *"fieu,"* hence "fief," "feod," or "feud"). By the eighth century such grants were made not only to secure for a vassal the economic security to which he was entitled but were intended to enable him further to provide the equipment for the knights and mounted soldiers needed to perform the military duties expected of him by the lord. Originally vassals were people of little significance, but in the course of time, men of noble birth became the vassals of some great lord, often a king, and large landed estates and manors were granted them as fiefs. In this way a feudal system emerged in which a hierarchy of personal bonds between magnate and king, minor and major lords, was combined with military organization and land ownership.

A feudal relationship was derived primarily from a contract between free men by which the vassal surrendered himself to the lord. Stated summarily, the contractual obligations consisted in mutual aid and advice. The vassal was bound to assist his lord in wars, feuds, and raids as well as to perform escort and guard duties. The more powerful vassals were also expected to supply, equip, and lead a military force composed of knights (who were usually their subvassals), servants, and common foot soldiers. These private armies occasionally numbered several thousands of men. Other obligations included managing the lord's manor, performing important services in the lord's household, and lending financial aid in case of need. The obligation to give advice consisted mainly in attendance at the lord's law court. The duties of the lord were of a similar nature. He had to defend his vassal when the latter was unjustly attacked, and to act as his attorney in a lawsuit. He was also bound to advise him and to act fairly and justly toward him. Finally, the lord was responsible for his vassal's sustenance either by maintaining him in his own household or—more commonly—by providing him with a fief.

As a rule the fief consisted of land—the principal means of production at that time. Its size varied from small parcels to thousands of acres. But a fief might also be a castle, a church, a political office, the right to tolls and market dues, or any other source of income. In principle, the lord retained direct ownership of the fief while the vassal acquired the right to use it and appropriate its produce; he might neither alter its substance, diminish its value, nor alienate it.

Originally, political power, including the administration of justice, remained a royal prerogative, just as the land remained the king's property or "eminent domain." In due course, however, territorial lords often succeeded in setting up their own courts of justice and in exercising almost autonomous political power; their fiefs became inheritable property. In this way the structure of an empire tended to dissolve into a hierarchy of relationships between minor and major lords, while political power was widely dispersed over a variety of jurisdictions. The paramount ruler retained only as much real political authority as he was able to maintain in dynamic opposition to his most powerful vassals (the "barons" of English history), namely, through the actual power that he possessed by virtue of his direct control over natural and human resources.

THE MANORIAL SYSTEM

When we pass from kings and lords to the common people, we find a different situation. Though many vassals and knights were modest in their style of living, they belonged to the same small elite who lived not from manual labor but from the products of others, particularly the peasantry. Elite and folk, otherwise worlds apart, met and interacted directly at the level of the local community. We shall now describe its basic structure in a highly simplified manner.

In the feudal age, a village consisted of the homes and barns of the peasants as well as the huts of landless cotters and of the lord's enclosure ("court") built around his mansion (occasionally a castle). The village territory that belonged to the fief of the lord, was divided into land set aside for common use (such as pastures and forests) and arable land. The latter included "servile" land, which was burdened with a variety of dues and was farmed by peasant families individually, and the demesne, which was under the direct management of the lord.

Relations between the lord of the manor and his tenants or serfs (that is, the holders of servile land) were similar to those between a feudal lord and his vassals. In return for protection and the hereditary usufruct of some of the lord's land, the serf was obliged to surrender a part of his produce, to pay rent and other fees, and to render certain services, which included labor on the lord's demesne. The manor was not only a closed and largely self-sufficient economic system, it was a political and ecclesiastical unit as well.

THE NORMAN EMPIRE

When studying the internal structure of a feudal empire, one should not concentrate on the Holy Roman Empire, for some of its outstanding features are unique. Instead, the Norman empire, which emerged on both sides of the English Channel, at the height of the Middle Ages, appears to be more suitable for this purpose.

The Normans came from Scandinavia to Western France as seafaring raiders. Like the Franks before them, they settled among the native Celtic population as a dominant elite. Bonds of vassalage were established with the West-Frankish king. Eventually, the Norman nobility adopted the French speech and culture of their Frankish peers. The Duke of Normandy united two functions in his person: he was the feudal overlord of the Norman nobility and also the prince of a largely autonomous territory whose paramount ruler was the king of France. By conquest, inheritance, marriage, or purchase, the Dukes of Normandy acquired England as well as an empire that stretched from the Pyrenees to Scotland. After the loss of all French possessions, their erstwhile empire was finally reduced to the British Isles.

ENGLAND BEFORE AND AFTER THE CONQUEST

Conditions in England before 1066 require a few words of preliminary explanation. Before the country was occupied by suceeding waves of Germanic invaders, its military and political organization, like that of Gaul, followed the Roman pattern and was largely in charge of Romanized Celts. We must picture the invaders as bands of predatory warriors recruited from different Germanic tribes. Once they were settled in the eastern parts of the island, several tribal chiefdoms emerged, each of which claimed descent from one of three ethnic societies: Jutes, Saxons, or Angles. Eventually, these early tribal societies united under one paramount ruler, the English king, in order to counter more effectively the threat of further invasions by Vikings and Danes. The elite consisted of landowning thanes who were the personal followers of the paramount ruler. The political administration of subdivisions was entrused to earls and sheriffs having broad military, judicial, and fiscal functions.

When William the Conqueror, Duke of Normandy, invaded the British Isles, he claimed to be the legitimate successor to the kings of England. He did not at first touch the traditional political and social structure. Several uprisings, however, forced him to entrust positions of power to his own companions who, besides his Norman vassals, included knights from Flanders, Brittany, and other parts of France. Some of the Anglo-Saxon thanes were also accepted as vassals and eventually absorbed by the Norman nobility, while others lost their aristocratic status and became indistinguishable from the free peasants. The most profound changes, however, were brought about by the introduction of feudalism to England by the Normans.

FEUDALISM IN ENGLAND

At first the new ruler maintained his power through what amounted to an expeditionary force of occupation. To his most important vassals and tenants-in-chief he granted large estates which were widely scattered throughout the country. In addition, royal castles were built at strategic points, forming a network of fortified strongholds through which the native population could be effectively controlled. The elite of the new political power structure consisted of some two hundred powerful barons together with their vassals and knights. This alien nobility, though of diverse ethnic origin, was French in culture and speech. Some of them held fiefs on both sides of the English Channel, and it was not uncommon for them to move from one part of the Norman empire to another. They saw military service in far-flung expeditions such as the Crusades, intermingled with the elites of other countries, and frequently shifted allegiance. Thus, the English barons were identified with an elite that was international in character; it had a culture of its own that effectively distinguished its members from the common people in every country.

Overlapping the hierarchy of feudal bonds we find a political superstructure. The administrative subdivisions of the kingdom were in charge of royal officers. As these, however, were usually appointed from among the high nobility, royal commissions and feudal bonds were not always clearly distinguishable. The most important common institutions that brought the people into direct contact with the political superstructure were the royal law courts, the system of royal taxation and the levies for the local militia.

The social structure of feudal England is characterized above all by a caste-like division between the nobility of the Norman empire and the people of England. There was, however, a finer differentiation within these broad classes. Prelates, bishops, and abbots were often feudal lords or high officers of the crown. The lower grades of vassals, such as knights and "serjeants," tended, regardless of their particular ethnic origin, to move closer to the native population. They developed common interests and solidarities with the local communities in which they had their personal holdings. In this way a landed gentry came into being which was more closely identified with England and the English people than with the international nobility of the Norman empire. The common people were divided first and foremost into freemen and bondsmen. Similarly to the free townsmen the free peasants were organized in corporations headed by elected reeves who were responsible to the royal authorities.

From this very sketchy outline of one historical case—which is nevertheless sufficient for our purpose—we pass on to a more general discussion of interethnic relations in medieval empires. It is well to note at the outset that our account will follow the sociological method of ideal types.

MEDIEVAL SOCIETY

Foci of Identification. When trying to understand the role played by ethnicity in medieval society, we do well to remind ourselves that none of the vital and viable social units we can distinguish approximate the closed and self-sufficient social system commonly associated with a global society. Christendom as a whole was too loosely knit to fit this concept. The village or the manor, though a little closed world for the peasant, did not embody the whole social fabric with which the elite was identified. In any discussion of medieval social structure, the essential duality between elite and common folk must be strictly kept in mind. Another important point is that political and economic institutions were so closely interwoven as to be barely distinguishable in many cases. But genealogical and spatial relationships lost the strategic importance that they had had in earlier periods. Kinship ties were largely replaced by feudal bonds of mutual aid and advice. The significance of a shared territory was bound to diminish as social distance hardened into castelike divisions, and the interests and aspirations of the elite were defined in a supraterritorial context.

Students of constitutional law have characterized the medieval political system as a *Personenverband* (a social unit based on personal relationships) as distinct from a *Territorialverband* (one based on common territory) such as the modern state. This is true as long as one concentrates on feudal relationships; for one local community or region could comprise the fiefs of many different lords, and one lord could hold fiefs in many different, and often very distant, places. Moreover, contracts of vassalage could be terminated for various reasons, and allegiances were often switched in defiance of law and custom. Thus, lords living in the same neighborhood, and even one and the same lord, may have owed allegiance to a variety of overlords who were not subject to the same paramount ruler. But feudal bonds did not always supersede the loyalties owed to king and country, and the specific powers wielded by the paramount ruler and his divisional lieutenants, however weak they may at times have been, were defined in terms of territorial jurisdiction rather than personal relationships. More significant still is the fact that the feudal system, symbolized by an intricate web of personal relationships, was confined to a small power elite; it affected the common people only indirectly and remotely.

Unlike the elite, the masses were relatively immobile. At the height of the Middle Ages, serfs were legally bound to the soil. Together with the land they could be sold, inherited, donated, or otherwise transferred from one lord to another. Manor, village, and parish, and even large domains held by the magnates or the church were, for all practical purposes, politically autonomous, economically self-sufficient, and socially closed. There were few contacts between their population and the outside world, except indirectly through the mediation of the lord, the nobility, and the clergy. As far as the common folk were concerned, the relatively small territorial units, nowhere embracing a whole kingdom or empire, provided the principal foci of social identification and solidarity.

Social Stratification. Among the common people the basic differentiation was between the free and unfree legal status, which was heritable and ascribed. Yet there existed a certain margin of upward and downward mobility. Free peasants might be reduced to servility; slaves and servants might be freed and occasionally even raised to noble rank. In addition, differences of wealth erected barriers between the peasants as well as between the urban freeman. At the lowest end of the status scale were household servants, day laborers, and paupers, who had really no social standing at all and were just one notch above the slaves.

The principal strata of the elite included territorial princes, high nobility, and minor aristocracy. A distinction was made between the nobility of birth, scions of conquering tribal chiefs; the nobility of the sword who had acquired land and power through military achievement; and the nobility of service, appointees of king or emperor who, by virtue of public service, had gained property and rank. Yet where status is mainly ascribed, nobility acquired by accomplishment or appointment is apt to become, in time, a nobility of birth. Moreover, large estates, however gained, and the virtual power that goes with them tend to open the gates to the elite. Preeminent among the nobility were the territorial princes who, by virtue of their military power, property, and legal authority, had won independence from their feudal overlord and paramount ruler. Many of these eventually became sovereign monarchs of modern states. Minor aristocrats, like the English gentry of whom we have spoken, held intermediary positions between elite and commoners. Clergy and monks formed a separate hierarchy whose highest ranks paralleled those of the secular elite, while the lower clergy and the friars ranked with the common people.

Although politically organized society was based on feudal bonds rather than on kinship relationships, genealogies nevertheless continued to play an important role when it came to the inheritance of property and of positions of power. At all times, genealogies have been a preoccupation of royalty and nobility. This is easily understood when one recalls that rules of succession stress legitimacy of birth as well as position in a genealogical system. Also among the common people, all those who have a claim to heritable rights—and in the Middle Ages most privileges were of this kind—are concerned with genealogies, although their lineages are as a rule shorter than among the nobility. Only the propertyless and those who have nothing to leave to their heirs have no genealogy reaching beyond their immediate family and relatives.

There were significant differences between elite and commoners with regard to social identification and solidarity. The ranks of nobility were established on a truly international scale, cutting across territorial and political structures. Nobles and knights, who hailed from different lands, were of quite diverse ethnic origin. As time went on, they developed a common way of life, a common code of conduct, a common culture, common interests, and a strong sense of solidarity. Their womenfolk also provided a pool for preferential marriages. Their common identity was defined first and foremost by social status rather than by kinship, shared ethnicity, or common territory.

But the common people were spatially immobile. Their identification was not so much with a lord—for lords changed and often were many lords in one locality—nor with a paramount ruler to whom they were but loosely bound through a hierarchy of officials and intermediaries. Identity and solidarity among the common people were, first of all, spatially defined: The social unit that counted was the village, the valley, or the region—in short, a collectivity of people who shared common interests, who cooperated, who interacted directly and frequently, who intermarried, and who were isolated by physical and social barriers from the multitude of similar small territories into which the kingdoms and empires were divided.

The Structure of a Medieval Empire

Let us compare the structure of medieval empires with the model of inter-locking levels that we used in Part I. A number of similarities soon become apparent. On the lowest level we find a multitude of local communities and territorial subdivisions. These were, to a considerable degree, self-contained and closed social units. On a higher level were the larger territorial units— kingdoms or other principalities. Here the situation was highly complex be-cause of two concurrent systems of power relations: the feudal system of personal bonds, and the royal system of territorial jurisdiction and administra-tion. A paramount ruler was not only a feudal overlord, but also a territorial prince who generally had the right of eminent domain over natural resources, especially land, and who was also in control of administrative, judicial, mili-tary, and fiscal institutions effective in the whole territory. Although feudal obligations strengthened royal power, feudal privileges severely curtailed it. There were innumerable "immunities" (exemptions from legal obligations such as taxes) and "freedoms" (special rights granted to persons and corporations). Administrative offices were held as feudal fiefs. Military forces at the king's disposal were only partly under his control, their cooperation depended on the allegiance of vassals and allies—often his near-equals in power. In addition to the geographical fragmentation of political units, we find a segmentation of the entire social structure which was divided, not only between conflicting centers of power, but also between castelike status groups.

At the highest level was the imperial superstructure. Among all the paramount rulers of constituent units the emperor held a position of supreme dignity and moral authority. He was the empire's representative and the symbol of its unity. Yet the emperor himself was also a territorial prince. His effective power strongly depended on the political weight of the constituent units that were under his direct control. It also depended on the military forces and the economic means at his disposal. Finally, it depended on the support of the other magnates which the emperor was able to command because of the benefits he could grant or withhold.

The main functions of the emperor and his staff consisted in the maintenance of peace and order among all the constituent units, the protection of the integrity of the whole as well as of its components, and the promotion of the general well-being of the people. To this end a separate set of imperial institutions—military, administrative, judicial, fiscal—were at his command. The minting of money and the exploitation of mineral wealth, for instance, were among his prerogatives: the promotion of internal commerce and foreign trade as well as the upkeep of roads and waterways were his responsibility. The conflicting interests of the component units and their rulers, the dispersion of power and responsibility among many agencies, and the segmentation of the social structure were the principal weaknesses of empires. Their outstanding advantage consisted in their great flexibility and a capacity for expanding the political organization indefinitely; for there was no limit to the number and variety of components that could be added to an empire.

The links between the different levels were furnished by the elite. The lords of the manor constituted the dominant core of the larger territorial unit whose ruler was himself a feudal lord. The territorial princes formed the power elite of the empire, while the emperor himself was a prince in his own territories and also the lord of his personal domain. This framework resembles the pyramidal structures studied in Part I.

Ethnicity in the Medieval Empire. Under these conditions, ethnicity could have only a limited scope and saliency. Traditional ethnic units had been disrupted during the great migrations, and people of diverse ethnic origin inhabited the same territories. But new ethnic formations were slow to emerge since the dominant reference groups were based on fragmented and ever-shifting political power, and status divisions retarded identification between the common folk and an elite that was often of alien origin.

Secondary ethnic units emerged mostly among the masses of common people living together in their self-contained worlds. Within limited areas, endogamy, brought about by isolation or enforced by authorities, resulted in a distinctive web of kinship relations. Cooperation, intensive interaction, common experiences and traditions generated a subcultural variety, a particular dialect, a sense of identity. Outside contacts hardly went beyond neighbors who were of only a slightly different cultural shade and ethnic composition. Interethnic relations were limited to rare occasions—military expeditions, long-distance trade, pilgrimages. Ethnic contrasts were more obvious in border regions and in areas of more recent colonization. Generally, political fragmentation and social segmentation prevented an awareness of a wider ethnic identity and permitted the emergence of secondary ethnic societies only on a small scale. During the tenth and eleventh centuries the French, German, Italian, or English peoples, as we think of them today, were unknown. Each one of the territorial populations, which are now the ancestors of the present ethnic societies, had been ethnically heterogeneous and ethnically differentiated, and the process of their eventual ethnic unification and homogenization has been gradual and devious.

Previously, we stressed the cosmopolitan character of the feudal elite. Their world ended with the confines of Christendom rather than at territorial or political boundaries. To them, shared social status rather than shared ethnicity provided a motive and legitimization for identification and solidarity. Yet even a mobile, status-conscious, and exclusive elite needs a home base and permanent residence; which generally leads to interaction and affiliation with the local folk. Their closest associates, above all in the formative years of childhood, were commoners rather than peers: nurses and playmates, priests and teachers, servants and clerks, escorts and guards, companions of the chase and comrades at arms.

Ethnicity, however, also played an important role in the political designs of the power elite. Whenever regional groups of noblemen or territorial princes sought greater autonomy, they were prone to activate latent ethnic divisions and to legitimize demands for freedom in ethnic terms. It is significant that the adoption of vernaculars coincided with the coalescence of regional opposition against centralized political power. The new literary languages appearing in the Middle Ages were not the idioms spoken by the common people, though they were derived from these. They were deliberately created as a regional *koine* or *lingua franca* to symbolize emancipation from a political superstructure. The so-called national literatures written in these languages were not spontaneous creations of the *Volksgeist* (ethnic spirit or culture), but were created in support of emancipatory and secessionist elites. Indeed, until relatively recent times, the term "nation" referred to a territorial nobility sharing political power and vying for it with the paramount ruler, rather than to the entire population.

The Empire as an Ideal Type. An imperial power structure comes nearest to the pure type of political system in that its essential function is the coordination of a great variety of collectivities by establishing relationships of submission, allegiance, and support among their elites. The empire allows a wide margin of autonomy in its component units, which may be tribal societies, local communities, territorial states, monarchies or republics, aristocracies or democracies; their people may speak one or many different languages; they may be of the same or of diverse ethnic origin and race; their culture may be of almost any type. In fact, the internal conditions of its constituent units are of no immediate relevance to the maintenance of the imperial superstructure. As long as no serious conflicts disturb the peace, and as long as military and financial obligations to the imperial government are met, there is no reason to interfere with the institutions, the traditions, or the culture of the constituent units. The same is true of their ethnic composition. Because social integration in an empire depends on the elite not on the common people, there is no need for cultural uniformity or ethnic homogeneity. Ethnic societies and their folk cultures may be left undisturbed, as these societies continue to function independently from each other and their members interact with each other collectively through group agents rather than individually and directly.

The traditional chief of any major unit or subdivision included in the empire is, as the symbol of its unity, the prime focus of identification. At the same time, he participates in the imperial superstructure. Thus, members of the elite represent not only the particularistic interests of their own peoples, they also pursue universalistic interests related to the proper functioning of the imperial superstructure. A common purpose, cooperation, and common action orientation are sources of common sentiments of solidarity and of a common subculture and *lingua franca,* which may differ from the folk cultures and folk dialects found in their separate regions. The members of the elite are the mediators between the political superstructure and the diverse populations that are included in its components. Collectively, they form the "national" nucleus of the empire together with the officers of the imperial army and the imperial bureaucracy. To these one must add the ecclesiastical and secular intelligentsia, who are the creators and propagators of universalistic ideas and of the cultural values identified with and symbolized by the empire, the long-distance traders, and the bourgeoisie who flourish under its protection.

To sum up, within a political power structure of the empire type we may expect to find mutually exclusive homogeneous societies with separate traditions and folk cultures in addition to an ethnically heterogeneous mediating elite with a dynamic "national" civilization (or "high culture").

REFERENCES

Barrow, G. W. S., *Feudal Britian: The Completion of the Medieval Kingdoms, 1066–1314.* London: Edward Arnold, Publishers Ltd., 1956.

Bergel, Egon E., "The European Estate Systems," in E. Bergel, *Social Stratification.* New York: McGraw-Hill Book Company, 1962, pp. 99–151.

Bosl, Karl, "Staat, Gesellschaft, Wirtschaft im deutschen Mittelalter," in *Handbuch der Deutschen Geschichte*, ed. Bruno Gebhard, vol. I (8th ed.). Stuttgart: Union Verlag, 1958a, pp. 585–684.

———, "Reich," in *Sachwörterbuch der deutschen Geschichte*, eds. H. Rössler and G. Franz. Munich: R. Oldenbourg, 1958b, pp. 969–973.

———, *Die Gesellschaft in der Geschichte des Mittelalters*. Göttingen: Vandenhoeck & Ruprecht, 1969.

Brunner, Otto, *Land und Herrschaft: Grundfragen der territorialen Verfassungsgeschichte Südostdeutschlands im Mittellalter* (4th ed.). Vienna: Rudolf M. Rohrer Verlag, 1959.

———, "Feudalismus," *Abhandlungen der Geistes- und Sozialwissenschaftlichen Klasse*, Jahrgang 1958. Wiesbaden: Akademie der Wissenschaften und der Literatur in Mainz, 1959, pp. 589–627.

Clapham, J. H., and Eileen Power, eds. The Cambridge Economic History of Europe from the Decline of the Roman Empire, vol. I: *Agrarian Life of the Middle Ages*. Cambridge: Cambridge University Press, 1942.

Coulborn, R., ed., *Feudalism in History*. Princeton, N.J.: Princeton University Press, 1965.

Eisenstadt, Shmuel N., *The Political Systems of Empires: The Rise and Fall of the Historical Bureaucratic Societies*. New York: The Free Press of Glencoe, 1963.

Emerson, Rupert, *From Empire to Nation: The Rise of Self-Assertion of Asian and African Peoples*. Cambridge, Mass.: Harvard University Press, 1960.

Ganshof, François L., *Feudalism*. London: Longmans, Green & Co., 1952.

Handelsmann, M., "Le rôle de la Nationalité dans l'histoire du Moyen Age," *Bulletin of the International Committee of Historical Sciences*, II, no. 2 (1929), pp. 235–246.

Hugelmann, K. G., *Stämme, Nation und Nationalstaat im deutschen Mittelalter: Nationalstaat und Nationalitätenrecht im deutschen Mittelalter*, vol. I. Stuttgart: W. Kohlhammer Verlag, 1955.

Kämpf, Hellmut, ed., *Herrschaft und Staat im Mittelalter*. Darmstadt: Wissenschaftliche Buchgesellschaft, 1964.

Lemberg, Eugen, *Geschichte des Nationalismus in Europa*. Stuttgart: Curd E. Schwab, 1950.

Wenskus, Reinhard, *Stammesbildung und Verfassung: Das Werden der frühmittelalterlichen Gentes*. Köln: Grünauer Hermann Böhlau Nachf. Verlag, 1961.

Prelude to Nation-Building

6

The preceding discussion of the role of territorial princes within an empire has paved the way for a closer investigation of the relationship between nation-building and the state-type of political power structure. The modern state not only laid the foundations of the modern nation, but the nation-state that emerged in the Age of Nationalism was itself a modification or variety of the more basic type of territorial state, of which the Age of Absolutism provided the most perfect examples. Thus, the analysis of the prenational type of modern state will give us a better understanding of the national type, and should help us to visualize a postnational stage of political organization, the outline of which can already be discerned in our own day.

THE RISE OF TERRITORIAL STATES

At the end of the Middle Ages we find forces working towards an emancipation from authority, a concentration of power, and a consolidation of contiguous territories. The actual outcome of this movement depended very much on circumstance. If a paramount ruler was able to increase his power over the princes of territorial subdivisions included in the imperial superstructure, he himself became a sovereign monarch unhampered by traditional curbs on his power, and the segmented empire type of power structure was transformed into the comprehensive state type. Such was the case in England and France. If, however, the princes of the constituent units succeeded in shaking off the imperial authority while suppressing similar emancipatory tendencies among cities and nobility within their own territory, the superstructure dissolved into a plurality of independent territorial states under the rule of sovereign monarchs and/or of sovereign city republics. Such was the case in Italy and Germany.

SOCIAL CHANGE

The formation of territorial states by either one of these processes was marked by profound changes in the body politic.

1. The intermittent exercise of particularistic power by a variety of political authorities was changed to the continuous exercise of universalistic power by one authority.
2. As internal peace and external defense became the sole responsibility of the territorial prince, he tended to monopolize the use of force. Instead of relying on the private armies of vassals and allies in addition to local militias, he organized a standing army of professional soldiers, often foreign mercenaries.
3. The administration of justice was unified under the authority of the prince. At the same time, the existing codes of traditional law and custom (and there were many of them) were formalized and consolidated. Gaps or inconsistencies were corrected by the enactment of positve laws. This, however, did not yet imply a uniform legal system or the "rule of law." Customary privileges and inequalities were, in fact, legalized and emphasized so that traditional status divisions became more conspicuous and rigid. The whole country was administered directly by a hierarchy of bureaucrats. Offices were no longer held by members of the local nobility, but were filled by professionals; as a rule, urban commoners, often graduates of Italian law schools, and foreigners. The formalization of law and the bureaucratization of government required an expertise that the companions and vassals of the king, his traditional counsellors, and the former aristocratic administrators often did not have. The new corps of civil servants was deliberately separated from both elite and people so that their decisions would be guided entirely by the rule of law in the general interests of state, prince, and people, without any regard to traditional bonds and particularistic interests.

The State and the Estates. The expansion of state functions required a drastic increase of financial resources. As income from the private domains and other property of the prince did not meet the mounting costs, it became imperative to introduce new taxes, to increase tax rates, and to ensure a more regular flow of income into the treasury. At this point, the estates, whose political functions had been curtailed by the territorial princes and who had rarely been assembled by him, gained a new importance. For any new levy or taxation (apart from feudal and customary obligations) required the consent of the magnates and prelates assembled at the court of the paramount ruler. The increased financial needs of the state offered them an opportunity to reassert their political influence. A new balance of power was struck between the prince and the estates, to which the cities had been added. This power system remained typical for a transitory period from the late Middle Ages to the Age of Absolutism. The assemblies of the estates became permanent institutions and developed a strong sense of corporate solidarity. In return for financial assistance, they demanded redress of grievances and a greater share in government through officials whom they themselves nominated. In some countries, notably England, even legislation became the joint concern of king and parliament: in others, it remained the sole prerogative of the king-in-council.

The Estates and the Nation. The early territorial state had two separate centers of power: the executive (the prince, the council, and the ministers) and the estates. The officials employed by the prince as administrators were often aliens or had been alienated from the people because of their training, employment, and residence. The prince himself often ruled over several different countries; frequently, he held his position by the historical accident of dynastic succession, marriage, inheritance, or outright purchase without, in many cases, being bound to the country by birth or by traditional solidarities.

The estates, however, were natives and close to the people. They were, in their own estimation, the genuine representatives of the country, the defenders of the law, the guardians of the native culture and language. The assembled estates were addressed as the "nation" when, in the name of the whole population including the common folk, they exercised political power jointly with or even in opposition to the territorial prince who ruled the country through the bureaucracy. Thus, the "nation," in this sense, consisted of the politically active nucleus of a territorial population as distinct from the "people." The latter comprised the broad masses of lower status who had no part in the affairs of state. In another sense, however, the "nation" that the estates represented, was taken to be the equivalent of the ethnic core of the country.

ABSOLUTISM

The better the territorial prince was able to free himself from control by the estates, the more absolute he became. However, the more that ultimate power was concentrated in his hands, the greater was his reliance on the state machinery at his command, without which he could not govern. This meant that the state gradually became independent of the prince until, finally, the state could altogether do without the prince. Eventually, the sovereign monarch was replaced by the sovereign nation. Yet the power wrested from the king was not restored to the estates as the embodiment of the nation, but ideally to the people at large, realistically to a new power elite claiming to be the true representatives of the nation.

The adage ascribed to King Louis XIV of France, *"L'état, c'est moi,"* is widely regarded as expressing the quintessence of absolutism. What Louis XIV really wrote was this: "The king represents the nation; all the power is in his hands . . . in France the nation is not a corporation (of estates) but resides exclusively in the person of the king" (quoted by Hertz, 1957, p. 314). Eventually, the word "nation" acquired new meanings; one of them was equivalent to "estates," another referred to the corporate body of the "people" from which—in the language of the Revolution—not only the king but also nobility and prelates now were expressly excluded. The terminological shifts reflect not only changes in political ideas, but in the actual power structure as well.

To recapitulate: The more the prince succeeded in eliminating the co-rule of the estates and in concentrating the functions of government in the hands of his appointees, the greater became the part played by the state bureaucracy in the exercise of absolute power. For without its cooperation, the monarch was powerless. When finally "the Court shed responsibility for the practical as distinct from the ceremonial functions of kingship" (Beloff, 1956, p. 23), an abstract principle was concretized in the persons of the state agents with whom the king's "subjects" were confronted. Even after the ultimate, often only nominal, control of the state machinery had passed from the sovereign king to elected representatives of the sovereign people, regimentation by the all-powerful state remained almost unchanged. At this point, a new term intruded itself into the political discussion: "society" as distinct from the "state." It stood for that sphere of economic and social life that should be free from state interference.

The Doctrine of the Absolute Power of Monarchs

According to Bodin's classical formula, the power of the monarch was supreme and not subject to laws. This meant that the monarch had unlimited freedom of action, subject to no control whatsoever; and that he was entitled to tax his subjects without asking for the consent of the estates. It was never suggested, however, that all decisions should be made arbitrarily by him alone. Actually, the absolute monarch continued to take advice from councillors and ministers appointed by him, although he was not bound to accept it; his decision was his own and final. Moreover, executive action was taken on many levels by subordinate officers. Although royal approval of such actions was implicit rather than explicit, they were subject to revision on appeal. No appeal, however, was possible in the case of a royal decision or command, and in this sense the king's word was indeed law. Normally, the absolute monarchy tended to preserve existing inequalities in the distribution of wealth, power and prestige, and even multiplied them.

Neither in theory nor in actual practice was the absolute monarch above the law. He was expected to respect private property as well as rights to offices and titles. Even his power of legislation was curtailed, for instance, by domestic laws of the royal family regulating the succession to the throne. Above all, the king was supposed to observe divine and "natural" law. Although there was no human authority before whom he could be held responsible, the legitimacy of his authority was impaired if he acted contrary to what was considered right. During the *ancien régime* in France the royal ordinances had to be registered with the Parlement de Paris, a kind of Supreme Court. If it censured a royal ordinance on the grounds that it was contrary to traditional law, the verdict was, as a rule, respected by the Crown.

Enlightened Absolutism. The philosophy of Enlightenment propounded a new conception of state functions, which had a more direct influence upon interethnic relations. According to this school of thought, the monarch was not above the law but subordinate to the state, its "first servant," as Frederic II of Prussia expressed it. The theory of social contract provided the legitimation of state authority. The ultimate political criterion was to be "reason," which enabled statesmen to recognize the general principles of natural law and the justice and practicability of every political transaction. As long as the state conformed to these general principles and took rational and efficient steps toward their realization, its authority could not be challenged. State power was still "absolute," qualified only by the rule of law.

Statecraft. As monarchs and statesmen proceeded to realize their political aims in accordance with the doctrines of absolutism, a new type of statecraft emerged. It was conceived as a technology that required scientific knowledge of the general laws of nature, especially human nature, as well as adequate empirical information about actual conditions. The one was supplied by the new "cameral sciences" (including budding sociology), the other by inquiries, surveys, and statistical compilations prepared by a network of government bureaus. They provided the basis for rational policy decisions to be carried out by a hierarchy of administrative officials. Since physics, especially mechanics, served as a model for social science, the state population (the object of internal politics) was conceived analogically as the sum total of equivalent atoms. This was not only consistent with the individualism that had sprung up among the elite since the Renaissance, but it was also welcomed as a justification of the efforts made to deprive the traditional elites of their political power.

Before investigating the effects of absolutist statecraft, we should make clear that etatism survived the downfall of the absolute monarchs. Its practices were continued by the statesmen of the Revolution and their successors. The nation-state, after all, is itself only one variety of the modern state. In the following summary, we are therefore compelled to anticipate some of the effects of absolutist statecraft that were actually manifested in later times.

Centralized Administration. Absolutist statecraft built up a centralized system of bureaucratic administration with a single hierarchical chain of command

and with channels of communication through which, ideally, every single individual was reached from the top without the mediation of the traditional elites; that is, to the exclusion of intermediary powers, so called by Montesquieu. This had a profound effect on popular attitudes toward political authority. During earlier periods people had been confronted with authorities who, however cruel, unjust, and arbitrary, were still human beings like themselves; their actions and reactions at least seemed intelligible. Now the officials with whom the common man had face-to-face relationships were not only strangers to the community, but appeared to be the unfeeling instruments of a remote and abstract power called "the state" and "the law." There was no way of persuading superiors to change their minds, nor could one obtain redress of grievances or gain benefits and acts of grace except through a hierarchy of bureaus manned by faceless bureaucrats. Without the protection of their kin, close associates, and patrons, the people felt at the mercy of a dehumanized power which reached into every corner of their personal lives.

It was precisely those bureaucratic features that were meant to guarantee the rationality, efficiency, and legality of public administration, that resulted in the alienation from the state. The impression was mitigated by the myth that represented the prince as the strict but benevolent father of the country—a mundane version of the Christian God. Still, the state, which did not ask for consent and active cooperation but for passive obedience, was felt to be an alien force arbitrarily interfering with people's destinies. Instead of a manmade institution created for his benefit, the state appeared as a machine which, like other mechanisms, operated in accordance with inexorable laws to which even its operators professed to be subject. The alienation reached a dangerous climax when the state extended its functions to the regimentation of the personal economic activities of its subjects.

Heterogeneity of the State Population. The population of absolutistic states had been politically united by historical accident and were generally, with the exception of smaller states, highly heterogeneous. This is true not only of the common people but also of the elites. Their common civilization and literary language, which differed from the folk culture of the masses, were as often "international" as they were "national." By and large, the refined culture of a territorial elite was that of the court. Where princes imitated the King of France, as in Germany, the culture and language of the court were French. Differences between the various folk cultures and dialects were of no immediate concern to the state. Nevertheless, administration and economic policy suggested the adoption of one official standard language throughout the state territory which could be understood by high and low, in town and country, by officials and their charges alike.

Frequently, the language adopted by the bureaucracy for internal use (in Hungary Latin until the last century) differed from that used in dealing with the people, which was usually one of the regional vernaculars discussed earlier. We recall that communication posed no major problems to the government as long as mediating elites transmitted the intentions of the central administration to their constituencies, not just by translating laws and ordinances literally into the local dialects, which often did not even possess appropriate words for highly technical terms, but by interpreting their meaning. The same elite also transmitted the wishes and sentiments of the common people to higher authorities (cf. Montesquieu, 1965, pp. 133–136). This state of affairs changed, however, when positive law and written regulations replaced old custom and personal command and when alien bureaucrats took over the political functions of traditional elites. Now the state had to decide which of the several idioms spoken by the common people should be adopted for official use. The introduction of an official *lingua franca* has the added advantage of facilitating business transactions between different parts of the country and different sections of the population.

While etatism helped to overcome internal differences and barriers, it tended to throw up and heighten barriers along international boundary lines. The sovereign state suffered no alien authority and permitted no outside interference with its internal affairs. It jealously guarded its resources by prohibiting emigration, limiting travel through strict passport laws, and controlling the traffic of goods through customs and export regulations. It even restricted the flow of ideas across its frontiers through censorship. Every opportunity was seized to emphasize differences between the closed world within the state and the strange, and potentially hostile, world without. To the political closure epitomized by the principle of sovereignty was added an economic closure propagated by mercantilism, as well as a general social closure against foreign countries. This was later completed by the linguistic and cultural closure brought about by the state-controlled system of public or "national" education. Thus, after fragmented and segmentalized social structures had prevailed for centuries, the entire population of a sovereign state came to resemble a closed system of social relations. It was this situation created by the modern state that suggested the novel concept of "society," understood as the most comprehensive social unit.

International Relations. The theory and policy of the modern state also had their repercussions in the sphere of international relations. As all effective power was concentrated in the government, the only conceivable subjects of international law and politics were sovereign states. Relations between them were regulated by treaties (that is, contract); conflicts were resolved by war and/or negotiation and arbitration. International order could be maintained only if contractual obligations entered into by state governments were binding for all. Accordingly, every man and every inch of ground were assumed to be subjects of some government having absolute jurisdiction over a territory defined by fixed boundaries. The people were regarded as pertaining to the territory in much the same way as were its natural resources. It thus became the foremost concern of the state to protect its territory against any division from within and from any violation from without.

Demotic Unification. The long-term effects of etatism played a crucial role in the demotic integration of the entire state population. A common government and economy, common institutions and laws, a common language, common interests and experience, statewide mobility, communication and interaction leading to intermarriage and the establishment of kinship ties over wide areas, as well as barriers put up against other countries and intense differentiation between natives and foreigners; all this contributed to the general homogenizing and levelling processes that preformed the modern nations. The state and its people, that is, the "nation," tended to become the principal focus of identification and solidarity. Patriotism, implying service and attachment to the state, became a supreme value, which tended to supersede allegiance to traditional social units.

Mobilization. Mobilization (or activation) was another, even if incidental, effect of etatistic policies. By this we mean primarily the release of latent energies for social, economic, political, and cultural change. A mobilized segment of society includes those who are not only capable of imagining a polity different from the existing one but are also ready to accept radical change and to take an active part in remolding the social fabric. Three factors seem to have contributed to the mobilization which took place in the absolutist state:

1. Increased mobility tended to broaden the people's outlook and to produce a greater objectivity towards their own native culture.
2. Alienation and dissatisfaction with inequalities in the distribution of social rewards increased the readiness to accept new standards of value and even utopian goals.
3. The modernizing tendencies of state politics—which amounted to a veritable "revolution from above," particularly in the spheres of the internal administration and the economy—had a generally unsettling effect, creating a good deal of social disorganization among both the common people and the traditional elites. When traditional political units were deprived of their functions, many people were torn from their social moorings and searched for a new psychological anchorage and reference group. It was no accident that the fathers of the French Revolution were, in large part, of privileged status. Nor was it an accident that the people at large were ready to recognize them as their representatives.

In conclusion, it may be said that the homogenization and mobilization of the state population set the stage for the national movement and the emergence of the nation-state.

R E F E R E N C E S

Beloff, Max, *The Age of Absolutism, 1660–1815*. London: Hutchinson's University Library, 1956.

Bühl, Walter L., "Zur Typologie der nationalen Ordnungen und das Problem der Soziologie," *Sociologia Internationalis*, VII (1969), pp. 1–31.

Clark, Sir George N., *Early Modern Europe from About 1450 to About 1720*. London: Oxford University Press, 1966.

Heller, Hermann, *Staatslehre*. Leiden: Sigthoffs Uitgevermaatschappij, 1934.

Hertz, Frederick O., *Nationality in History and Politics: A Psychology and Sociology of National Sentiment and Character*. London: Routledge & Kegan Paul, 1957.

Hofmann, Hanns Hubert, ed., *Die Entstehung des modernen souveränen Staates*. Köln: Kiepenheuer & Witsch, 1967.

Lemberg, Eugen, *Nationalismus*, vol. I: *Psychologie und Geschichte*. Reinbeck bei Hamburg: Rowohlts Taschenbuch Verlag, 1964.

Montesquieu, Charles-Louis de Secondat, dit de, "Les Pouvoirs Intermédiaires," in Jean Ehrard, *Politique de Montesquieu*. Paris: Armand Colin, 1956, pp. 133–136.

Parry, J. H., *Europe and the Wider World, 1415–1715* (3rd ed.). London: Hutchinston & Co., 1966.

Strayer, Joseph R., "The Historical Experience of Nation-Building in Europe," in K. W. Deutsch and W. J. Foltz, eds., *Nation-Building*. New York: Atherton Press, 1966, pp. 17–26.

Nationalism and the Nation-State

7

During the nineteenth century, the Age of Absolutism gradually faded into the Age of Nationalism; the absolutist state was transformed into the nation-state. In the West the national movement gained momentum earlier than in Eastern Europe, where vestiges of an imperial power structure survived in Turkey, Russia, Austria, and to some extent, in multiethnic Prussia. During the Age of Absolutism, the groundwork was laid for the demotic structures on which the nation-state was founded. It was during this period, then, that the nation in embryo was formed, and slowly, with the help of a political power instrument inherited from the absolutist state, the nation-state evolved. This whole process has been described in the preceding chapter. Let us now examine the principal ideas that gave impetus and direction to the national movement.

The territorial state suggested a new focus of identification but failed to arouse strong sentiments of solidarity. Integrity, power, and aggrandizement—the concern of princes, elites, and bureaucracies—were not values to be readily grasped by the alienated masses. Their interests were economic rather than political. Changes in the economy, such as an increasing division of labor, pointed in the direction of organic solidarity (as understood by Durkheim). But a new inclusive interpretation of societal unity was missing which might help express this solidarity, help integrate it with the allegiance required by the state, and provide it with moral legitimation. Once the idea of Christendom symbolized by the Roman Church and Empire collapsed under the schisms of the Reformation and the partitions into sovereign states, the spirit of secularism triumphed. The humanistic conception, offered as an alternative to religion by the philosophers of the Enlightenment, was far too abstract, far too remote from the experience of the common man to arouse any strong sentiments outside certain intellectual circles. There was a need for a new ideology comprehensible to all. This was provided by an intellectual movement which in various ways combined three basic trends: democratism, liberalism, and nationalism.

Democratism. Democratism is concerned with the relationship between the few who exercise political power and the many who are subject to it.[1] The problem became particularly acute with the concentration and depersonalization of state power when, after the masses had been freed from traditional bonds, this question was no longer just a concern of emperors, princes, and nobility, but became a universal problem that had to be solved on a broader basis. Democratism provided an answer by suggesting that the sovereignty of the ruler be replaced by the sovereignty of the ruled.

Liberalism. Apart from the question as to who should make ultimate policy decisions is the problem of how much power should be vested in the state. It concerns the proper functions of the state, the spheres of social life to be excluded from state-interference, the rights of individuals and collectivities in their dealings with the state, the methods of exercising state power, and the control to prevent its abuse. The policy of placing restrictions on the scope and power of the state may be called "liberalism."

Nationalism. Democratism and liberalism, which have been described as the twofold heritage of the Great Revolution (Kohn, 1962, p. 8), focus on the internal order. Yet the nation, which according to democratism is supposed to determine its own political destiny, and the democratic state, whose power according to liberalism should be restricted, exist only within a larger social context. So here we have a problem of external order. Moreover, the very boundaries separating one nation from the other require definition. The question of what constitutes a nation and of who should be included in or excluded from it touch directly the central concern of this book.

This is not the place to analyze the various meanings which the word "nation" has been given in politics, law, or in the social sciences (cf. Francis, 1965, pp. 69–87). It would be utterly futile to look for any common denominator. Karl Renner insisted that it "is neither a scientific nor an ethnological nor a sociological but a political concept" (Renner, 1958, p. 7; transl. by E.K.F.). A political concept does not serve to state facts but to express intentions. It is not meant to convince rationally but to persuade emotionally. It does not call for intellectual agreement but for practical action. Vagueness and ambiguity are its virtues: it should appeal to diverse interests and be applicable to many different situations.

Nationalism cannot be considered to be simply an ideology reflecting vested interests and justifying ulterior motives. It is more than that. It is also an active

---

[1]The original term used to designate political theories of this type was "republicanism"; it has become unsuitable through its association with the formal head of state. It makes no provision for the fact that a monarch may be more than the ceremonial head of a democracy, or that democratically elected presidents may wield absolute power. The term "democracy," on the other hand, has become controversial due to contemporary ideological disputes over its proper meaning.

ingredient of social reality; a moral postulate or principle of social action orientation. Perhaps it would be less confusing if we described nationalism as a political doctrine, a system of political ideas. As Eric Voegelin has pointed out,

> what welds the diffuse mass of individual life into a group unit are the symbolic beliefs entertained by the members of a group. Every group has its symbols which permit of concentrating into an emotional and volitional substance that, if viewed empirically, is a stream of human action, articulated by behavior and purposes of highly questionable unity . . . . It is not the function of an idea to describe social reality but to assist its constitution (Voegelin, 1940, p. 294).

Ideas are guidelines of human behavior; they set goals, value standards, and norms of conduct. Political doctrines aim at a system of ideas by which scattered intentions are drawn together into a consistent whole, strenghtening the sense of conviction and purpose, offering rational support and legitimation to the social order which is the goal of our actions.

By "nationalism" we may also understand a social movement aiming at the realization of such ideas. In common with any other social movement it has its origin in a vague dissatisfaction with existing conditions. The general unrest that results from disenchantment may express itself in groping attempts to relieve frustration, vexation, and misery; to redress particular grievances of immediate concern; and even to design an entirely new and better social order. As leaders and action groups stir up passions, mobilize support, and induce ever-wider sections of the population to cooperate towards definite goals, unrest turns into a social movement with a revolutionary potential. At this point the ideological aspect of a social movement assumes major significance. An ideology supplies pseudoscientific and seemingly rational arguments for a variety of motives and intentions that are not stated openly but are actually obscured by rhetoric. Its purpose is to offer spurious proofs of the righteousness of a cause and the ultimate success of a proposed course of action. Finally, when we speak of the Age of Nationalism, we refer not only to the prevalence of national ideas but to actual social change brought about by national movements.

PLAN OF CHAPTER

In the following pages we shall first deal with two aspects of the national movement: the freedom movement and the movement for national self-determination. Next, we propose to show how the principles propounded by these movements served as instruments of power politics and how political aspiration and national ideology influenced each other. Depending on local conditions and power constellations, the national movements in different countries embraced typical variations of nationalist ideology. In the West, demotic nationalism, born in the liberal and democratic ideas of the Enlightenment, remained prevalent. The philosophy of German idealism and romanticism gave birth, however, to another type of nationalism which stressed the political relevance of shared ethnicity. According to the "principle of nationality," every ethnic unit was entitled to its own nation-state. Risorgimento nationalism, a third type, combined both demotic and ethnic principles; its achievement was "the great national awakening of peoples," which revolutionized the map of Europe. In the final paragraphs of this chapter we shall present a multidimensional matrix of variables that relate certain types of nationalism to situational factors and social classes.

THE FREEDOM MOVEMENT

The freedom movements that ushered in the Age of Nationalism crystallized around several different issues. In the movement for constitutional rights one finds a continuation and expansion of the struggle between the estates and the absolute prince. The "freedoms" that had been lost and were to be restored included not only traditional privileges and exemptions of church, nobility, and cities, but also the right of the "nation," represented by the estates, to participate in state government. Yet the "nation," that is, the politically active part of the state population, had changed its complexion. As the economic weight of the rising bourgeoisie increased, it seemed only reasonable that it should demand a voice in state affairs commensurate with its financial contribution. The commoners were not satisfied with the mere restoration of their traditional right to be represented in the assembly of estates. They aimed at a statement of principles, which would limit the sphere of the state, and which neither prince nor parliament could rightfully disregard or infringe upon.

Such principles had been embodied in the doctrine of natural law which had played an important role in defining the divine rights of kings as well as in establishing the proper functions of enlightened monarchs. Now, however, they were to be restated and adjusted to changed social conditions. What was assumed to have been the content of the original social contract between the ruler and the ruled, was now to be specified and expressed in a solemn declaration agreed upon by all parties concerned. Documents that listed the inalienable "freedoms" of every human being—"freedom" that was not to be violated by any human institution—became known as "declaration of human rights," "bill of rights," or "constitution." Other legal provisions that were considered basic enough to be included in the constitution concerned either specific grievances, widely voiced at a particular time, or the conditions necessary for the proper functioning of democratic government, such as the freedom of the press or the right of assembly.

THE DOCTRINE OF GENERAL WILL AND THE NATION

The radical wing of the freedom movement was not so much concerned with limiting state power in favor of individual freedom as with the question of who should ultimately determine state policy. The Swiss writer-philosopher, Jean-Jacques Rousseau, expressed an age-old aspiration to which the excesses of absolutism had given particular urgency: "Men are born free and equal, and everywhere they are in fetters and chains" (Rousseau, 1962, p. 454). The doctrine of the sovereignty of the nation attempted no less than to resolve the fundamental antinomy between the desire for individual "emancipation" and the "repression" involved in all human association. The argument, when deprived of its metaphysical trimmings, runs roughly as follows:

Man is free when he acts in accordance with the moral law which in his own conscience he feels to be evident and unquestionable. It entails social responsibilities and obligations that guarantee not only the individual's own well-being, but that of all others, and thus the common good. Positive laws issued and enforced by the state are legitimate only insofar as they implement moral law and apply it to concrete situations. Individual freedom and self-determination can only be safeguarded if the commands of the state do not express the will of one man—neither that of the prince nor that of any other "alien"—but if they are in conformity with a collective decision, freely arrived at by those who are subject to the state: the "nation." In other words, if the sovereignty of the monarch is replaced by the sovereignty of the nation, the general will of the ruled becomes identical with the will of the ruler. Any other form of government, even the most beneficial, must be considered despotic. In this same spirit Kant declared that self-government is better than good government. The crux, of course, is the problem of how it can be realized.

The notion of general will implies the existence of a collective substratum or quasi-person having a will, and the notion of self-government presupposes a society that is capable of governing itself. It was easier to find a symbol for the postulated collectivity than to reach clarity about its nature. The term "nation" suggested itself because of its earlier usage at the period when the Estates General claimed to represent the nation. This concept became questionable, however, when an ever-widening segment of the common people achieved social and economic weight significant enough to warrant its inclusion into the "nation." A tug-of-war ensued over the question of which category of estates—the first and the second (nobility and clergy) or the third—was in a better position to represent the entire political community. The commoners, in their struggle for political ascendency, favored an expansion of the term "nation." Eventually, the third estate claimed to be the true representative, not only of the broad masses, until such time as they should be enlightened and mature enough to exercise the franchise in their own right, but of the entire state population taken collectively. The commoners in parliament insisted that they alone were entitled to be the interpreters of the "general will."

LIBERAL AND RADICAL DEMOCRATISM

Early nationalism has been characterized by Hans Kohn as

a movement of . . . emancipation from the closed world of the past, the promise of an open future in which tolerance and liberalism would integrate various, formerly separated, religious and ethnic groups, classes and castes (Kohn, 1962, p. 19f).

Liberalism aimed no further than the emancipation of the individual from traditional bonds and absolute obligations, and the reduction of the scope of the state sphere to a minimum. Humanity was envisioned as the universal community of free men, which was only accidentally divided into states for superficial administrative purposes. The doctrine of the sovereign nation propounded by radical democratism, on the other hand, implied that whatever was decided in the name of the general will, and however such general will was ascertained, the decision arrived at should have the same unchallengeable authority that the *fiat* of the absolute monarch was supposed to have had. The absolute power of the sovereign nation replaced that of the sovereign prince, and the state machinery inherited from the king was used to complete building up the nation.

The homogenization of the state population, which the absolutist state had initiated by accident rather than by deliberate design, became a task of the utmost urgency for the nation-state. For the state was now viewed as the politically organized nation. The spatial extension of nations was marked by the geographical boundaries of already existing states. As the jurisdiction of the state covered the entire population included in its territory, the politically active core of commoners (the "nation" in its concretized meaning) had to be expanded to its limits. Furthermore, the legitimacy and proper functioning of democratic government required that the citizens should form a viable societal unit having a corporate will. It was therefore the right and duty of the nation-state to remove all obstacles to this unity of purpose; to eradicate—if need be, by brute police force—all the traditional identities and particularistic solidarities, including those based on shared ethnicity, which divided the state population. In order to avoid any misunderstanding, we shall qualify this concept of nation and of national policy as "demotic."

A telling example is supplied by the language policy of the French Revolution and the immediate post-Revolutionary period. In keeping with the principles of absolutist statecraft, language was treated as an administrative problem. To ascertain the actual situation, a survey was carried out by Abbé Grégoire, who, in 1794, reported that in only fifteen departments was the French language in exclusive use. In all probability, the majority of French citizens was either unable to speak French at all or spoke it with great difficulty, and could neither read nor write it. In the south of France, not only the peasants but also the nobility and the burgesses spoke vernaculars almost exclusively, which, though related to French, could not readily be understood by French-speaking persons. In addition, France comprised many regions in which alien languages, such as Spanish, Basque, Italian, Flemish, English, and German were both the sole idiom of daily intercourse and the accepted language of the region.

In view of this veritable confusion of tongues the authorities hastened to have the constitutional law and the most important ordinances translated into the languages spoken in the thirty provinces. As this method proved impracticable, however, it was deemed preferable in the interest of the state to ban from the territory of the republic all languages other than that spoken in the national convention ". . . in a democracy it is treason to the fatherland to let the citizen remain ignorant to the national[!] language," exclaims the orator. "Among a free people language ought to be one and the same for all," comments a second. Another politician of the Revolution concludes:

> In order to exterminate all the prejudices, to develop all the truths, all the talents, all the virtues, to weld all the citizens into the national mass, to simplify the mechanisms and to facilitate the play of the political machine, an identity of language is necessary . . . unity of speech is an integral part of the revolution" (cf. Brunot, 1905, pp. 207, 210).

To achieve this unity, drastic measures, amounting to outright terrorism in the case of Alsace, were taken. The principal means by which the victory of the national language was finally achieved, however, was through the introduction of a general public school system supported and supervised by the state (cf. Francis, 1965, p. 120).

THE EMANCIPATION OF NATIONS

Demotic nationalism had international aspects also. The principle of the sovereign state, regardless of whether the sovereign will was embodied in the monarch or the nation, excluded any outside interference. Nation-states, so it was thought, would never fight each other; only foreign despots had an interest in aggressive wars in order once again to curb the freedom achieved by the citizens of nation-states. Yet it was the duty of free citizens and patriots all over the world to support others in their struggle for freedom. In this vein, Danton announced before the Convention of 1792 that "by sending us as deputies here, the French nation has brought into being a grand committee for the general insurrection of peoples" (Quoted by Kedouri, 1961, p. 92). The political rhetoric of the freedom movement justified not only interference in foreign states, but even the annexation of their territories if this was necessary to free their people from despotism. It also seemed reasonable to help the subjects of foreign despots to attach themselves to a democratic state if they so desired. Thus, the French Constitution of 1790 denounced wars of aggression: it declared that the French nation would never use their armies to suppress the freedom of other people. Yet it was maintained that not every use of force against other countries was to be considered aggressive. The French nation, it was said, would not hesitate to defend a free people against the unjust aggression of a despot nor to give aid to peoples fighting for the cause of liberty.

Perhaps we should not give too much credence to declarations of noble purpose or to political arguments that are prone to be settled in the battlefield or by diplomatic compromise, reflecting more accurately the existing power constellations than the political doctrines. Yet the principles of democratism and nationalism, even if they lend themselves to convenient rationalizations of conflicting goals, have proved to be a potent factor in arousing strong sentiments, in providing moral support to particular policies, and in conceiving radical political designs. Once the idea of national freedom had captured the public mind, obvious acts of brute force and solid self-interest acquired a legitimacy that made political strife, if anything, more acrimonious and political conflicts more vicious. Any struggle for particularistic goals tended to escalate into a holy war for a universalistic ideal, which could only be settled either by the conversion or annihilation of the enemy.

Once the national movement had embarked upon a course of international politics, it was confronted with intellectual problems which could only partially be mastered in terms of liberalism and democratism. The nation was conceived in analogy to the individual and thus was thought to have, as a corporate person, the same inalienable right to self-determination. In countries where the absolutist state had laid the foundations for a demotic nation, the notion of self-determination readily blended with the older doctrine of the external sovereignty of the state. The application of this principle to other situations, however, required a reformulation of the concept of nation answering the question as to how the territorial extension and the personnel of the nation-to-be could be recognized which was to determine its own self-constitution as a nation-state. In Germany and Italy, with their multitudes of small territorial states and city-states, the national movement aimed at political unification; in surviving empires, such as Turkey, Austria, or Russia, at partition according to the principle of nationality.

In both cases the nation, instead of simply taking over an already existing state and defending its freedom to determine its internal political affairs against external interference, had to be assumed to exist as a corporate person prior to the state. Any social movement that raised political demands in the name of such a nation was confronted with the task of developing an ideology that would provide a legitimation for its right to self-determination and, at the same time, a practicable method of identifying the territory and population exactly.

From this we gather that the elaboration of the doctrine of national self-determination had not only theoretical but also eminently practical aspects. We shall first describe the historical developments of international power politics that influenced the new conception of the nation and of its right to self-determination.

NATIONAL SELF-DETERMINATION AND POWER POLITICS

The idea of national self-determination proved to be a potent, yet double-edged, sword of power politics. Napoleon Bonaparte, heir to the Great Revolution, was the first to wield it on a European scale; he was also the first to suffer from its boomerang effect. The fate of Poland had attracted the early sympathies of those who advocated the principles of liberalism and democratism. When Napoleon decided to invade Russia, he enlisted Polish support by playing up to nationalist sentiments. He promised the restoration of Polish statehood and set up the Duchy of Warsaw as a first token. At an earlier date, after he had occupied Venice, he employed special agents to encourage the Greeks of the Ionian Islands to rebel against their Venetian masters by awakening in them memories of the ancient glories of Sparta and Athens. In his struggle against the Austrian Emperor, Napoleon pursued a similar course of action. He reminded the Hungarians of their national culture and language and suggested that they free themselves from alien rule. In Italy and Germany, Napoleon merged a multitude of ministates into larger political units. When the Napoleonic system of satellite states threatened to break down, one of his henchmen, Murat, King of Naples, mobilized resistance against the Austrian armies by proclaiming the union and independence of all Italy (which, since Roman times, had never been politically united).

Napoleon's enemies used the same ideology to their own advantage. The insurrections in 1809 of the Spaniards and the Tyrolese peasants (who under the leadership of priests faced up to superior military forces) were later interpreted in national terms to serve as an inspiration in the Wars of Liberation. England advocated the national freedom of Spain and the Netherlands; Czar Alexander of Russia assembled in Vilna a "Tribunal of Nations" in an attempt to represent the Grand Coalition of European monarchs as a league of oppressed peoples. In 1813, the allies enlisted national sentiments for a war against despotism. After his defeat, Napoleon himself proposed a peace on the basis of the independence of nations. When the Holy Alliance finally succeeded in restoring the order that Napoleon's imperialism had broken up, Czar Alexander declared the nations of Europe to be brethren and the monarchs to be their representatives. He also granted national autonomy to Finland and made similar promises to Poland and the Balkan countries. From that time on, the principle of national self-determination has remained a mainstay of political rhetoric and a leitmotif of world politics. It has served to legitimize particularistic aspirations as well as universalistic goals of the kind expressed in Wilson's Fourteen Points, Roosevelt's Atlantic Charter, or the programs of the League of Nations and the United Nations.

THE FREEDOM MOVEMENT IN GERMANY

The new conception of the nation, mentioned earlier, first took shape in Germany. The symbol and its moral appeal remained unaltered; its content, however, was radically changed when it was adopted by German patriots to legitimize their struggle against French dominance and domination. Actually, the freedom movement in Germany (despite the fact that the Napoleonic occupation had contributed to its mass appeal) was older than the French Revolution. The first to rebel against the cultural dominance of France were men of letters. In the seventeenth and eighteenth centuries French was not only the recognized language of diplomacy and erudition, it was also used by the privileged classes in their homes. Scholars—unless they continued lecturing and publishing in Latin—wrote and corresponded in French in order to gain international attention and to exchange ideas with the foremost thinkers of the time. Frederic II of Prussia considered it natural to think, write, and converse in French, and he was also steeped in French culture, drew inspiration from French thinkers like Voltaire, and surrounded himself with French advisors. Moreover, he invited Hugenot refugees to help with his mercantile policies.

Everywhere, French manners, etiquette, fashion, and refinement were imitated, and the new revolutionary ideas were eagerly embraced by many, not so much because they answered a genuinely felt need, but because they were French and thus a mark of good breeding and sophistication. Intellectuals of more humble birth, however, to whom language was their tool of creative activity and the source of their livelihood, and who found the avenues to social prestige and public influence blocked, gave vent to their frustrations by purifying their native tongue from alien, particularly French, elements. Societies for the cultivation of German language and literature became rallying points of German nativism and xenophobia.

The dramatic events in France and the ideas of the Revolution nevertheless had their impact upon German literati and philosophers. The Wars of the Coalition, conducted originally against republicanism and then against French expansionism, found German states pitted against each other in opposing camps. Defeat and occupation, particularly of Prussia, gave impetus to the German freedom movement. While liberalism and democratism had a certain influence, nationalist tendencies counted for much more. The fervent desire to restore German unity and greatness and to liberate the Germans from French influence and domination, however, was not easily expressed in an idiom that was more adapted to conditions in France or England. Above all, any national ideology would have to provide a cogent proof that the Germans, just as the

French, constituted a nation. None of the smaller states, however, provided a realistic focus of national identification, whilst the most powerful ones, Prussia and Austria, included populations with diverse cultural traditions and ethnic identities. Despairing of ever attaining an early renewal of political unity as it had existed in the Middle Ages, men of letters turned to symbols of national identity and solidarity other than the state. There are good grounds for the contention that the political philosophy of German idealism reflects the effort to master intellectually the complex German situation in the Age of Nationalism.

ETHNIC NATIONALISM

We shall call the type of nationalism that first emerged in Germany and then spread east and south, *ethnic nationalism*. For, generally speaking, the nation is identified here not with the demotic unit of a given state population, but with an ethnic unit supposedly antedating any particular state. The roots of this doctrine go back to the German poet and philosopher, Johann Gottfried Herder. He and his followers conceived the nation to be a collective personality endowed with a soul or a spiritual substance called *Volksgeist,* which found expression in a distinctive culture of its own. The unity and greatness of the nation consisted, not in a common state, but in a unique "culture," that is to say, in "higher" spiritual achievements, such as language, literature, art, science, religion, morality, and law. If ever the Germans were to be reunited politically, they had to be made aware of their national identity. Cultivation of German language and literature and immersion in the history of the Middle Ages when German prestige and leadership were at their height were recommended as means to promote national consciousness.

Ethnic nationalism was not only seen as an ideology supporting German interests, but as a doctrine of universal validity equal with demotic nationalism. All ethnic nations have a right and sacred duty to preserve and unfold the distinctive culture that is their heritage and the expression of their "spirit." Any recognizable ethnic unit was viewed as a potential nation which, if it proved at all possible, should be united in a nation-state of its own. Thus, the idea of national freedom and self-determination assumed a new meaning. In Western Europe it meant that the demotic nation took over the government of an existing sovereign state, thereby safeguarding its self-determination. In the freedom movement that spread from Germany east and south, however, the term "self-determination" meant the liberation of a preestablished ethnic society from alien influence and foreign domination. The one freedom movement revolutionized the internal structure of societies, the other revolutionized the map of Europe—and eventually of the world.

The problem of how an ethnic unit, that is to say, a nation-to-be, was to be recognized, and how its boundaries were to be defined with sufficient exactness as to permit the political and legal implementation of the doctrine still remained unsolved. Several criteria were suggested, of which the following have been the most commonly used, either singly or in combination: (1) a territory occupied by an ethnic unit which at one time was politically united; (2) the manifest will of a population regarded as belonging to a particular ethnic unit; (3) a distinctive language; and (4) a common "racial" origin. When applied to concrete situations, none of these criteria proved to be unequivocal; moreover, conclusions differed widely and often contradicted each other. As we shall return to this point later, it suffices here to single out for brief inspection two arguments used to establish the existence of a distinctive ethnic unit.

In the *Addresses to the German Nation,* which the idealist philosopher, Johann Gottlieb Fichte, delivered in the darkest days of French oppression, we read: "We give the name of people to men whose organs of speech are influenced by the same external conditions, who live together, and who develop their language in continuous communication with each other" (Fichte, 1955, 62ff). He also taught that, unlike the French who spoke a composite idiom in part derived from a dead language (Latin), the Germans were an *Urvolk* (primordial ethnie) which had never been corrupted by the influence of alien languages and races. They alone were therefore capable of the highest cultural perfection and destined to world leadership. This line of thought was later revived under the influence of Darwinism, when "races" were viewed in analogy to biological species struggling for survival and supremacy. Now each race was supposed to be endowed with specific mental characteristics that could not be changed except by a hybridization, which necessarily led to its degeneration.

THE AWAKENING OF NATIONS

So far we have concentrated on national ideology; the time has come to consider its effects on practical politics. The most explosive mixture of national ideas and the most virulent combination of ethnic and demotic principles of political action may be seen in risorgimento nationalism. The word *risorgimento* (derived from *risorgere* which means "to rise again") was adopted in Italy to describe the efforts made to awaken national sentiments among the Italians who were divided into several states. The Italian risorgimento movement envisioned not only the political union of the Apennine Peninsula, but the reorganization of Europe into ethnically homogeneous nation-states, involving as its first step the dismemberment of the Austrian empire.

To the Italian risorgimento we owe two political terms that have gained considerable importance in the national movement and ideology. The union of Italy, which was accomplished between 1860–1870, left certain territories inhabited by Italian-speaking populations outside the national boundaries: Trieste,

Istria, and the Trentino remained part of Austria; the Tessin was a Swiss canton; Nice and Corsica belonged to France. These areas were considered *terra irredenta* or unredeemed territory, and the movement that worked for their liberation has become known as "irredentism."

Another political term adopted by risorgimento nationalism was "nationality." It was used to describe an ethnic unit aspiring at independent statehood. The word was given a somewhat different meaning in situations where national claims were recognized as valid without going to the length of granting the ethnic units full political independence. Leaders of a nationality were occasionally satisfied with a reduced program of national autonomy because they could not hope for complete emancipation or because in countries with an ethnically mixed population it was impossible to separate ethnic units geographically. In the case where political autonomy within an existing state was granted to a nationality (including its recognition as a corporate entity, guaranteeing the preservation of its language and culture as well as taking appropriate administrative measures to protect it from assimilation and loss of substance), it could be regarded as an imperfect nation.

The strategy of risorgimento nationalism may be summed up as follows: Ethnic arguments were usually adopted in its initial stages, demotic arguments in the period of consolidation. The compact settlement of a people speaking a distinctive language served mainly as indicator of a potential national unit. Occasionally, ethnic units so defined turned out to be nothing more than small agrarian societies, which could not hope for more than recognition as permanent nationalities. National claims of this kind, moreover, carried no great conviction unless a distinctive language group occupied at least an administrative subdivision of a major political power structure. Still more plausible was the situation whenever it was possible to identify an ethnie with some political unit which, at one time, had played a major role in history but had subsequently lost its independence. If it could be shown that its original population still occupied the territory in question, it was considered sufficient proof that the country belonged to them by right, and that it should become a nation-state or at least an autonomous administrative subdivision of the state exercising jurisdiction over it. Whatever argument appeared most favorable to a particular national cause and most convincing in a given domestic and international situation was advanced in order to arouse or "awaken" the people envisioned as a potential nationality or nation.

As soon, however, as the immediate goal had been accomplished, either full sovereignty or limited autonomy, a diametrically opposed position was taken up by leaders of the risorgimento movement. From now on the entire population of the territory in question was treated as a demotic nation, one and indivisible. The dominant ethnic unit was taken to represent its true core, and its language and culture were declared the national standard. If any portion of the charter ethnic unit was left outside the new political unit, irredentist movements were encouraged, or else steps were taken to protect and support the "separated brethren." Whatever principles and arguments were adopted, however, the national aims remained very much the same: maximation of internal and external power; expansion of the national territory to the greatest extent that, in one way or another, could be justified in terms of an ambiguous national ideology; and defense against any loss of the demographic, territorial, and economic substance. In addition, the promotion of national culture loomed large in an age when international prestige depended on great achievements of the "national genius."

SOCIAL FACTORS ASSOCIATED WITH NATIONAL IDEOLOGIES

Our historical survey has revealed that nationalism is not a homogeneous phenomenon, but a congeries of diverse, often conflicting, ideas and policies clustered around a common symbol with broad emotional appeal. Most general theories of nationalism have concentrated on its demotic version, and have explained it largely by way of economic factors (cf. Deutsch, 1966, p. 71; Lemberg, 1964, vol. I, p. 171).

Yet a much more complex, multidimensional matrix of variables seems to be required to explain diverging national tendencies, and to enable us to predict behavior under specified conditions. To this end, we shall first recapitulate the various types of nationalist movements as the dependent variables, and then suggest a set of independent variables that seem to be empirically correlated with them.

DEPENDENT VARIABLES: TYPES OF NATIONALISM

The advocates of *demotic nationalism* took the state, including its administrative structure and territorial extension, as given. Their main concern was with the proper relationship between the ruler and the ruled and with the liberation of the people from a despotic rule. The sovereignty of the people was to replace the sovereignty of the prince; "alien" rule was to yield to self-determination. These principles, however, could not be realized unless a reasonably homogeneous and culturally integrated society, comprising the whole state population or at least a significant part of it, provided the ground for the formation of a general will. This type of nationalism, therefore, tended to continue and intensify the process of transforming the state population into a demotic unit, a process that had been initiated by absolutist statecraft.

Integral nationalism was adopted when, in demotically conceived nations, a crisis arose due to defeat in war or excessive outside pressure; when national aspirations were blocked; when doubts as to the legitimacy of the national cause were raised; or when feelings of inferiority became widespread. The leaders of this movement enriched demotic ideology with elements of ethnic ideology to demonstrate that the nation was a stark reality prior to the state, and that its existence did not depend on political accident.

Ethnic nationalism included two main subtypes, neither of which was primarily concerned with the principle of self-determination within a given state, or with national sovereignty without. On the contrary, they challenged the sovereignty of existing states and determined collective self-determination for entities that had as yet no actual political existence or had lost it. Ethnic nations of this kind were supposed to be constituted by common descent, a common history, and a common culture, but not necessarily by a common state. This type of national movement strove to make the people concerned aware that they were part of such a unit and that they had a right to be politically united in a single nation-state. The subtypes of ethnic nationalism are characterized by the different factors that were assumed to be constitutive of an ethnic unit or by which the the existence of such a unit could be readily ascertained. Leaders of this movement appealed primarily to linguistic and cultural affinities that were often spurious as symbols of shared ethnicity.

Restorative nationalism applied the term "nation" to a formerly independent political unit that had been submerged in a supernational and multiethnic political power structure of the empire type. The political unit that had once existed in history was conceived as having been a kind of forerunner of a nation-state and as coinciding with a distinctive ethnic unit. The principal aim of this type of national movement was the restoration of a historic nation-state to be accomplished by arousing the collective will of the people concerned.

Risorgimento nationalism may be regarded as the most comprehensive type of nationalism, combining the ambitions and ideas of demotic, ethnic, and restorative nationalisms. It was most influential in the heyday of nation-building in central and eastern Europe. National ideas of the ethnic and restorative type were most effective during the formative period of nations; ideas of the demotic type were propagated to consolidate the new nations or nationalities.

INDEPENDENT VARIABLES: SITUATIONAL FACTORS

Among the factors that influence the ideology adopted by national movements are three situational variables that require special attention: (1) economic, (2) demographic, and (3) political.

The Socioeconomic Situation. Two types of socioeconomic situation seem to have had a bearing upon the emergence of national ideas, one relating to the industrial, the other to the agrarian type of society.

1. Nationalism in industrial society. Commercialization and industrialization and the concommitant transformation of the social structure contributed to the rise of demotic nationalism.
2. Nationalism in agrarian society. National movements in agrarian countries, at least in their initial phase, rarely operated with ideas of the demotic type. For these latter originated in a world alien to both the peasantry and the land-owning elite, in the world of commerce and industry, of urbanism and bureaucracy, of abstract principles and doctrinaire thought. Thus, to the upper as much as to the lower strata of agrarian society, new ideas could become acceptable only if they were made to conform to the traditional interests. The concept of a demotic nation was highly abstract; its meaning could not be grasped easily by illiterate and uneducated people whose way of thinking was intuitive rather than abstract, and who perceived social institutions and collectivities in terms of personal relationships.

The ethnic ideology, on the other hand, represented nations as extended kinship structures and enlarged territorial communities. It also emphasized traditional values that had deep roots in folk culture. The society envisioned by demotic nationalism was of the *Gesellschaft* type; ethnic nationalism thought in terms of collective organism and of a *Gemeinschaft* type of solidarity that corresponded more closely to the daily experience of people living under agrarian conditions. Demotic nationalism worked for the radical break with the past, but ethnic nationalism aimed at the renewal of the old order and its rejuvenation. Ethnic nationalism thus appealed more strongly than did demotic nationalism to the social strata that were fundamentally traditionalist.

Nevertheless, nationalism in agrarian countries cannot be understood as a simple reaction to threats emanating from demotic nationalism. Reactionary forces based their arguments more often upon prenational doctrines, such as the ideology of legitimate rule. In an agrarian society it was often the regional nobility who justified its particularistic tendencies with arguments culled from ethnic and restorative ideologies. The national movement that it initiated or supported was one aiming to restore independence to the native population and to increase the power of its traditional elite.

Among the peasantry, xenophobia and nativism, which are much older and more universal tendencies than nationalism, lend themselves to rationalization in terms of ethnic nationalism. This provided opportunities to arouse popular sentiments, not only against alien conquerors, but also against a central government whose power had become more strongly felt under the absolutist regime.The agrarian population even turned against alien elements in their own midst such as Jews, town folk, and settlers of foreign stock. Furthermore, the upgrading of folk culture by advocates of ethnic nationalism strengthened a solidarity between the peasantry and the elite such as had rarely existed before.

But the main interest of peasants was a more favorable distribution of land and the removal of servitude. When liberal leaders made the peasants' emancipation a national goal, an important step was taken towards winning the agrarian masses over to the national movement, and eventually towards integrating them into the new nation. As the old agrarian order dissolved, the nation was substituted as the prime focus of identity and solidarity in place of the traditional communities.

The Demographic Situation. Nationalism of whatever type had little difficulty in applying its principles to areas with an ethnically homogeneous population. For here the territory of the nation-state coincided with a territory occupied by a population having a common language, culture, and history. Where a territorial population was of diverse ethnic origin, the situation was different. Demotic nationalism was confronted with the task of homogenizing the state population and with the risk of arousing resistance in the name of ethnic nationalism.

Advocates of ethnic nationalism faced other problems. The modern state is defined by its territorial jurisdiction. The territory of a nation-state, which (according to the ethnic doctrine) was to embrace only one complete ethnic unit, had to correspond with the territory occupied by that ethnic unit. But, as we have seen, shared ethnicity and shared territory are different dimensions of social organization. The intermingling of heterogeneous populations raised the question of how to draw the boundaries of nation-states in such a way that they could best conform to the ideology of ethnic nationalism. Many different and contradictory answers appeared justifiable in terms of the same general doctrine. The so-called national problems to be discussed in the next chapter may be regarded as resulting from the fact that national doctrine does not present a consistent body of principles providing unequivocal guides to practical political action, but rather an assemblage of vague and often conflicting ideologies and political recipes.

The Political Situation. Our historical survey has shown that wherever an economically viable and militarily defensible state of the absolutist type succeeded in transforming its heterogeneous population into a reasonably homogeneous unit with one language and one culture, nationalism was, as a rule, of the demotic type. The situation was different where vestiges of the empire-type of political power structure survived the initial period of nation-building. During the later stages of the national movement, empires were invariably broken up by the national movement or transformed into a different type of political power structure, which will be discussed in the following chapter. As we have already noted, empires tend to include a variety of politically organized collectivities, each having dissimilar ethnic origins. They also fail to homogenize ethnically mixed populations. Accordingly, national movements arising in former imperial power structures were confronted with a particularly tricky task when it came to identifying ethnic units and their territories. This problem gave rise to grave, almost insoluble, conflicts.

INDEPENDENT VARIABLES: CLASS INTERESTS

We now turn to the question: Which collective interests are behind the socioeconomic, demographic, and political conditions associated with the one or other type of nationalism? We shall concentrate on the elites: bourgeoisie, nobility, clergy, and intelligentsia. Historically, these have been the creators of national ideologies as well as the organizers and leaders of national movements; they have also occupied positions of power and influence in national units, once these had come into existence.

The Bourgeois Middle Classes. This group has generally been assumed to be the principal instigator and supporter of nationalist tendencies and movements. To make this claim, we must first clarify the meaning of "middle classes," and then distinguish between the different types of nationalism advocated by this group. The commoners, that is, the property-owning, self-employed merchants and industrialists, have indeed played a leading role in the building of nations during the early period of the national movement. Later on, however, this same bourgeoisie mingled with the nobility; together with the latter, the "barons" of finance and industry must be counted among the new power elite.

In the heyday of nationalism, the so-called middle classes included a wide range of better-educated, urbanized people who had been torn from the moorings of an old and mainly agrarian social order and had become highly mobile—spatially, socially, and intellectually. These classes, above all others, found a new focus of identification in the nation as well as a new *Weltanschauung* and a common value standard in the national ideology. They became the leaders of the national movements and saw in the nation-state the principal means of achieving economic and political power. They were among the foremost advocates of demotic nationalism whenever the political and demographic situation was such that a nation-state, which would be viable and strong in the political and military as well as in the economic sphere, held the promise of advancing their class interests.

In multiethnic states, competition within the middle classes for economic opportunities and political supremacy tended to follow ethnic cleavages. Those actually wielding power were inclined to adopt demotic principles of nationalism; those who felt their aspirations thwarted were apt to legitimize their particularistic and separatistic tendencies in terms of ethnic nationalism. Having once achieved autonomy or independence, however, they behaved like any dominant middle class and embraced a demotic type of nationalism. We, therefore, conclude that risorgimento nationalism, combining ethnic and demotic elements, is most typical for the educated, mobile, and urbanized middle classes, and is linked to the rise of a modern commercialized and industrialized economy.

The Nobility. In the present context this term implies not the many titled persons who, for all practical purposes, had been absorbed by the middle classes, but those who still had to defend an economic, political, and social position sufficiently stable as to develop collective interests. Where the nobility constituted the power elite, or a significant part of it, they rarely embraced nationalism with any great enthusiasm. Whenever they adopted its idiom (they rarely adopted its principles), it was in order to adapt themselves to the political climate of a changing age. If the nobility had lost their power or had suffered setbacks; if their leading and privileged position was threatened, either internally through the centralizing tendencies of an absolutist state or through domination by a foreign conqueror, they tended toward the restorative type of nationalism. In some countries, notably Italy, only that section of the nobility associated with a political unit that was in process of becoming, or had already become, the core of the unified nation-state, participated in the risorgimento movement. Thus, the nobility of the Kingdom of Sardinia strongly supported the risorgimento movement which was to unite Italy under their own monarch. Elsewhere, the Italian nobility was far less attracted by prospects of an Italian nation-state.

The Clergy. Inasmuch as the clergy belonged to the traditional power elite, they could be expected to behave much like the nobility. Yet clergymen have played a very influential role in almost every type of nationalism, except perhaps integralism. The lower ranks of the parish priests or ministers of congregational churches sided most readily with the collective interests of their charges. In agrarian societies, such as Mexico, priests frequently became the outstanding leaders of populist movements and supported a demotic type of nationalism. In other instances, members of the lower clergy cooperated with the secularized intellectuals in upholding the national movements prevalent in the urban middle classes. The higher clergy, however, tended to side with those in power. But when particularistic and regional interests followed ethnic divisions, the clergy, in common with the nobility, were not opposed to adopting the idiom and aspirations of restorative and, with more reluctance, of ethnic nationalism. Whenever ethnic divisions coincided with religious cleavages, all sections of the clergy tended to support that type of nationalism that, in the given circumstances, was likely to protect their flock from contamination with competing religions.

The Intellectuals. The so-called intellectuals can hardly be said to form a definite social class. Usually they are placed in the middle classes. They include not only the creators of higher cultural values and their mediators, but also college-trained specialists in a great variety of professions, especially in science and technology, law and medicine, education and mass communications, economy and the civil service. When focusing our attention on their role in the development of nationalism we have to distinguish between initiators and propagators of national ideas, leaders of national movements and parties, and supporters of nation-states in actual existence. Thus, we can hardly expect to discover any general line followed by intellectuals as such. Nevertheless, they too seem to have their own collective interests, which need not be the same as the interests of those whom they may serve in an official capacity, either by inclination or in the expectation of rewards. The intellectuals as a class have shown a tendency to foster a castlelike self-recruitment and to uphold the prestige and privileges associated in modern society with higher education. Political leaders, members of parliament, and statesmen have been frequently chosen from among them. For this reason, it could be expected that they advocated the type of nationalism that promised them the opportunities of participating in political power, the gaining of prestige, and economic advantages.

Intellectuals, just like other classes, have supported particularistic and separatistic tendencies, whenever the supremacy of competing groups could be challenged in terms of ethnic nationalism. For when an ethnic unit was granted political autonomy or independence, intellectuals speaking its language and identified with it by descent and culture gained new opportunities of employment in politics, the civil service, education, the press, and the fine arts. Many of those who had formerly held important positions were consequently disqualified as aliens—discriminated against or even expelled. Some of the most radical forms of nationalism have undoubtedly had their roots in the collective self-interest of intellectuals.

CONCLUSIONS

We shall sum up our historical findings in a few general hypotheses that may prove useful in understanding more recent developments in nation-building—developments that are discussed in Part IV.

1. Any elite that actually exercises political power in a given state, or that can hope to attain power within the existing framework, will tend to interpret the situation in terms of demotic nationalism, and to identify itself with the nation or its active core.
2. Given an economically viable state, the middle classes that are in ascendancy, although frustrated in their ambitions, can be expected to advocate the ideas of demotic nationalism. They are likely to promote the unitarian

nation-state in which the middle classes assume power in the name of the nation.

3. If the state in question, however, is not economically viable, or if the economic and military resources can be increased by adopting other principles of nationalism, and if the middle classes are not strong enough to attain their ambitions without cooperating with the traditional elite, the middle classes will be inclined to advocate risorgimento nationalism.

4. Whenever different power elites, including sectional interest groups in the middle classes, compete for supremacy, it is likely that they will adopt different types of nationalism; the minority or otherwise weaker groups are liable to chose ethnic nationalism.

5. Restorative nationalism is likely to be embraced by traditional elites, including nobility and clergy, when they feel that their position is being threatened. The liberation of their country from the dominance of an alien elite promises a restoration and improvement of their own prestige, power, and economic situation.

R E F E R E N C E S

See also the Selected Bibliography at the end of the book.

Bendix, Rinehard, *Nation-Building and Citizenship: Studies of Our Changing Social Order*. New York: John Wiley & Sons, 1964.

Brunot, F., *Historie de la langue Francaise des origines à 1900*, vol. IX, part I. Paris: Armand Colin, 1905 ff.

Delos, Joseph T., *La problème de la Civilisation: La nation* (2 vols). Montreal: Editions de L'Arbre, 1944.

Deutsch, Karl W., and William J. Foltz, eds., *Nation-Building*. New York: Atherton Press, 1963.

———, *Nationalism and Social Communication: An Inquiry into the Foundations of Nationality* (2nd ed.). New York: John Wiley & Sons, 1966.

Fichte, Johann Gottlieb, *Reden an die Deutsche Nation*. Hamburg: Felix Meiner, 1955. (*Addresses to the German Nation*, translated by R. F. Jones and G. H. Turnbull 1922).

Francis, Emerich, "Die Nation—Politische Idee und Wirklichkeit" in Francis, *Ethnos und Demos: Soziologische Beiträge zur Volkstheorie*. Berlin: Duncker & Humblot, 1965, pp. 61–121.

Hayes, Carlton J., *Nationalism: A Religion*. New York: The Macmillan Company, 1960.

Heraud, Guy, *Die Völker als Träger Europas*. Vienna: Wilhelm Braumüller, 1967.

Hertz, Frederick O., *Nationality in History and Politics: A Study of the Psychology and Sociology of National Sentiment and Character*. London: Routledge & Kegan Paul, 1944.

Hyslop, Beatrice Fry, *French Nationalism in 1789, According to the General Cahiers*. New York: Columbia University Press, 1934.

Kedouri, Elie, *Nationalism* (2nd ed.). London: Hutchinson's University Library, 1961.

Kohn, Hans, *The Idea of Nationalism*. New York: The Macmillan Company, 1961.

———, *The Age of Nationalism: The First Era of Global History*. New York: Harper & Bros., 1962.

———, *Nationalism: Its Meaning and History* (rev. ed.). Princeton, N.J.: D. van Nostrand Company, 1965.

Koppelmann, H. L., *Nation, Sprache und Nationalismus*. Leiden: A. W. Sijthoff's Uitgeversmaatschappij, 1956.

Laun, Rudolf, *Der Wandel der Ideen Staat und Volk als Äußerung des Weltgewissens: Eine völkerrechtliche und staatsrechtliche Untersuchung auf philosophischer Grundlage*. Barcelona: Institució Patxot, 1933.

Lemberg, Eugen, *Nationalismus* (2 vols). Reinbeck bei Hamburg: Rowohlts Taschenbuch Verlag GmbH, 1964.

Renner, Karl, *Das Selbstbestimmungsrecht der Nationen in besonderer Anwendung auf Österreich*, Teil I: Nation und Staat (2nd ed.). Leipzig: Franz Deuticke, 1918.

Rousseau, J. J., *The Political Writings*, ed. C. E. Vaughn. Oxford: Blackwell, 1962.

Smith, Anthony D., *Theories of Nationalism*. London: Gerald Duckworth & Co. Ltd., 1971.

Snyder, Louis L., *The Meaning of Nationalism* (2nd ed.), New York: Greenwood Press, 1968.

Sulzbach, Walter, *Imperialismus und Nationalbewußtsein*. Frankfurt/Main: Europäische Verlagsanstalt, 1959.

Veiter, Theodor, "Volk, Volksgruppe, Nation", in Veiter, *Das Recht der Volksgruppen und Sprachminderheiten in Österreich*. Vienna: Wilhelm Braumüller, 1966, pp. 1–168.

Voegelin, Eric, "The Growth of the Race Idea," *Review of Politics* II (1940).

Ziegler, Heinz O., *Die Moderne Nation: Ein Beitrag zur politischen Soziologie*. Tübingen: J. C. B. Mohr/Paul Siebeck, 1931.

National Problems

8

The preceding chapter provided insight into the intellectual problems that are bound to arise when the ideas of nationalism are applied to real-life situations. The present chapter is concerned with patterns of political action rather than with patterns of political thought. By "national problems" we understand conflict situations between states as well as within politically organized societies, which are incidental to efforts to adopt national principles as guidelines to political action. Such problems generally originate in the imperfections of the national doctrine itself and in the difficulties encountered in an attempt to apply it to the realities of a given situation. It is sometimes found that certain principles cannot be applied without violating others, or that different parties adopt conflicting principles that are equally implicit in the doctrine.

Moreover, the use of specific indicators to ascertain the precise territory or population of a particular nation or nationality may be inapplicable, may fail to produce conclusive results, or the results may conflict. Finally, the situation to be ascertained may itself be subject to manipulation and change. Yet a given power constellation, economic conditions, strong interests, and so on may suggest political actions that, in the historical context, are incompatible with the principles of nationalism or which lie entirely outside their scope; nevertheless, by way of national symbolism they are presented in such a manner as to be apparently legitimized by the ideology. The existing power constellation may also prevent the full realization of legitimate national aspirations. These are frequently suppressed or dropped when it seems that their realization would endanger the existing social order or bring about serious calamities.

By and large, such conflicts and ambiguities are less liable to arise when nations are constituted in accordance with demotic nationalism, but they are frequent whenever principles of ethnic nationalism are applied. The restoration of a historical nation, for instance, poses the question as to which particular period of history is to be selected in defining national boundaries. This is usually one reason why in addition to ethnic arguments, economic, military, or geographical arguments unrelated to the principles of nationalism are advanced in support of historical claims. Moreover, national problems are more likely to emerge in ethnically heterogeneous areas than in homogeneous areas where it is easier to make the territory of a demotic unit coincide with that of an ethnic unit. In the following pages, we shall therefore concentrate on national problems that are likely to arise when the ideas of ethnic and/or restorative nationalism serve as guides to political action in countries with an ethnically mixed population. In particular, we are interested in practical attempts to remedy national problems. The Austro-Hungarian monarchy has been chosen as a prototype because several methods of problem-solving had actually been experimented with.

AUSTRIA—A MULTINATIONAL EMPIRE

The name "Austria" is derived from that of the eastern marches of Bavaria which, in the twelfth century, were made an independent duchy within the Roman Empire. The first Hapsburg emperor enfeoffed (invested with a fief) his two sons with Upper and Lower Austria, Styria, Carinthia, and Carniola. Later enlarged by Tyrol and Gorizia, these principalities became the hereditary domain of the Hapsburgs who continued to rule as Holy Roman Emperors, at least nominally, until 1806. In the sixteenth century they acquired by marriage Bohemia, Hungary, and Croatia, which had been independent kingdoms with a long history. As the Holy Roman Empire declined, the Hapsburgs emerged as the most powerful territorial princes in Central Europe; their sovereign rule eventually extended from the Elbe to the Adriatic and from the Russian plains far into Italy.

The dawn of nationalism found Austria a power structure of the empire type with a highly differentiated administrative system. Its political identity was mainly concentrated in the person of the ruler who controlled the army, foreign relations, and the expanding state machinery. Austrian centralism, nursed by absolutist statecraft, aroused the resistance of the provincial estates, which found ideological support in the national movements. This reached historical proportions, particularly in the countries of the Bohemian and Hungarian crowns, where memories of political independence remained strong. Unlike the original possessions of the Hapsburgs with their predominantly or exclusively German populations, Bohemia and Hungary were ethnically mixed, and are thus of particular interest to the present study.

The Countries of the Bohemian Crown

In the Middle Ages the Czech rulers of Bohemia had come under the political and cultural influence of Charlemagne's empire. As one of the seven Electors, the King of Bohemia played an important role in the later affairs of the Holy Roman Empire. Ever since the eleventh century, when German merchants and craftsmen were invited by the king to settle at the foot of his castle, considerable numbers of knights, burgesses, miners, and farmers immigrated from Germany. Yet the privileges and favors granted to these foreigners were resented by the Czech natives.

The religious movement of Hussitism was not only directed against German professors and students, who eventually emigrated to found the University of Leipzig in nearby Saxony, but also against the German towns and German influence in general. The political struggle taken up by nobility and estates for the birthright of the Czech nation was supported by the religious fervor of the broad masses, and remained a leitmotif of Bohemian history. Foreigners were now required by law to learn and use the Czech language; German preachers and teachers were replaced by Czechs. When the Hapsburg Ferdinand I succeeded to the thrones of Bohemia and Hungary, he confirmed these language regulations, although according to the customs of the time, the royal administration was expected to use the German tongue of the prince in its internal proceedings.

The Thirty-Years' War of Religion was sparked by a rebellion in Prague that was directed as much against the Catholic Hapsburgs as against German supremacy. After the defeat of the Protestant Union, the leaders of the Bohemian uprising and almost the whole native nobility were executed, banished, or deprived of their property. The new Bohemian aristocracy was mainly of German descent and culture, but partially of Spanish, Italian, and even Scottish origin. The country became Catholic again, constitutional rights were rescinded, and a central administration was established. Henceforth, the lower law courts and administrative bureaus conducted their business in German or Czech according to the native tongue spoken by the parties concerned. Yet German became the only official language for internal use. Because a thorough command of German was highly advantageous for anybody seeking office, the elite showed little interest in cultivating the Czech language, which in time degenerated into a mere peasant dialect. The upper and middle classes, regardless of their ethnic origins, spoke German and wholeheartedly embraced the German culture. The Bohemian elite even participated in the German emancipation from French influence and cultural dominance.

Joseph II attempted to transform the sprawling Austrian empire into a modern state with a strongly centralized administration. To this end, he promoted the general use of German as the most advanced literary language (excluding Italian) spoken in his realm. In the universities German replaced Latin as the language of instruction; wherever feasible, German was also used in primary schools. The precipitous reforms, though in keeping with absolutist statecraft, inadvertently favored German speakers and made them the object of widespread resentment. The Bohemian nobility fought against the concentration of power in Vienna and for the restoration of the Bohemian Estates to their former position. These aspirations converged with the national movement, which had captured the imagination of the Bohemian intellectuals and middle classes.

Inspired by the ideas of Herder and German romanticism and by the ferment caused by the French Revolution, Napoleonic imperialism, and the Wars of Liberation, scholars and literati, regardless of their ethnic origins, began to take an interest in Czech folklore and history. They worked for a renewal of language and literature and advocated the restoration of the Bohemian "nation" to its ancient "freedoms."

The Risorgimento Movement. The risorgimento movement in Bohemia eventually split along ethnic and linguistic lines. Bohemian Czechs and Germans found themselves in opposing camps, each advocating its own version of nationalism, namely, the one most favorable to its sectional interests and ambitions. In the revolution of 1848, Czech and German patriots still fought side by side for emancipation from the absolutist Vienna government. Faced with an invitation to the Frankfurt Parliament, however, the Czechs explained that they had no interest in the union of German countries, but they felt as one with the other Slav peoples under the protection of Austria. While restorative nationalism had briefly united Germans and Czechs, the progress of ethnic nationalism soon deepened an age-old rift; it was never again closed until, in the aftermath of World War II, the Germans were forcibly expelled while the Czechs were so much weakened economically and politically that they succumbed to Communist Russia.

Ethnic History of Hungary

We now turn to developments in Hungary before the crucial year of 1848. From the period of the great migration of peoples onward, the Pannonian Basin was invaded by various raiding parties and tribes of Teutonic, Slav, Finno-Ugric, and even Mongol origin. In the ninth century the Magyars, mounted warrior nomads of Finno-Ugric stock under the leadership of Turkish warlords, established their rule over the ethnically mixed yet sparse native population of what was to become Hungary. King Stephen the Saint, crowned in 1001 by the Pope, finally organized the country after the pattern of a medieval empire. Throughout the centuries the nobility remained the core of the Hungarian nation. Its origin may be traced to the corporation of Magyar freemen who, in time, absorbed noblemen of other ethnic stock. Far into the modern age the nobility remained strictly separated from the ethnically heterogeneous masses of peasants.

The Turkish occupation (sixteenth to eighteenth century) principally affected the Magyar regions of Hungary, while the areas inhabited by Germans, Slavs, and other non-Magyars suffered less under its ravages. After the Austrian Hapsburgs had succeeded to the crown of Saint Stephen in 1526, they gradually freed all Hungary from Turkish occupation, and resettled the depopulated regions mainly with German peasants. Thus, by 1778, no more than 39 percent of the Hungarian population was of Magyar stock. This posed a serious problem for the integrity and cohesion of the country, and also jeopardized the Austrian policy, which was to administer the non-Magyar regions directly from Vienna. As early as 1781, considerations of statecraft rather than nationalism induced the magnates to demand the assimilation of the non-Magyar population. In this they found support among Germans, Slovaks, Jews, Ruthenians, and Rumanians who formed a new middle class and identified with the Hungarian nation and its Magyar aristocratic core.

Resistance to Viennese centralism and a desire to restore the political unity and independence of Hungary gave birth to a national movement that played a decisive role in the revolution of 1848. Its aim was a demotic nation-state with a culturally homogenized population. Such leaders as Lajos Kossuth refused even to recognize the existence of non-Magyar ethnic groups, let alone to grant them any separate status as nationalities. Latin was replaced by Magyar as the official language of the administration, but instruction in the parish schools was to be in the local language. No discrimination on ethnic or religious grounds should be allowed in the employment of civil servants. Only Croatia was granted a special status, but strong pressure was applied to assimilate her Slav majority as well as her German and Italian minorities.

AN AUSTRIAN NATION

By 1848, Austria was becoming a modern state. Had it not been for her unsolved national problems, she might have been transformed into a demotic nation-state rivaling France. But by the time national ideas of the ethnic type had captured the public imagination and risorgimento movements had flared up everywhere, it was too late to mold a multiethnic state population into a demotic unit. Nevertheless, during the following decades the development of its essential prerequisites continued: a centralized government, an efficient bureaucracy, an ever-widening franchise, common institutions, a *lingua franca,* and free movement throughout the country. Peasants and Jews had already been emancipated. In many sections industrialization was progressing rapidly, giving rise to a capitalistic bourgeoisie as well as to a growing proletariat, a dynamic labor movement, and a spirited socialist party. Compulsory public education was rapidly diminishing illiteracy; a complex system of schools reached out into the remote corners of the country; intellectual and cultural life was flourishing.

Despite the assertions of partisan historiography to the contrary, we should not underrate the growing body of Austrian citizens whose ultimate allegiance was to the common fatherland symbolized by emperor and dynasty. The image of an Austrian nation inspired not only civil servants and army officers with a sense of identity and solidarity but also—regardless of ethnic background—large sections of the nobility, clergy, and middle classes. These attitudes, which were propagated by church, school, patriotic associations, and during service in the standing army (which for the common man lasted several years), also influenced the broad masses.

German Dominance. There is no doubt that the German element formed the core of the Austrian "nation." The monarch was a German prince; the dominant elite included a German or Germanized nobility, clergy, and bourgeoisie, as well as a growing corps of civil servants and army officers. German was the official language, widely understood and used as a *lingua franca* almost everywhere; intellectual and cultural life remained within the German sphere of influence; and strategic positions in the institutional framework were manned by persons who spoke German as their mother tongue or were at least thoroughly familiar with it.

It would be an oversimplification to assume that nationalism pitted all non-Germans against the overpowering block of German vested interests. The situation was much more complex. Nationalist aspirations turned some Germans against the established order, as they sought their fulfillment in Germany rather than in Austria. And the ambitions of non-German ethnic units often clashed with each other; some of them even entered into alliances with the Germans. Moreover, different social classes in each of the ethnic units had different ideas of what nationalism involved, and specific class interests cut across ethnic dividing lines.

The Power Structure. The Austrian power structure had at its apex the emperor who, with his house and close associates, symbolized the Austrian nation. A group of persons, which at that time was called "high society" and would probably be described today as "establishment," had the greatest influence upon public affairs. It included nobility and prelates, who always had access to the court; the cream of the financial, commercial, and industrial bourgeoisie; the upper ranks of the army and bureaucracy; the scholars and the educators.

With the introduction of democratic institutions, a new dimension was added to the political power structure, which provided the principal forum for the national struggle. In the central and provincial legislatures and in party caucuses, national issues were formulated and debated. Organized nationalism found its expression in civic associations, boards of trade and commerce, student fraternities, glee clubs, and professional unions. The *Turnerbunds* and associations supporting schools and cultural activities came to play the most prominent role. Finally, we should mention the opinion-makers and educators: journalists, political writers, professors, teachers, and the lower and middle ranks of the clergy. Apart from political parties, national organizations and public opinion leaders were, in fact, the only means by which an ethnic unit, having no corporate legal existence, could form, express, and carry out its "general will."

Constitutional Rights. National problems are primarily political issues requiring legal and government action.[1] Accordingly, they were generally formulated in terms of "rights of nationalities." Among the principal issues, constitutional and state rights took precedence. The quarrel about the rights of the
so-called historical nations concerned mainly the extent to which autonomy
should be granted to provincial legislatures and administrations. Hungary
achieved almost complete sovereignty in 1876. Her remaining links with Austria were limited to the person of the emperor, who was also king of Hungary,
and a common foreign policy, treasury, and army.

Henceforth, Austria became known as the Dual Monarchy, with a Trans-
leithanian portion dominated by the Magyars and a Cisleithanian portion where
the Germans were supposed to remain dominant. Both portions, however,
included large populations of different ethnic origin, even "historical nations"
such as the Kingdom of Croatia, the countries of the Bohemian Crown, and the
Austrian parts of former Poland. The Czechs objected most violently to the
Austro-Hungarian Compromise, and demanded equal rights with Hungary.
Plans for a triple monarchy and even for a loose federation of a still greater
number of nation-states were hotly debated until, after 1918, the Danube
Monarchy was finally dismembered partly, but only partly, by restoring the
"historical nations" to complete political independence.

While the Austro-Hungarian Monarchy lasted, the struggle for the constitutional rights of the historical nations engendered a host of new national problems. The greater the autonomy granted to the crownlands (provinces) representing historical nations, the weaker became the position of the central
government representing Austrian unity and of the numerous ethnic groups
living in these crownlands. Moreover, there was no historical nation—now
defined in ethnic terms—that did not have some of their members living under
the jurisdiction of some other historical nation: Germans and Hungarians in the
lands of the Bohemian Crown, Slovaks (claimed to be ethnically one with the
Czechs) and Germans in Hungary, Czechs in Lower Austria (Vienna), and so
on.

All these ethnic groups, especially those that were not recognized as belonging to any of the historical nations—Rumanians, Ruthenians, Italians,
Slovenes, Jews—were counted as "nonhistorical," or "small nationalities."
To repeat: The historical nations were demotic nations identified with a formerly independent administrative unit, having one distinctive ethnic core. The
small nationalities, on the other hand, were ethnic units that were not identified
with any particular province. Since language was, in both cases, considered the
principal mark of a nationality, it became one of the most hotly debated national issues. Of this more will have to be said presently.

---

[1] It should be pointed out that nationalist terminology was not always consistent. In the present
context the terms will be used as defined earlier in this book regardless of which German, Czech,
Magyar, or other equivalents had been actually adopted in the controversies of the time.

The Magna Carta of Nationalities. The Austrian Constitution of 1876, which can be described as the Magna Carta of Nationalities in Cisleithanian Austria (Hungary having become by then an almost sovereign nation-state), declared that all nationalities had equal rights; and that each of them had the inalienable right to the preservation and cultivation of its identity, culture, and language.[2] In this way nationalities were recognized at law as corporate bodies. The recognition of collective rights, in addition to the "natural" rights of individuals incorporated in all Western constitutions, was a most significant step. The legal concept of corporate rights of ethnic units, however, also had practical implications that were to create serious difficulties.

One major national problem, for instance, concerned the organs through which a nationality officially expressed its collective will, promoted its interests, maintained itself, and improved its condition. A historical nation, in the same way as a demotic nation, was in control of political institutions, having jurisdiction and control over a definite territory and its population. This was not the case of ethnic "nationalities" that were not identified with a particular political or an autonomous administrative unit. Leaders of the small nationalities, therefore, demanded that the whole country be divided by the central government into administrative subunits in such a way that each nationality enjoy political autonomy at least on a local and regional level. This policy was at times also advocated by German leaders. For the vital interests of both the Germans and the "small nationalities" were threatened by the prospect of a partition of Austria among sovereign historical nations operating according to demotic principles. This would have meant the loss of large numbers of Austrian Germans living outside the Alpine crownlands. Moreover, it would have weakened the political superstructure through which the Germans were able to promote their interests throughout the whole monarchy.

Language Problems. Another important issue was language. This problem, too, had several aspects. One concerned the language to be used for communication with government agencies; in parliament and in councils on the community, county, and provincial level; in the army, in law courts, in public conveyances; and in the promulgation of laws and regulations. A distinction was made between the language used internally by various bureaus and departments and the language in which clients and patrons communicated with administrative officers, judges, policemen, railroad conductors, mail clerks, and others.

---

[2]The actual wording was somewhat ambiguous in that the Constitution referred to the nationalities as ethnic groups (*Volksstämme*), which had the right to preserve their *"Nationalität."* In the terminology adopted here, however, an ethnic unit is a politically neutral social fact; it becomes a nation or a nationality once definite political consequences are drawn from the simple statement that a particular ethnic unit exists. The phrase, "all nationalities have equal rights" (*sind gleichberechtigt*), implied equality before the law. The word *"Nationalität"* on the other hand, referred to the cultural manifestations of an ethnic unit rather than to its political character.

The language that was chosen for official use, however, put all those persons at a disadvantage who knew it imperfectly or not at all. Moreover, if knowledge of a particular language was required for employment, those unfamiliar with it were discriminated against. Language also had a great symbolic value. It made a difference to the prestige and stature of an ethnic unit whether its language was the standard language of the country, or just a tolerated or ignored folk dialect. Finally, if it was advantageous or necessary to learn another language well, people might be inclined to forget their native tongue and even wean their children from it. Together with the alien language, the alien culture was also bound to be adopted, resulting in corresponding losses to the numerical strength of the ethnic unit.

Of equal, if not greater, importance was the language of instruction in the schools. Attempts to promote bilingualism, or at least to make some other language spoken in the country a compulsory subject, met with nationalist resentment and resistance. To each nationality their schools meant not only protection against losses in human and cultural substance but also jobs for teachers of their own group, better trained leaders in the national struggle, and intellectual centers and bastions for defense and aggression. Even with the best of intentions, it was impossible to do justice to all the various aspects of the language problem. Although law and practice were, by and large, as liberal as anywhere in the world, and were in many respects the most tolerant and considerate, reasons could always be found to represent Austrian language policies as unjust and oppressive.

Administrative Problems. The Moravian Compromise of 1905 probably included some of the most advanced laws trying to cope with the national problems typical of those modern states that have ethnically mixed populations. It deviated from the usual practice of granting national rights to the majority of a territorial population. Instead, these rights were granted to all the inhabitants of Moravia who were entered in the national register without regard to actual residence or relative numbers. This was called the "personal" as against the "territorial" principle.[3] Although praised by some as the most satisfactory way of dealing with national problems, the method has its drawbacks, too. It does indeed tend to protect any nationality that is not dominant in a particular community or territorial jurisdiction from loss of substance; but it also "freezes" the ethnic distribution as it exists at any given time. An ethnic, for instance, who might want to merge into the dominant society would find legal barriers added to the usual social obstacles of prejudice and discrimination to prevent him or his children from becoming assimilated. Thus, the rights of

---

[3]Among the most significant contributions to this theory are the writings of the Austrian social democrat, Karl Renner (cf. Renner, 1918; 1964).

nationalities often infringed upon individual rights constitutionally guaranteed to all citizens.

The problem as to which particular criteria were to be used in order to determine a person's nationality was always highly controversial. The choice of criteria had not only legal and political consequences, it also directly affected personal lives; for it made a difference when one's chances of employment, one's right to send children to a particular school or to vote for a particular party, depended on the ethnic category under which one was officially subsumed. By and large, the decision as to membership of a particular ethnic unit was left to public opinion. Census data about the language used in public served as an additional criterion.[4]

When controversies arose, Austrian review boards and courts of appeal applied a variety of criteria in addition to data on language. At first the authorities relied on what people said they were. When language was treated as the most "objective" criterion, the question arose as to which language was meant; that customarily spoken in public, that spoken at home, or the mother tongue. Results were not always unequivocal. Sometimes impartial investigators were ordered to check reports of local authorities. Additional inquiries were made as to membership of voluntary associations or political parties, place of origin, schools attended, and so on. The results often differed widely. It always remained highly controversial as to what weight should be given to which criterion. Each interested party claimed the greatest objectivity and reliability for those findings that corresponded most closely to their particular ideology and which supported their own national aspirations. So much for the situation in Cisleithanian Austria.

Hungary after the Compromise of 1867

In the regions that had been surrendered to Hungarian supremacy in 1867, national policies conformed to the demotic rather than the ethnic type. The dominant Magyar group insisted on the integrity of the country and on its Magyar character. Corporate rights of other nationalities were neglected and eventually denied. Only individual rights were to some extent recognized. After a period of transition Magyar was made the sole official language; all positions in the centralized bureaucracy were manned by Magyar-speaking officials; place names were Magyarized; Magyar culture and intellectual life were generously subsidized; and strong pressure was exerted to expand the Magyar school system.

Eventually, the mere fact that somebody insisted on speaking his non-Magyar mother tongue made him suspect of treason. But any non-Magyar

---

[4]The item "racial origin," included until recently in the Canadian census, was not used in Austria.

sufficiently familiar with the Magyar language was admitted to the national institutions of higher education, and was thereby eligible for public service and even for the highest offices. Ethnics with adequate training and ability, particularly after they had Magyarized their names and wholeheartedly embraced Magyar culture, filled the ranks of a growing bourgeois and intellectual middle class that adopted the mentality of the traditional aristocratic elite.

The peasantry, however, was only superficially affected by these policies. A deep gulf existed between the dominant elite, emphatically Magyar in character, and the broad masses, mostly of peasant stock, who preserved their folk culture and speech. Because social advancement depended on entering Magyar urban society, the non-Magyar ethnic groups were deprived of most of their leaders.

If we compare the situation in Hungary after the Compromise with that in France after the Revolution, we find striking similarities. Lagging about a century behind the West, Hungary attempted to catch up with economic and social developments, and to create a centralized demotic nation-state after the French model. But the process of nation-building in France had been accomplished at a time when national movements of the ethnic type were in their infancy. When Hungary embarked upon the same course, risorgimento nationalism was in full bloom, and even in Cisleithanian Austria, the rights of ethnic collectivities were widely recognized. International public opinion thus looked with a highly critical eye upon Hungarian policies (which in an earlier age would have been praised as the epitome of wise statecraft), and tended to criticize Hungary for dealing with national problems in a manner that in Western Europe—as well as in America—had been readily condoned.

THE MULTIETHNIC NATION-STATE

Hungary and Austria tried to solve their national problems in two different ways. Hungary's attempt to enforce the demotic integration of her ethnically heterogeneous population was undertaken too late to forestall the disruptive effects of ethnic nationalism. Austria, however, experimented with novel methods of political organization, which would safeguard the proper functioning of a modern territorial state, and at the same time make allowance for the legitimate aspirations of diverse ethnic units to self-preservation and undisturbed development. The type of political power structure exemplified by Cisleithanian Austria between 1876 and 1918 has been called by German authors *Nationalitätenstaat,* a difficult word to translate into English. We propose to use the rather colorless phrase "multiethnic nation-state" (cf. Bühl, 1969), although this does not convey the implication of the German term that such a state is constructed in accordance with the principle of nationality.

A nationality, we have said earlier, may be regarded as an imperfect nation. Although a nation is sovereign in exercising political power through its state, both internally and externally, the political power exercised by a nationality within an administrative subdivision of the state is limited. At the same time, however, the nationality participates collectively in the policy decisions of the central government in all matters concerning the entire state population, especially as regards internal relations between different nationalities and external relations with other nation-states. An ethnic unit is transformed into a nationality when the following three conditions are realized:

1. Corporate participation in the exercise of state power on equal terms with other nationalities.
2. Relative self-determination in administrating the subunit identified with it.[5] In the demotic nation-state there is but one national core to which the state "belongs" in a specific manner; but in the multiethnic nation-state, there are several nationalities that are formally equal. However, within the limits set by the inalienable rights imputed to the ethnic units in accordance with a mutually acceptable national doctrine, these are free to compete in the struggle for political power and even supremacy.
3. Protection of its vital interests, including its maintenance and advancement, both on the state level and on the level of all its autonomous administrative subdivisions, against whatever nationality threatens domination. This implies above all protection against being outvoted by a majority of different ethnic origin.

In conclusion, we may characterize a multiethnic nation-state as the political integration of imperfect nation-states into one sovereign nation-state. Internal sovereignty is limited on principle because both the superordinate state and its autonomous subdivisions have only limited and mutually complementary competences. The arrangement resembles a federal state whereby the boundaries of its components are determined with a view to the ethnic homogeneity of their population rather than to historical, economic, topological, or other considerations.

The failure of Austria to transform herself into a multiethnic nation-state, and to make nationalist principles work, does not in itself prove that the model is without merit. It was the interests and power politics of the Allies, rather than the internal breakdown under the stress of war, that was responsible for her eventual partition. This, as it turned out, multiplied the national problems in Central Europe, and thereby contributed to the outbreak of a second and still more disastrous world conflagration.

---

[5]The Moravian type of autonomy modifies the second item in that two or more nationalities united in an autonomous administrative subunit participate in the exercise of the limited power granted to the subunit in proportion to their relative number, but so that vital interests of none of them can be violated through majority rule.

Among numerous other attempts to solve the problems that are bound to arise when the ideology of nationalism is adopted by a modern state, Switzerland is frequently cited as having found the most successful solution. For this reason, we shall examine the problem faced by this country.

SWITZERLAND—MODEL OR SINGULAR CASE?[6]

With a population roughly divided into 70 percent Germans, 20 percent French, and 10 percent Italians (in addition to a small proportion of Rhaeto-Romans), Switzerland gives the impression of being a modern nation-state showing no serious signs of national conflict. The overwhelming German majority has neither made a sustained effort to impose its language and culture upon the French and Italian minorities nor have the latter developed strong separatistic tendencies. There have been occasional pockets of unrest, notably in recent years in the French-Jura region of the predominantly German Canton of Bern, but that is all. Thus, one might ask whether a superior type of state-craft, perhaps a higher moral calibre, or a more rational approach have been in this case responsible or whether Swiss history provides the answers as to how, in analogous situations elsewhere, dangerous cleavages could possibly be prevented. The answer will depend on whether or not the situation in Switzerland is really analogous to that in other countries. This cannot be decided without taking historical developments into consideration.

PRENATIONAL ORIGINS

Historians usually project the origins of Switzerland, as one distinctive national entity, back into the thirteenth century. In reality, what we find at the root of her history is nothing more than a loose alliance for mutual aid concluded by the peasants of three Alpine valleys against infringements of their hard-won communal self-government by secular or ecclesiastical lords. Some city republics soon found it to their advantage to join the alliance. Neither communes of freemen standing up against their feudal overlords nor regional leagues were unusual in the Middle Ages.

Until the end of the fifteenth century, the Swiss Confederates were firmly embedded in the power structure of the Holy Roman Empire of the German Nation; they remained nominally part of it until the Peace of Westphalia in 1648. Before the turn of the eighteenth century, no Swiss state or a Swiss nation existed. The *Eidgenossenschaft* was precisely what the name indicates, a sworn confederacy of several sociopolitical units, later called cantons; it had neither a legislative body nor an executive authority, neither a common army

---

[6]Cf. Kohn, 1956; Weilemann, 1925.

nor common laws, and its sole purpose was the defense of its members' independence. Nor was there any doubt as to the German character of the charter cantons.

The Swiss distinguished between charter cantons, allied places, and subject territories that had been acquired through conquest, treaty, or purchase, which were colonies of an individual canton or of a group of cantons. Both charter cantons and allied places had to be of German character in order to be accepted into the Confederation. This stipulation often ignored the fact that a few cantons—Fribourg, the Valais, and the Grisons League—had, in part, a non-German population. The Pays de Vaud, subject land of Bern, and the Tessin, subject land of the whole Confederation, had, respectively, French-speaking and Italian-speaking populations. A further distinction was made between rural cantons with a democratic self-government of free peasants, and urban cantons which, like the city republics in Upper Italy or Germany, were ruled by patrician oligarchies or guilds of burgesses. Although the Swiss cherished the league that guaranteed them their hard-won liberties, no common identity or solidarity bound them together into one sociopolitical unit. On the contrary, they were divided along ethnic and religious lines, and also continued to display a pronounced parochialism and particularism centered on the local community and the canton. Before 1798, the only common institution was the *Tagsatzung,* a conference of cantonal representatives, whose deliberations could at the best result in a common agreement or in treaties between independent political units.

Impact of Nationalism. The stirring ideas of the Enlightenment also captured the imagination of Swiss intellectuals (of whom Rousseau was the outstanding figure). Absolutism had never assumed any extreme form in the government of Swiss cantons: democratism had struck a more familiar chord. The new ideas reinforced this democratic tradition and inspired a series of popular uprisings against the ruling oligarchies of numerous cantons. Nationalism was even more important; it served to strengthen the unity of the Swiss people and to confirm their country's standing as a distinctive nation equal to other emergent nations of Europe.

The national movement had no need to turn against a despot to create a nation-state of the demotic type, nor did it trigger the separatist tendencies of ethnic nationalism. In the first place, any kind of ethnic nationalism was bound to emphasize ties with neighboring countries from which the Swiss had separated, and thus to defeat its own purpose. Moreover, as in France or elsewhere in Western Europe, national ideology had succeeded in taking firm root before the ethnic principle of nationality began to dominate the political scene in Central and Eastern Europe or in Italy. Accordingly, Swiss nationalism assumed a somewhat unique character in that its principal and almost sole aim was the rejuvenation of a historical unity which, though enfeebled, had never wholly disappeared. This was achieved by awakening a consciousness of the common past and the proud accomplishments that were consistent with the then prevailing principles of demotic nationalism, without adopting its centralizing and homogenizing tendencies.

Centralizing tendencies were introduced from abroad, when, in 1798, the French Directory decided to occupy Switzerland for strategic reasons. Representing themselves as liberators, the French imposed upon the country a new constitution on the French model, which had been drawn up in Paris by a Swiss collaborator. As a French satellite, the Helvetic Republic became a state endowed with a parliament representing the whole country. It was divided into nineteen equivalent administrative districts with a highly centralized government, common citizenship, freedom of residence, commerce, trade, and religion, as well as a common system of education.

But the constitution was too centralistic, the executive power too authoritarian, to have any lasting success. Growing dissension, especially in the old rural, Catholic cantons, rendered the constitution unworkable. Three years later, Napoleon, by the Act of Mediation, restored the sovereignty of the cantons, with the *Tagsatzung* acting again as a conference of independent states. It was, however, given a permanent president and the sole right to decide over war and peace. After Napoleon's defeat the Swiss took eighteen months to negotiate a new federal pact. The Confederation, now comprising twenty-one sovereign states, could agree on only one major point—Swiss neutrality. They were willing to unite in order to maintain their security, to preserve their liberty and independence. During the following period Switzerland much resembled the Switzerland before 1798: no common citizenship, no common monetary system, no national postal service, no liberty of trade. The only progress made was the establishment of a federal general staff and federal inspection of cantonal armament, and so the way was clear for a federal army.

The transformation of Switzerland into a nation-state patterned on the risorgimento movement was carried out in two steps. Under the impact of the revolutions in 1830, a number of cantonal constitutions were "regenerated" in accordance with the liberal and democratic principles of the day. In another revolutionary year, the Constitution of 1848, which was modeled on that of the United States, but also enshrined many of the principles laid down in Napoleon's Act of Mediation, was adopted by popular vote. Although the cantons remained largely autonomous, federal power was greatly strengthened and expanded to assume many new responsibilities.

The new constitution, while seeking to preserve historical continuity and studiously avoiding all revolutionary measures which might have antagonized the more conservative cantons, introduced a number of fundamental and necessary changes. Switzerland became one nation with one citizenship; its territory was transformed into a political unit forming a custom's union and having one national economy and one foreign policy. It is of particular interest to note that only at this period did French and Italian become official languages on equal footing with German. As late as 1938, Rhaeto-Romance was added; this after it had developed from a set of related peasant idioms into a literary language. No further provision was made to guarantee the equality of the three national language groups. But since education and cultural affairs remained in the hands of local and cantonal authorities, they were sufficiently removed from centralized political power to generate severe national problems.

Ethnic Conflict. We should not, however, imagine that Switzerland has remained entirely free of ethnic antagonism or of controversies about the official use of different languages, which often reflected a class struggle for political dominance. There are instances when conflicting interests, not always motivated solely by ethnic but also by economic or religious differences, were resolved simply by dividing a canton into sovereign halves. In 1597, for instance, under the impact of the Reformation, Appenzell was divided into a Protestant, mainly industrial part and a Catholic, mainly agricultural part. The French Pays de Vaud was liberated from domination by the German canton of Bern with the help of revolutionary France and was later annexed by her. When the Congress of Vienna restored to the Federation the regions that had been lost to France, Vaud became an independent canton, while Bern was idemnified with the Jura, whose French population has never ceased to protest against this arbitrary decision.

A Multiethnic Canton. In 1481, bilingual Fribourg (Boschung, 1963) was accepted into the Confederation, which was still wholly German, only because, for political reasons, it gave itself out to be a state of "German character." There was a considerable German population in the town, and the original nucleus of Fribourg was German-speaking. Moreover, the ruling patriciate was strongly oriented towards Bern. Had this not been the case, the Canton of Fribourg with its French-speaking majority could not even have become an allied place. From the beginning of the fourteenth century until Fribourg's acceptance into the Confederation, there had been duality; the rich merchant class had spoken French, which had also been the language of the administration. After this period German became not only the official language but also the only one tolerated in the churches and schools of the city. The rural hinterland, however, continued to be administered and its church services conducted, in French, which remained the idiom of the majority of the canton.

Although the dominance of the German patricians during the sixteenth century brought with it a trend towards Germanization, this was counteracted when, in the wake of the French armies, the ideas of modern democratism and nationalism were propagated and the language of the majority became once again the official means of communication. Although the Constitution of Fribourg does not postulate the equality of the German minority and French majority with regard to the official use of their languages or proportionate representation in government, administration, or law courts as clearly as do the Constitutions of other multiethnic cantons or the Confederacy as a whole, the sources of controversy have remained limited and localized.

The Swiss Nation-State. Our initial question has been whether Switzerland might serve as a successful model of a multiethnic nation-state. In the nineteenth century Switzerland had indeed been transformed into a modern nation-state. It appears, however, that in spite of its ethnically heterogeneous population, Switzerland has neither experienced the same kind of national problems that have beset other countries in a similar situation, notably Austria, nor has it experimented with the type of legal and administrative measures that would entitle us to consider it a multiethnic nation-state. It would be more correct to maintain that, for reasons to be investigated presently, Switzerland has been able to prevent problems of nationality from ever reaching a level of virulence.

Leopold Kohr (1957) suggests that Switzerland's unity and peaceful functioning has been praised for the wrong reasons; not all member units are lacking in strong separatist tendencies, nor is the overwhelming German majority entirely devoid of ambitions or even power potential. It is only because Switzerland is a union of states, none of which is strong enough to challenge federal authority, that such tendencies have been successfully suppressed. Switzerland, Kohr adds, has repeatedly anticipated the emergence of minority problems by creating minority states rather than by recognizing minority rights. Thus, when internal differences developed in a canton that would have necessitated a greater degree of submission by a minority to the dominant majority, without any hesitation such cantons were subdivided into mutually independent political units. Kohr's argument, however, does not explain how the balance of power was achieved in the first place nor why it has been adhered to in the face of rising nationalism elsewhere. While under its impact the Swiss have been transformed into a demotic nation with which they identify and feel solidarity, they have never adopted the ideology of ethnic nationalism to any significant extent or considered ethnicity as being of major political relevance. Why?

Swiss national unity was not initiated under the auspices of the modern ideologies of democratism and nationalism in the same way as was the French, German, or Italian national unity. Its roots are to be found rather in the accomplishments of a prenational period and in a social myth that had developed under the conditions of a premodern, agrarian society. When the influence of nationalism made itself felt, the Swiss did not attempt to found their unity on the myth of common descent or language but on common political traditions and institutions. They turned for inspiration to their past struggles for constitutional liberty—back to the thirteenth century. They revived the memory and glorified the interpretation of those foundations: William Tell became the national hero. The Swiss had no choice, for the pursuit of ethnic or linguistic nationalisms could only have brought about a dismemberment of Switzerland. Her unique past and her love of liberty have repeatedly been brought back to memory to mobilize greater cooperation and stronger feelings of solidarity in times of national crisis.

Today, the Swiss consider themselves indeed a demotic nation and the Helvetic Confederacy a modern nation-state, having an international standing equal to other politically organized national societies. Yet their strong parochialism has been preserved; allegiance is paid directly to the canton and indirectly to the confederacy. Political union is to them more a liaison of convenience than based on romantic love. Although sanctioned by eternal vows, the relationship is primarily based on common interest in their safety and prosperity, an interest that seems best served by their neutral position at the crossroads of three powerful neighbors and influential cultures. The same cantonal "nationalism" has also prevented them from seeking allies among ethnically related populations either of other cantons or of neighboring nation-states. The French Swiss of one canton, it is said, feel no greater solidarity with the French Swiss of other cantons than with German or Italian Swiss. Thus, ethnic conflicts remain intrasocietal affairs whose spread is checked at cantonal boundaries. Although industrialization has contributed to the social interdependence of the whole Swiss people and thus given a new meaning to national solidarity, it has also decreased the significance of ethnicity.

We conclude that, for reasons that have no parallel anywhere else, Switzerland, contrary to common opinion, does not fit the model of a multiethnic nation-state. Accordingly, the manner in which their so-called national problems have been solved or circumvented does not permit a more general application. We would have to look to other parts of the world for cases resembling the Austrian prototype more closely; a few examples are Canada, Belgium, or Nigeria.[7] It would be beyond the scope of this book to analyze additional cases. Only the following suggestions may be offered.

CONCLUSIONS

It has been a rare exception to grant ethnic units included in a modern nation-state the kind of constitutional recognition as "nationalities" which our discussion of the Dual Monarchy has revealed. But a similar effect has, on occasion, been achieved indirectly through legal and administrative measures, which do not seem to be inspired by nationalism. For instance, the Constitution of Canada does not contain any provisions that would recognize the

---

[7]The cases of Canada (up to 1945) and Nigeria (before the secession of Biafra) have been analyzed by the author under this viewpoint (Francis, 1965, pp. 178–194; see also Francis, 1963).

French-Canadians as a nationality, protect them collectively against loss of ethnic substance, or provide funds for their proper development as a distinctive ethnic society. To a considerable extent, however, this protection and support have been achieved through provincial federalism, the rights granted to religious groups, and a particular political situation which, until the end of World War II at least, gave the French-Canadians a greater weight than their numbers alone would have warranted.

Still, wherever the population is divided into several relatively large ethnic units, the ideology and political principles on which the modern nation-state is based are bound to lead to a clash between national aspirations of the demotic and the ethnic type, unless a balance of power has become firmly established in political traditions and social myth long before the ideas of modern nationalism have captured the public mind. But such exception from the rule can hardly be expected to occur today, least of all among the new nations of the postcolonial age.

The lesson we can learn from the foregoing studies is this: As long as the nation-state itself has not been replaced by a novel type of political power structure that would be more in keeping with the requirements of industrial society, the most promising device for minimizing perpetual unrest, violent oppression, or secessionistic and separatistic movements may be seen in the recognition of all major ethnic units found within the state population as corporations after the manner of nationalities coupled with a rather generous federalism. Yet even the multiethnic nation-state, representing a political federation of nationalities, cannot achieve more than a labile equilibrium. Apart from international developments, its relative stability depends above all on the mobile middle classes of the different nationalities. They are likely to acquiesce if they realize that any feasible alternative would serve their interests to a lesser degree, and if they are unwilling to shoulder the cost of a more radical change.

NATIONAL MINORITIES

The model of the multiethnic nation-state has not been foremost in the political thought and practice of recent years. Ever since World War I, the older word "nationality" has more and more been replaced by the expression "national minority," not only in political discussion and controversy but also in international law. The significance of this shift in the terminology will be best elucidated by briefly recapitulating the historical developments that led to it. We realize that national problems are strongly influenced by international power politics. Ethnic units, for instance, are likely to embark upon a course of *irredenta* only when they are encouraged and backed by a powerful nation-state which claims them as an integral part of its own national core. Moreover, it is rare indeed that territories have been reapportioned in accordance with the principle of nationality, unless there was a special occasion for doing so (wars, peace treaties, serious boundary conflicts) or unless international constellations were particularly favorable. This has to be kept in mind when we try to determine the precise meaning that the concept of minority has acquired.

Theodore Roosevelt, and not—as one might expect—Woodrow Wilson, was the American president who, early in the century, proclaimed that Europe ought to be reconstructed on the principle of nationality. "The Austro-Hungarian and the Turkish empire," he said, "must be broken up if we intend to make the world safe for democracy." The President was mistaken, as subsequent events have proved; for when the opportunity came to follow his concepts in dismembering first the Ottoman, later the Austrian and, in part, the Russian empires, new problems were created that led to the Balkanization of Eastern Europe and provided fuel for Hitler's imperialism. During World War I, the idea of reconstructing Central Europe on the principle of nationality was incorporated in the peace aims of the Allies, and these were summed up in Wilson's "Fourteen Points." The Allied program of territorial settlements after the war was guided by the principle that "all peoples and nationalities" had a "right to self-determination" and "national independence."

The victors, however, never agreed to apply this principle to themselves, nor did they venture to force it upon countries that were not parties to the peace negotiations. Moreover, it soon turned out that any territorial settlement that was at all practicable would leave numerous ethnic groups outside the boundaries of their proper nation-states. Thus, the provisions for the protection of national minorities, which were included in the peace treaties and in the charter of the League of Nations, had their roots in efforts to correct the fact that the right to self-determination had been denied to many ethnic groups. Thus, minorities may be said to be the result of bad conscience.

From this it also becomes evident that "minority" is not just another word for "nationality." In its legal sense it is a residual category; it obviously refers to the fact that even if the principle of nationality were carried to its logical consequences (which in most instances was not the case), a residue of national problems would remain.

The origin of the concept explains the difficulties that have been encountered in defining it. They reflect the great variety of conflicting interests involved in the issue of minority rights, on the one hand, and the diversity of partly contradictory principles employed in legitimizing opposing claims, on the other. Let us take a simple illustration. If the population of a nation-state includes elements who are ethnically different from the national core, the claim may be made that this "minority" has been denied the right of self-determination. Yet any effort to join its territory to the state to which, according to the principle of nationality, the group "belongs" will be considered as high treason if it comes from the inside, or as a violation of national sovereignty and territorial integrity if it originates from the outside. Quite apart from the principle of self-

determination, which has proved to be not only ambiguous but largely unworkable, there still remains the question of whether an ethnic group has an
inalienable right to the preservation of its substance and to its collective self-
development, possibly with the active support either of the state into which it is
politically incorporated, or of the state whose national core is of the same
ethnic origin; and whether such rights should be guaranteed by bilateral agreement or sanctioned by international bodies such as the League of Nations or
the United Nations.

NATIONAL AUTONOMY

The full recognition of collective rights leads in its practical consequences to
some form of national autonomy. A minimal program of this kind is embodied
in the notion of cultural autonomy. It implies that ethnic groups, represented by
self-appointed agencies, should be entrusted by the state with the autonomous
management of their schools and cultural affairs. In addition, the state should
be responsible for the financial support of separate educational, cultural, and
even charitable institutions of the ethnic group, in proportion to the group's
share in the total population. During the period between the two World Wars,
Esthonia, for instance, provided an outstanding example for such an arrangement. The Law of Cultural Autonomy, enacted in 1925, authorized each minority to draw up a national register. Those entered in it were entitled to elect a
"Cultural Council" which was empowered to manage all the educational, cultural, and charitable institutions of the minority; to receive and administer
public funds for their maintenance; to enact bylaws; and to levy taxes for these
purposes.

By and large, however, it has been the exception rather than the rule to grant
autonomy and similarly far-reaching special rights to ethnic minorities collectively. One reason behind the long-time refusal of the United Nations to incorporate an article on the collective protection of minorities in its Universal
Declaration of Human Rights has been expressed in one document:

> The right to preserve ethnic, religious or linguistic traditions or characteristics differ-
> ent from those of the rest of the population is . . . an exceptional right and claims to
> it enjoy a diversity that renders them difficult to meet by measures that are worldwide
> in scope.[8]

It was also widely thought that a statement of general rules, even the mere
attempt to define the term "minority," was apt to create problems where none
as yet existed by arousing aspirations of hitherto satisfied groups:

---

[8]Proposal of the United Kingdom submitted to the Subcommission on Prevention of Discrimination
and Protection of Minorities, on October 8, 1951. Cited by Ermacora, 1964, pp. 46f.

to artificially prolong the existence of minorities[9]

to hinder by any action spontaneous development of minority groups towards integration with the rest of population of the country in which they live, which takes place when impacts such as those of a new environment, or that of modern civilization, produce a state of rapid racial, social, cultural, or linguistic change[10]

or to invite the intervention by other states, which might use alleged infringements of minority rights as a pretext for aggression and annexation.

Minority Rights

Instead, the theory and practice dealing with minority problems since the conclusion of World War I have developed in quite different directions. The very term "minority" is related to the democratic principle of majority rule; and rights of minorities are derived from those human rights and individual freedoms that have been repeatedly declared as fundamental and inalienable, and that are widely recognized by democratic state constitutions and international covenants. The basic meaning of "minority" refers to categories of citizens who are unable to advance their rightful interests because they are bound to be outvoted by the dominant majority. When it comes to the protection of national minorities, the tendency has been to emphatically restate precisely those universal human rights which—because of the minority position of an ethnic unit—are in a particular danger of being violated under majority rule.

Since World War II, especially, such violations of rights that are due to individual human beings in general have been summarily described as "discrimination"—a term that implies unequal treatment. In this sense, the United Nations have been wont to deal with minority problems in terms of "prevention of discrimination" rather than of "protection of minorities." Still, what benefits individual ethnics may indirectly also contribute to the protection of ethnic collectivities. This can be gathered from the wording of the Draft Covenant on Civil and Political Rights whose article 25 is as follows:

In those States in which ethnic, religious or linguistic minorities exist, persons belonging to such minorities shall not be denied the right, in community with the other members of their group, to enjoy their own culture, to profess and practice their own religion or to use their own language.[11]

Generally speaking, however, there is a tendency to regard only the protection of individual rights as a proper concern of that international body, and to leave

---

[9]Cf. an intervention by the United Kingdom representative, Samuel Hoare, Commission on Human Rights, Summary Records 369, p. 5. Cited by Ermacora, 1964, p. 55.

[10]Resolution F of the Subcommission on Prevention of Discrimination and Protection of Minorities, in Ermacora, 1964, p. 80.

[11]Ermacora, 1964, p. 56.

the matter of collective rights to internal state legislation or to bilateral conventions and treaties.

There are two basic types of protective measures: the prevention of unequal treatment of individuals and the preservation and advancement of collectivities. Ethnic units aspiring to the political recognition of their separate identity within a given state population obviously have but a remote interest in antidiscriminatory laws. For their preservation requires unequal treatment and the recognition of particularistic rights rather than equality and the recognition of universalistic rights, though on occasion they may utilize the principle of nondiscrimination as a means to further their own ends. Ethnic units taking this stand are, as a rule, viable subsocieties with a long history of independent existence, which have fallen under the sway of a nation-state not their own. Immigrants to a foreign country, on the other hand, are less concerned with the prosperity of the ethnic collectivity than with the individual enjoyment of social rewards on equal terms with the majority of their compatriots. This type of minority is also the principal beneficiary of provisions preventing discrimination.

The difference between the two basic types of national minorities, which we have found to be significant on the political level, will once more occupy our attention in Part III when, in a broader sociological context, we shall make a distinction between primary ethnic groups, secondary ethnic groups, and ethnic categories.

REFERENCES

See also the general references to the preceding chapter.

Boschung, Peter, ed., *Der Staat Freiburg und seine sprachliche Minderheit: Dokumente 1958–63,* Schriftenreihe der Deutsch-freiburgischen Arbeitsgemeinschaft. Freiburg, 1963.

Bühl, Walter L., "Zur Typologie der nationalen Ordnungen und das Problem der Soziologie," *Sociologia Internationalis,* VII (1969), pp. 1–31.

Chadwick, Hector M., *The Nationalities of Europe and the Growth of National Ideologies.* Cambridge: Cambridge University Press, 1945.

Claude, Inis L., *National Minorities: An International Problem.* Cambridge, Mass.: Harvard University Press, 1955.

Ermacora, Felix, *Der Minderheitenschutz in der Arbeit der Vereinten Nationen.* Wien: Wilhelm Braumüller, 1964.

Francis, Emerich, "Der Nationalstaat und seine Alternativen," in *Das Geschichtsbild im deutschen und italienischen Sprachraum: Gegenwärtiger Stand und Probleme im Rahmen der europäischen Kultureinheit.* Auszüge aus den Akten der 4. Internationalen Tagung deutsch-italienischer Studien. Meran: n.p. 1963, pp. 326–346.

———, "Dreimal Nationalitätenstaat," in Francis, *Ethnos und Demos.* Berlin: Duncker, 1965, pp. 178–194.

Hugelmann, K. G., ed., *Das Nationalitätenrecht des alten Österreich.* Vienna: Wilhelm Braumüller, 1934.

Janowsky, Oscar I., *Nationalities and National Minorities: With Special Reference to East-Central Europe.* New York: The Macmillan Company, 1945.

Kann, Robert A., *The Multinational Empire*. New York: Columbia University Press, 1950; revised edition under the title: *Das Nationalitätenproblem der Habsburgermonarchie: Geschichte und Ideengehalt der nationalen Bestrebungen vom Vormärz bis zur Auflösung des Reiches im Jahre 1918*, 2 vols. Graz: Verlag Hermann Böhlaus Nachf., 1964.

————, *The Habsburg Empire: A Study in Integration and Disintegration*. New York: Frederick A. Praeger, 1957.

Kohn, Hans. *Nationalism and Liberty, The Swiss Example*. London: George Allen and Unwin, 1956.

Kohr, Leopold, *The Breakdown of Nations*. London: Routledge and Kegan Paul, 1957.

Macartney, C. A., *National States and National Minorities*. London: Oxford University Press, 1934.

Renner, Karl, *Das Selbstbestimmungsrecht der Nationen in besonderer Anwendung auf Österreich*. I. Teil: *Nation und Staat*. Leipzig: Franz Deuticke, 1918. (Completed in December 1917; no second volume has appeared).

————, *Die Nation: Mythos und Wirklichkeit*, ed. Jacques Hannak. Vienna: Europa Verlag, 1964.

Turegg, K. E. v., *Minderheitenrecht: Untersuchungen zum Recht der völkischen Minderheiten*. Köln: Kölner Universitätsverlag, 1950.

United Nations, *The Main Types and Causes of Discrimination*. Memorandum submitted by the Secretary General. Lake Success, New York: United Nations, 1949.

————, Commission on Human Rights, Subcommission on Prevention of Discrimination and Protection of Minorities, *Definition and Classification of Minorities*. Lake Success, New York: United Nations, 1950.

Veiter, Theodor, *Das Recht der Volksgruppen und Sprachminderheiten in Österreich*. Vienna: Wilhelm Braumüller, 1966.

Viefhaus, Erwin, *Die Minderheitenfrage und die Entstehung der Minderheitenschutzverträge auf der Pariser Friedenskonferenz 1919*. Marburger Ostforschungen. Würzburg: Holzer, 1960.

Weilemann, Hermann, *Die vielsprachige Schweiz: Eine Lösung des Nationalitätenproblems*. Basel: Rheinverlag, 1925.

Ethnicity in Different Political Settings

Part II has prepared us for the task we have set ourselves in the main body of this book, namely, to discover and explain regularities in the interethnic relations that confront us in contemporary society. The historical survey has shown the manner in which the role of ethnicity varies in different types of social settings. Our main emphasis has been the political dimension. We believe that political power relations tend to be dominant in societal units more complex than "primitive societies," which are mainly based on genealogical and spatial relationships, but which antedate the emergence of "modern society," in which economic relationships generally determine societal identities and solidarities.

In the empire type of power structure we have found ethnic differences or similarities to have no direct political relevance. An empire is capable of organizing a great variety of peasant and folk societies, which are allowed to persist undisturbed, into one political superstructure through a hierarchy of personal relationships and through a network of political and economic interdependences. At the same time, the elites, mediating between the political superstructure and the common folk of great ethnic diversity, tend to develop literary languages and high cultures that draw upon the traditions of related folk dialects and peasant cultures, but which are not identical with any one of them. The languages and cultures of regional elites are apt to engender particularistic solidarities over wider areas and, at the same time, promote the social integration of a territorial population into a larger political unit; they become thereby the seedbed of modern national cultures and societies.

The prenational state, emerging from the major territorial subdivisions of empires, is likewise not directly concerned with the ethnic composition of its subjects. However, considerations of rational statecraft ultimately suggest a drastic interference with traditional social structures; its aim is the increased efficiency of the state administration and economy. In this way, the modern state, at its prenational stage, sets processes of homogenization in motion throughout the entire state population, which tend to transform it eventually into a demotic unit. We have used the term "nationalization" to describe these processes of demotic integration; for the cultural unification of a state population accomplishes the indispensable preformation of the nation due to emerge at the following stage of development under the impact of nationalism.

The type of political power structure that is considered normal in contemporary political and legal thought and practice has been found to be the nation-state where ethnicity has a very high saliency. All the efforts made to replace the sovereign nation-state by new forms of international organization and political power structure, which would be more in keeping with economic and social reality, have to take into consideration the factual existence of a multitude of nation-states. Moreover, new political units emerging in former colonies have been able to take their place in the world community of sovereign nations only by following their example, and this despite the fact that more often than not the model has proved to be unsuitable to cope with the actual situation found in the developing countries. The self-constitution of a demotic nation, however, is based on existing political units, such as states, administrative subdivisions, or colonial territories whose boundary lines are supposed to be inviolable. Consequently, demotic nation-building involves the policy of eradicating all particularistic ethnic traditions within a given state territory, except those of the national core that enjoys dominance and paramouncy.

The homogenizing pressures exerted by the nation-state upon ethnically diverse components of its population tend to call forth an opposition which finds its ideological expression in the principle of nationality. According to it, ethnic units antedating the state formation, or added to the state population later by way of annexation, are supposed to have a right to be organized politically in nation-states of their own. This right of national self-determination, however, if carried to its logical conclusion, is bound to create serious disturbances of the international order. The principle has, in fact, only been realized under exceptional circumstances, particularly in the aftermath of wars, when a defeated country has had to accept secession and dismemberment.

Nationalism, in both its theoretical and practical dimensions, has not only been shown to be fraught with inconsistencies and contradictions, but also to be often unworkable due to particular geographic and especially demographic conditions. This has given rise to specific "national problems" that are political in nature. They concern the claims of ethnic units, if not to complete political emancipation, at least to territorial autonomy, adequate participation in overall state policies, and protection of their substance with regard to personnel and culture. The multiethnic nation-state appears to offer a practicable solution to the dilemma that arises when the granting of full national self-determination, for one reason or another, proves unfeasible.

In addition to the pure nation-states constructed according to demotic or ethnic principles, which are bound to violate either the integrity of ethnic units or the sovereignty of the state, and the organization of multiethnic nation-states that are highly vulnerable and labile, Walter L. Bühl suggests a fourth possible type of political power structure which he calls *"Mehrstaatennationalität"* (multistate ethnic society) (Bühl, 1969). By this he understands an ethnic unit that is not politically united and which intersects several states. He believes that the gradual emergence of a European, possibly also of an African "superethnos" might point in this direction, but he insists that the legitimacy and effectiveness of each of the four equivalent forms (demotic nation, ethnic nation, multiethnic nation-state, and multistate ethnic society) depends on the actual ethnic and demotic conditions.

Where either the full self-determination of a nation or the limited self-determination of a nationality has been denied to ethnic units, the concept of national minority has been introduced as a residual category. Its applicability to real-life situations, however, is limited. For national phenomena, though primarily located in the political dimension, have their wider social implications and repercussions. A nation, a nationality, or a national minority may be conceived of either as a global society or as a division of a global society; in this sense we speak of "national societies" and "subsocieties." Yet modern society, to repeat an earlier contention which has yet to be substantiated in the following chapter, is dominated not only by political but even more by economic values and relationships. Accordingly, in Part III, we shall transcend the political and legal implications of interethnic relations and consider social processes in other significant dimensions, which constitute the phenomena we have so far discussed under the heading of nationalities and national minorities. Finally, in Part IV, the lessons learned in the remainder of this book will be applied to the novel problems of nation-building that arise in former colonies. There we shall find not only a similar conflict between demotic and ethnic principles of nationalism as exists in Europe and which is reflected in the clash between tribes and nation-states, but also secondary ethnic groups emerging in the modernized urban centers. It will also become evident that the intellectual tools provided by international law for the solution of minority problems are as inadequate to cope with the actual situation there as they have been in Europe.

INTERETHNIC
RELATIONS IN
INDUSTRIAL
SOCIETY
III

The Problem

9

When scholars speak of "ethnic groups," they are generally concerned with those social problems that originate in the unequal treatment of permanent residents of a nation-state who are socially defined as being ethnically different from the national core of the state population. Such problems of malintegration into a global society are congenital in the modern nation-state, but unknown in other types of political power structures. For it is only when the prinicples of democratism and nationalism are introduced that ethnically diverse elements of a state population require special protection against the effects of cultural homogenization and the danger of being permanently outvoted by a numerical majority representing the national core. This protection finds its expression in the notion of "minority" rights.

Yet the problems created by the ground rules of modern society have broader social implications, which are not susceptible to correction only by political and legal measures. To cope with these more general problems it seems advisable at this point to replace the expression "national minority" by the term "ethnic group."

THE CONCEPT OF ETHNIC GROUP

Up to now we have applied the term "ethnic unit" in preference to "ethnic group" to any collectivity whose personnel is defined in terms of common descent and thereby distinguished from other collectivities of a similar type. In precisely this sense, E. C. and H. M. Hughes maintained that "ethnic means people unlike ourselves, and since we are all unlike some other people, we are all ethnics" (Hughes, 1952, p. 7n). The trouble with this definition is that it offers about the same heuristic advantages as when somebody is described as an "air-breather" or a "social-rules-observer." Obvious human qualities do not attain practical or theoretical relevance unless, in some way, they become controversial or problematical. The quality of social-rules-observing is interesting only if there is a possibility of nonobservance. Similarly, the quality of ethnicity only becomes sociologically relevant if, in a given

118

situation, some people are treated differently or behave differently because of ethnic differences.

The negative and equally important aspect of ethnicity, then, is what may be called the "contrast effect." This notion is reflected in Warner's definition:

> The term "ethnic" refers to any individual who considers himself, or is considered by others, to be a member of a group with a foreign culture, and who participates in the activities of the group (Warner, Srole, 1945, p. 28; see also Loiskandl, 1966).

Thus, ethnicity becomes salient when contrasting groups interact in a given social context and when ethnic differentiation is felt to disturb the proper functioning of society. It is in this sense that we shall speak of "ethnic community," "ethnic subcommunity," "ethnic subsociety," or "ethnic category." For rhetorical reasons, we shall use the unspecified term "ethnic group" when indicating any collectivity whose integration into a modern society creates a problematical situation because of ethnic cleavages or conflict.

THE CONCEPT OF MODERN SOCIETY

In the political dimension we have found that processes of nationalization mark the emergence of modern societies. The corresponding processes in the economic dimension may be summarily described as industrialization. Both processes are interdependent results of modern statecraft. As we have seen, economic improvement became a primary concern of the modern state because of the financial requirements of its administrative and military establishment. By rounding up and expanding its territory, by emphasizing frontiers, by restricting and controlling the traffic of persons, goods, and ideas across them, at the same time breaking down regional and local barriers within its confines, the centrally administered state created the large protected markets that were necessary for the rise of an industrial economy.

Another requirement of a "modern" or industrialized economy is the availability of a mobile labor force, which the state helped to provide in several ways, partly accidentally, partly intentionally. Its principal contribution was in the tearing down of the traditional social barriers and of dividing lines cutting through the state population. By freeing individuals from traditional solidarities, they became linked all the more firmly and directly to the ruler and his administrative staff. To weaken the power of lords and nobles, the significance of status ascription on the basis of birth and descent was played down in favor of an increasing emphasis on individual ability and achievement as a more rational standard for social placement and for the utilization of manpower. As rational government tended to deal with individual subjects rather than with corporate units, disregarding traditional solidarities in favor of relationships based on utility and purpose, it prepared the way for the kind of contractual relationships that are typical of modern society.

IMPACT OF MODERN SOCIETY ON INTERETHNIC RELATIONS

In Part II we studied the impact of modernization on interethnic relations in the political dimension. Demotic nationalism works toward the minimization of ethnic differences. Resistance to state centralism and cultural homogenization, on the other hand, finds its expression in ethnic nationalism. Particularistic tendencies, separatism, and regionalism—all these may be expressed in ethnic terms. Consequently, ethnicity acquires a new political saliency leading to the emergence of nationalities, national minorities, and ethnic groups.

In the economic dimension, the impact of modernization on interethnic relations is linked to the industrialization of agrarian economies as well as to the further expansion of industrial economies. In both cases, the mounting need for an adequate labor supply promotes urbanization; it sets in motion large-scale population transfers from rural agrarian areas to urban industrial areas within a relatively short period. Such migrations may be confined to one state territory or may transcend international boundary lines. International (especially trans-oceanic) migrations, but often just intranational migrations, are apt to bring distant and ethnically unrelated populations into close contact. This, however, disturbs the homogeneity that a modern society requires for its proper functioning. For, as we have seen, the smooth working of democracy presupposes a reasonably homogeneous state population with a common identity, a sense of solidarity, and a common core culture. The increase of ethnic diversity brought about by industrial migrations, however, makes national unity again problematical.

The ethnic heterogeneity of the labor force also proves a disturbing factor in an industrial economy. Before turning to this crucial problem, it is advisable to outline the general nature and specific social implications of an industrial economy. Basically, industrialism indicates the mass production of material goods made possible by technological inventions which are based on new insights in the natural sciences. Production in an industrial economy is characterized by mechanization and utilization of inanimate energy. Cooperation is regulated through the institutions of property, contract, and occupation. It presupposes a common means of communication and a common core culture. Yet industrial economy requires conformity only with value standards and norms that are essential to its efficient operation while tolerating diversity in other respects. But national polity aims at a more comprehensive cultural uniformity.

Moreover, segmental industrial culture is basically the same for all industrialized national societies, while comprehensive national cultures are more-or-less mutually exclusive. Among the essential requirements of an industrial culture are a dominance of economic value orientation; a prevalence of the profit motive; replacement of traditional solidarities by contractual relations; technical and social skills appropriate to particular occupations; discipline of work; and submission to functional authority. Industrial culture, like any other, lays down the general rules according to which social rewards are to be distributed. A social reward may be any benefit that a person or a group of persons gains by participating in a particular society at a particular time with regard to any kind of goods and services (including power and prestige). The overall result of the differential distribution of social rewards according to social status is reflected in the social structure. The concept of social status refers to the rights and duties of a category of persons, which may or may not also form a subgroup of a society. The concept of social position refers to the social rights and duties of a person.

THE STATUS SYSTEM OF MODERN SOCIETY

The social structure that is typical of an industrial society may be best described in terms of the criteria by which status is socially assigned. The distinction between ascribed and achieved status has become a stock-in-trade of contemporary sociology. Before we adopt it for the present purpose, some refinement of the conventional terms seems to be called for. Ralph Linton, who introduced the simple dichotomy, defined the concepts as follows: Achieved statuses, he wrote, "are not assigned to individuals from birth but are left open to be filled through competition and individual effort" (Linton, 1939, p. 115). Ascribed status, on the other hand, "can be predicted and trained for from the moment of birth," according to a variety of criteria. Besides age and sex, Linton mentioned being born into a particular family or a "socially established group," such as a class or caste. Obviously, sex and age are not of the same order as the other criteria on the basis of which status may be "ascribed." Apart from sex and age, the common denominator of all other criteria mentioned by Linton appears to be status inheritance on account of descent from a particular family, kinship group, or ethnic unit. However, Linton's concept of achieved status seems to cover too much ground: it is meant to include any status that is not determined either by biological differences or by descent; it may be acquired by virtue of some individual quality or accomplishment (e.g., intelligence, business acumen, education, successful performance of a task, a particular skill, even sheer good luck).

By modifying Linton's terminology slightly, and by neglecting sex and age as factors that have no direct bearing on interethnic relations, we arrive at three principal types of status assignment affecting the unequal distribution of social rewards: inheritance, acquisition, or accomplishment.

Inherited status is derived from the status of parents as well as more remote ancestors. Inheritance is the mechanism that guarantees the orderly transfer of rewards acquired by one generation to succeeding generations. Inherited status is a principal factor in safeguarding the continuity and stability of a social system. It tends to preserve a given social structure, to establish a system of social stratification, and to keep social mobility at a minimum. A society in which the criterion of descent prevails in assigning status to its members may be properly called a "closed society." Its social categories and ranks are closed not only to other members of the same society occupying different positions, but also to all nonmembers of this society: strangers remain outside the status system.

Those enjoying superior status have an interest in maintaining it through generations; they tend to favor the distribution of social rewards on the basis of inheritance. Those striving for improvement of their status, on the other hand, are interested in replacing the automatic transfer of status from generation to generation by adopting some other criteria of status assignment more favorable to themselves. Such criteria may be any quality or accomplishment that is highly valued in that society, and is suitable for distinguishing clearly between social categories or subgroups without referring to the status of their ancestors. This is generally meant when sociologists speak of "achieved status." Yet the expression is misleading. The relevant criteria need not be actually based on any accomplishment through individual or group effort, but include also qualities like physical strength, health, beauty, charisma, good luck, "unearned money," and many others, which a person gets without any particular effort or merit of his own. The term "acquired status" thus appears to be more appropriate.

In modern society a particularly high value is attached to individual effort: not what a man is—but what he does—counts. Accordingly, accomplishment is widely used as a criterion in assigning status. Status by accomplishment is therefore an important subtype of acquired status. An "open society" may be said to be one in which status is acquired rather than inherited; an "achieving society," one in which stress is put mainly on accomplishment.

Legitimacy of Status Assignment. In modern society we find a tendency to consider status assignment by way of inheritance as less legitimate than by acquisition, in particular, by accomplishment. Among the principles on which modern society is based we also find the idea of equality. If equality is meant to include a more equal distribution of social rewards, one is forced to admit that the substitution of acquired status for inherited status does not necessarily make for more equality. Because a more open society admits a greater differentiation of the social structure, often inequality is actually increased. Moreover, greater equality in one dimension, as for example, the political, may be accompanied by greater inequality in another dimension, such as the economic. Today, neither "capitalistic" nor "socialistic" societies are truly egalitarian in the sense that all kinds of social rewards are evenly distributed among all individuals, social categories, and subgroups.

The problem that concerns us at this point is not so much equality as distributive justice, which implies that there should be a definite relationship between the socially relevant activities performed by the members of a society and the rewards they bring. The ideas of justice differ from one society to another and from one period to another. Moreover, patently unjust arrangements are frequently rationalized by way of ideologies that seek to prove that such arrangements somehow contribute to the well-being of society and its members. Whatever the ground rules of a culture may be, their net result is bound to be the uneven distribution of social rewards among the structural components of society.

When, for instance, the nobility was forced to yield to the bourgeoisie, acquired wealth rather than inherited titles became the principal criterion for the distribution of most social rewards. But wealth acquired in one generation by one's own effort and efficiency becomes wealth inherited in the next. In the same way that the aristocrats had maintained their status level by dint of the principle of inheritance, the rich tended to maintain theirs on the basis of the same principle, so that society once more became closed—although, because of the operation of a market economy, to a lesser extent perhaps than before. Another criterion of status assignment that has gained importance in modern society is education, particularly training for higher skills and occupations. Again, new avenues for upward mobility were opened to those willing and able to increase their level of formal education.

Foreigners in American Society. Let us take another example: Among the basic tenets of the "American Creed" (Myrdal, 1944, p. 3) are included the inalienable rights of every man "to life, liberty, and the pursuit of happiness"; these rights are supported by the Christian (and humanistic) idea of the universal brotherhood of man. To the notion of a basic identity of man's very nature is added the moral postulate of equal opportunity for "the pursuit of happiness" without any regard to religion, race, or ethnicity. If we try to translate these phrases—repeated over and over again until they acquire a ritual symbolism—into the language of sociology, we might substitute for "pursuit of happiness" the attainment of social rewards. The handicap that should be removed clearly refers to barriers put up by status assignment on the basis of inheritance.[1]

This fundamental principle upon which American society is based—and which is also accepted with certain modifications by other modern societies—has a direct bearing on interethnic relations. In order to fully understand its implications, we have to remind ourselves that the ground rules of a global society are meant to regulate primarily intrasocietal and not intersocietal rela-

---

[1] Inherited status may also be based on religious differences insofar as religion, though formally a matter of individual choice, more often than not is actually transferred from generation to generation as a social heritage not to be easily changed at will.

tions. Social status indicates status in a particular society; assignment of a status is tantamount to membership in that society. A person without a recognizable status is excluded from society, he does not belong to it. National society has become the contemporary basic unit to which a given status system applies. Members of other societies are, by definition, excluded from the full enjoyment of its benefits. In the political sphere we call members of a national society "citizens," nonmembers "aliens." If we think of the broader aspects of social life, we prefer to speak of "natives" and "foreigners." Foreigners may be either permanent residents or nonresidents, such as visitors or tourists.

If we return to our example, we find from the very beginning, that the United States has been thought of as an open society; open not only with regard to the different social categories and subgroups in their relations to each other, but open also toward other peoples. In the earlier period of its history, this country was conceived of not as one nation-state among others but rather as a utopian society, where the past mistakes and shortcomings of Old World societies should be avoided: a model of a good society, a New World, a haven of freedom and opportunity for all those who wished to escape the oppression and persecution they had to endure in the old country. In a sense, there were no foreigners in America—only residents. And as all men were considered to be born equal, those who came to this country from abroad were supposed to have a start in the race for rewards equal to those who had come earlier: title, family, background, religion, property—in short, nothing that had afforded them social status in the old country—should count, only what they were able to acquire and accomplish through their own effort, skill, and good luck after they had arrived.

In due course, however, conditions became consolidated, and the population of the country, at first held together rather loosely by its utopian blueprint for a new society, was welded together into a modern nation on an equal footing with the other modern nations of the Western world (Kohn, 1957). More and more native Americans felt that the indiscriminate admission of foreigners was a threat to what they had achieved through hard toil and much suffering. The wish to transfer their possessions, including their status, to their children and children's children was reflected in the notion that natives had a special birthright to the country, and that to them alone the benefits that they had made possible should be reserved. Accordingly, the tendency to impose disabilities on all newcomers, on foreigners, and also on freed Negro slaves, grew. In this way the principle of status assignment by descent was reintroduced. The trend was intensified through the aftermath of the Civil War, through the closure of the frontier, and finally through the immense influx of foreigners from Eastern and Southern Europe in the wake of industrialization.[2]

---

[2]This trend, however, was temporary and has not succeeded in displacing the ideal of equality of opportunity (cf. Baltzell, 1964; Parsons, 1965).

Ethnicity in a Modern Status System. The American case illuminates the role played by ethnicity in the status system of a modern society. To repeat: Industrialism tends to increase the ethnic diversity of the state population, and to bring forth an industrial culture that is not tied to any particular national society. Nationalism, on the other hand, aims at the absorption of ethnically diverse populations into the national core; it also tends to exclude or to reduce the influx of ethnically diverse immigrants and to prevent the formation of ethnic groups. Participation in an industrial economy is ideal-typically governed by a competitive system of distributing social rewards according to acquired status. Full membership in a national society is confined to those who are identified with the national core. The status of natives is basically inherited through descent, but it may be acquired by foreigners when they adjust to the national core culture sufficiently to be accepted on equal terms.

Industrialization and nationalization have partly opposite effects on interethnic relations. The operation of the industrial system of distributing social rewards is curtailed by the national system of distributing social rewards. The inherited status of foreigners serves to exclude them from free competition with natives in the economic sphere. Moreover, neither the principles of industrialism governing the economic sphere nor the principles of demotic nationalism governing the political sphere regulate the totality of social relations including those which are epitomized by *commensalitas* and *connubium* (see below, p. 396). Thus, an ethnic who has become a citizen of a modern state and participates in its economy may still be excluded from the social rewards enjoyed by natives, such as participation in convivial activities or choice of a mate.

Integration of a society may be said to be accomplished when all its structural components have been assigned a definite status according to general criteria. Ethnic problems arise in a modern society when the recruitment of ethnically diverse elements for the industrial economy impedes their direct integration into the national core through absorption. In this case a compromise is offered by cultural pluralism. On the one hand, it insists upon uniformity with regard to those aspects of the culture that are essential requirements for the functioning of the polity and the economy. On the other hand, it permits diversity in other aspects of the culture that do not conspicuously affect political solidarity and economic cooperation. To preserve national identity, however, those cultural elements, which are extraneous to the national core culture and its carriers, are assigned an inferior value. Nevertheless, cultural pluralism permits the toleration of particularistic ethnic institutions as long as they do not interfere with the requirements of the industrial economy or the political order. In the course of the following discussion we shall discover several typical mechanisms by which ethnically diverse population elements are integrated into a modern society.

Agrarian versus Industrial Societies. A last point calls for special attention. Rural sections of a modern society and the parent societies of migrants to urban centers of industrial production are frequently prenational and preindustrial. We propose to call them "agrarian," for the predominant occupation is agriculture, animal husbandry, or other forms of primary production, such as forestry, fishing, and so on. Commercial and industrial activities in agrarian societies are complementary to the primary sector of the economy, and thus do not affect fundamentally the general style of life.

Industrialism tends to weaken primary, including ethnic, solidarities, but agrarianism tends to preserve them. Whenever the agrarian way of life and the coherence of the community are threatened by the pressures of industrialization and nationalization, ethnic differentiation is more strongly emphasized, and assimilation is conspicuously resisted. Thus, peasant traditions and folk cultures persisting in agrarian regions tend to block modernization unless they are rendered innocuous and socially ineffective by way of "stylization."

By contrast, migrants from agrarian countries or regions to the industrial sectors of modern societies are immediately compelled to accomodate to the culture of the host society. When they suffer disabilities, they tend to draw together to protect themselves against discrimination and, through collective effort, to gain a fair share in the economic and social rewards that industrial society has to offer. Yet the resistance put up by an agrarian population against the pressures of industrial society is frequently expressed in ethnic terms. Almost anything that is threatened by industrialization—religion, kinship solidarity, community organization, ethnic traditions, and cultural distinctions—may be represented as a morally superior value to be defended even at the cost of economic disadvantages.

PLAN OF PART III

The preceding discussion suggests that interethnic relations in modern society be studied on different levels to arrive at sociological generalizations. For they involve a variety of typical situations resulting in different behavior patterns. When the frame of reference is a local community, ethnically diverse people interact in a different manner than when a national society is taken as a whole. The former situation is the general topic of Section A, the latter of Sections B, C, and D. A second viewpoint concerns typical differences between the behavior of ethnics who are transferred collectively to the host society, for instance, by way of annexation, forming viable subsocieties or primary ethnic groups (Section B), and the behavior of immigrants who form secondary ethnic groups because of difficulties obstructing their direct integration into a host society by way of individual assimilation (Section C). Finally, a distinction has to be made between the processes by which ethnic groups are integrated collectively into the host society (Sections B and C), and the direct integration of individual ethnics, who either do not form an ethnic group or leave it at a later stage, into the host society by way of assimilation and absorption (Section D).

REFERENCES

Baltzell, Digby E., *The Protestant Establishment: Aristocracy and Caste in America*. New York: Random House, 1964.

Hughes, Everett C. and Helen M., *Where Peoples Meet: Racial and Ethnic Frontiers*. Glencoe, Ill.: The Free Press, 1952.

Kohn, Hans, *American Nationalism: An Interpretative Essay*. New York: The Macmillan Company, 1957.

Linton, Ralph, *The Study of Man*. New York: Appleton-Century, 1936.

Loiskandl, Helmut, *Edle Wilde, Heiden und Barbaren: Fremdheit als Bewertungskriterium zwischen Kulturen*. (Munich doctoral dissertation). Mödling bei Wien: St. Gabriel Verlag, 1966.

Myrdal, Gunnar, *An American Dilemma: The Negro Problem and Modern Democracy*. New York: Harper and Bros., 1944.

Parsons, Talcott, "Full Citizenship for the Negro American?" *Daedalus*, November 1965, reprinted in: Talcott Parsons, *Sociological Theory and Modern Society*. New York: The Free Press, 1967, chap. 13, pp. 422–465.

Warner, Lloyd W., and Leo Srole, *The Social Systems of American Ethnic Groups*, Yankee City Series, vol. III. New Haven: Yale University Press, 1945.

A. Ethnicity on the Community Level

INTRODUCTION

In the following five chapters we shall be dealing with interethnic relations within the framework of local communities: villages, country towns, industrial cities.[1] The approach has a definite advantage because ethnic phenomena appear most tangible, most transparent, and most directly observable on this level.

Plan of Section A. In Chapter 9 we studied a local community which, at the same time, constitutes a distinctive ethnic community. In Chapter 10 a local community will be analyzed which is divided into two subcommunities, in each of which a different ethnic group is dominant, Chapter 11 deals with the more common case of a local community whose dominant group corresponds to the national core of society at large, but which, in addition, comprises a relatively large population of ethnics of diverse origin. Although the dominant as well as the ethnic populations are integrated into one common status system, their relative positions in the social structure of the community are largely determined by ethnicity. The local community treated in Chapter 11, though it is similarly structured, offers the additional opportunity to investigate the relationship between ethnicity and religious affiliation. This theme is treated more fully in the final chapter of Section A, which deals with the peculiar situation of different Jewish immigrants to a large industrial city who are not of the same cultural background.

---

[1]As in Part I, we shall mostly use the present tense, although the materials on which our case studies are based have been collected years ago, occasionally up to half a century.

The Experience of Ethnicity: Atrisco

10

Atrisco is a tiny, Spanish-American village in New Mexico with a population of 157.[1] The community is ethnically homogeneous with the exception of the Catholic parish priest and the trader and his family, who are the only Protestants. The majority are peasant-farmers; some supplement their meagre farm income by wage-work, others earn their entire living as laborers. The local community is coextensive with a Catholic parish, but is incorporated in a larger unit of civil administration—the county, which includes many settlements with ethnically diverse populations. Thus, civil administration is both spatially and socially far removed, and does not support or symbolize communal unity.

The *patrón*, the trader, a few more prosperous farmers, and the parish priest may be considered as belonging to the upper class. The lower class is subdivided into farm-owners and wage-earners; residents and transients; families known to be partly of Indian origin and the others. A transient is considered a member of the community only when he marries into a resident family. Though intermarriage with Indians is generally regarded undesirable, it sometimes occurs.

ETHNIC DIFFERENCES

The Atrisqueños, forming a small community with meagre resources and surrounded on all sides by ethnically diverse communities, have numerous outside contacts. Many of them are forced to make a living as day laborers in the nearby country-towns or on some large livestock ranch as cowboys and shepherds. Just to the south of Atrisco is Homestead, a thriving village on which the Atrisqueños depend for many services. Its population consists mainly of immigrant farmers from Texas. Contacts are also maintained with the Mormon community of Rimrock and with the Indian pueblo of Zuni, where

---

[1]Abstracts of empirical materials included in this chapter are adopted with the permission of the publishers from Florence Rockwood Kluckhohn and F. Strodtbeck, *Variations in Value Orientations*. Evanston, Ill.: Row, Peterson & Co., 1961.

many villagers do their shopping and use the facilities of the government hospital. The best relations, however, are with Navajo Indians, who are frequently nired for seasonal work and herding, although no Atrisqueño considers an Indian to be his social equal.

Thus, ethnicity is not only a matter of everyday experience but is of vital concern for the Atrisqueños, as such contacts are usually fraught with tensions and frequently lead to open hostility. The people of Atrisco and other Spanish-Americans define themselves as *Mejicanos*; for their ancestors were citizens of the Estados Unidos de Mexico until 1848, when they were annexed by the United States of America, and thereby became "Spanish-speaking Americans of Mexican descent." For brevity's sake, we shall call them "Hispanos." The Indians, with whom the Atrisqueños maintain social relations, are ethnically divided among themselves and speak different native languages, but use Navajo as a *lingua franca*. Older Indians still know some Spanish; the younger ones have been taught English in school. Some Hispanos know a few Navajo words; the younger generation have attended schools where English is the language of instruction, although they rarely speak it well. Everyone using English as his normal means of communication, even if it is not his mother tongue, is socially defined by the Atrisqueños as an "Americano."

Besides language differences, however, other marks of distinction serve to identify members of the different ethnic groups at a glance: dress and haircut as well as "racial" characteristics. This is particularly true of Pueblo and Navajo Indians. Since Hispanos are frequently part-Indian, they sometimes may be mistaken for an Indian; indeed, Anglo-Americans, especially Texans, are inclined to view them as "colored," ranked only slightly higher than blacks. The average American, however, is readily distinguishable from either Indians or Hispanos. Although neither a Mexican nor an American race exists, it is an incontestable fact that, in a given heterogeneous population, the natives are quite able to recognize (with the help of subtle, often not easily determinable, clues) to which ethnic group an unknown person belongs, and they are rarely mistaken (cf. Part III, Chapter 21).

Besides biosomatic, there are cultural differences that assist an Atrisqueño in recognizing members of various ethnic groups. Not all of them have been observed directly by every Atrisqueño but each has at least heard others discussing them. In fact, partly due to curiosity, cultural differences are a favorite topic of conversation everywhere.

Such knowledge is however also highly functional: To get along with different people, to protect oneself against unpleasant and even dangerous reactions, one must know in some way what to expect from them. Thus, children are told in early youth about the habits of various categories of strangers they might meet. This knowledge often does not go very deep nor is it always correct. On the contrary, heterostereotypes are highly simplified and slanted. They do not conform with the scientific rules of objective description and interpretation. *They are not meant to do justice to other people, but only to serve the very practical purpose of getting along with them when one meets them* (cf. Part III, Chapter 21).

As an example, when people go hunting for mushrooms they observe certain rules by which to distinguish edible from noxious species. One popular yardstick is that when you cut the trunk of a mushroom and it runs blue or green, you should not eat it. Although botanists will tell you that there are many mushrooms of this kind that are perfectly safe, the generalization is the result of long human experience and can serve as a useful rule of thumb. The main thing is that you may eat mushrooms and stay alive, not that you recognize by sight all the mushrooms which can safely be consumed; it is important to avoid all the poisonous ones; it is decidedly less important to eat all the nourishing ones. It is also unnecessary to know all the species of mushroom in the world that are possibly edible; one need only recognize most edible mushrooms that grow abundantly in one's neighborhood. In the same way, one only needs general rules for those people with whom one is likely to have contact. An Atrisqueño is not interested in the character and culture of the Swiss or Turks, as he will probably never meet one. But he is vitally concerned with the character of Navajos, Pueblo Indians, or Tejanos of Homestead. He must have learned some easy cues by which to distinguish them readily; than he must know what to expect of them in a given situation.

From what we have said so far, we realize that the assertion and specification of differences in the culture and character of different people is a necessary ingredient of interethnic relations. Unless there is a common understanding within a given group about characteristic differences that distinguish one from others, interaction between members of various groups personally unknown to each other, and thus interaction between groups *qua* groups, becomes impossible. The collective representations that groups have of each other are mostly asymmetric. Although this gives rise to frictions, misunderstandings, and conflicts, it does not exclude intergroup interaction. In fact, it is constitutive of interethnic relations.

History and Ethnicity

This excursus should no longer detract our attention from our primary problem: Which collective experiences and representations explain why Atrisqueños consider the Tejanos or Indios as ethnically different and treat them accordingly? Apart from different locality, a low frequency of interaction, a lack of intimacy, weak kinship ties, and, above all, language differences, real or imputed differences in culture, behavior patterns, and "character" are among the most effective factors. Finally, we have to consider history. History may be called the memory of a people, but it is sociologically irrelevant whether a historical account is based on fact or myth, as long as it is believed and influences behavior. The Atrisqueños do have a notion (however vague) that the

Indians are the aborigines of New Mexico; that they were conquered by the Spaniards, their own ancestors; that the Spaniards were the first European settlers; that they have been conquered by the Americans, who took away much of their land and have forced upon them a new system of government as well as other institutions. The Artrisqueños are also well aware that their present school is an American school—the school of a foreign people.

They know that Homestead was established in relatively recent years by immigrants from Texas who were supported by the government of the United States. Whereas the Indians are remembered as former subjects of the Hispanos, the Tejanos are considered interlopers and intruders. One group is looked down upon; the other resented. These sentiments, generated by historical events, also effectively color the image that Atrisqueños hold of the two groups and their ideas about their own relations with them. Thus, events long past and of no immediate significance for present conditions and different situations—history, as told and transmitted from generation to generation—is another factor providing orientation in interethnic relations.

CONCLUSIONS

The relations of the Atrisqueños to the people with whom they are in frequent, almost daily, contact is strongly and vitally influenced by an awareness of shared ethnicity. And the notion of ethnicity, as we already know, necessarily implies contrast: marked differences in speech, culture, historical memory, political dominance, and economic status. It is this specific contrast effect that entitles us to describe Atrisco as an "ethnic community." This term implies a local community that is socially defined by reference to ethnic differences from other local communities and from the national society within which it functions.

The next case on our agenda is also concerned with a local community, but one which is in many respects different from Atrisco. This peasant community conformed to an agrarian type of social organization. Cantonville, on the other hand, marks the transition from the preindustrial to the modern type. It is a small city in which many vestiges of its agrarian origin as a country-town are still preserved; in which, however, industrialization and modernization have concurrently progressed so far that they have come to determine the character of the local community as a whole. The theme of ethnic distinctions and interethnic relations also looms large in Cantonville, whose population is divided between French-Canadians and English-speaking Canadians and Americans. But the two ethnic groups do not live in separate local communities; they form two distinctive ethnic communities within one local community. What is the evidence?

Ethnic Subcommunities: Cantonville

11

Cantonville is a place of about 20,000 in the Eastern Townships of Quebec.[1] Its earliest European settlers were not French, as in most other parts of the province, but English. This is still reflected in the administrative system: the basic unit is not the parish comprising a peasant village, but the township combining scattered farms with a trading center. Cantonville is thus the name of both the town and its rural hinterland. As occurred everywhere in the Eastern Townships, which was the portion of Quebec originally settled by the English, French-Canadian *habitants* soon began to migrate into the area so that by 1911, more than nine-tenths of the township's total population of 2605 was French. Throughout the nineteenth century the old-stock English, mostly Anglicans, remained dominant in the trades, professions, and industries typical of a country-town; they also dominated the local community politically and gave it its cultural character. By the turn of the century the original English families had relinquished their power and influence to a new elite of French merchants and professionals. The common people were now almost exclusively French in speech and culture, and Catholic by religion.

INDUSTRIALIZATION

Industrialization once again changed the character of the local community. The new industries were run on quite different lines from those which prevailed in the original country-town. The sawmill, tannery, and smelting furnace had been owned by local people, and had served mainly local needs. The new textile mills, mass producing for large national and international markets, were in the hands of British and American companies; management and personnel

---

[1]This chapter is based on empirical materials adapted with the permission of the publishers from Everett C. and Helen McGill Hughes, *French Canada in Transition*. Chicago: University of Chicago Press, 1943.

down to the level of foremen, skilled workers, and clerks were recruited outside French Canada. As a result of industrialization, considerable numbers of mainly Protestant migrants from England, the United States, and Anglo-Saxon Canada were added to the local community. At the same time, industrial expansion stimulated migration from a wider, mostly rural, region of Quebec to Cantonville.

Despite these developments, Cantonville was not completely transformed into an industrial city. It became a local community, cradling two subcommunities clearly distinguishable from each other, yet united in a kind of symbiosis, remaining separate in some respects yet merging in others. Basse-Ville, the old town, includes the original business district and the old residential areas; across the railroad tracks lies New Town with a new business street, new residential areas and, still further out, the big factories.

THE OLD FRENCH SUBCOMMUNITY

What is left of the former country-town and of its people remains concentrated in Basse-Ville. It still fulfills some vital functions as a trading and service center for the agrarian hinterland. Characteristically, these business units are owned and operated by the French and, occasionally, by the bilingual descendants of the original English families. The subcommunity that has its natural center in Basse-Ville is French and Catholic.

This older French subcommunity has retained many characteristics of the preindustrial community, including its social structure: the old French families of importance at the top of the status scale, the French laboring and servant class at the opposite end. The French subcommunity is firmly anchored in the larger society of French Canada and its general culture; it also carries weight in provincial politics. Still, the French subcommunity remains an integral part of the local community. Its elite is prominent in local politics from which the new English arrivals are, for all practical purposes, excluded. Its businesses also cater to the new industrial community. In this respect, however, French merchants of the old stock find themselves in competition with French businessmen who have arrived since, and because of, industrialization, in addition to chain-stores controlled by outside interests, usually English or Jewish. Ecologically as well as economically and socially, both subcommunities interlock and form one larger local community. Even Basse-Ville has been invaded by Anglo-Saxon newcomers with their houses, offices, stores, clubs, tennis courts, and golf courses.

THE INDUSTRIAL SUBCOMMUNITY

In the new industrial subcommunity the Anglo-Saxons are clearly dominant, although their number in 1940 amounted to no more than 7.5 percent of the

Cantonville population. The majority of them belong either to the Anglican church, as do the old English families of Basse-Ville, or to the United Church of Canada. About 4 percent of the Catholic population are Anglo-Saxons who tend to send their children to the English Protestant school and take little or no interest in organized church activities out of fear that they might become identified with the French. But even relations among Anglicans are sometimes strained; the old stock English resent the new arrivals chiefly because the latter introduced many changes in the church. So we can see that tensions between the two subcommunities are not entirely due to ethnic or religious differences but also to the contrast between the old and the new. This is also reflected in the changed social structure of the local community. French businessmen and professionals not only represent the elite of the French subcommunity but are also prominent in the Catholic church and in town politics. The new English elite, on the other hand, is prominent in industry as well as in certain civic associations and clubs, which are partly open to both English and French. In these organizations and also in the Chamber of Commerce there is some intermingling of both French and English upper classes; some intimate friendships are formed and even intermarriage occurs. In addition, a new French upper class has emerged which is more oriented toward the new industrial subcommunity. This "sporty clique" is fully accepted by its Anglo-Saxon opposite number, but is regarded by the old French and English elites as being "cheap."

Although the dividing line is vague, the new industrial subcommunity is composed mostly of newcomers, both English and French, migrants from other parts of Quebec and Canada, from the United States, and from overseas. In addition, the younger generation of the original population, both of the town and of its rural hinterland, are being drawn more and more into the orbit of the new industrial community. Thus, social change in Cantonville is brought about by both migration and reorientation. The old community is constantly losing its younger people to the new community, whilst concurrently, the latter is also growing through the addition of outsiders and thus—by the sheer weight of numbers—is inevitably gaining ground. The new subcommunity is much more directly linked to industrial society at large and to the Canadian national society rather than to French Canada. The big factories, which are owned by outside corporations and produce for outside markets, constitute its economic base. Economic power is vested in people identified with the Anglo-Saxon society. Anglo-Saxon values and ways of life prevail, to which also the French working in the new industries, or dependent on them in some other way, must adapt.

Relations Between the Two Subcommunities

Viewing the local community as a whole, it may be said that its traditional section is dominant in the polity, its modern section in the economy, and that the modern section is rapidly gaining ground in the local community. The

French constitute the overwhelming majority of Cantonville's population. Yet (disregarding the spheres of home and church), they have to adjust their ways of life to business practices, work discipline, and even to recreational habits typical of the Anglo-Saxon newcomers whose culture is generally closer to that of industrial society than are the traditions of the French-Canadians. Thus, the Anglo-Saxons, by and large, are better equipped to live and make a living in an industrialized society. Those French who want to succeed in the industrial section of the community must follow their example. It is the French who have to change, not the English—who, as the Hughes' report, "continue their customary occupations" (Hughes, 1943, p. 44) and, by the same token, their way of life.

As the industrial subcommunity gains in importance, the community as a whole becomes oriented toward values and norms represented by the Anglo-Saxons. If language is a significant index of dominance, Cantonville is still not an English town and probably never will be. Yet the Anglo-Saxons need not learn French to obtain goods and services in town or to keep their positions in industry. Many of the French, on the other hand, are bilingual; they must know English in order to deal with most of their superiors at work or with English customers and clients. In industry, the Hughes' remark, "the pressure is on the subordinate, whose mother tongue is French, rather than upon the superior, whose mother tongue is English" (Hughes, 1943, p. 82). Some Anglo-Saxons justify this attitude by saying that Canada is, after all, an English country, and it is up to the French to learn English.

We find the same situation with regard to the proportion of French and Anglo-Saxons in occupations that are more or less desirable, which have a higher or lower prestige. "Generally speaking, English do not work under French authority" (Hughes, 1943, p. 73). Typically, unskilled industrial laborers are recruited from the lower French classes. Children of upper- and middle-class French families are accepted for minor clerical work without much hope of advancement. The prestige of the few French found in the higher positions, though never at the top, is not in reality derived from their occupation. Their social status is not "achieved": they are employed in better positions in industry because of their ascribed status as members of better-class French families.

Power on all levels of industry is clearly in the hands of the Anglo-Saxons. There are, however, other reasons why the Anglo-Saxons as a whole, including the relatively small number of laborers, attain a higher prestige in the community: They stand for the values that are typical of industrial society. As industrial society has succeeded in opening up new avenues for advancement and new opportunities for the enjoyment of goods and services hitherto unknown or unobtainable, their way of life is considered by many as superior. There is therefore a tendency to emulate, or at least to envy, all those who are typical carriers of industrial culture—once more the Anglo-Saxons.

INTERETHNIC RELATIONS

Although we have emphasized ethnicity throughout, the time has come to deal more specifically with interethnic relations in Cantonville. ". . . the ethnic factor is so important and apparent that almost everyone accounts for things in terms of it. It is in the air" (Hughes, 1943, p. 64). The English have definite opinions about the French in comparison to themselves, and vice versa. The French resent the effective superiority of the English in industry, their competition in business, that they are generally better off, their conspicuous consumption, and their style of living. There is also active resistance to the progress of the industrial and national culture for which they stand. Some of the French voluntary associations, such as the Retail Merchants' Association, engage in propaganda against their competitors. Strikes have been called against the big companies, mainly in protest against Anglo-Saxon control.

The Anglo-Saxons are no less opinionated. They patronize the one general practitioner in town who is English; if they need specialized medical work, they will drive to Montreal to consult English doctors, even though there are French specialists in Cantonville. The English look down upon the French inability to adjust to industrial society and to make their way in industry except as manual workers. They also resent their political power in town and in the province. Most of all, the English resent being forced to live in an unfamiliar milieu. Language differences, in particular, are a constant reminder of being different.

The French of Cantonville, in order to think and communicate in a manner adapted to life in industrial society, are forced to learn English and to modify even their own French speech to fit new conditions. They are under a stress to become "Anglicized" or "Americanized." To rise in the system, it is necessary that they become less traditionally French. This, in spite of the opposition of priests and intellectuals who extol the glories of the past and the virtues of French agrarian traditions.

CONCLUSIONS

The term "ethnic community" is unsuitably applied to Cantonville, which should be considered a local community forming part of a global society—the French-Canadian society, which we are inclined to describe as an ethnic society in the process of becoming a national society. But scientific concepts should not be used for purposes other than those for which they are meant. The French-Canadians certainly identify themselves with the country in which they were the first white settlers. They call themselves *"les Canadiens,"* but are inclined to consider other Canadians to be foreign intruders and call them *"les*

Anglais.'' English-speaking citizens of Canada, on the other hand, reverse the argument. They distinguish the French-Canadians as a particular ethnic group.

Though popular terminologies are revealing, they should not detract our attention from the real situation. The claim to a country advanced by ethnically different sections of its population may be grounded on various principles of legitimacy, such as priority of occupation and permanent settlement, effective political power, or cultural superiority. Depending on which standpoint one prefers to take on the issue of such conflicting legal and moral claims, the one or the other people may be regarded as "ethnically different" from the national core, and therefore as an "ethnic group" in our terminology.

Seen in this light, we might consider the Anglo-Saxons in Cantonville to be an immigrant ethnic group, and the French a distinctive nationality within the Canadian state population. Nevertheless, we have to realize that the Anglo-Saxon minority is becoming more dominant in Cantonville, just as, and partly because, the Anglo-Saxon majority has become dominant in the Canadian national society as a whole. This draws attention to the essential dynamism of interethnic relations. The typical character of a population persisting through time is subject to change; thus, *we must not hesitate to apply different analytical concepts to one and the same people at different stages of its history.* Such changes may be due to political and economic factors. In the case of Cantonville, we have found that industrialization brought about several changes, which are of immediate relevance for our investigation.

The addition of alien migrants to the local community not only produced ethnic heterogeneity but has made ethnicity all the more significant. This led to the formation of a new subcommunity with a different social structure and culture, which was superimposed upon the old ethnically homogeneous community and tended to replace it. As the division of labor increased, the social structure of the community became more complex and assumed a class character. Cultural and subcultural differences among a variety of population elements—rural and urban, agrarian and industrial, French and English— which were integrated into one local community, promoted a pluralism permitting different value systems and ways of life to coexist side by side.

Still, economic developments exerted pressures upon the preindustrial, and in this particular case French, culture. These pressures clashed with the nationalizing tendencies in French-Canadian society, which were in part a reaction to the general nationalization of Canada during her transformation from a British colony into a sovereign nation. As a result of these counter-pressures, exerted not only by political forces but by the Catholic church as well, the Cantonville French made the following concessions while adapting to industrialization: Without relinquishing their ethnic identity, they collectively adopted those Anglo-Saxon culture traits that enabled them to function properly in an industrial setting, including a working knowledge of the English language.

Because of their sense of superiority and actual power, the English have no interest in identifying themselves with French Canada. To them Cantonville is just a place in which to make a living. Their psychological anchorage is elsewhere in Canada, in the United States, or in England. Should the French ever decide that Cantonville no longer offers them enough scope, they can find full satisfaction of their social and emotional needs elsewhere in French Canada. Only the very ambitious might look to the United States or Anglo-Saxon Canada for the benefits of a more advanced industrial society.

As the town population grows and the occupational diversification and the complexity of the social structure increases, social relations have tended to become depersonalized. Social categorization has become increasingly important in determining social action orientation. Social rank has gained greater significance than membership in primary groups. These facts require a few additional remarks of a more general, theoretical nature.

Social Categorization. Group membership always implies a social classification. The perception of groups necessarily implies the social definition of its personnel in terms of individual qualities typically shared by other members. In other words, social classification (or categorization) draws attention to the typical qualities of the members of one group (the "in-group"), which distinguish them from all other groups (the "out-groups"). Accordingly, one can maintain that groups are social categories of a special kind. Frequently, however, the term "social classifciation"—though equally serving the purpose of social action orientation—does not imply that the persons classified as belonging to a particular social category actually interact as one social group. The shared qualities of individuals, which are considered socially significant enough to call forth differential behavior, depend on the situation and the culture of the interacting groups. Social classifications correspond to the assignment of social roles: Persons classified as belonging to a particular social category are expected to behave in a manner considered appropriate for that category.

In a local community like Atrisco or agrarian Cantonville, most people know each other, or at least of each other, as persons. As a new generation grows up, community members are pointed out to the children, who also gather further information about them by overhearing the conversation of their elders. As long as the number of newcomers remains small, every one of them is an object of curiosity and a topic of gossip until he, too, becomes sufficiently familiar to everybody to be treated as any other member of the community. The number of people with whom one can be on terms of familiarity and maintain personalized relations is, however, limited. If the limit is exceeded, social categorization (a mental device by which we are able to interact socially with people personally unknown to us) comes into play. As size, spatial mobility, and the occupational diversity of a community increase, more people will be unknown to each other, and the mechanism of social categorization will increase in importance.

The people of Cantonville who migrated there because of industrialization are strangers to most of the original inhabitants and also to each other. Even if, in time, some of them become personally acquainted, most interaction is still based on categorization. Inasmuch as categorization determines social relations, these tend to become more abstract and impersonal, less intimate and more segmentalized. People interact much less often as "persons" and more often as "types." Industrialization has brought to Cantonville new activities and new people; both have disrupted the original social structure that was comparatively transparent and simple. The social structure has now become so complex that few people are able to grasp it as a whole, or are at all aware that it has any pervasive pattern. Rather, each individual is limited to a knowledge of those categories with which he is confronted and to which he has to respond in everyday life.

In ethnically heterogeneous communities like modern Cantonville, status tends to be linked to ethnicity. Not only is the status system different for the French and the English population, but the relative rank of people assigned to the same status category according to the criteria generally recognized in modern society (power, wealth, education, and so on) is influenced by their social definition as French or Anglo-Saxon. *Thus, ethnicity may be considered as a special type of social category.* This problem will occupy our attention in the following chapter. Finally, people having the same status tend to associate with each other and, once they begin to interact in a specific manner, they—by definition—have begun forming a group. A group thus formed on the basis of shared status we propose to call a "status group." Just as people who interact in a specific manner on account of shared ethnicity may be called an "ethnic group," and just as their social status in their own community is greatly influenced by ethnic differentiation, so we may consider ethnic groups in a modern setting as a special type of status group. The following chapter will offer an opportunity to examine this point more closely.

Ethnicity and Social Status: Yankee City

12

Founded in the early sixteenth century, Yankee City, Massachusetts, has grown into an industrial community with a population of 17,000.[1] Although serving an agrarian hinterland much like old Cantonville and living largely from fishing, it must be considered a city in the technical sense of the word since long-distance sea trade and shipbuilding have been its principal sources of income. Modern industries (producing silverware, shoes, and textiles) were introduced in the middle of the last century. As the demand for labor could no longer be satisfied locally, immigrants from abroad were attracted in steadily increasing numbers. Between 1840 and 1850 the Irish arrived, later the French-Canadians; they were followed (in this order) by Jews, Italians, Armenians, Greeks, Poles, and finally (between 1910 and 1920) by Russians.

In 1940, slightly over one-half of the population were "Yankees" (descendants of the original city population), or else standard "Americans," that is, white, Protestant, and Anglo-Saxon. The other half consisted of ethnics[2]: 23 percent French-Canadian, 2 percent Jewish, 1.7 percent Italian, 1.5 percent Polish, 2.5 percent Greek, 4 percent Armenian, 0.9 percent Russian, and 0.5 percent black. Ethnic differentiation is greater than in Cantonville, but the economic base of Yankee city is more clearly industrial (one-fourth of the working population is employed in the shoe industry alone). Its overall cultural character is definitely Anglo-Saxon, and its industrial economy conforms to that of the American national society.

The parent societies of these ethnics were predominantly of the preindustrial, agrarian, and even prenational type at the time of their migration to Yankee City. Their reasons for emigrating, however, differed. Armenians and Jews

---

[1] This chapter is based on empirical materials adapted with the permission of the publishers from W. Lloyd Warner and Paul S. Lunt, *The Social Life of a Modern Community*. Yankee City Series, Vol. 1. New Haven: Yale University Press, 1941.

[2] The noun "ethnic" is a convenient term introduced by Warner to indicate one belonging to an ethnic group or category.

fled from oppression and violence—massacres in Turkey, pogroms in Russia; they came with their families and had no intention of returning. In the other ethnic groups, the men were usually attracted by economic opportunities that would allow them to support their indigent families at home; they hoped to return eventually, though they rarely did. After a while, their families followed them to settle permanently in America. They tended to live each in their own neighborhood, usually some slum section with which they remained identified for decades.

They accommodated to the host society as far as was necessary in order to make a living and avoid conflict, but they retained as many of their folkways as were permitted. Each ethnic group organized voluntary associations, especially mutual-aid societies, which served recreational and convivial as well as utilitarian purposes. The establishment and support of their own religious congregation was a priority: a church building, a priest, a hall, a parish school. The church became the most important center of the ethnic subcommunity—a symbol of ethnic identity, a common meeting place, a generator of sentiments of solidarity, a custodian of folk traditions, and a mediator of national culture. Consequently, the threads of religion and nationality were so highly interwoven that it becomes practically impossible to distinguish them clearly.

SOCIAL STRUCTURE AND ETHNICITY

For the analysis of the Yankee City system of ranked status categories, Warner adopted a scheme of six social classes (lower-lower, upper-lower, lower-middle, upper-middle, lower-upper, upper-upper), which has become a stock-in-trade of social science. With the help of this classification he ascertained the typical distribution of ethnics among the different status categories as well as the relative degree and speed of upward mobility. Generally, every ethnic group upon arrival started at the bottom of the scale as common laborers. Yankees, that is, descendants of the original population, stayed at the top of the social pyramid. The higher the pyramid grew due to occupational diversification, and the more ethnics filled its lower ranks, the greater became the opportunities for members of the national core to rise ever higher in the status scale. Thus, Warner found that all the highest and 95 percent of the following class were "Yankees," but only 38 and 43 percent of the two lowest classes. Some ethnics have invaded the lower-upper class of the new rich and, in increasing numbers, the upper and lower middle classes, while the highest percentage of ethnics (61 percent) is found in the upper-lower class, which Warner describes as the "honest workmen" and "clean poor" class. The bulk of the Yankee City population (62 percent) belongs to this and to the next higher class of "good common people" who are concerned about their respectability, careful with their money, and cling to the "Protestant ethic." The lowest class, which makes up one-fourth of the total population, is commonly considered to consist of "shiftless Yankees" and "ignorant immigrants;" actually a smaller proportion of ethnics, but a larger proportion of Americans are found in this class than in the next higher class.

A COMPARISON WITH CANTONVILLE

In our discussion on Cantonville, we emphasized that the relative frequency with which one meets a certain type of person has an influence upon the impression gained about the general character of a local community. In most cases, the "better people" of Yankee city are Yankees. Although three-fourths of the ethnics belong to Warner's two-fold lower class, one cannot overlook the fact that nearly half the Yankee population is also to be found there. Still, there are good grounds for labeling this community "Yankee City." It is as "Yankee" as Cantonville is "French-Canadian," not only by virtue of its history and geographical location, but by its general character. The most significant difference between the two cities is not that one is French and the other Anglo-Saxon, but is due rather to the effects of industrialization on the two communities. In Yankee City the natives have remained dominant despite the addition of large numbers of ethnics, proportionally a much larger group than in Cantonville; and the natives have been able to take full advantage of the new economic opportunities.

The main labor force in Cantonville is ethnically homogeneous and native to the region. By contrast, in Yankee City a higher percentage of ethnics than Yankees are employed in half the major industries. The Yankees are also significantly fewer in the retail business. Moreover, the ethnics are not a homogeneous group. Of course, the Anglo-Saxons in Cantonville are not strictly homogeneous either, but they still constitute one socially effective category and even form a distinctive subcommunity. In Yankee City the ethnics, taken as a whole, represent a large proportion of the total population and they make up a substantial part of the three lowest social classes. The various ethnic categories are concentrated in certain industries, businesses, and occupations.

Although Yankee city is ethnically much more differentiated, the structure of the local community is actually less complex and the status system more uniform than in Cantonville. Cultural pluralism in Yankee City is similar to that in the American national society; it bears little resemblance to the uneasy coexistence of two national cultures in an enclave of a country where the French "nationality" struggles for its survival in a sea of Anglo-Saxons. The old French of Cantonville improved their status because of the influx of French migrants at the bottom of the scale. Yet, concurrently, strangers joined the top and so partially blocked the upward mobility of the French. Precisely because they moved to Cantonville, the Anglo-Saxons generally rose in status, whereas the French migrants were given fewer chances for advancement. In Yankee City, on the other hand, the position of the Yankees at the top of the scale remained unchallenged by later immigrants.

A further difference may be seen in the ecological distribution. In Cantonville we found only two clearly distinguishable ecological areas, Basse-Ville and New Town. The situation in Yankee City is much more complex. Warner reports of twelve areas over which the city's nine ethnic groups are distributed in different proportions. Five areas are inhabited predominantly by Yankees with a sprinkling of all other groups except blacks. Each of the other ethnic groups is clearly concentrated in certain areas. Some are occupied by a typical combination of French, Pole, and Russian; Italians and Armenians associate preferably with the Irish; the blacks are almost wholly confined to one area, which also includes heavy concentrations of Irish, Italians, Armenians, and Greeks, but almost no French, Jews, or Yankees.

SOCIAL MOBILITY OF ETHNIC GROUPS

The degree to which different ethnic groups have been integrated into the local community of Yankee City, and the rate at which they have advanced in status, reveal considerable variations. The Jews and Armenians, who came with the intention of settling permanently in America, became adapted faster and attained upward mobility sooner than groups like the Italians, Greeks, or Poles, who originally planned to stay only temporarily. Groups like the French or Irish, whose peasant culture and Catholic religion protected the traditional family structure, tended to adapt themselves more slowly. The chronological order of a group's appearance in the city also affected the time needed for integration and assimilation; thus, the Irish took longer because they were the first and helped clear the way for subsequent groups. The large size of an ethnic population tends to retard social mobility; this was evident with the Irish and French. If an ethnic group is similar in culture to Armenian society, its social mobility is accelerated. Thus the Jews, whose economic background was commercial rather than agricultural, and the Armenians, whose religion had some affinity to the Episcopalian church, experienced greater and faster upward mobility than other groups.

CONCLUSIONS

The preceding analysis of empirical materials permits us already to draw several more general conclusions:

Proposition 1. The members of a community (society) are differentiated according to social status. Social rewards are distributed unequally among them in accordance with definite criteria.

Proposition 2. Ethnics differ from other members of the community (society) with regard to the distribution of social rewards. As in Yankee City they tend to be underrepresented in the higher status categories, overrepresented in the lower. This fact suggests but does not yet prove discrimination. By discrimination we mean unequal treatment contrary to the general rules governing the distribution of social rewards among the members of a community (society). The specific disability of ethnics obviously consists in being treated "less equally" than natives. In this sense, ethnicity appears to be a disturbing factor in the "normal" distribution of social rewards. From a purely analytic standpoint, we can treat ethnicity as a status category that modulates the operation of all other status categories.

Proposition 3. This modulating potency is brought about by the different degrees of "belongingness" to a community (society). No other group mentioned by Warner is fully accepted by the dominant group, the Yankees, as belonging to the community. They are not only popularly called "foreigners," they actually share to some extent the fate of nonmembers of a society. Long-term residence, citizenship, and even native birth do not in themselves seem to alter substantially their status as foreigners. The same is true of the blacks. The ex-slave was not accepted as a full member of American society; in fact, the membership status of blacks in the South was drastically reduced several years after emancipation. In the North, on the other hand, they tended to share the lot of foreign immigrants, even if they actually came from other parts of the United States. If we draw a scale between full membership and nonmembership in the community of Yankee City, we find that only Yankees enjoy full membership, but that ethnic groups are granted lesser degrees of membership.

Put more abstractly, nonresident foreigners are entirely excluded from the normal operation of the system for distributing social rewards. Only certain forms of courtesy and hospitality are extended to them as well as certain legal rights, such as the protection of life and property, granted to everyone. Resident foreigners, especially those of long-established residence who make their living in the country, gradually become integrated into the community (society); they are granted an increasing degree of membership status. The higher the degree of membership the more the regular status system becomes applicable to them.

Proposition 4. In the same way as status is assigned according to definite criteria, there exist also general criteria for determining the degree of membership. Warner has drawn up a list of such criteria for Yankee City. Basically, the degree of membership depends on the degree to which immigrants (foreigners) and their descendants conform to the ideal type of American (popularly referred to as the "full-blooded American"). This ideal type is expressed by the phrase "white, Anglo-Saxon, and Protestant" (WASP). In Yankee City this type is perfectly represented by the Yankees.

THE SOCIAL SITUATION

The social situation of an ethnic group in American society has been investigated by Warner in terms of (1) its relative exclusion from the system of the distribution of rewards applicable to charter members; (2) the coherence of the group measured by the degree of control exercised by the ethnic group over its members, primarily through its particular religious and educational institutions, as well as through voluntary associations; and (3) the time required for ethnics to become assimilated by the host society.[3]

These three factors are correlated by Warner with the degree of deviation from the American prototype, measured in terms of race and culture. The degree of racial deviation reaches from "white like old Americans" through dark Caucasoid, Caucasoid mixtures, Mongoloid, to Negroid. With regard to culture, Warner distinguishes between language and religion, crediting religion with the greater importance. He arrives at the following scale: Protestants who speak English, Protestants who do not speak English, non-Protestant Christians who respectively speak or do not speak English, the two lowest categories are Christians who speak English and those who do not. By combining the two scales he arrives at thirty possible combinations of which only eighteen exist in actual fact. Thus, religion appears as one of three principal factors that determine the degree to which foreigners are admitted to full participation in the American status system on equal terms with natives. (For the moment we disregard American Negroes and Indians who, strictly speaking, are not foreigners in the accepted meaning of the term.)

In the light of our own conclusions, Warner's scheme does not appear to be entirely satisfactory. Although it focuses attention upon the statistical association between three characteristics of ethnic groups (race, language, and religion) and their social status in the host society, it fails to consider that such characteristics alone (or any combination thereof) cannot in themselves make an ethnic group what it is, but they serve rather as indicators for the presence of a major descent group. It would, for instance, be incorrect to assume that all white non-Protestants or even non-Christians who speak English form ethnic groups in American society.[4] We are therefore inclined to keep the factor of religion separate from "ethnicity."

Moreover, Warner often speaks of "ethnic groups" when he actually means ethnic categories. *Ethnic categories consist of people socially defined as being*

---

[3]The list of criteria mentioned by Warner for determining the "strength of the ethnic group" and for the "timetable of assimilation" are not quite consistent.

[4]Although individuals are not assigned to ethnic groups simply because they deviate from the American prototype, it is quite a different matter to maintain, as Warner does, that the degree to which members of ethnic groups deviate with regard to race, religion, and language has some influence upon the extent to which they are admitted to the American status system. The two problems—factors indicating the presence of ethnic groups and factors influencing the assimilation of individual ethnics—should be kept separate. As will be seen in Chapter 19, the two sets of variables are not complementary or symmetrical.

in varying degree foreigners who, accordingly, are excluded from the status system applicable to charter members. Foreigners *are strangers (defined in terms of social distance and lack of familiarity) who, by virtue of their descent from people identified with another country, are refused membership of the social community.* Natives or charter members, *on the other hand, are socially defined as belonging to a major descent group identified with a given place or territory.* Newcomers to a community who belong to the larger descent group identified with the country of which the community is considered to be a part, may also experience resistance and discrimination but definitely to a lesser extent than foreign immigrants.

In the following chapter we shall try to establish a link between ethnicity and religion, both of which seem to operate in a similar way with regard to the distribution of social rewards. For this purpose we shall present two more community studies, one specifically related to the social position of ethnics belonging to different Christian churches, the other to that of Jews.

Ethnicity and Religion: Paper City

13

Religion, as it is commonly understood, is not a homogeneous social phenomenon.[1] First, a clear distinction should be drawn between two levels. Analogous to the difference between global society and local community, we must distinguish between the church and the religious congregation (occasionally referred to by theologians as *"ecclesia"* and *"ecclesiola"*—the large and the little church). It is at the congregational level that religious life can be most concretely experienced and religious unity most directly expressed. At the level of the church, abstract ideas take precedence over expressive behavior, and the interaction between persons is replaced by formal organization. There are, of course, degrees of generality, abstractness and formality between the two poles, but we shall confine ourselves to the ideal type.

At the church level we find (1) general beliefs from which are derived shared interpretations of reality, value standards, and norms of conduct; (2) practices typical of all the subdivisions of the church, such as meetings, offerings, services, rites of transition, sacraments, instruction, and other collective activities; (3) an organization, that is, groups of agents charged with the task of coordinating, regulating, and controlling beliefs and practices (hierarchies of priests, conferences of ministers, synods, provincial and ecumenical councils).

Distinctive beliefs, practices, and organization are also found on the congregational level. But in a local community, differences in expressive behavior, especially in ritual and other collective activities, are more important when it comes to distinguishing different religions and their members from each other. For these are more readily perceived than are specific beliefs, which are not always dogmatically fixed with sufficient precision, and whose subtleties are rarely appreciated by the rank and file. The general beliefs and collective practices typical of a large church are bound to be modified and supplemented through local customs and observances, the degree of variation depending on the strictness of control exercised by the central organization over local con-

---

[1]This chapter is based on empirical materials adapted with the permission of Marjorie F. Underwood, from Wilson Kenneth Underwood, *Protestant and Catholic: Religious and Social Interaction in an Industrial Community*. Boston: Beacon Press, 1957.

gregations. Among the customs and usages peculiar to religious communities, or regional clusters of such communities, one should also take into account the linguistic vehicle used in ritual and instruction.

TYPES OF AMERICAN CHURCHES

The particular role that religion plays in American ethnic groups depends largely on the type of church. Whenever a territorial population belongs not only to one national society but also predominantly to one church, we may speak of an "established church," regardless of whether its paramountcy is legally recognized by the government and law. Several types can be distinguished among the churches operating in the United States: (1) The American core churches whose members include the bulk of old stock "Americans." The religious tolerance postulated by the Declaration of Independence referred primarily to the mutual toleration of the American core churches. It is the membership of these churches and their later offshoots that is meant when the typical American is described as "Protestant." The principal core churches are Baptists, Methodists, Presbyterians, Congregationalists, and Disciples of Christ; they include more than a third of all Americans registered as belonging to some organized religious body.[2] (2) Ethnic churches (like Catholic, Jewish, Lutheran, Orthodox) have been brought to America by later immigrants and have remained linked to particular ethnic groups. (3) The reform and protest churches include revivalist churches and new sects, such as Adventists or Pentecostals, as well as more recent movements, sometimes referred to as the Second Reformation. (4) Some sects have been transformed into denominations, for instance, Mennonites, Moravian Brethren, Mormons. Like the ethnic churches, most of the former sects have a definitely ethnic base; they were imported by foreigners of non-Anglo-Saxon origin or are largely confined to members of certain ethnic groups. (5) Finally, there are upper-class cults like Christian Science, Theosophy, or Bahai.

With this in mind we turn to the investigation of the role played by religion in interethnic relations at the community level. Paper City will serve as a first type case, the Jews in Minneapolis as a second (see Chapter 13).

THE SETTING

Paper City is an industrial community in Massachusetts with a population of some 54,000. The town, founded in 1849, owes its origin to New England textile interests. Later, paper became its major industry. As in Yankee City,

---

[2]The Episcopalians do not really belong to the American core churches, although they include many of the old stock Americans. Their intermediate position, however, does not require special attention in the present context. Locally, the Episcopalian church is frequently dominant, but so are occasionally churches of types 2 and 4. The Negro and other "non-white" churches are not pertinent here.

the labor force was largely recruited abroad; within twenty-five years the majority of the population was foreign-born. Although the proportion of foreign-born has decreased to the extent that they now only compose a quarter of the population, the majority today are nonetheless descendants of Catholic immigrants. The first to arrive (1850–75) were the Irish, who settled in the least expensive city sections. After them came immigrants from French Canada and Germany, still later, Poles. As the Irish resented the newcomers, particularly the French-Canadians, two ethnic subcommunities emerged between 1870 and 1890: the Irish Catholics and the French Catholics. The Germans, arriving in the 1860s, were predominantly Lutheran. They were mainly skilled workers and better educated than the Catholics. They settled in the same section of the city as the other two ethnic groups, but otherwise kept aloof from them. Other immigrants who came from England, Scotland, or Scandinavia never formed ethnic subcommunities, but merged with the general "American" population.

THE IRISH

In many respects the situation in Paper City is similar to that in Yankee City: there are ethnic neighborhoods, ethnic clubs, a concentration in certain occupations, differential rates of advancement in social status. One point, however, calls for special attention: the role of the Irish in the local community. They are not only by far the largest ethnic group, to some extent they have even become dominant in Paper City. During centuries of English domination the Irish had become adjusted to Anglo-Saxon ways; they spoke English and were familiar with English culture and institutions, which are not so very different from American institutions. Why is it then that the Irish did not behave like other immigrants from the British Isles but remained a distinctive group, and for a long time kept themselves apart from the American population of the city?

Because of cultural affinities and because they were the first foreign group to arrive, the Irish achieved more upward mobility and that at a faster rate than the French-Canadians, Poles, and German Lutherans. They even developed a status system of their own. The "venetian blind" Irish are found in the upper and upper-middle class of the city population; they are rather well off and respectable and live in the same neighborhoods as other Americans of comparable status. The "lace curtain" Irish belong to the broad lower-middle class of Paper City. They tend to scorn or ignore their Irish past and to keep aloof from the masses of low-class Irish. They are well on the way to becoming completely assimilated. Their endeavor to rise further on the status scale and to blend into the general American population is indicated by their tendency to mingle with the "venetian blind" but not with the "shanty" Irish, and even to associate with upper-middle-class Yankees. The character of a separate ethnic group has best been preserved by the "shanty Irish" who belong to the lowest class of unskilled or semiskilled workmen and continue to live in the poorer sections of the city.

RELIGION AND ETHNIC IDENTIFICATION

We now turn to the main topic of this chapter, the role of religion in ethnic identification. As we shall see, the most important factor in this connection is the organizational aspect of religion in combination with the activities that are shared by church members and tend to separate them from members of other churches. This requires a brief review of church development in Paper City.

Most of the Yankees belonged—and still belong—to American core churches, which as a rule, are organized along congregational lines. Unlike "parishes," which are organized along territorial lines, churches of the congregational type do not recognize membership solely on the basis of residence. Members of such churches are free to join any of the congregations present in a given local community, or even to organize a new congregation. Thus, in a larger community where there are several congregations of the same Protestant church, these are apt to draw their membership mainly from particular status or ethnic categories.

Catholic parishes, on the other hand, have jurisdiction over all Catholics living in a local community or a quarter of a larger community, regardless of ethnic or class divisions. They only make provisions for special services if a great number of church members are not sufficiently familiar with the local language to follow sermons, say prayers, sing hymns, or make confession. The first Catholic parish in Paper City catered to the needs of the Irish immigrants. When the French-Canadians arrived, they were repelled and frustrated by the fact that the language used in all Catholic activities was English, and that the Irish, including their priests, showed even less understanding and sympathy than had many native Protestants. It was only after a separate Catholic parish was organized for the French-Canadians with priests of their own ethnic background, separate parochial schools, and separate church-linked associations, that their religious life began to flourish. Some years later, the Poles also obtained their separate parish. Eventually, there were six "regular," that is, territorial, English-speaking parishes in Paper City that were dominated by the Irish; in addition to these, there were three French "national" parishes and one Polish "national" parish.

Despite the cosmopolitan character of the Catholic Church, "national" parishes whose members are recruited from one foreign-language group regardless of residence, and which serve their needs exclusively, have the same effect as Protestant churches of the ethnic and sectarian type. Both tend (1) to support the ethnic identity of their members; (2) to increase interaction between them, thereby strengthening sentiments of solidarity and group coherence; (3) to promote their social and ecological segregation, thus isolating them from outside influences; and (4) to provide them with powerful agencies of social control, inhibiting the assimilation of individual members to the host society.

THE GERMAN LUTHERANS

The situation of the German Lutherans in Paper City resembles that of the Catholic ethnic groups. The church and the manifold activities carried out under its auspices are at the center of a segregated subcommunity in which, however, not all the Germans in town participate. Lutheran churches generally have strong links to particular national societies. In America they are mostly German or Scandinavian. Even after the adoption of the English language for religious practices, sentimental ties with the countries of origin persist, and membership is largely restricted to people coming from those countries. Thus major shifts, for instance, from a German to a Swedish or Finnish congregation are rare. In preference to joining a Lutheran congregation having a different ethnic affiliation, Lutherans are inclined to turn to one of the Americn core churches, and thereby better their chances of becoming accepted into American society. Until the first World War, services in the Lutheran church in Paper City were held in German; a reform group then broke off and switched to English. Since then both congregations have adopted English and subscribe to a policy of assimilation, although the more conservative group still refuses to cooperate in interdenominational Protestant organizations which, of course, have an Anglo-Saxon character.

RELIGION AND SOCIAL MOBILITY

For over thirty years, Grace Congregational Church, located in a working-class quarter and financed by the better established American congregations in Paper City, endeavored to attract immigrants, mostly Catholics; it "held a series of services planned with a special appeal to particular nationalities" only to abandon it eventually "because of lack of interest. . . . 'The people want to be called Americans,' the . . . pastor . . . observed" (Underwood, 1957, p. 220). It would seem that immigrants who have no opportunity of joining a congregation of their own nationality, or have no desire to do so, prefer membership of an outright "American" church in order to become more easily accepted into American society. Identification with Grace Congregational Church, catering only to foreigners, would not have served their purpose.

To Catholic ethnics who did not wish to abandon their faith, membership in an Irish parish was also a means of social advancement. The regular territorial parish did not serve the Irish as a rallying point and symbol of identification to the same extent as a national parish did for the French-Canadians or Poles. Though largely identified with and dominated by the Irish, the territorial parishes of Paper City were obliged to admit Catholics of any ethnic and cultural background (including old stock Americans who happened to be Catholic). Moreover, the language used besides the ritual Latin in the regular parishes was not only the *lingua franca* that the Irish had adopted in Europe but also the official language of America and the vehicle of American culture. Thus, any Catholic ethnic who relinquished the privilege of attending his national parish church and submitted to the territorial jurisdiction of the regular Catholic parish moved closer to American society. Not only did he expose himself to the forces of acculturation and assimilation, he also found new avenues to the social rewards that the host society offers to its charter members but tends to withhold from foreigners.

AMERICAN ATTITUDES TOWARD CATHOLICS

As long as Catholicism remained a foreign religion in the eyes of old stock Americans, complete acceptance of Catholic ethnics, including the Irish, was not to be expected. Moreover, there is a long history behind the traditional attitudes of Protestant Americans toward the Irish Catholics. This history has found its expression in folk traditions and strong emotions that can easily be triggered off by such symbols as Irish and English, Catholic and Protestant. The struggle of the English against the Catholics in the Old Country, their fear of Popish conspiracy, their cruel persecution of the Irish, not only because of their resistance to alien domination, but also because they were staunch Catholics—all this has left deep marks in the memory of both peoples. The latent antagonism flared up as soon as the Irish immigrants appeared in large numbers on the American scene. The Yankees despised the Irish and were suspicious of them because they were Catholics and were considered traditional foes. The Yankees, in turn, were dreaded and hated by the Irish because they were Protestants and because they were descendants of their English arch-enemies. The general stigma on Catholicism was gradually removed as increasing numbers of Catholics rose in the American status system, primarily by way of transculturation, economic success, and political power.

ADVANCEMENT OF CATHOLICS

Catholics in Paper City have benefited from the improvement in the general religious climate just as ethnics in general have benefited by the expansion of the industrial economy. With each new arrival, the first-comers—the Yankees above all, but also the Irish—saw their chance of rising a notch higher in the status system improved, both individually and also as a group. As the Irish (and some of the other Catholics) advanced socially, their religion tended to gain prestige. Although the Catholic Church perhaps has not yet achieved full equality with the Protestant core churches, it is nevertheless recognized as one of a plurality of churches to which any good American may belong without seriously jeopardizing his social standing and chances in American society. Accordingly, a Catholic ethnic is now in a position to become fully Americanized and even president without leaving his church. In Paper City, a French-Canadian or a Pole may achieve a large measure of social mobility simply by transferring allegiance from his "national" Catholic parish to the regular Catholic parish run by Americanized Irish. In contrast to "national" Catholic parishes the regular territorial parish tends to function as a mechanism by which foreigners are integrated into the status system of the host society without being forced to change their religion.

INDICES OF ETHNIC IDENTITY

With all this in mind the following question becomes imperative: How is ethnicity, as an effective factor in social action orientation, defined in a local community like Paper City? This is closely connected with the definition of the criteria by which people are assigned to particular ethnic categories. The simplest way of ascertaining the ethnic background of a stranger is by asking: "Where were you born?" The method, however, is only reliable in stable and homogeneous societies where a close and permanent association exists between place and people. For mobility and the intermingling of heterogeneous people often makes even a truthful answer ambiguous.

The multitude of questions usually included in registration or application forms is necessary not only to incontestably establish the legal identity of registrants; the information is often also intended to indicate their genealogical and ethnic background and perhaps their social status as well.

In most encounters with strangers, however, it is not possible, and often contrary to good manners, to require that complete background information be provided. To know what sort of a person one's partner is, what to expect of him in social intercourse, which rules of proper conduct should be applied, more indirect and abbreviated methods are generally used. Most effective indicators of ethnic origin are external characteristics, which can be ascertained at a glance and procure reasonably reliable results. We have spoken at length of this in the chapter on Atrisco. We have also explained why the selection of traits does not depend on whether they are important, irremovable, or essential attributes of a descent group, but only on whether they have sufficient discriminatory power in a practical situation.

One indicator of ethnicity that occasionally can be used with a high degree of reliability is religious affiliation. One does not have to ask a person outright to which church he belongs when one is in a position to observe him avoiding meat on Friday or work on Saturday, attending certain religious functions regularly, sending his children to a parochial school, joining certain clubs, and the like. When we look for an explanation of this particular effectiveness of religious symbols in determining ethnic origin, we are reminded that religion, like language and other important features of a culture, is more often than not passed on from one generation to the next through the socializing agency of the family. It is the family that exerts strong controls over its members to preserve the social heritage; and religion is widely felt to be among the most crucial and significant factors in maintaining family coherence.

But religion can only serve as a suitable symbol of ethnic identification if, in a given social context, it is exclusive or peculiar to one group, and if religious practices are clearly differentiated from those of other groups. We shall now try to construct a few simple models to illustrate various ways in which religious affiliation and ethnicity may be associated.

Let us assume that two ethnic groups (E_1 and E_2) within a given local community have the same religious affiliation (R). Here ethnicity cannot be ascertained by means of religious symbols. If, however, each ethnic group has a different religion (R_1 and R_2), religious symbols possess a high discriminatory power with regard to ethnicity: R_1 may be substituted for E_1 and R_2 for E_2. This typical situation is approximated in Cantonville and probably existed in Paper City at the time when only Protestant Yankees and Irish Catholics were present in the community. Religion alone was sufficient to identify the members of the ethnic group within the community.

Next we shall consider a hypothetical situation in which there are two ethnic groups in a community, the membership of each group being fairly equally divided with regard to religious affiliation, so that each religious group is also fairly equally divided with regard to ethnic affiliation. Here, too, religion cannot serve as a symbol for the identification of ethnicity, although the religious division may contribute to status differentiations within the community on the basis of wealth, power, prestige, and so on. Now, let us assume that one ethnic group (E_1) in a community is associated with one religion (R_1), and that the members of the other ethnic group (E_2) belong either to the same religion (R_1) or to another religion (R_2). In this case religion R_2 will suggest ethnic identification (all R_2 belong to E_2), while religion R_1 will not be suitable to serve as a symbol of ethnicity (some R_1 belong to E_1, others to E_2). Moreover, religious activities shared by all members of E_1 and some of the members of E_2 will tend to draw these together, while differentiation within E_2 will be intensified along religious lines.

In Paper City we are confronted with two segments of the population affiliated to religion, the Protestant (Yankee and German), and three ethnic groups affiliated to the Catholic religion (Irish, French, and Poles). If the German Protestants were not present, "Catholic" could serve as a generalized symbol of foreigners, "Protestant" as a symbol of natives. The addition of the German Protestants theoretically should result in three significant categories: (1) Catholics (all foreigners), (2) Protestant natives, and (3) Protestant foreigners. Actually, the Catholics were further subdivided into Catholics attending the regular parish churches identified with the Irish, on the one hand, and French-Canadians and Poles who attended their respective national churches, on the other.

CONCLUSIONS

We come to the conclusion that where religious congregations are identified with one particular ethnic group, ethnicity is frequently symbolized in religious terms, and vice versa. In Paper City the ethnicity of the Irish is not as clearly symbolized through religious affiliation as that of the Germans, French-Canadians, and Poles; these three groups have separate church organizations mostly using their native language in religious ritual. It is the ethnic group which sanctions a particular church affiliation, and which supports a religious congregation and its institutions as an effective means for its own maintenance and the preservation of its cultural traditions. Thus, when religious affiliation and ethnicity are coextensive, both tend to support and sanction each other. In other cases, however, instead of increasing the unity and coherence of an existing ethnic group and of protecting it against the influences of the social environment so that assimilation is inhibited by religious taboos on intermarriage and apostasy, religious differences may weaken and divide ethnic groups, promote union with different ethnic groups, and facilitate transculturation, assimilation, and eventually absorption.

Ethnicity and Religion: The Jews in Minneapolis

14

The following case was chosen to throw some additional light on the role played by a common religion in the formation of an ethnic group.[1] It raises, however, a taxonomic problem: Is it legitimate to treat the Jews in Minneapolis as an ethnic group in the same way, for instance, as the German Lutherans or Irish Catholics in Paper City? Are the Jews generally to be considered an ethnic unit like the Germans or Irish? Would it not be more meaningful to think of them as a religious body, a church, like the Lutherans or Catholics? Some may even be inclined to classify them as a racial group like the Negroes or Orientals. The issue has two different aspects that should not be confused with each other: the nature of a distinctive subgroup within the host society, and the nature of the parent society from which the subgroup is derived. Let us consider the first aspect.

In the present context, the term "ethnic group" is applied to any distinctive subgroup which, because of its alien origin, is being treated differently from the charter members of a national society. Some authors draw a line between ethnic, religious, and racial groups. Robin Williams for instance, defines an ethnic group as "one possessing continuity through biological descent whose members share a distinctive social and cultural tradition." He qualifies a racial group as "one whose members, through biological descent, share distinctive common hereditary physical characteristics" (Williams, 1947, p. 42). Obviously, the terms are not mutually exclusive. But since the significance of "race" will be discussed elsewhere, we shall confine ourselves here to the problem of whether the American Jews should be classified as a religious rather than an ethnic group. A religious group is defined in such a way as to focus attention on some shared religious beliefs and practices or membership in a

---

[1]This chapter is based on empirical materials adapted with the permission of Mrs. Albert J. Gordon, from Albert J. Gordon, *Jews in Transition*. Minneapolis: University of Minnesota Press, 1949. See also Louis Wirth, *The Ghetto*. Chicago: University of Chicago Press, 1958 (First Edition 1928).

particular church organization, or else focused on participation in a religious movement having no formal organization. Yet, it becomes clear that Williams has not in mind all groups that are covered by his definition. While the Jews, Mormons, Mennonites, Lutherans, and Catholics in America are often spoken of as religious groups, the same is not true of Baptists, Methodists, or Disciples of Christ. Why?

In modern times a common religious orientation or membership in a particular church is not, as a rule, linked to identification with a societal unit—a people or a nation. Nor does the fact that some differ in this respect from the general population make them a distinctive subgroup or subsociety.[2] When we compare people professing a particular religion who simultaneously constitute a distinctive subgroup with others who do not, we find that they define themselves, and are defined by others, as a societal or subsocietal unit, tied together not only in the religious but in other important dimensions of social life as well. They constitute, in fact, a particular "religious group" only to the extent that they are distinguished from the charter population through their alien descent.

Apart from terminological considerations, however, the distinction between ethnic and religious groups does not appear particularly useful for our purpose. For subgroups defined as ethnic and subgroups defined as religious tend to behave similarly and to follow the same empirical laws in analogous situations. Neither specific differences in national culture nor specific differences in religion have any significant influence per se upon the formation, maintenance, and dissolution of ethnic groups.

We have found that ethnicity is essentially based on a contrast effect; ethnic groups emerge only if readily distinguishable differences exist between parent and host society. Such differences are manifested in the combination of many factors: language, habitat, racial appearance, and also religion; but none of these factors, if isolated from the rest, is in itself decisive. Each only serves to indicate the more fundamental fact of imputed common descent.

We have called an "ethnic unit" a societal unit that is differentiated from its environment through common descent. A subgroup may be called an "ethnic group" inasmuch as parent and host society are ethnically different. This raises the question of which society should be considered the parent society of the Jewish ethnic group in America. Is there any one ethnic unit from which they are derived? Are the Jews one people in the same way as are the Germans or Poles? Are the German Jews just Germans, the Polish Jews just Poles who believe in the Jewish religion? Or should we think of them as members of ethnic subsocieties in Germany or Poland which are derived from one and the same parental ethnic unit: the Jewish people? Expressed in this general way such questions are difficult to answer. The Jews became a distinctive societal unit in

---

[2]The most conspicuous exception to the rule are modern nations formed on the basis of the Islam, like the Arab nations or Pakistan, which have not been treated in this book.

much the same manner as the Tswana, Ganda, German, or French people. At one time they certainly constituted a demotic unit; their common religion—as in most premodern cultures—was both an expression and a strong support of this unity. Although the Jews, like all other peoples, were originally composed of heterogeneous elements, their religion created and propagated a social myth of common origin, which has helped model them into a secondary ethnic unit.

But this is not the salient point here. If, at one time, they were ethnically distinct from their environment, did they remain so after their dispersal; and did they remain one ethnic unit after forming ethnic subcommunities and subsocieties in many lands? From an analytical viewpoint, it is meaningless to assign a people throughout all the stages of its development and in all situations to one sociological type simply because it seems to display historical continuity and is called by one name (sometimes only a scholarly invention). As we know, such situations are continually changing and so are the typical patterns of social interaction that entitle us to apply different sociological concepts, such as nation, ethnie, ethnic group, to a social or political structure. Today, the Israelis have certainly become a "national society" but the Jews in America have hardly been transformed by this fact into a "national minority" (as the terms have been used in this book). Before the foundation of the Jewish nation-state, the Palestinian Jews as well as Jews who lived in Germany, Russia, or elsewhere, in accordance with the teachings of their religion, defined themselves as one people, the "People of God," and not just as believers in one religion. Because of this belief in a common descent, we are entitled to consider the Jewish subcommunities and subsocieties in the disaspora as parts of one ethnic unit.

As we shall see, after their emancipation, some Jews, especially in Western Europe, became so fully assimilated to their respective host societies that they lost their specific ethnic character—only their religious affiliation remained. It is therefore appropriate to classify the various Jewish groups that were affected by the migrations to the United States at the turn of the century quite differently, taking into account in each case the situation in which they found themselves in their countries of origin. Although the Jews in Russia or Poland formed distinctive ethnic subcommunities and subsocieties before their migration, their position in Germany or France was more that of Germans or Frenchmen professing the Jewish rather than Christian faith. Before coming to any final conclusions, however, the data presented on the following pages should best be studied.

GERMAN AND EASTERN JEWS

The first Jews who, with other German immigrants, arrived in Minneapolis after 1869 on the eve of industrialization, came to the United States in search of economic opportunities, political freedom, and religious toleration. Most of the

German Jews were merchants; they had been either fairly well-off in Germany or had acquired some capital in other American cities before moving to Minneapolis. As did other urbanized immigrants from Germany, they tended to conform to the American culture pattern. Besides religious instruction they received little more than elementary Hebrew training, and they formed no special clubs. All told, they were not easily distinguishable from the motley crowd of Americans moving to the new West.

The Orthodox East European Jews arrived amidst the waves of immigrants who almost swamped America between 1880 and 1920. Most of them had been driven from Russia as a consequence of the discriminatory May Laws; some were young men trying to escape military conscription. On arrival they usually began by peddling wares, even though they knew little or no English. When their earnings increased, they arranged for the transportation of their wives, children, and parents to America. The families then settled in different parts of the city, often according to their countries of origin; each group organized its own synagogue and voluntary associations. Unlike the German Jews, the Eastern Jews came from predominantly agrarian parts of Europe, as did the majority of peasants who formed the bulk of the "new immigration."

In their community life and in their relations to the American host society, they followed a general pattern similar to other immigrant groups from agrarian countries. This pattern is already familiar to us and need not be described again, although significant differences should be pointed out. Throughout the centuries—ever since they had migrated from Germany to various countries of Eastern Europe—the Eastern Jews had remained quite isolated from their host societies—Polish, Rumanian, Ukranian, Lithuanian, and so on. They had lived in segregated ghettos; social interaction and sentiments of solidarity were confined to their own people; and they were excluded from *commensalitas* and *connubium* with gentiles. More significant still, their way of life, world view, value standards, and norms of conduct, their dress and outward appearance, religious observance and ritual, their folkways—in short their whole culture—was conspicuously different from that of all the peoples with whom they had actual contact. Their language was also unique—a peculiar German idiom interspersed with Slavic and Hebrew words, spoken with a peculiar accent, and written in Hebrew script. This language, Yiddish, was not easily understood, even by German Jews who used literary German or one of the folk dialects spoken in Frankfort, Berlin, or Vienna.

They remained an ethnic group after their arrival in Minneapolis. In reality, their transfer from the ghettos of Eastern Europe (forced upon them by Russian law and tradition) to the slums of a Midwestern city (into which they were forced by American society and its ideology) did not bring about conspicuous changes in their social situation. In America, as in Europe, they were segregated from their environment by their observance of the Sabbath, which excluded them from holding regular jobs; by dietary laws, which precluded convivial association with neighbors; by their keen interest in religious ritual and Talmudic studies, which left few opportunities for recreational activities together with gentiles. At every turn, their Orthodox traditions sealed them off into a subcommunity.

Jewish Religion. There hardly exists any formal organization in Jewish religion—no central administration, no priests, no hierarchy. Wherever a minimum of ten male Jews gather for prayer, religious disputation, or to study the Torah and the Talmud, there is a "synagogue," a Jewish congregation. The rabbi is not a priest but a teacher, a scholar, and an arbitrator in matters concerning the ritual law, which covers almost every phase of daily life. Nevertheless, a basic unity and uniformity has persisted through the many centuries of dispersal.

Because the word of God is the common law strictly binding on all Jews and because there has always been a lively exchange of opinion about this law between Jewish congregations throughout the world, a common and all the more rigid core culture has been preserved, which has bound together all the Jews in one social unit despite spatial separation. To the Jews, therefore, ethnicity and religion is one inseparable whole. According to their self-interpretation, they are the Chosen People, united forever through a collective covenant with God. Descent from common ancestors more than voluntary membership in a particular congregation assures latter-day Jews that the Covenant, which gives meaning to their lives, direction to their activities, and promise of salvation, remains valid for them too. Thus their image of self as much as their actual behavior proves our point, which is that it is more correct to consider the Jews an ethnic rather than a "religious" group similar to the Disciples of Christ or Pentecostals.

Group Interaction. The German Jews, we have said, were really more German than Jew. They had become transculturated and even in part assimilated to their German host society; so much so that they were generally looked upon by Americans as Germans and treated more or less in the same way. Thus, the original Jews in Minneapolis, when they learned of the arrival of masses of Eastern Jews, who were almost as much strangers to themselves as to their gentile neighbors, were reluctant to associate with them or even to recognize them as their equals. In fact, they were afraid that the new arrivals would stir up anti-Semitism; subsequent events proved this fear to be fully justified. Still, as Jews, they could not avoid taking an interest in them; they actually did a great deal to help them become self-supporting. Yet the East Europeans resented their aid, for it was not given in the traditional personal manner; instead, formal inquiries were made before aid was dispensed through agencies.

The Eastern Jews did not harbor any sense of kinship with the more prosperous and partially assimilated German Jews who could not speak Yiddish. To the Orthodox, the German Jews were worse than the *goyim* (unbelievers), they were in fact *meshumeds* (apostates).

REFORM JUDAISM

The religion of the German Jews was significantly different from that of the Eastern Jews, and this difference may be traced to the reform movement started in Germany during the early nineteenth century. The followers of Reform Judaism rejected the authority of the Rabbinic tradition of interpreting the law collected in the Talmudic writings; they no longer regarded the Torah as the literal word of God. They further maintained that each generation should practice only those laws that it found essential. Even the ritual of the synagogue was altered. The movement corresponded to the critical trend in Christian theology; its aim was to bring the religious services into accord with the customary procedures of Christian churches—organs, mixed choirs, and the use of the vernacular in religious practices. Moreover, services were held on Sunday instead of Saturday; the requirement of thrice-daily prayer was dropped in addition to dietary laws that had become impracticable; intermarriage was no longer a serious offense. In other words, Reform Judaism dropped those elements of their religion that made Jews outwardly a "peculiar people." Yet it was these marks of distinction that continued to be regarded by the Orthodox Jews as essential to their religious belief and experience.

CONSERVATIVE JUDAISM

Shortly after 1910, when significant numbers of East Europeans began to enter the American middle classes, another Jewish group emerged from the Orthodox synagogues. Conservative Judaism, which had also originated in Germany, intended to conserve the Jewish heritage, but at the same time to enable Jews to live as American a life as possible. Consequently, the Conservatives modified the traditional ritual and practices, but to a lesser extent than had the Reform group. From that time, there were three types of Jewish congregation in Minneapolis comparable to the different kinds of Christian churches. The religious division, however, did not separate the Jews in the same way as it does gentiles who, under similar circumstances, often split into entirely separate groups. Significantly, the differences between German and Eastern Jews tended to decrease with time. This was not so much the result of their intermingling or uniting in common synagogues and voluntary associations, but rather because the Eastern Jews slowly adapted to the American way of life. Moreover, the pressures exerted by American society on both groups were alike.

ADJUSTMENT TO AMERICAN SOCIETY

The Reform Judaism of the German Jews had already helped them to adjust to life in a modern Christian society—the national and industrial society of

Germany. From there, it was a relatively short step to adjust to American society. The Americanization of the Reform Jews followed the same patterns as that of members of Christian churches with strong ethnic ties, namely, through the adoption of English as the church language and of religious practices patterned after those of the American core churches. The Eastern Jews eventually followed the example of the German Jews who, by modernizing Jewish religion, had gained conspicuous economic and social advantages.

The Americanization of the Orthodox Jews, initiated by the so-called Conservative reform, suggested itself not only because new pressures were brought to bear upon immigrants by the host society. Social pressures in Europe had tended toward the opposite direction: In America the pressure was on integration, in Eastern Europe it had been on segregation. But Americanization was also accepted because of the new opportunities of social advancement offered by an industrial and open society which extended religious toleration, however reluctantly, even to Mormons, Catholics, and Jews. As religious orthodoxy, the prime obstacle to transculturation and assimilation, lost its hold on a steadily broadening section of the Jewish population in Minneapolis, the situation of the Jews became similar to that of any other ethnic group.

Both groups, the German and the Eastern Jews, were about equally exposed to the cultural influences of American society. Command of the English language was a requirement for business and employment, and for many other daily pursuits. The strongest impact was exerted on the younger generation, who were compelled to attend American public schools where teachers and classmates were Americans or at least Americanized ethnics. Only the short after-school hours were spent with their own group in Hebrew schools. The Jewish family lost its patriarchical pattern in much the same way as had the family of other immigrants coming from agrarian societies. In both cases, secularization decreased the authority of religious traditions. American customs with regard to birth, marriage, and burial ceremonies were adopted, as well as accepted practices regarding the participation in civic affairs and voluntary associations.

Both kinds of Jews became increasingly integrated into community life, closely associating and interacting with the general population. They were now no longer treated as strangers but as members of the local community and of American society, and were thus assigned a definite place in the social structure. Accordingly, their status was determined by the rules operative in the general American status system. By and large, all Jews were assigned to the same status category, regardless of differences in their national background or in the degree of adjustment. It was a seemingly rational social definition that worked out very much to their disfavor, more so for the German than for the Eastern Jews, as the latter had experienced this kind of discrimination in Europe.

The social definition of Jews and their corresponding treatment on the part of the gentiles (which is commonly summed up by the term "anti-Semitism") was partly imported to America by East European immigrants. Among the Anglo-Saxons, the problem had less urgency or actuality: Jews had been excluded from the British Isles in 1290, and after their readmission in the seventeenth century, their numbers remained relatively small. Before the middle of the nineteenth century there were in America some long-established colonies of Sephardic (Spanish-speaking) Jews and a few other Jewish immigrants who were popular and respected. But in the countries of Eastern Europe, with their relatively large Jewish populations, there was a long tradition of hostility, hatred, and open violence, often kindled and supported by governments pretending Christian convictions.

An analysis of anti-Semitism exceeds the scope of this book. Suffice it to say that in a community like Minneapolis, the fact that one was known to be a Jew was apt to activate traditional antagonisms on the part of Christians, above all, among East European immigrants. When Jews of a type familiar to these immigrant gentiles appeared on the local scene, anti-Semitic sentiments and behavior patterns, learned and internalized in the Old World, were not only reinforced but gained apparent legitimacy through experience in the New World.

CONCLUSIONS

This evaluation of the situation on the part of the community at large, and the attendant discrimination and disabilities with regard to the distribution of social rewards, affected the relationship between German Jews and Eastern Jews. Their exposure to the same exigencies led to mutual identification. This case illustrates the essential dynamism of group formation and group transformation: As a result of the processes just described, the German Jews changed their collective character and identification. They became more Jewish and less German-American than they had been before. If assimilation is seen as the process by which strangers become accepted by, and absorbed into, the host society, the striking reversal suffered by the German Jews may be described as dissimilation. Just as Nazi persecution and the Nuremberg race laws brought about the dissimilation of the Jews in Germany from the German people, the situation in Minneapolis turned the German Jews from members of a different but acceptable religion into ethnics.

REFERENCES

Gordon, Albert J., *Jews in Transition*. Minneapolis: University of Minnesota Press, 1949.
Williams, Robin M., Jr., "The Reduction of Intergroup Tensions: A Survey of Research on Problems of Ethnic, Racial, and Religious Group Relations," *Social Science Research Council Bulletin,* LVII (1947).
Wirth, Louis, *The Ghetto*. Chicago: University of Chicago Press, 1958 (First Edition 1928).

B. Primary Ethnic Groups

INTRODUCTION

The preceding chapters have revealed a variety of situational factors that affect ethnic phenomena in modern society. When we are trying to discover regularities in ethnic group behavior, however, we find that community studies have their inherent limitations. For not only are local communities an integral part of some larger society, but the typical situation of ethnics is also determined by their relationship to the host society taken as a whole. Moreover, ethnic groups in one locality are frequently associated with kindred groups in other localities; together they may form an ethnic subsociety within the host society. We shall therefore come closer to reality if in the following chapters we view ethnic problems in the broader context of global societies: the host society as well as the parent societies from which the populations in question are derived. Our attempt to make empirical generalizations concerning interethnic relations in a modern society will be facilitated by distinguishing different types of ethnic groups.

CLASSIFICATION OF ETHNIC GROUPS

Within a theoretical framework, classifications serve to divide a more comprehensive species of phenomena so that the subspecies become more homogeneous. Earlier, we made the point that the more conventional classifications that distinguish between ethnic, racial, and religious groups appear to be inadequate because empirical evidence does not reveal any typical differences in their behavior. But classifying them together under one heading does not solve our difficulties, either; behavior patterns that are found in some ethnic groups are missing in others. Moreover, ethnics who derive from the same parent society often behave differently from others having the same origin, while the behavior of ethnics who are descended from different parent societies is frequently similar. Such observations suggest that ethnic groups cannot be considered as one simple and homogeneous class of social phenomena equal in all the respects that bear on the solution of the theoretical problem on hand.

In searching for a more satisfactory classification, we realize that fundamental similarities and disparities can be established only if we divide ethnic groups according to constitutive properties. Neither specific cultural or racial differences between ethnic group and host society nor historical developments meet the requirement; specific cultures and unique events are not comparable and are thus unsuitable for sociological generalizations. The same is true of "external" characteristics; the mere fact that a particular language, a sectarian religion, certain racial features, distinctive cultural traditions, or any combination thereof, are shared by many people does not make them a distinctive social group. Moreover, there is no obvious connection between them and the formation, maintenance, and dissolution of ethnic groups. To avoid the difficulties involved in the use of external characteristics as criteria of classification, it seems preferable to adopt formal properties that are closely associated with typical variations in the actual behavior of ethnic groups.

For the present purpose, a simple dichotomy will be adopted which is based on the manner in which ethnic groups are formed (cf. Francis, 1954). For if it can be shown, as we contend, that ethnic group formation results in two distinctive types, then we may also expect that the subsequent behavior of these groups, particularly in their relations to the host society, will differ. But even if this were not so, only ethnic groups that have already come into being can serve as a base line for the discussion of the processes that are operative in their maintenance or dissolution.

We recall that ethnicity is fundamentally a relational concept. The emergence of groups on account of ethnic differentiation implies changes in the relations of a population to the societal environment. These changes may be due either to endogenous factors which originate in the internal system of the society, or to exogenous factors which originate in its external system. The term "external system" has been adopted from George C. Homans, who understands by it the state of the elements of group behavior, insofar as it constitutes a solution to the problem: How shall the group survive in its environment? He adds: "We call it 'external' because it is conditioned by the environment; we call it a 'system' because in it the elements of behavior are mutually dependent" (Homans, 1950, p. 90).

Endogenous Factors. With regard to the endogenous factors leading to the formation of ethnic groups we can be brief; for we have dealt with this problem at length in Part II. There we have seen that the processes of nationalization, set in motion within a given state population, are apt to transform ethnic units that differ from the national core into nationalities and national minorities. We have also indicated that this transformation need not affect all ethnic components of a state population; some of them may simply submit to the pressures exerted upon them and become "nationalized," that is, absorbed into the national core without giving rise to specific social problems. Other ethnic units may be too politically insignificant to create any public interest in their nationalization. Such groups are often allowed to withdraw from active participation in national affairs, and to lead a secluded life in a self-chosen ghetto. As an object of folkloristic curiosity and political indulgence, they may altogether escape the influences of nationalization and industrialization, and, for a considerable length of time, remain prenational and agrarian enclaves within a modern society. In some respects they resemble the primary ethnic groups brought about by exogenous factors. To these we turn next.

Exogenous Factors. The principal exogenous factors leading to the formation of ethnic groups are changes in political boundary lines and migrations. The annexation of territory by a modern state always involves the extension of direct social control over its permanent population. As a consequence of this transfer from one state jurisdiction to another, the territorial population may be transformed into a primary ethnic group. The conditions under which this is likely to occur will be discussed below.

More often than not, migration leads to the formation of secondary rather than primary ethnic groups. What is the basic difference between the two types? Both come into being when people are transferred from one to another society, and when marked differences exist between the transferees and the host society so that the population transferred can be readily identified with the parent rather than with the host society. In both cases the people concerned have been enculturated into the parent society so that conditions in the host society are unfamiliar to them. At this point, however, the similarity ends. For ethnics of the primary type are less affected by an unfamiliar environment than are those of the secondary type. After their transfer they still remain firmly embedded, at least on a subsocietal level, in a web of familiar social relationships. These are more important for the satisfaction of ordinary social needs than are relationships with society at large, which are mainly confined to the political and economic sphere and, moreover, touch directly upon the interests of only some of the group.

Ethnics of the secondary type, on the other hand, who enter the host society as isolated individuals or as small bands of migrants, depend entirely on the host society for the satisfaction of almost all basic needs. They are at once forced to adjust to an unfamiliar social setting, to acquire a plethora of new social skills, and to submit to the usually painful process of transculturation in order to function properly and to find their niche in the host society. Accordingly, a primary ethnic group gives the impression of being a fragment of the parent society, maintaining some segmental and relatively loose relationships with the host society. Not so a secondary ethnic group, which is exclusively the result of processes originating in the host society itself. A more detailed discussion of the conditions under which secondary ethnic groups are being formed will have to be left to Section C.

At a first glance, one might conclude that annexation tends to lead to the emergence of primary, migration to that of secondary, ethnic groups. While empirical evidence seems to support the hypothesis, it would still miss the point. For primary, unlike secondary, ethnic groups are characterized above all by their ability to maintain their original identity and solidarity, to preserve their particular social structure and institutions, and to continue functioning in the host society in much the same way as they did in the parent society. For their members are not compelled to rely entirely on the cooperation with the host society in order to satisfy their most pressing economic and social needs. While primary ethnic groups are most likely to be formed when an agrarian population is being transferred into a modern society by way of annexation, under exceptional circumstances migration may also lead to the formation of a primary ethnic group. This problem is the topic of Chapter 15.

The expressions "formation of a primary ethnic group" and "transfer of an ethnic group from parent to host society" used in this context require a word of caution. Strictly speaking, they fit some cases only and should be adopted with circumspection in others. Whenever endogenous factors lead to the emergence of such a collectivity, it must have already been in existence before assuming the typical character of a primary ethnic group. Also in the case of group migration, the group in question must have been in existence before its transfer from parent to host society. On the other hand, if the emergence of a primary ethnic group is due to annexation, the population concerned cannot have constituted a distinctive social unit at all before their transfer from the parent to the host society, but an arbitrary section of the parent society, being indistinguishable from the rest of the population. It is only by virtue of the transfer that their situation is changed in such a way that it now becomes possible to perceive them as a particular group. It is because of these new situational factors that their typical character is changed and that they are transformed into a primary ethnic group.

ETHNIC INTEGRATION AS A PROCESS OF SOCIAL CHANGE

The primary ethnic groups in which sufficient empirical evidence is available were usually formed under preindustrial conditions and often resemble survivals from a premodern age. Their inclusion under the heading "Interethnic Relations in Industrial Society" is justified, not so much by their specific difference from similar phenomena in prenational and preindustrial society, as by the fact that the presence of viable ethnic subsocieties, which function in a manner similar to ethnic units in premodern society, notably in the empire, is now felt to be an anomaly. Attempts to neglect or to overcome such deviations from the prevailing political doctrine and social myth are apt to cause typical social problems. The crucial issue concerns the integration of a modern society in which ethnic groups, primary as well as secondary, are regarded as a disturbing factor rather than as a constitutive component of the social structure. The problem is as much an intellectual as a practical one.

In the following pages, attention will be paid to the processes of social change that result in the integration of primary ethnic groups into a host society of the national and industrial type. Offhand, one might be inclined to say that complete integration is accomplished when an ethnic group has been dissolved by way of absorption, as this conforms ideal typically with the ultimate goal of nationalization. Yet *we may also speak of "integration" whenever both ethnic group and host society have become so adjusted to each other that major conflicts or disturbances in the total social fabric of the host society are avoided without the ethnic group losing its identity and solidarity; or, in other words, if the continued presence of the primary ethnic group is not felt by either party to constitute a social problem.* But even in cases where a primary ethnic group apparently has ceased to exist as a viable subsociety, its dissolution rarely results in the traceless absorption of all its members into the host society; more often, it will be transformed into a secondary ethnic group or an ethnic category.

We now turn to the analysis of some case studies of primary ethnic groups.

REFERENCES

Francis, E. K., "Variables in the Formation of So-Called 'Minority Groups,'" *American Journal of Sociology,* LIX (1954), pp. 6–14.
Homans, George C., *The Human Group*. New York: Harcourt, Brace and Company, 1950.

Group Formation as a Result of Migration

15

The Mennonites in Manitoba

At the conclusion of World War II there were some 40,000 Mennonites in Manitoba, over 5 percent of the population of the province and 9 percent of the rural population. No less than 83 percent of the Manitoba Mennonites lived in rural areas; of these, 80 percent on farms. They were the sixth largest component of the ethnic mosaic of the province, concentrated in a region of great economic importance between the provincial capital, Winnipeg, and the American border.

ORIGINS

The designation, "Mennonites," refers primarily to a religious body which, in the early sixteenth century, was founded by Menno Simons among Anabaptists in the Netherlands. The Counter-Reformation forced him and many of his followers to seek refuge in Northern Germany where they made further converts. Substantial Mennonite settlements sprang up along the lower Vistula River in a country which, at the time, belonged to the Kingdom of Poland. Although its members were mainly of Frisian, Dutch, and Flemish origin, this Mennonite group became assimilated to its German neighbors. With the first partition of Poland it was incorporated into the Kingdom of Prussia.

Political and economic changes launched by the new government caused such anxiety among the West-Prussian Mennonites that about 18,000 migrated to the Ukraine between 1788 and 1810. The colonial policy of Czarist Russia was directly responsible for the transformation of this group of German Mennonites into something like a new ethnic unit that was clearly set apart, not only from Russian society, but also from non-Mennonite German settlers. In those days Russia still conformed to the empire type of political power structure. Accordingly, her government had no difficulties in granting special corporate

172

rights (or "privileges") to groups of foreign immigrants without insisting on their integration into Russian society. On the contrary, every effort was made to isolate them politically and culturally. The sole aim of Russia's immigration policy was to improve the economy by filling the vast spaces, left depopulated after the Turkish occupation, with skilled peasant farmers. Like other homogeneous groups of settlers, the Mennonites were allowed to settle in compact colonies where they enjoyed a high degree of political autonomy and economic self-sufficiency.

THE FORMATION OF A NEW ETHNIC SOCIETY

The Anabaptist doctrine, to which the Mennonites subscribed, made a clear distinction between the voluntary brotherhood of the true believers and the world of sinners. Within their own communities, authority had to be exercised by the congregation of the faithful under the guidance of self-chosen lay ministers. For the rest, the faithful were entreated to submit to the authority of those in power. Yet the law of the Czar, which brought fulfillment of their desire to withdraw from the world as a religious brotherhood, at the same time compelled them to take care of all the wordly affairs within their settlements. This created some tricky problems. Since Anabaptist doctrine insisted upon the strict separation of church and state, the Mennonites were now required to set up additional secular institutions and authorities. This arrangement was bound to change the character of the Mennonite church. Contrary to Anabaptist convictions that admission to the brotherhood depended on spiritual rebirth and personal commitment, anyone born of Mennonite parents now had to be admitted to church membership; for he could otherwise not legally live in a Mennonite colony or partake in the rights granted to the Mennonite group collectively. In this way the voluntary brotherhood was transformed into an established church, and the group of Mennonite settlers as a whole into a distinctive ethnic society which occupied a definite though not contiguous territory. It was endowed with a fairly comprehensive set of separate institutions and had a culture clearly distinguished from that of its environment.

As Russia gradually became exposed to the processes of modernization, this method of integrating an alien group into the political and economic system became impracticable. The emancipation of the peasants in 1869 may be regarded as a turning point. If affected the Mennonites directly. Under the old system they had held the legal status of peasants of the Crown. Following the emancipation, the separate administration of crown lands was abolished and, with it, the once-privileged districts of colonists became incorporated as regular *volosts* (counties) into the general administrative system. Above the village and *volost* level the Mennonites became a powerless national minority, whereas before they had been a nearly self-governing societal unit. They also lost most of their economic privileges; finally, even their exemption from military service was put in jeopardy. This was the signal for many of them to prepare for emigration to a country that would permit them to live once again in segregated communities in accordance with their conception of Christian life.

THE MIGRATION TO CANADA

The Canadian government and the United States railroad interests vied with each other to attract the Russian Mennonites by promising them that they would find in the New World all that they were afraid of losing in the Old Country—promises which were later broken. Between 1875 and 1877, 1200 Mennonite households comprising 6140 persons were transferred from their villages in Southern Russia to Manitoba where two parcels of land, called "Reserves," had been set aside for their exclusive use by the Dominion government. Two entire Mennonite colonies in Russia, Fürstenland and Bergtal, were involved in the movement. Another group consisted of the members of a dissident religious community, who had lived among other Mennonites in Russia without forming a colony of their own. Upon their arrival, the Fürstenland group took over the West Reserve and the Bergtal people the East Reserve.

Both Reserves were at once organized after the pattern of a Russian *volost;* villages were laid out in the same way as in the Old Country. Thus, the Mennonite settlements in Manitoba became exact replicas of those in Russia, with the same persons assuming the various ecclesiastical and civil functions. Even the natural scenery of the Canadian prairie had a striking resemblance to the Russian steppes, so that the migrants, after a few years of transition, found themselves once more in a thoroughly familiar environment where they continued their traditional way of life almost as if nothing had happened.

A group migration of this kind was made possible by the fact that, during the pioneering stage, the political situation in Manitoba was not yet stable enough to interfere with the Mennonite settlements. No efficient provincial bureaucracy existed, and so the Mennonites were left almost completely free to arrange their internal affairs after a pattern that the Russian colonial administration had institutionalized almost a century earlier. During the first decade after their settlement in Manitoba, neither the internal nor the external social system of the Mennonite group underwent any significant changes despite the transfer of political allegiance from one to another imperial power structure, both of which were on the verge of becoming modernized. This remark requires some explanation. Our readers will probably accept the characterization of conditions in Russia, but will fail to see any similarity with Canada. True enough, the United Kingdom was already well on the way to becoming a national and industrial society, but the British Empire was still organized along prenational and preindustrial lines. After the British possessions in North America had been united under the Dominion government, it took many years before the colony developed into a modern nation-state.

The Mennonite institutions, which were transferred to Manitoba together with the people, represented the cultural heritage of an agrarian and prenational societal organization. Few of them conformed to the type of modern society that Canada intended to build up on the newly settled Prairie Provinces, which was also envisaged by her legal system; for the latter followed the model of Great Britain and, in part, of the United States, two of the most advanced industrial societies.

THE CHALLENGE TO TRADITION

Introduction of the Canadian Administration. The first challenge to the integrity of the Mennonite institutional system in Manitoba came when a modern, rational, and uniform administrative system was put into operation. The changeover from a Russian *volost* to a Canadian municipality was achieved without great difficulty in the East Reserve. Lasting dissensions, however, arose in the other settlement between the very conservative Fürstenland people and a group of more progressive Bergtal people who had moved from the East Reserve to better lands in the West Reserve. As the former abstained from voting and continued to informally maintain a *volost* administration in their area of settlement, the Bergtal people assumed official control of the entire municipality.

One of the most important functions of a municipality consisted in the organization and maintenance of schools, which had been the responsibility of the church among the Mennonites. The Fürstenland people rejected the new school system and continued to maintain their own church-supervised private schools; but a large part of their taxes was now used for the upkeep of public schools frequented almost exclusively by children of the Bergtal group. More important than the ensuing strife between different Mennonite groups were the changes brought about in other dimensions of Mennonite life by the modernization of the administrative setup. These concerned primarily the problem of social controls and formal sanctions.

THE MENNONITE FARMING COMMUNITY

In the traditional Mennonite system, as it had been developed in Russia and transferred to early Manitoba, the basic unit was the semiautonomous village commune, which was also an almost self-sufficient economic unit. Arable land was divided into several open fields in which each family homestead received a strip for perpetual usufruct. Pasture and woodlands were managed collectively. Innovations in the farm economy, working conditions, or even style of life could only be introduced by general consent. This kind of economic system required a great deal of cooperation and collective management. Its maintenance depended on strict social controls and effective sanctions enforced by legitimate authorities. Civil authority was vested in the Mennonite reeve of the *volost*. In addition, the established Mennonite church in each settlement exercised important social controls, which also extended to secular matters, such as conformity to the traditional economic system and obedience to the village and *volost* authorities. If a Mennonite left his community or was excluded from it, he not only lost his share in the communal lands, he also lost his civil status as a Mennonite together with the privileges granted to the group as such, including exemption from taxation and from military service.

Canadian officials did not interfere with the Mennonites when they tried to institute village habitat and field community. In contrast to Russia, however, Canadian law and government neither legitimized Mennonite institutions nor supported their authorities. Nobody was coerced into abandoning the Mennonite way of life but, if a Mennonite preferred to withdraw from the cooperative economic system, to move from the village site to his homestead or to neglect the Mennonite rules of inheritance, he was fully protected against any claim that Mennonite authorities might put forward against him. But whenever this happened, the whole delicate balance of interlocking communal institutions was threatened.

There was, of course, still the authority of the Mennonite church with a set of religious controls at its command. Of these, excommunication had always proved the most potent and consequential. Yet religious sanctions also lost their power in Canada. It was extremely rare that a Mennonite would withdraw altogether from intimate association with other Mennonites, as life in Canadian society at large was too unfamiliar to seem at all bearable. But it was a very easy matter for a whole group of Mennonites, who were dissatisfied with the policy of an established church and unwilling to submit to its controls, to form a dissident congregation. Similarly, a disgruntled Mennonite could simply move to another section of the Reserves where the policies of the church authorities were more to his liking. Neither dissension nor switch of church membership had any legal consequences, as had been the case in Russia.

Adjustment to the Host Society. Our simplified outline has shown how changes in the administrative setup were brought about, not by direct interference on the part of the host society, but by their failure to support the Mennonite authorities, thus weakening traditional social controls. It has further affected Mennonite economy. Economic changes could not fail to influence cultural life. By the outbreak of World War I the whole Mennonite community had become integrated into the capitalistic system of the host society with consequent benefits in prosperity. Yet cultural modernization progressed much more slowly and, above all, more selectively.

The Mennonites had always considered a frugal way of life as farmers to be most fitting to the moral precepts of their faith, and to be the surest safeguard for preserving the Mennonite group in an alien environment. Participation in a modern economy, of course, not only brought many technological innovations within their reach, but they were even forced to adopt them to compete successfully with non-Mennonites. Some of the church groups were more conservative than others in permitting the adoption of modern culture traits from the host society. None of them, though, became fully acculturated to modern Canadian society. More important still, formal social controls, particularly of a religious kind, remained strong enough to prevent individuals from embracing modern ways of life wholeheartedly. It was always the Mennonite group as a whole, or else entire subgroups organized in a particular church, who finally accepted one or the other innovation; and because cultural change was always carried out collectively, it was not felt to be an adoption from an alien culture but a spontaneous development of their own social heritage. This goes far to explain why the Mennonite societal unit never lost its separate identity as a distinctive ethnic group within the Canadian society.

Nevertheless, great differences in the readiness and speed with which social change was accepted by different Mennonite groups led to a break that went so far that even intermarriage between members of different Mennonite churches was forbidden. The rift became almost complete over the issue of public schools. As we have already noted, the school is a powerful instrument of nationalization and of modernization in general. Early attempts of Canadian authorities to replace Mennonite church schools by district schools under provincial supervision was motivated by the realization that the Mennonite children had been left without the kind of schooling that would prepare them adequately for life in modern society. About the time of World War 1, however, nationalist ideologies began to make themselves strongly felt, and assimilation of minority groups became the accepted policy of the Manitoba government. Accordingly, it was decided not only to suppress private church schools that mediated the language and culture of minority groups but even to abolish the system of bilingual public schools that had been allowed in ethnically heterogeneous districts. It was the avowed purpose of this measure to indoctrinate alien groups with the ideals and values of Anglo-Saxon society, and thus to promote national unity through cultural uniformity in order to speed up the formation of a homogenized Canadian nation.

SOCIAL CHANGE

Regroupment. The more conservative Mennonites were unwilling to accept the alienation of their schools; they were afraid to lose control of their children and to expose them to modernizing influences that were contrary to their religious convictions. Between 1921 and 1930, approximately 6000, or one-third of the Mennonite population in Manitoba, emigrated to Mexico and Paraguay.[1] Once more, entire church groups were involved in the movement, especially the Fürstenland and the East-Reserve Bergtal people. Yet the vacuum that they left was quickly filled by about 8000 refugees from Soviet Russia who were admitted to Manitoba at about the same time. These were members of the same Mennonite commonwealth from which the earlier immigrants had broken away. Both had undergone profound changes in the intervening period. Both had become modernized without losing their ethnic identity. In reality, those who had stayed in Russia had progressed farther and had adjusted better to a modern society than had those who left earlier.

The regroupment of the Mennonites in Manitoba had several significant consequences. Due to the loss in population, the original group became so disorganized that their resistance to modernizing influences on the part of the host society and of the new arrivals was weak. Of the latter, only a fraction were able to settle in the original colonies, while the remainder were widely dispersed over the whole province. These scattered Mennonite groups became more reliant on the host society; they were also better equipped for the new conditions because of their superior education. They developed a conscious ethnic nationalism, but their native brethren still defined themselves primarily in terms of a distinctive religion. Nevertheless, the identity and solidarity of the whole Mennonite population was maintained despite differences in the degree of modernization they had undergone.

CULTURAL MODERNIZATION

Let us pause to reconsider the concept of modernization, which we defined earlier in terms of nationalization and industrialization. Is the meaning of modernization quite so evident if applied to the cultural subsystem? Up to now we have spoken of cultural modernization above all in the sense that it made the Mennonite group more like the host society with regard to their general outlook on life. Our tacit assumption was that the host society was of the "modern" type. The conclusion that suggests itself is that "modernization" in this sense means very much the same as "acculturation" in the language of older cultural anthropologists. On the other hand, we have insisted that the cultural modernization of the Manitoba Mennonites did not result in the loss of their ethnic distinctiveness. Thus, a premodern group apparently may become acculturated to a modern host society *formally* without becoming acculturated *materially* in all respects.

In a somewhat different sense, we also used the concept, "modernization of the cultural system," in relation to the processes that are liable to put a collectivity in a better position to function properly in a modern economy. Any

---

[1] A similar exodus occurred after World War II, when between 2,000 and 3,000 emigrated to Latin America.

culture change, therefore, that is required by industrialization and/or commercialization may be described as cultural modernization. One of the most important changes consists in the establishment of schools that equip people for life in industrial society. Another aspect of this process pertains to the kind of change in the religious culture that is commonly described as secularization. For the present purpose, it seems least controversial to adopt the term "cultural modernization" in the second sense. But both meanings may coincide if the host society itself is of the modern type. Nevertheless, the adjustment of a subculture to a modern economy does not necessarily involve material acculturation to the host society. This will help us to understand further developments in the Mennonite ethnic group.

By the early 1930s social change had become quite noticeable. Most conspicuous was the adoption of a capitalistic farm economy and the kind of rural life that had become typical of Western Canada in general. There was even a certain amount of urbanization and industrialization. The Mennonites participated actively in public affairs and politics; they also went to "nationalized" public schools which mediated the "modern" Anglo-Saxon culture typical of the host society. In addition, they began to adopt voluntary associations as well as various forms of commercialized recreation which tended to break the monopoly of family and church on the social life of the community. Even their churches adopted beliefs, cult forms, methods of religious instruction and so on from Anglo-Saxon Protestant churches.

THE THIRD PERIOD OF READJUSTMENT

Reversal of Acculturation. From this brief account we gather that the Mennonites experienced modernization in most dimensions and, by the same token, were becoming acculturated. Yet the process was halted and in part reversed when the Depression threw the host society into a serious crisis. The immediate reaction of the Mennonites was the revival of traditional patterns of subsistence farming, coupled with a reduction of inventories, farm expenses, and cash living costs. Even so, many of them lost the titles to their land. Nevertheless, they were better able to weather the period of stress than their non-Mennonite neighbors.

With the reorientation of their economy went a reassessment of the whole capitalistic system and the "modern" culture that goes with it. As long as it had proved successful, the Mennonites had—even if cautiously—followed the example of the host society. As its fallacies became apparent, they began to go their own way, which was more in keeping with their traditions. They learned to look down upon their Anglo-Saxon compatriots who appeared unable to weather the crisis. Once the myth of Anglo-Saxon superiority was shattered in the economic sphere, the Mennonites tended to reconsider their attitude towards other aspects of the host society. They gained a new pride in their own social heritage and new confidence in the resources of their group.

This does not mean that they completely reverted to their traditional institutions or cut off all ties with the host society—if such a course of action had been at all feasible. The trend expressed itself in a much more selective acculturation than before and in a tendency to rely more on their own inventiveness than on the example of others. At the end of this process the differences between the Mennonite group and the host society were in many respects greater than they had been before the crisis, and the distinctiveness of the ethnic group once again approached the level of the period prior to their disorganization.

Economic Reorganization. Economic reorganization was completed when Mennonites not only took over the railroad towns in their settlements from the non-Mennonite founders but also established small and medium-sized businesses and industries in their old farm-operator villages and in the open countryside. In this way they managed to increase the division of labor and socioeconomic interdependence within the whole Mennonite group. By joining a large area of Mennonite concentration into a solid regional unit, they were, at the same time, able to restore some of the partial autarchy of their compact settlements. This, in turn, increased once again social self-sufficiency and, at the same time, encouraged segregation from the host society. In so far as the Mennonite economy differed from that of the larger society, it put a new emphasis on the distinctiveness of the ethnic group and served as an added symbol of its identity when other symbols were lost. Moreover, the *organic solidarity* which, according to Durkheim, goes with a more elaborate division of labor proved superior to the *mechanic solidarity* typical of the preindustrial type of subsistence farming, by preventing fissions along religious lines, which had split up the Mennonite group in the earlier days. Despite the multiplication of Mennonite churches, the internal solidarity and coherence of the whole Mennonite group became, if anything, stronger than it had been in the last half century.

Religion and Ethnicity. In the religious sphere, too, there were many changes. Considering the great variety of beliefs, practices, and organization that commonly exist among Christian communities, it is difficult to say exactly in what respect Mennonite churches have become "modernized." It must suffice to point out that, because of different degrees of acculturation, various branches of Mennonitism differ from each other today just as much as other Protestant churches differ among themselves, and that some Mennonite churches bear a closer resemblance to some non-Mennonite churches than to each other. It is, in fact, difficult to say precisely which distinctive religious traits are equally shared by all Mennonites. Nor is there any common church organization or specific confession of faith recognized by all. Moreover, some individuals who are still socially defined as Mennonites are not members of any Mennonite church.

This poses the question of what promotes this sense of religious identity that prevents individual branches of Mennonitism from giving up the designation "Mennonite" altogether; for, in reality, the name indicates little more than a common derivation from Evangelical Anabaptism. The injunction on bearing arms and taking oaths as well as the insistence on adult baptism have always been considered specific marks of Mennonite churches; yet even these practices are not exclusive to them and have not been enforced equally by all their churches at all times. Much more important in maintaining a sense of identity among Mennonite congregations has been the shared experience of problems that they had to face, which required cooperation. Above all, we have to think of recurrent persecutions and threats to what they considered the sacred trust of their faith.

In World War I the imposition of the public school seemed, at least to some church groups, to be a challenge calling for cooperative effort. Shortly afterwards, a new challenge arose when the sufferings of their brethren in Communist Russia required relief. Mennonite churches in Manitoba, in Canada as a whole, and even beyond formed committees to help the refugees settle in the New World. In World War II the churches cooperated in the defense and relief of conscientious objectors. The war was barely over when the care for another batch of refugees from Russia again called for a common effort. Of these, about 8000 came to Manitoba alone, requiring assistance by Mennonite organizations under the auspices of the churches. Again and again, there arose the need for common action, which did not allow the members of the several Mennonite churches ever to forget that in a crisis they depended on mutual aid, sacrifice, and solidarity for sheer survival as a religious group.

The Role of the Public School. Since the 1920s the grade schools have been taken out of the hands of Mennonite churches and have been integrated into the provincial school system. Nevertheless, they continued to add to the coherence of the Mennonite group. This statement requires a few words of explanation. By and large, the Mennonites took a keen interest in educational affairs; school attendance and scholastic achievements were above the provincial average. In their compact settlements the school was run by Mennonite trustees, manned by Mennonite teachers, attended by children belonging to various Mennonite churches; the school was also an important center of community life. It was thus felt to be a genuine Mennonite institution. Not even the Canadian culture it mediated was considered an alien intrusion. This situation can be properly appreciated only if one realizes that *ethnicity is not a fixed state of affairs but an intermittent process, which is activated solely when ethnic differentiation becomes salient.* By the end of World War II, the Manitoba Mennonites had become as much Canadian as they remained Mennonite. And in common with all Canadians, Canadian culture was theirs even if it was modified by a Mennonite subculture that emerged from latency whenever they acted with specific reference to their church and/or ethnic group. In addition, we should remember that *acculturation to the host society need not endanger the identity and solidarity of a primary ethnic group—in fact, it may help to maintain it*.

INDICES OF ETHNICITY

Let us put the question this way: Since the Mennonites have become acculturated to Canadian society, and since differences between the Mennonite group and the host society were no greater or more significant than among other sections of Canadian society, in what respect are we entitled to consider them a distinctive ethnic group at all? What are the external characteristics that symbolize their distinctiveness today? We have already indicated the rather ambiguous role that Mennonite religion plays in this respect. We should add that English has become not only the language of instruction in schools and a vehicle of values shared with other Canadians, it also serves as a generalized means of communication. Still, all Manitoba Mennonites speak their West Prussian Platt and understand High German to a greater or lesser degree. Their German speech certainly serves as a mark that distinguishes them from the general run of Canadians and symbolizes their unity. But it cannot explain why they have also remained distinct from other Germans in the province.

ECOLOGICAL CONCENTRATION

We have already spoken of the solid territorial base of the Mennonite group with its distinctive regional economy. The importance of their identification with a definite region is further underlined by the fact that the ecological concentration of the Mennonite population in Manitoba is greater today than it has been at any time since the disturbances of the 1920s. As soon as they were able to do so, the scattered groups of new Mennonite immigrants tended to move into the Reserves and adjacent areas. By 1941, more than 80 percent of the Manitoba Mennonites were concentrated south of Winnipeg. In two densely populated regions comprising thirty-nine of the one-hundred thirteen subdistricts of the province, the Mennonite population amounted to almost a third of the total population. Although their settlements were not entirely contiguous and were not always ethnically homogeneous, modern means of transportation helped maintain frequent interaction, face-to-face relationships, *commensalitas,* and intensive cooperation.

THE ROLE OF THE FAMILY

A still more important factor, however, in maintaining the ethnic group must be seen in the kinship system. The vast majority of Manitoba Mennonites answer to approximately three hundred family names, of which about forty are not only most common among them but also relatively rare among other Germans. There are, indeed, typical Mennonite names. The family and the extended family group still play an outstanding role in Mennonite social life, which is even more crucial than that of the church. Visits of relatives and family affairs still draw more people together at regular intervals, and more closely than any other form of recreation. And it is still very rare for Mennonites to marry non-Mennonites. *All this gives the impression that the whole group of Russian Mennonites consists of one intricate web of kinship ties; and this, according to our definition, is the distinguishing mark of an ethnic unit.* Mennonites are also keenly aware of their historical traditions; their history emphasizes their common origin, the sufferings that they had to share, the ideas which are common to all branches, even if they may have sought their realization in different ways. It provides them with a social myth that transcends all particularistic divisions, which conceives of the whole group as an indivisible unit.

We may conclude that the following factors have proved decisive in preserving the identity and solidarity of the Manitoba Mennonite group: an ideology centering on religion; a concatenation of kinship relations maintained through endogamy; territorial concentration allowing for a high degree of social and even economic self-sufficiency; and a set of separate institutions able to exercise adequate social controls.

CONCLUSIONS

The study of the Manitoba Mennonites has provided us with an object lesson of how primary ethnic groups may emerge and maintain themselves in an alien environment. The principal condition for their formation was apparently the effective segregation of a relatively large population from its societal environment. The motivation for this withdrawal was religious. Theoretically, any other strong motive, nationalism or specific class differences, for instance, would have served the same purpose. But the segregation of particularistic subsocieties has a real chance of success only as long as the pressures of nationalization and industrialization on the part of the host society have not yet become paramount. Once formed, the resistance against absorption is strengthened in proportion to the contrast between the segregated group and its societal environment. Again, this contrast may refer to a variety of group attributes: a distinctive religion, a distinctive language, a distinctive economic system, or even distinctive somatic differences. If several such characteristics combine they tend to fortify each other. *The principal function of differentiating characteristics appears to be symbolic. The more readily the differences can be perceived and the greater their discriminatory power is, the better they can serve as symbols for the distinctiveness and unity of the group.* This helps to explain why characteristics that had played a role in the formative stage may be replaced by other differentiating characteristics at a later stage, in order to maintain the group. In fact, partial acculturation to the host society may increase the chances of survival as a group.

Apart from the cognitive aspect of the problem, we have seen that the exercise of internal controls is essential for the maintenance of a primary ethnic group, as it is indeed for all collectivities. Anything that keeps social controls in the hands of group leaders to the exclusion of representatives of the host society is bound to prevent or retard the dissolution of the ethnic group. Accordingly, political autonomy is the most important safeguard for its maintenance. But any other institutions exercising strong social controls—for instance, economic or religious institutions—may work in the same direction, *if and only if the group has a monopoly of them.* It is not even necessary for such separate institutions to be germane to the group; *they must only be confined to it in a given situation and different from the corresponding institutions of the societal environment.* The Manitoba Mennonites gave up their separate institutions and even some of their distinctive cultural traits. They accepted the more modern and effective institutions of the host society, as long as they were sure that there were still sufficient other social controls, old or new, at their disposal to maintain the group and set it apart from the host society.

Ecological concentration serves several functions in the maintenance of an ethnic group. Its territory becomes identified with the group and thus an added symbol of it. Compact settlement increases the opportunities of frequent and intimate interaction and decreases the need of associating with others. If *commensalitas* can be confined to members of the group, *connubium* follows, even without any particular taboos on exogamy. When regional economic autarchy is added, the exclusiveness of the group may become nearly comprehensive. But even if self-sufficiency is not possible under the condition of a modernized economy, division of labor, creating a system of regional interdependences, gives the impression that in the sphere of *commercium* the group collectively deals with the host society as such, each individual acting as the representative of the entire group. In their transactions with members of the host society, individual gains and losses are perceived as gains and losses of the group.

The Mormons as an Ethnic Group

That Mormons might be considered an ethnic group seems, on the face of it, a preposterous suggestion; for is the Church of Latter-Day Saints not simply one among many other Protestant denominations which, in the course of time, have separated from the American core churches? If we think only of recent decades, the query seems justified; but it was not always so. We recall that in the middle of the last century a Mormon state existed for a few years in the Great Basin of the Rocky Mountains. And as late as the 1930s, a reputed sociologist included a chapter on Alberta Mormons in his study of "Ethnic Communities in Western Canada" (Dawson, 1936). Even in the comparative study touching upon interethnic relations, which was undertaken by a Harvard research team in western New Mexico after World War II, a Mormon village was selected along with a Spanish, Texan, Navajo, and Pueblo Indian community.[2]

To some extent the story of the Mormons parallels that of the Mennonites in Russia. In both cases the formation of the ethnic collectivity was due to the opportunity offered to a group of religious dissenters to separate from the parent society and to establish itself as a self-sufficient agrarian community without interference on the part of the societal environment, particularly of the central government. Unlike the Mennonites, however, who achieved their full status as a distinctive ethnic unit after they had left the jurisdiction of their parent society, the American Mormons remained within the territory of the United States, and were confronted with a host society that had also been their parent society. Moreover, the contrast effect was never as pronounced in the case of the Mormons as in that of the Mennonites, whose ethnic distinctiveness was obvious in Russia as well as in Canada. While both, at one time, approximated the type of a separate ethnic unit, their further transformation was different: The Mennonites became an ethnic group, the Mormons became a religious denomination. The analysis of the Mormon case, though necessarily brief, offers a further opportunity to specify the conditions under which group migration may lead to the emergence of a primary ethnic group.

MORMON RELIGION

Mormon religion was not a foreign intrusion but a genuine product of the American scene in the first half of the nineteenth century. After the political

---

[2]A list of publications of the "Comparative Study of Values" project will be found in Smith, Roberts 1954.

and economic emancipation from Great Britain, nationalism mainly developed along two lines among the settler population of the former colony: completion of emancipation in the cultural dimension and territorial expansion. American nationalism was supported by a religious enthusiasm that inspired the broad masses. Two moral problems immanent in the postcolonial situation challenged the ingenuity of creative religious leaders: Negro slavery and the birthright of the aborigines. To both dilemmas, Joseph Smith, founder of the Mormon church, provided an imaginative answer, which was in keeping with a widespread Fundamentalism, Revivalism, and Chiliasm. The divine revelation divulged by the Book of Mormon, which he claimed to have discovered, explained the racial and ethnic differences found on the American continent by elaborating on the Biblical story of the Chosen People. The pith of the argument was the reinterpretation, in religious terms, of the differential treatment of the white, Indian, and Negro races in American society, and the call for the founding of a new Zion where the Chosen (the "Saints") should await the second advent of the Lord. Thus, the religious beliefs of Mormonism offered a comprehensive social myth, claiming general validity for all Americans, which clashed not only with the ambitions of other churches but also with the social and economic interests underlying the traditional treatment of Negroes and Indians. The ideology of the Mormons also explained their strong missionary zeal and their contribution to the settlement of the New West. For it was only beyond the reach of the established American society that they could hope to realize their vision of a perfect society, the City of God.

MIGRATIONS

Resistance on the part of the societal environment, inspired as much by religious as secular competition, together with the practical goals of the movement initiated a series of migrations to the more remote areas of the continent. From upstate New York, where the church was formally founded in 1830, about one thousand Mormons moved to Kirtland, Ohio; in short intervals, new migrations followed to Missouri and Illinois, where by 1842, no less than fifteen thousand of them lived in agrarian village communes of their own. These communes still depended economically and financially on their non-Mormon neighbors and were subject to the United States legal and administrative system, but they remained segregated from the societal environment through strict taboos on *commensalitas* and *connubium,* as well as a fairly comprehensive set of local institutions under their own control. Moreover, their culture pattern was already in conspicuous contrast to that of American society at large. In 1842, the trek got under way to the Great Basin of the Rocky Mountains; eventually twenty thousand Mormon pioneers arrived. In view of the endogamy enforced by the leaders, the rapid increase of the Mormon population was, of course, mainly due to energetic missionary activities which also extended to Europe. Yet the ensuing heterogeneity was not greater than that of the general American population, which increased no less rapidly through the steady flow of mostly rural immigrants.

THE EMERGENCE OF A MORMON ETHNIE

In the case of the Mennonites we have already seen how migration to a sparsely populated territory, formally claimed by a state but not yet effectively controlled by it, improves the chances of the independent development of a sectarian group. In time, lack of association and feeble communications, as well as self-reliance in meeting all basic social needs within the group, tended to give it the character of a global society and to deepen cultural differences, thereby emphasizing the contrast effect that is at the bottom of ethnic differentiation.

Although the Mennonites had been already socially defined in ethnic terms upon their arrival in Russia, and became ethnically distinct also from the parent society as a consequence of migration and spatial separation, ethnicity had initially played no role whatever in the relations of the Mormons to the American society whose influence they fled. Nevertheless, factors similar to those that were at work in the Mennonite case nearly succeeded in transforming the Mormons into a separate people.

Political Autonomy. The ineffectiveness of political control at the outer reaches of the pioneering fringe left Brigham Young (successor to the charismatic founder, who had been murdered in an Illinois jail in 1844) and his fellow leaders free to establish a political power structure and administrative system of their own design for the State of Deseret, which extended far beyond the later boundary lines of the State of Utah. They even declared its secession from the Union when the central authorities interfered with its internal affairs. Sovereign rule of the United States over the territory could be restored and made effective only after federal troops had overcome the resistance of the Mormons and their Indian allies.

Economic Autarchy. The agrarian economy based on subsistence farming permitted the organization of village communes after a pattern which was at variance with the pattern common among other American settlers in the West. The Mormons, like the Mennonites, not only preferred close habitat to scattered homesteads, they also adopted communal land ownership similar to that which had prevailed in the Middle Ages or in pre-modern Russia. In addition, they propagated and partly achieved authoritarian control by the church leadership over the profits gained by individual accomplishment, and established a system of distributing economic rewards in accordance with the collective interests of the Mormon theocratic commonwealth. The irrigation system, on which most of Mormon agriculture and its conspicuous successes were based, also made for a higher degree of cooperation and solidarity in Mormon community life than was known among most of their American neighbors who specialized in cattle ranching and dry farming.

Cultural Distinctiveness. Deviations of Mormon culture from the general American pattern were initiated by a religion that regulated all aspects of social life. Mormon ideology was not in keeping with the American social myth. Their religious cult contained strong elements of secrecy, which was contrary to the practices of other American churches. Similarly, the authoritarian organization of their theocracy differed widely from American democratic ideas. Finally, in addition to taboos not only on *connubium* but also on every form of *commensalitas* with non-Mormons, the religious sanctioning of polygamy, which in many ways affected both family life and the social structure as a whole, set the Mormons apart from the general run of Americans and violated fundamental moral principles that were incorporated in the common Christian tenets of the New Testament. These appeared to be suspended by the special Divine Relevation which Joseph Smith claimed to have received. With regard to marriage a particularly crucial and emotionally charged issue was raised. Although the language of the Mormons remained that of other Americans, differences that extended to most aspects of culture created a contrast effect which—together with social self-sufficiency including a considerable amount of self-recruitment, identification with a particular territory, political autonomy, and economic autarchy—furnished them with the distinguishing characteristics of a separate ethnic unit.

Reversal of the Trend. The trend, however, was reversed before the Mormons had a chance of establishing themselves as new politically organized society, which eventually might have been defined in ethnic terms. One reason was that Mormon territory was soon swamped by non-Mormon migrants from the interior of the United States, mainly because of the new economic opportunities offered by mining. Violent conflicts between the new arrivals and the locally dominant Mormons, in fact, necessitated the restoration of public order by Federal authorities. This intervention put the first decisive dent in Mormon independence by depriving them of the chance of organizing themselves into a sovereign state.

Economically, they were forced into an ever-tighter network of interdependence with their societal environment. They tried to meet the threat to autarchy by a boycott of non-Mormon businesses, which was organized by the church. The only permanent result was a kind of cooperative which, under the name of "Church Welfare Plan," proved useful, especially during the Great Depression. The construction of the transcontinental railroad and the relative increase of the non-Mormon population in their area of settlement finally put an end to social isolation and economic independence.

The Mormons remained a foreign body within American society as long as their territorial concentration, deviating behavior, and inner cohesion were felt to be a threat to the homogeneity of the emerging nation. The issue of polygamy provided a symbol for all those who were bent on eliminating the threat. When it was forbidden by Federal legislation, the Mormons made a last stand against complete control by the national society—they clung all the more tenaciously to the practice, which they defined as a religious matter exempted from state interference by constitutional law. This provided a convenient pretext for the suppression of the Mormon church by the American authorities in 1887. When the president of the Mormon church declared the United States law to be binding on the Mormons in the moral sphere of marriage relations, he managed to save the Mormon church as a religious institution, but the Mormons had to abandon their mission to build Zion as a global society.

Before attempting to come to any more general conclusions concerning the formation, maintenance, and dissolution of primary ethnic groups, we shall do well to consider a far more common situation that arises when such groups are the result of territorial annexation rather than migration.

REFERENCES

Dawson, Carl A., *Group Settlement: Ethnic Communities in Western Canada*. Canadian Frontiers of Settlement, Vol. VII. Toronto: The Macmillan Company of Canada, 1936, pp. 175–272.

Francis, E. K., *In Search of Utopia: The Mennonites in Manitoba*. Glencoe, Ill.: The Free Press, and Altona, Manitoba: D. W. Friesen and Sons Ltd., 1955.

Nelson, Lowry, *The Mormon Village: A Pattern and Technique of Land Settlement*. Salt Lake City: University of Utah Press, 1952.

O'Dea, Thomas F., "Mormonism and the Avoidance of Sectarian Stagnation: A Study of Church, Sect, and Incipient Nationality," *American Journal of Sociology*, LX (1954), pp. 285–293.

————*The Mormons*. Chicago: University of Chicago Press, 1957.

Smith, Watson, and John M. Roberts, *Zuni Law: A Preliminary Study in Values*. Peabody Museum of Harvard University Papers, vol. 43, No. 1, 1954.

Kluckhohn, Florence Rockwood, and Fred L. Strodtbeck, *Variations in Value Orientations*. Evanston, Ill.: Row, Peterson & Co., 1961, pp. 175–257.

Group Formation as a Result of Annexation

16

The Hispanos in New Mexico

The Mennonite immigrants to Manitoba were transformed into a primary ethnic group as a result of their transfer to a territory over which the emerging Canadian nation exercised social control through law. In the case of the New Mexico Hispanos, however, a preexisting regional subsociety of the emerging Mexican national society was transformed into a primary ethnic group after its territory had been annexed by another (emerging) national society—that of the United States. It is important to note that we are dealing with emerging nations. The group migration of the Mennonites to Manitoba had at first resulted in their establishment of a quasi-independent, regional subsociety. It was only after modern state administration became effective and particularly after the public school was introduced and the influences of a modern economy made themselves felt, that ethnic differentiation gave rise to specific problems. Similarly, it was the process of nationalization set in motion some time after the transfer from one state jurisdiction to another that transformed the regional subsociety of New Mexico into a primary ethnic group. This transformation, which is the subject matter of the following analysis, was not fully achieved until almost a quarter of a century after political annexation.

NEW MEXICO IN COLONIAL TIMES

The present territory of New Mexico was conquered by the Spaniards and incorporated by them into their colonial empire at the turn of the sixteenth century. About one hundred years later they established a military settlement there in order to protect the northern frontiers of their American possessions against the French. Unlike the British (and later the Americans), who tended to isolate the aborigines from the European settlers by pushing them into remote places and finally into segregated reservations without making any sustained

190

attempts to integrate them into the colonial (later, national) society, the Spaniards (later, the Mexicans) favored the Hispanization of the aboriginal population and their amalgamation through intermarriage. In New Mexico, in particular, the Spanish settlers, who had been recruited for the economic support of the Catholic mission, the garrison, and the civil administrators, associated freely with the sedentary tribes of Pueblo Indians. This symbiosis resulted primarily from a common need to defend themselves against the nomadic Plains Indians who raided Spanish and Indian villages indiscriminately. In addition, the agrarian economy of the geographically isolated settlement required close cooperation. Finally, the Christianization of the aborigines led to a common participation in important religious ceremonies. Intermarriage became not only legitimate but was actually enforced by church and state where sexual intercourse could not altogether be prevented.

THE SOCIAL STRUCTURE

After Mexico's emancipation from Spain in 1821, the New Mexicans became part of the new nation. On the eve of the American conquest, a quarter of a century later, the regional subsociety was made up of the following components: (1) a small elite of feudal estate owners, military and civil officers, parish clergy, and missionaries; (2) a broad peasant substratum of Spanish settlers, Hispanized Indians, and mestizos; and (3) partially acculturated Pueblo Indians who retained their separate community organization but were linked to the Mexican society through a variety of social bonds. Since the opening of the Santa Fe trail in 1822, immigrants from the interior of the North American continent also settled in the border towns; these were socially defined as foreigners. They were members of the American society, ethnically distinct from the Mexicans, and potentially a fifth column. The Treaty of Guadalupe Hidalgo, which concluded the war between the United States and Mexico in 1848, sanctioned the annexation of New Mexico. All Mexicans who did not chose to leave the country became American citizens. With few minor exceptions, no special provisions were made to grant them corporate rights, such as the Mennonites had been granted in Russia or early Manitoba. Thus the maintenance of the Hispanos as a distinctive ethnic unit was guaranteed neither by law nor by agreement.

Social Change Due to the Annexation. The annexation did not immediately threaten the continued existence of the regional subsociety in its traditional form. However, there were changes in the political sphere: American institutions replaced those of Mexico, and the Federal government had a more than usual influence on internal affairs before New Mexico became a full-fledged member-state. And this did not happen till 1912, at a time when the Hispanos could not longer challenge American dominance. The limited autonomy of the

Territory offered some Hispanos an opportunity of participating in its adminis-tration along with Americanos, though not in proportion to their relative num-bers; for actual political power was heavily weighted in favor of the Americano minority.

In the economic sphere, changes were at first far less pronounced than in the political. Before 1879, when the Santa Fe Railroad linked New Mexico with the interior of the United States, and before the vast intervening spaces had be-come pacified and settled, economic exchange beyond the border of the Terri-tory remained almost as limited as it had been previously with the interior of Mexico. The agrarian economy of the region, mainly subsistence farming, remained for all practical purposes autarchical. Nor did the moderate influx of American traders, professionals, and speculators with their strange business practices cause major changes. Apart from the geographical isolation, the small native population (which at the time of the conquest included about 70,000 Hispanos and 10,000 Indians) and its concentration in a continuous area of the Upper Rio Grande Valley increased the capability of the regional subsociety to function in much the same way as before the annexation.

THE MORAL BASIS OF LEGITIMATE POWER

The transfer of a territory from one nation-state to another does not, in itself, change the moral basis of the legitimate exercise of political power. Before the annexation, the decision-making power had been vested in representatives of the Hispanos. Its legitimacy rested on the notion that a territory that has been effectively occupied by a group of people "belongs" to them. The identifica-tion of place and people implies a right of priority or "birthright"; in other words, those who are first in a place have more right to determine what hap-pens there than those who came later. Yet priority rights may be challenged by concurrent "rights," for instance, those of the stronger, the wiser, the ones better able to promote the general welfare.

The ideology of nationalism, too, provides a moral basis of legitimate power, which may conflict with the birthright of a territorial population. Typical con-flicts of this kind arise when a nation-state annexes a portion of another nation-state. Such conflicts cannot be settled simply by positive law that the conquerors impose upon the conquered. In the beginning, at least, the situation requires certain adjustments (such as exemptions from the general laws of the conquering nation-state or the enactment of special laws for the annexed terri-tory) in order to increase the chances that the conquered acquiesce and open conflict be avoided. The gradual nationalization of a conquered people involves persuading them that the compromise reached between their birthright and the paramount rights of the conquering nation is legitimate. Before the conquest, the birthright of the Hispanos in New Mexico coincided with the rights of the Mexican nation of which they were a regional component. Now, however, the

Americanos represented the right of the national society, which conflicted with the birthright of the Hispanos. Although the latter had legally become American citizens, they were not socially identified with the national core of American society. They were nevertheless expected to recognize the dominant role of the Americanos which was legitimized by the principles of demotic nationalism. This is, of course, another way of expressing the fact that the Hispanos were being transformed into a national minority.

THE INTEGRATION OF AMERICANOS INTO HISPANO SOCIETY

Yet the changes in the power structure took almost a generation to complete. At first, American power was primarily represented by a weakly developed bureaucracy, the law courts, and the garrison. In a premodern agrarian society their scope was limited. Despite new arrivals after the conquest, the number of resident Americanos remained relatively small. They included adventurers, hunters and trappers, truckers, traders, professionals, and clergymen. Many of them were recent immigrants from Europe who were themselves not yet properly Americanized. The Americanos thus were not a homogeneous group; they were even inclined to recognize not only the birthright of the Hispanos but also their cultural superiority. In view of their own inferior educational status, they were neither anxious nor able to impose their own culture upon the Hispanos. Because of their isolation in a strange country, they professed to seek attachment to the native Hispano society. This proved all the more attractive to them as their ethnic affinity to the new rulers, their familiarity with American institutions, together with their business acumen and economic success endowed them with a higher social standing than they had enjoyed before they came to New Mexico, and made them eligible for *commensalitas* and even *connubium* with the Hispano upper class. Americanos tended to marry into native families, and it was they and their children rather than the Hispanos who were acculturated. In time the resident Americanos became identified with the elite of New Mexico, developed a genuine appreciation for its traditions, and even became fully accepted as an integral part of New Mexican society.

THE AMERICANIZATION OF NEW MEXICO

The real "conquest" of New Mexico, that is, its effective Americanization, did not take place till 1870–90. It was a result of economic and demographic changes. Geographical isolation broke down when transportation between New Mexico and the interior of the continent was improved, and when contiguous American settlement reached the borders of the Territory and spilled over them. Large-scale immigration, both from other parts of the United States and from abroad, coincided with the great migratory movements which, after the Civil War, transformed the general character of American society. Added to this, New Mexico became integrated into the American economy and participated in its modernization. Vast stretches of pasture land became available for exploitation, which so far were barely populated and used as hunting grounds by nomadic Indians. When the autochthones were subdued and confined to remote reservations, both Americanos and Hispanos were able to take full advantage of the rapid expansion of American agricultural economy. Some members of each group acquired fabulous riches. Mining became a major industry, and new urban centers sprang up along railroad lines and highways.

Ethnic Divisions. Because of these developments, ethnicity acquired a saliency which it did not have before. This manifested itself most conspicuously in an ecological sectionalization of New Mexico which was both economic and ethnic. The principal dividing line ran between a contiguous area of compact Hispano settlement and the rest of the country which was rapidly being occupied by in-migrants. In addition, there were further subdivisions. From the old Hispano settlement, whose economic basis remained peasant farming in irrigated valleys and on humid mountain slopes, the Hispanos spread over the semiarid hinterland, where they achieved a monopoly in sheep grazing. In the old and most of the new Hispano settlement, the regional subsociety remained intact during the period of transition which lasted from the third quarter of the nineteenth through the first quarter of the twentieth century. Relations with the New-Mexican Anglos, and the host society in general, followed a pattern that had developed after the occupation and changed only gradually. In the marginal areas of the new Hispano settlement, however, social disorganization and fierce competition with the advancing Americanos created interethnic conflict.

In the hitherto unsettled areas, which were now occupied either by Americanos or European immigrants, American dominance was unchallenged. The economic base here was cattle ranching and dry farming. One section was nothing other than an extension of Texas across an administrative boundary line that had no social significance. The Hispanos made a distinction between the Tejanos (Texans) and the other Americans, whom they called "Anglos," as if they were ethnically different. The Anglos, who mostly came from the northern states or abroad, were by and large ready to regard the Hispanos as equals and to respect their culture. The Tejanos, on the other hand, tended to apply to them the same social norms of conduct which, in the South, govern relations between "white" and "colored" people. To them, all "Mexicans" were barely above Negroes and Indians. In the extreme south of New Mexico, finally, the population continued to maintain closer ties with Mexican society just across the border than with the more distant Hispanos settlements farther up the Rio Grande.

The ecological distribution of the urban population did not follow the same sectional dividing lines. In the old and new Hispano settlements, several country towns were situated that remained integrated into the regional subsociety, although the urban population included a greater proportion of Anglos than did the rural population, which in many communities remained purely Hispano. On the other hand, new urban settlements that had been started by the in-migrants did not differ from American towns in general. Yet the character of some old Hispano towns also changed in much the same was as in Cantonville: The Americans who migrated to these towns soon became dominant not only economically and politically but culturally as well; the nucleus, however, remained affiliated with the Hispano regional subsociety.

So far we have paid attention to the ecological distribution of the New Mexican population, which followed rather definite ethnic dividing lines. If we consider the social structure, we find the following situation. While the Hispano lower classes, particularly farmers and ranchers, remained clearly segregated in compact settlements, their politicians, professionals, entrepreneurs, as well as the urban middle classes tended to participate more directly in American society. For a time their role was that of a "colonial society" as well as that of a "mediating elite." At this level there was a good deal of association and cooperation with the corresponding strata of American society, which resulted in mutual acculturation, intermarriage, and bilingualism. After a period of transition, however, the progress of modernization weakened the dominant position of the old Hispano power elite in favor of the Americanos.

Loss of Economic and Political Dominance. One reason for this development must be sought in the diminishing economic power of the Hispano elite, another in their involvement in American party politics. Both factors were related and tended to support each other. Added to this, Catholic church policy deprived the Hispanos of their native clergy. Simultaneously, the activities of American Protestant churches in New Mexico retarded the emergence of a new set of national leaders among school teachers and other intellectuals. Economic development is too complicated for a thorough analysis here. In part it is due to climatic and other aspects of the physical geography, in part to general economic trends and fiscal policies in the host society that put the Hispanos at a definite disadvantage.

The most important single reason for the economic setbacks suffered by the Hispanos must be seen in the manner in which landed property in New Mexico was handled under American law. The original land titles were mostly derived from grants of the Spanish Crown to *conquistadores* and other feudal lords. Yet before the annexation, only a minor part of the land grants had been actually utilized for farming purposes, while the rest remained little more than a vague claim for the benefit of future generations. Once the in-migrants started arriving in large numbers, however, they began to occupy the seemingly owner-less spaces without much regard for ancient property titles. New economic opportunities and the increase of the Hispano population soon turned what hitherto had been almost worthless into valuable real estate. This situation led to countless litigations against the squatters. In most cases it was, however, difficult to prove property rights in American courts which had been obvious under Spanish and Mexican law. When violence and terror were added to the common practices of corruption and nepotism, the Hispanos found themselves without sufficient natural resources to compete successfully with the Anglos.

Effective relief could come only from participation in the freewheeling kind of party politics typical of the "Wild West." Lawyers, judges, and administrators not only yielded to political pressures, but tended to reward Hispano bosses for votes that they alone were able to deliver. Hispanos were found in both parties, and the political strife was carried on more with an eye to particularistic interests than to the general well-being of the ethnic group. The disunity among the Hispano elite, their corruption and personal enrichment, alienated them from their own people. The few native Hispanos who, within both parties, tried to resist American dominance were unable to accomplish very much and occasionally even met with violent death.

THE ROLE OF THE CHURCH

Still more directly than by economic and political losses, the integrity of the Hispano group was jeopardized by the activities of the churches, both Catholic and Protestant. The Catholic church had always played an important role in Mexican society. Her priests not only took part in the struggle for independence from Spain, but were among the leaders of the New Mexican uprisings against the American army of occupation. The situation, however, changed radically after 1848. In accordance with the Constitution, the Catholic church was disestablished so that American Protestant churches were from then on free to organize their own missions among the Hispanos. The long-range effects of Protestant activity will be described later.

Of more immediate significance were the changes that took place within the Catholic church herself. With a speed unusual in church history, the Roman hierarchy transferred all the territories annexed by the United States from the jurisdiction of Mexican dioceses to that of the Archbishop of St. Louis. Soon afterwards, the Bishopric of Santa Fe was created; its first head was an immigrant priest from France who, with great missionary zeal, went about to make up for the previous long neglect of religious affairs. In his eyes the native clergy was not only unequal to its task but constituted an obstacle to any reforms. To strengthen his position, the new bishop deprived one Hispano priest after another of their parishes, and replaced them by French missionaries. He and his two French successors, in whose opinion the native Hispano youth were altogether unsuited for the priesthood, made no effort to provide any theological training for them. Instead, all the parish clergy and missionary orders working in New Mexico were recruited from outside. Although the majority were recent immigrants and barely Americanized, they identified themselves with American rather than with Hispano society. In any event, their preoccupation was with religious affairs; they took no interest in Hispano culture or the maintenance of the ethnic group. This attitude was apt to add to the school problem, to which we turn next.

The School Problem. On several occasions we have emphasized the strategic role played by the school in interethnic relations. As far as the maintenance of the Hispano ethnic group was concerned, these questions were of crucial importance: (1) the kind of schooling necessary to successfully compete with Americans in an economy rapidly undergoing modernization; (2) the control of the schools; (3) the ethnic composition of the teaching staff; (4) the language of instruction and the culture transmitted through the school; and (5) the training of a new type of educated leaders who could make up for the loss of the old elite.

The new bishop of Santa Fe, who was well aware of and also in sympathy with modern educational trends, induced American and French religious orders to establish parish schools and private boarding schools in the major urban centers. But this did not solve the problem of public education in rural areas, which was complicated by three conflicting pressures on the Catholic church; namely: (1) Anglos and liberals demanded a system of public education that would follow the general American pattern; (2) American Protestant churches set about establishing private mission schools in Hispano communities; and (3) the Hispano estate owners were not interested in an educated peasantry and opposed taxation for the upkeep of rural public schools.

In contrast to the Protestant missions, which were generously supplied with financial means and teachers by their parent congregations in the interior of the United States, the Catholic church had neither the money nor the personnel to counter the threat with sufficient private and parish schools of her own. Faced with the dilemma between the pastoral necessity of improving the education of the broad masses and the danger of exposing Catholic children to hostile influences of teachers and textbooks, the bishop adopted a rather cunning policy: He saw to it that the speed with which public schools were introduced to Hispano communities was proportionate to the number of Hispano Catholic laymen who became available for teaching positions. This solution, which was inspired by purely religious considerations, had the effect that the American public schools, made general after 1891, did not become a serious threat to the maintenance of the Hispano ethnic group or to their cultural traditions.

Protestant Mission Schools as Agents of Americanization. From then on, there were three separate school systems in New Mexico, all of which were obliged to comply with the same official curriculum and to use textbooks printed in English: (1) Catholic private and parish schools; (2) private Protestant mission schools (both (1) and (2) were located mostly in Hispano communities); and (3) public schools, part of which served the growing Anglo and Tejano population, while in the others, Hispano teachers took care of the Hispano pupils. Of the three systems, the Protestant mission schools contributed most directly and consciously to the Americanization of the Hispanos. Above all, the Methodists and Presbytarians placed their mission schools in rural communities, often in inaccessible mountain villages, where due to the lack of priests and schools, the influence of the Catholic church was feeble or social controls were weakest. The poor Hispano peasants gladly accepted the excellent free education offered to their children, although the number of converts remained small.

Hispanos who were exposed to the Americanizing influence of Protestant schools, particularly secondary boarding schools, were usually better fitted for life in modern society than were those who went to Catholic or public schools. While some of them took advantage of the economic opportunities open to them outside the Hispano settlements and were thus lost to the ethnic group, a considerable proportion of the better educated, more progressive, and leading members of Hispano society, particularly teachers, were eventually recruited from among the graduates of Protestant mission schools. They formed the nucleus of a new middle-class elite who, although they did not favor any conscious resistance to American dominance, nevertheless improved the chances of the Hispano ethnic group of becoming better adjusted to American society without losing their ethnic identity.

Together with religious pluralism, the presence of Hispano Protestant congregations in their midst was eventually accepted by the Catholic Hispanos. Although this has facilitated their acculturation to the general American pattern, ethnic dividing lines have not been conspicuously blurred by it. Since World War II, the Protestant core churches themselves, having accomplished their intention of seeing a satisfactory system of American public schools firmly established among the Hispano population, have tended to withdraw outside support, and have left their Hispano congregations to their own devices. Catholic church policy has also changed in recent years. Once the notion that Hispano culture and Catholic religion formed an inseparable unit had proved untenable, new pastoral practices were adopted that were better suited to a modern, pluralistic, and secularized society. Nowadays, the Catholic church in New Mexico operates in much the same way as elsewhere in the United States. This has been an added factor in reducing the self-sufficiency of the Hispano ethnic subsociety and in softening their resistance against the forces of social change.

Penitente Brotherhoods. We have not yet completed the analysis of the role that religion played in the maintenance/dissolution of the Hispano ethnic group.

We have still to consider a sectarian movement within the Catholic church: the Penitentes. It is not their ostentatious and occasionally violent ceremonies that makes them so interesting to us, for these are only part of old Spanish traditions preserved here longer than in most other places because of the isolation of the country and the relatively weak controls that ecclesiastical and civil authorities have been able to exercise. Even before the American conquest, the secret brotherhoods of New Mexico Penitentes caused trouble to the Mexican church. The alien bishops and priests who came afterwards could not be expected to be more indulgent with the crude folkways and superstitions of the native peasants. When they felt themselves abandoned to the wiles of the conquerors: to oppression, fraudulent expropriation, and ruthless exploitation, the Penitentes became more recalcitrant against censure and discipline. At the height of their power, they could rightly have been described as an underground freedom movement against foreign domination. Later, they continued the struggle by taking an active role in party politics; political bosses and wealthy estate owners joined their lodges.

Despite the numerous conflicts between the brotherhoods and individual bishops and clergymen, the Penitentes continued to assert their orthodoxy and to consider themselves the champions of the Catholic church as well as of the Hispano people, which in their eyes were identical—a unity imperiled by alien interlopers and usurpers. Some of the native and even a few foreign priests recognized the potential of the movement for maintaining the Hispano ethnic group. Yet, in the same way as the church authorities had deprived the Hispanos of their natural leaders, they now neutralized and stunted a protest movement that was able to mobilize strong religious sentiments in support of national or, at least, nativistic goals.

TYPICAL CHANGES IN ETHNIC RELATIONS

The preceding historical outline has revealed marked changes in the relationship between the Hispanos of New Mexico and the American host society. During a first period after annexation, the internal social system of the regional subsociety continued to function very much as before. The small number of Anglos were integrated into the Hispano subsociety and were partially absorbed by its elite. American dominance was primarily political. In the following period of transition, the contacts between the Hispano subsociety and the host society were greatly multiplied. This was because the subsociety became engulfed by large masses of Americans and even some areas of compact settlements and some of the urban communities located within them were penetrated, and taken over.

Integration into the modern American economy and participation in the benefits of its expansion brought about far-reaching changes. Economic dominance by the host society was now added to political dominance, which became more pronounced and more direct. The cohesion of the Hispano subsociety and its power of resistance suffered when it was deprived of leadership. During a fifty-year period of transition, the Hispano regional subsociety was transformed into a primary ethnic group within the American host society. This applies to the majority of Hispanos who, in their compact rural settlements and country towns, continued to live under conditions typical of premodern, agrarian society. Others, however, who moved to "American" sections of the country experienced the same fate as, for instance, French-Canadian *habitants* moving to Toronto or Yankee City; they were transformed into secondary ethnic groups.

The processes of social change during the most recent period may be summed up as follows: Mass communications, temporary migration of laborers, military service, tourist traffic, economic interaction, participation in political parties and voluntary associations such as labor unions, cooperation with Federal agencies—these are some of the reasons for an increased communication and interaction with the host society. This has happened so widely that the ethnic group, taken as a whole, has lost its relative independence, self-sufficiency, and viability. The ecological divisions have become blurred as the Hispanos became steadily more integrated into the American social structure. Superior wealth, power, and prestige are, for all practical purposes, confined to the Anglos. The center of interethnic conflict has shifted to the middle classes where Anglos find many more opportunities than Hispanos, whose principal chances of social advancement are in the fields of politics and education. The lower classes continue to be composed mostly of Hispano farmers and laborers.

The Hispanos themselves have accepted American social definitions. They now strive as individuals to improve their lot within the framework of American society. They resent discrimination, but they have internalized, and accept as valid, the general principles according to which social rewards are supposed to be distributed in American society. Their handicap is not only due to prejudice and discrimination. Because of the poor instruction in their public schools, they remain ill-prepared for life in a modern society. Up to now (the time this survey was completed in 1960), few of them possess the qualifications recognized as indispensable for social acceptance and upward mobility.

The mood of the host society has also changed with the years. Forgotten is the birthright of the Hispanos who are now viewed in the same way as any other ethnic group of foreign origin to be integrated as rapidly as possible into the melting pot. If, in the formative period of American national society, political domination and economic exploitation were the immediate goal, cultural "imperialism" has now been added, which is no longer satisfied with accommodation and submission but demands uniformity and homogeneity. Even this standard of American society seems to have been accepted by most Hispanos, who do not see any particular value in the maintenance of the ethnic group or in the preservation of their culture; in any case, they do not see much realistic hope for it. There are still rural areas where the Hispano social system functions to some extent; but since the loss of its leaders and economic basis, dissolution seems to be the inevitable outcome.

We must still be careful in speaking of "dissolution." For the Hispanos have not only preserved their Spanish language and many cultural traditions, but ethnic differentiation is felt as strongly as ever; there is as yet little *commensalitas* or *connubium,* at least in the broad lower and middle classes. What has really happened is the transformation of a primary into a secondary ethnic group. The Hispanos have evolved from constituting a portion of Mexican society under American domination, first into a viable Hispano subsociety within the American national society, and finally into Spanish-speaking Americans who, because of their ethnic background, are not placed on an equal footing with other Americans.

A European Parallel Case:
The South Tyrolese Germans

In Europe, the emergence of ethnic groups has been more generally than in former colonies a consequence of annexation.[1,2] Among the numerous instances that have given rise to the nationality and minority problems typical of the Old World, South Tyrol has been selected for three reasons: (1) the situation bears a striking resemblance to New Mexico; (2) conditions in the Austrian parent and Italian host society are already familiar to the readers from Part II; (3) while the majority of primary ethnic groups in Central Europe have been dissolved following major political and economic changes or by violent means such as expulsion or genocide, the problem of South Tyrol is of current interest.

HISTORY

Although we shall confine ourselves to a few salient points that support or supplement previous findings, we cannot avoid mentioning some early facts of the country's history. The questions of birthright and of changes in the ethnic composition have played a considerable role in the ideological controversy over the legitimacy of conflicting claims to that part of Tyrol which, after World

---

[1]This secton is based on empirical materials adapted from Leidlmaier, 1958. See also Pan, 1971.
[2]The assumption is widespread among American social scientists generalizing on interethnic relations that annexation is typically a result of military action directly affecting a given territory. As often as not, however, foreign territories have been acquired by dynastic succession (donation, inheritance, or marriage), treaty ending a far-off war, negotiation, or purchase.

War I, was annexed by Italy. In Roman days the Alpine region, later included in the German principality of Tyrol, was inhabited by the Rhaetian descendants of Illyrian, Etruscan, and Celtic tribes, the forbears of the Ladins who became Romanized in speech and culture. Eventually the country was invaded by the Bavarians. In the thirteenth century Tyrol was politically united and was in 1363 acquired, through negotiation with the prince's widow, by the Hapsburgs, under whose rule it remained, with short interruptions, until 1918. Once the ethnic composition had been stablized, the southern part, called Trentino, was Italian in speech and culture, the Ladin peasantry was confined to a few valleys in the Dolomite mountains, and the major part, reaching north from about the city of Bozen, was solidly German. "South Tyrol" was nothing more than a geographical term applied to the German and Ladin-speaking regions south of the Brenner pass and the watershed.

National Conflict

Before World War I, South Tyrol was one of the many agrarian sections of Austria whose overall societal and economic structure, which we have described earlier, was well on the way to modernization. For some decades nationalism and ethnic conflicts had played a considerable role in Tyrolese affairs. This was mainly because the Italian risorgimento movement had made the Trentino a prime target of its irredentist aims. Even at that period, Italian nationalists laid claim to South Tyrol for various reasons: history, geography, and, above all, because of the assumed ethnic origin of the population. In actual fact, before World War I the resident population of South Tyrol was divided between over 221,000 Germans and 9,300 Ladins, while the Italians numbered no more than 7,000. The proportion in 1921 was approximately 203,000 : 9,900 : 20,300. The absolute and relative increase in the Italian population was mainly due to the replacement of Austrian by Italian civil servants and state employees.

In the Peace Treaties the Germans of South Tyrol, like those elsewhere in the defunct Austrian monarchy, were denied the right of national self-determination. Moreover, as a member of the victorious Alliance, Italy refused to enact legal provisions for the protection of national minorities such as had been imposed upon the successor states of Austria-Hungary. Instead they stuck steadfastly to the principles of demotic nationalism, which legitimized efforts to homogenize the entire state population including that of the annexed territories. The Germans of South Tyrol, on the other hand, upheld the principles of ethnic and restorative nationalism and continued to identify with rump Austria. From the beginning, the symbolism of the word "German" involved ambiguities that tended to make ethnic identification problematical. The South Tyrolese Germans hoped for a return to the (new) Austria whose population was not only, without a shadow of doubt, ethnically German, but by virtue of the right to national self-determination, clamored for a union with the German nation-state—the Deutsches Reich. The least to which the South Tyrolese felt themselves entitled was national autonomy within the Italian nation-state.

Under the rule of Fascism, Italy embarked upon a policy of enforced assimilation which eventually defeated its purpose. The German ethnic group was forcibly deprived of its symbols, such as place-names, landmarks, and folk costumes. More important, it was deprived of its separate institutions and voluntary associations; the school served exclusively the propagation of Italian language and culture; agents of the state from governor to postal clerks were Italians. The most effective instrument of nationalization, however, proved to be industrialization, which was initiated and subsidized by the Italian authorities. Its irreversible result was the partition of South Tyrol into an agrarian German and Ladin section, and a growing industrial section concentrated around the city of Bozen, which to this day has continued to attract thousands of laborers from the less-developed regions of Italy. As elsewhere, industrialization also fostered urbanization. Bozen, the capital and commercial center of the province, and Meran, an international health resort, were the principal targets of the rural-urban migration, mostly by Italians, while the original German population actually suffered losses through out-migration. On the other hand, few Italians have been able to settle as farmers; and even the Italian businessmen and artisans who invaded the coutnry-towns were unable to change their German character. If we consider the situation as it prevailed in about 1960, the division into a German agrarian and an Italian industrial section has remained very pronounced, *commensalitas* and *connubium* being the exception outside the modernized cities. Even more than their Austrian brethren in North Tyrol, the South Tyrolese Germans have stubbornly resisted urbanization and industrialization; their entire culture is strongly oriented toward the folk traditions of the peasants who represent the solid core of the ethnic group.

When it was seen that industrialization rapidly increased the proportion of Italians but failed to break German resistance against any form of Italianization, Hitler and Mussolini agreed in 1939 to evacuate the entire ethnic group. From both sides massive pressure was put on the South Tyrolese Germans to opt for emigration to the Third Reich. Eventually 83 percent did (including a considerable proportion of the Ladins). Before the breakdown of Fascist Italy and the occupation of South Tyrol by the German armies in 1943, 74,500 had actually left, mainly those employed in transportation, domestic services, trade, industry, and in the hotel and restaurant business. Of the farmers, however, only 9 percent actually emigrated. In this they were valiantly supported by the Catholic clergy who, ever since the annexation, were foremost in championing the preservation of the ethnic group.

Regional Autonomy. At the end of World War II, the Allies hesitated to humiliate the defeated Italians further by restoring South Tyrol to resurrected

Austria. They nevertheless took a hand in bringing about an agreement between Austria and Italy according to which South Tyrol was to be granted autonomy. Moreover, those who had left the country under the Hitler-Mussolini pact were allowed to return: about 21,000 actually did. By 1953, the ethnic composition was as follows: Over 214,000 Germans (and 12,000 Ladins making common cause with them) stood in opposition to over 114,000 Italians. To protect the Italian minority and economic and political interests, the two provinces of South Tyrol and Trentino were joined to form one autonomous region, despite the vehement protest of the South Tyrolese Germans and their Austrian protectors, who interpreted the agreement between Austria and Italy as guaranteeing autonomy to South Tyrol by herself. This and other controversies over the rights of the Germans in South Tyrol and their treatment by Italy has led to much social unrest, even acts of terrorism, until, in 1969, a package deal was offered by the Italian government, which the representatives of the South-Tyrolese Germans accepted by a small majority.

Conflicting Claims. Five decades of oppression have cemented the ethnic group into a viable and articulate subsociety whose predominantly agrarian character has been better preserved than perhaps anywhere else among Germans in Europe. German speech and culture flourish; the solidarity of the ethnic group benefits from a complete set of separate institutions, a galaxy of voluntary associations, and articulate political leadership. As before, national conflict is reflected in the incompatible definitions of the situation. In a test administered in 1960–61 by Doob (1962) to South Tyrolese schoolchildren, the following reasons were mentioned by both Italians and Germans to substantiate their claim to remain in South Tyrol: destiny, justice, superiority, priority, duration, nativity, living space, economic necessity; by Italians alone: legality, geography, achievement, accomplished fact, power, military necessity; by Germans alone: freedom, contribution to human values, ethnicity, solidarity, sentimental attachment, majority, efficient utilization of resources. This illustrates how both ethnic groups justify their contradictory claims by using a set of identical arguments based on assumed historical facts. The Italians put more emphasis on such criteria as legality, power, and geography, whereas the Germans on criteria derived from the principles of ethnic nationalism.

The younger people, who have no memory of the Austrian past, now tend to identify with the national society, politically organized in the German Federal Republic, where many of them go to study and work. A survey undertaken under the auspices of the Munich Sociology Department (Francis, Kellermann, 1963) has also revealed that the majority of middle-class high-school students has a strong preference for rural life and seems to see the culture of the ethnic group epitomized by the traditions of the mountain peasants. In view of the international situation and the inevitable decline of agriculture, such basic value orientations appear unrealistic. On the other hand, the young generation is bilingual, exposed to Italian cultural influences and the social forces of modernization. Opportunities for advancement within the German section of the country are limited. Now that the pressures of forced assimilation are at least mitigated, resistance against modernizing trends (including industrialization) is lowered. One may ask whether, under these circumstances, the primary character of the ethnic group will be maintained in the same way as in the past, or whether it will be transformed into a secondary ethnic group similar to the New-Mexican Hispanos.

CONCLUSIONS TO SECTION B

Primary ethnic groups are likely to emerge under the following conditions:

1. When there are marked differences between host and parent society so that their respective members can be readily differentiated in ethnic terms; for only then will the population, which has been transferred, remain socially identifiable for any length of time with the parent rather than the host society.
2. If there is resistance against nationalization, it may arise either among the population transferred or among significant sections of the host society; both kinds of resistance tend to reinforce each other.
3. Resistance against nationalization by and of itself, however, does not suffice for the actual emergence of a primary ethnic group; for this requires that the population transferred reconstitute themselves as a relatively closed and viable subsociety. Thus, it must be sufficiently large and sufficiently integrated. It will be transformed into a primary ethnic group to the extent to which it responds collectively to the new situation and takes appropriate collective action to meet it. This would entail the organization of separate political parties, measures to strengthen their own economic independence, and above all, refusal to extend *commensalitas* and *connubium* to members of the host society.
4. The chances of collective resistance to absorption into the host society, and consequently of being transformed into a primary ethnic group and of maintaining itself as a separate subsociety, are obviously increased if the population in question can satisfy basic economic and social needs without reliance on the resources of the host society. This is more likely if the group in question is of the agrarian type or has at least a strong agrarian core. Economic and social self-sufficiency is much less likely to be maintained under industrial conditions, as these characteristically require a more than regional economic cooperation, a considerable degree of spatial mobility, integration into a larger social structure with its mechanisms of

social advancement, acceptance of common cultural values and norms—in short, because social relations cannot be wholly confined to *commercium*.

Furthermore, agrarian societies based on mechanical solidarity can be fragmented almost *ad libitum*. Therefore, the transfer of agricultural settlements from one political unit to another is a relatively simple matter insofar as the social structure of such a settlement can remain unchanged for the time being. Industrial societies, on the other hand, cannot be so fragmented because they constitute an intricate web of social interdependences. If, therefore, ties are disrupted by political action, the total social and economic fabric of the portion cut off from its original social setting is disturbed and must be reconstructed in the host society by way of secondary ethnic group formation.

Although rural habitat seems to be a prerequisite for the emergence of primary ethnic groups, not all rural ethnic groups necessarily conform to the primary type. If the agricultural economy of the host society has been commercialized and/or industrialized to such an extent that the agrarian character of its rural sections has been lost, we may expect that migrants to farming areas will behave in the same way as do migrants to industrial cities, and will tend to form secondary ethnic groups.

There is, nevertheless, a difference between the conditions under which settlement in rural and urban communities takes place. Rural settlement is liable to impart a certain "primary" character to ethnic groups formed even in "modernized" rural areas, and to modify the subsequent processes of maintenance/dissolution. As will be seen in Section C, the laws governing the formation, maintenance, and dissolution of secondary ethnic groups become fully operative only under the condition of unhampered individual mobility. Migratory farm labor excepted, however, the ecological concentration of ethnics migrating to rural areas depends on the availability of relatively large parcels of contiguous farmland. State or private agencies controlling its sale are in a position to prevent or promote the formation of ethnic communities. Yet land may be bought by deliberate design in such a way that immigrants of a particular ethnic origin are directed to a definite locality. Once established ethnic settlements of farmers also tend to be more permanent than urban subcommunities because mobility is reduced by the greater difficulty involved in the selling of farm property and in establishing oneself economically in some other locality.

5. Annexation is more likely to lead to the formation of primary ethnic groups, migration to that of secondary ethnic groups. The transfer from parent to host society resulting from annexation is likely to involve viable regional subsocieties, while under modern conditions, immigration generally involves individuals or small groups. But migrations may also result in

primary ethnic groups if a population (1) had already formed an ethnic subsociety of the parent society; (2) is collectively transferred to the host society; (3) is allowed to establish agricultural settlements on contiguous tracts of land; (4) is able to restore its institutions and social structure upon arrival; and (5) enjoys legally or factually a considerable amount of local self-administration and cultural autonomy over a prolonged period thereafter.

Primary ethnic groups may be formed in yet another way. When a major dissident group is given a chance (1) to occupy land as yet unsettled; (2) to establish a complete set of separate institutions; (3) to remain isolated for some time from the parent society; and (4) when upon renewed contact the relationship is one of antagonism and hostility, there is a tendency for the group in question to become integrated into the national society as a quasi-ethnic subsociety. Such a situation may arise only before nationalization and industrialization have run their course. Modernization tends to retransform such a quasi-ethnic into a purely religious group, unless the contrast effect permits a definite differentiation to be upheld between the regional subsociety and the host society—as was the case with the Manitoba Mennonites but not with the American Mormons.

Thus, the probability that either primary or secondary ethnic groups will result from population transfers depends neither on whether the transfer has been brought about by migration or annexation, nor on rural/urban habitat as such. *The key factor is variation in the typical relationships between the transferees and their societal environment.* Primary ethnic groups are transferred as viable corporate units and continue to function in the host society as more-or-less comprehensive subsocieties able to satisfy all the basic social needs of their members; accordingly, association with members of the host society is likely to remain limited in all dimensions. Secondary ethnic groups, on the other hand, are formed in the host society in response to the social situation with which individual transferees are confronted; such groups, therefore, constitute segmental social systems. Social relations of the ethnics as pertain to *commercium* are largely with the host society, whereas relations pertaining to *commensalitas* and *connubium* tend to be confined to ethnics of the same origin. To this problem we turn next.

REFERENCES

Burma, John H., *The Spanish-Speaking Groups in the United States.* Durham, N.C.: Duke University Press, 1956.
Doob, Leonard W., "South Tyrol: An Introduction to the Psychological Syndrome of Nationalism," *Public Opinion Quarterly,* XXVI (1962), pp. 172–184.

Francis, E. K., "Religious Pluralism in a Peasant Community," *Religious Education*, (1955), pp. 23–26.

——, "Multiple Intergroup Relations in the Upper Rio Grande Region," *American Sociological Review*, XXI (1956a), pp. 84–87.

——, "Padre Martinez: A New Mexican Myth," *New Mexico Historial Review*, XXXI (1956b), pp. 265–269.

——, Paul Kellermann, et al., *Eine Umfrage unter Jugendlichen in Südtirol*. Unpublished manuscript, Soziologisches Institut der Universität München (Munich, 1963).

Leidlmaier, Adolf, *Bevölkerung und Wirtschaft in Südtirol*. Tiroler Wirtschaftsstudien. Schriftenreihe der Jubiläumsstiftung der Kammer der gewerblichen Wirtschaft für Tirol. Innsbruck: Universitätsverlag Wagner, 1958.

Pan, Christoph, *Südtirol als volkliches Problem: Grundriess einer Südtiroler Ethno-Soziologie*. Ethnos: Schriftenreihe der Forschungsstelle für Nationalitäten- und Sprachenfragen, Marburg/Lahn, Vol. 9. Wien: Wilhelm Braumüller, 1971.

C. Secondary Ethnic Groups

INTRODUCTION

Migrations of individuals over long distances, usually but not necessarily across international boundary lines, create conditions favorable to the formation of secondary ethnic groups. Yet similar conditions may be brought about by other factors. In Section B we have found instances in which primary ethnic groups were transformed into secondary ethnic groups because of endogenous changes, such as modernization, shifts in the balance of political power, transculturation, or loss of leadership. Even annexation may lead directly to the formation of secondary rather than primary ethnic groups; this seems to be the case when the population that is being transferred from one national society to another conforms to the modern industrial rather than to the premodern agrarian type.[1]

In this section we are confining ourselves to secondary ethnic groups that have been formed as a result of migration. This is the most common type found in the United States and in other highly modernized nations. Many of the ethnic groups discussed in Section A, particulary in Chapters 12 and 13, belong to this type. Again, not all migrations lead to ethnic group formation. In Section D we shall tackle the problem of what happens to ethnics who, after their immigration, do not form distinctive subgroups.

Before we can specify the general conditions under which secondary ethnic groups are formed by migrants, we should recall that large-scale migrations to modern societies have mainly been the outcome of industrialization and nationalization. As far as the receiving society was concerned, the expansion and modernization of the economy created a pressing demand for labor which could not be met domestically; it also increased the society's capacity to admit large numbers of people trying to escape the consequences of nationalization in their parent society. There are, however, other reasons for migration. Sometimes it is brought about through the use of physical force or the threat of violence. More common, however, is the voluntary migration that has been triggered off by social forces of push and pull.

---

[1]Although we have not found sufficient empirical material to study such a situation more closely, we are under the impression that after the annexation of Eupen-Malmédy by Belgium, for instance, or during the temporary French rule over the Saarland there were no indications of primary ethnic group formation among the German populations of those territories.

People are usually motivated to migrate because they are dissatisfied with conditions at home and/or because they expect to find more favorable conditions abroad. Their motives are sometimes expressed in terms of freedom from oppression. Occasionally, they are forced to leave at the point of the bayonet or because their lives and liberty are in grave danger. In other cases, nothing more is involved than a desire to escape military service or penal sanctions or the wish for new experience and adventure. More frequently, poverty and starvation or the necessity to care for destitute relatives plays a major role, or just the hope of finding the "pot at the end of the rainbow." For whatever reason individual migrants leave or chose a particular destination—and there are a great variety of motives—once they arrive their immediate and most pressing concerns are economic: to make a living and, in time, to better their lot. Thus we come to the conclusion that *economic factors are of paramount importance in secondary ethnic-group formation, whilst in primary ethnic-group formation political factors take precedence.*

CONDITIONS OF SECONDARY ETHNIC GROUP FORMATION

Ethnics who, in their quest for economic satisfaction, are confronted not only with the handicap of an unfamiliar social setting but also with the resistance of the natives, are inclined to seek the support of people with a familiar background and similar experience. In addition, they feel the need for more intimate social relationships on the level of *commensalitas* and *connubium* which, as a rule, are denied to them, at least on equal terms, by the host society. Finally, they have an urge to create for themselves a more familiar milieu than the host society can offer. The need for mutual aid and the desire for intimate social relations and a familiar social environment are likely to lead to an association with fellow countrymen and consequently to the formation of secondary ethnic groups *if the following conditions are fulfilled:*

1. There must be sufficient opportunities of communication between dispersed ethnics and sufficient freedom of movement to permit the concentration of a relatively large number of them in one locality.
2. Communication with the parent society must be restricted and the chance of returning home, either for short intervals or permanently, must be limited, so that the ethnics can find satisfaction of their basic needs only within the host society (which also includes all the subgroups of which it is composed).
3. The economy and institutional framework of the host society must be sufficiently elastic to accommodate considerable numbers of ethnics in one locality, and to permit them to function as a segmental subgroup of the host society.

NATIONAL CULTURE AND THE FORMATION OF ETHNIC GROUPS

The opinion is widespread that ethnic problems have their source in a clash of cultures: the culture of the immigrants' country of origin, on the one hand, and that of the receiving country, on the other. By implication, this suggests that the formation, maintenance, and dissolution of ethnic groups may be explained in terms of differences between the cultures of the parent and the host society. This viewpoint raises two difficulties. One concerns the concept of national culture that is derived from Herder's and Hegel's notion of "Volksgeist"; in this sense one speaks of a specific Polish, French, Italian, Russian, or American culture. *In the context of interethnic relations, such a generalized concept of national culture has negligible explanatory value; it neither lends itself easily to operationalization nor does it distinguish sufficiently between the manifold subcultural levels within a complex society.* We have shown earlier that typical differences between premodern, that is, prenational and preindustrial, societies on the one hand, and modern societies that are subject to the processes of nationalization, on the other, are of strategic importance in interethnic relations. These differences, however, are not linked definitely to any particular national cultures.

Furthermore, empirical evidence reveals that no constant relationship exists between variations in the behavior of different ethnic groups and specific differences in the "national culture" of their parent societies. In many instances, immigrants of the same national origin behave quite differently, while the behavior patterns of ethnic groups having another national origin resemble each other rather closely. Thus, the behavior of Polish immigrants who came to the United States, say in 1880, may be more similar to that of Italian immigrants who arrived at about the same time than to that of Poles who immigrated half a century later. In fact, Polish immigrants who arrived at the same time often behaved quite differently, some forming ethnic groups while others found their niche directly in American society at large without associating themselves with any Polish community. By contrast, the secondary ethnic groups formed by immigrants of quite different origin—Poles, Hungarians, Italians—may run through the same typical "life cycle"; this fact has been indicated by Warner in his study of Yankee City (Warner, 1941). As will be shown in the following chapters, *the crucial factors in ethnic group formation are not unique differences between particular "national" cultures but typical structural differences between parent and host society.*

STRUCTURAL DIFFERENCES BETWEEN PARENT AND HOST SOCIETIES

Most of the immigrants to the United States who eventually have formed secondary ethnic groups did have two things in common: (1) they had been peasants in Europe, more often poor landless folk than independent farmers; and (2) they were transferred to highly industrialized areas of America. This suggests that in speaking of their parent and host societies respectively we must not think in terms of an entire national society or a generalized national culture area. For at this period American society still comprised large sections in which the prevailing premodern and preindustrial conditions resembled those of the European peasant. Yet some of the European countries from which the immigrants came were becoming modernized and industrialized. Thus, we must focus our attention on the cultural type of local community and regional subsociety that constituted the immediate and socially significant milieu of the migrants, both in the country of origin and in the receiving country. We must picture the conditions under which the European peasants had been living in Poland, Italy, or Hungary. We must base our judgment not on what we know of modern Poland, Italy, or Hungary, but rather on what we have learned of the old Hispano core in New Mexico. And we must keep in mind that the European peasants who subsequently formed secondary ethnic groups settled in American cities where industrialization and modernization were farthest advanced.

Basic Theorems

In the following chapters we shall single out some of the factors that seem to influence the formation, maintenance, and dissolution of secondary ethnic groups. We shall proceed from the following assumptions:

1. Specific differences between the generalized national cultures of parent and host society may safely be neglected because they do not appear to be definitely linked to observable differences in the typical behavior of ethnics and ethnic groups.
2. The crucial factor in the formation of secondary ethnic groups and their subsequent behavior is to be sought in the difference between the premodern agrarian type of their respective parent societies and the modern industrial type of their host societies.
3. In speaking of parent and host societies we must focus attention on the particular section of a national society in which the migrants participate, especially on the local communities and regional subsocieties that constitute their immediate social environment.

PLAN OF SECTION C

To demonstrate the validity and heuristic value of these theorems we shall make use of a kind of *ex post facto* experimental design without however attempting any quantification. Our quasi-experiment rests on the selection of comparable cases which permit us to hold some factors constant while varying others. To test the theorem concerning the irrelevance of "national culture" we shall show that (1) the behavior of ethnics of Polish origin follows the same pattern in the United States, Germany, and Belgium; and (2) in the United States ethnics of different national origin (Italians, Hungarians, and so on) behave quite similarly to ethnics of Polish origin. In the first case we shall keep constant the "national culture" of the parent society of ethnics while varying the "national culture" of the host societies; in the second case the "national culture" of the host society (America) will be held constant while varying that of the parent societies. The result in both cases is the same type of secondary ethnic group behavior.

With regard to the theorem concerning the relevance of the structural differences between parent and host society it will be shown that in the cases studied, secondary ethnic groups have emerged when the host societies (the United States, Belgium, Germany) were of the industrial type, and when the ethnics, regardless of national origin, were of peasant origin.

Other cases to be treated in chapter 19, however, deviate from this general prototype of ethnic group formation. Among the Polish soldiers and refugees who were settled in England after World War II we shall find somewhat similar behavior patterns as among the other groups studied in Section C, although these immigrants do not conform to the peasant type; in addition, both parent and host societies have an analogous modern structure. In a similar manner the German expellees from Eastern Europe who were settled in Western Germany, as well as the Poles from Eastern Poland who, at about the same time, were settled in the Western Territories of Poland, tended to form quasi-ethnic subgroups within the German and Polish national society respectively, although remaining within one and the same national culture area. Here parent and host society appear to be identical. As these last three instances of ethnic group formation are not covered by our second theorem, they will require some supplementary hypotheses.

R E F E R E N C E

Warner, Lloyd W., and Paul S. Lunt, *The Social Life of a Modern Community*. Yankee City Series, Vol. I. New Haven: Yale University Press, 1941.

The Formation
of Secondary
Ethnic Groups:
The European
Peasant in America
17

In the United States secondary ethnic groups have emerged in the main since the conclusion of the Civil War, at a period when processes of nationalization and industrialization became fully effective. This time of transition also marks the dividing line between what has been called the "old" and the "new immigration." To the old immigration belong those ethnic elements, mainly German and Scandinavian, who arrived at a time when American society was still predominantly agrarian, and before it had clearly developed into a modern nation. Most of them took part in the colonization of what became the Middle West, along with the old stock American pioneers from the Atlantic Seaboard and New England States. Together they built the new American nation whose heartland was, for a century, those central regions of the country where descendants of the old immigration were most heavily represented. In cases where distinctive ethnic communities were formed, these were mostly of the primary type. Although the Irish chronologically belong to the old immigration, they conform in type to the new immigration; for, unlike other immigrants who came before the Civil War, they were deliberately directed by Catholic church authorities to the early urban industrial sections where conditions compelled them to form secondary ethnic groups.

During the period of the new immigration, which began in the 1870s and continued until the early years of World War I, nearly twenty million European peasants were attracted to the rapidly expanding industrial cities of the country, and once again threw out of gear an emerging national society which, only a few years earlier, had been reconstituted and consolidated in the cauldron of the Civil War. The natives countered the threat to social stability by a general suspicion of foreigners and a resistance to close association with them. When it became apparent that the majority of immigrants had come to stay and would have to be fully integrated into American society, the same homogenizing pressures were brought to bear upon them which we have found to be a concommitant of nation-building in general. After all, the ideology of Americanization and the "melting pot" is nothing else than the American version of demotic nationalism. American nationalism demanded the undivided loyalty of the immigrants as did the risorgimento nationalism, embraced at about the same period by their European parent societies. The propagation of national ideas which, in their practical consequences, were incompatible, created tensions and conflicts between the ethnics and their hosts that retarded the integration of the ethnics into the American national society.

In earlier sections of Part III our presentation followed this pattern: Starting with the description of a particular case, we proceeded to its analysis in order to arrive at some more general theoretical insight. In this and the following chapter we propose a somewhat different approach. It would be tedious first to digest a great variety of case studies on different European ethnic groups in America, which have already been adequately summarized by such authors as Schermerhorn (Schermerhorn, 1949; cf. also Francis, 1956; Handlin, 1959). For this reason we shall confine the descriptive part of our investigation to a synopsis of what has been found common to all these groups by many scholars writing on the subject. As a type case, however, we shall use the Polish peasant in America, and here again we shall rely heavily on a classical work by W. I. Thomas and F. Znaniecki (1958).

Before approaching the problem of secondary ethnic-group formation in the United States, three stages in this process should be clearly distinguished: (1) a preparatory stage lasting a few years after the first arrival of ethnics from a particular country; (2) a period of settling down permanently in American communities, during which ethnic groups and subcommunities were formed on the local level; and (3) a final stage during which alliances were organized to tie the local groups together into a "supraterritorial" or subsocietal system operating within American society at large.

THE PREPARATORY STAGE

The general background of the type of immigrants that is under scrutiny may be summed up as follows: The first arrivals were characteristically males; as they were mostly illiterate and unskilled (except in agriculture), they could only be employed as manual workers. They were propertyless strangers, unfamiliar with the language and culture of the host society. Only a minimum of accommodation, though, was required to integrate them into the industrial economy at the bottom of the occupational scale. As most of them expected to return eventually to their native villages with the savings made in America, they could hardly object to their hosts treating them as foreigners of temporary residence. The immigrants, who usually arrived singly or in small bands, tended to associate with chance acquaintances with whom they could converse in their mother tongue and share common interests. Frequently, males of the same ethnic background lived in cheap boardinghouses situated in the blighted districts of the city where they had found employment.

Soon, however, other countrymen followed. The reasons for this chain migration were mainly twofold. Immigrants often made a conscious effort to encourage relatives and acquaintances to join them. Moreover, favorable reports to the people back home were publicized in their native villages and adjacent areas, and influenced others to follow suit. Earlier immigrants, in their turn, welcomed any new arrivals from the Old Country as a relief from the isolation and loneliness that they had suffered in a strange and unfriendly environment. As soon as the immigrants realized that their stay in America would be more permanent than they had anticipated or feared, they sent for wives and children or asked their parents to arrange for a bride willing to join them in the New World. In this way people hailing from the same European region (even from one town) frequently concentrated in particular American communities.

THE FORMATIVE STAGE

Once sizable numbers of immigrant families with the same ethnic background had settled down in a given locality, the stage was set for the formation of a distinctive ethnic subgroup. As opportunities for extending mutual aid and also for more association on the level of *commensalitas* and *connubium* multiplied, a web of informal relationships began to tie together immigrants from one country. Thus, their sense of ethnic identity and solidarity was strengthened, and they were all the more ostensibly set apart from the host society and from other ethnic groups. As they tended to collect in one locality, concentrations of ethnics were soon found in particular streets and neighborhoods. In time, one ethnic group would occupy an entire city district, which had been abandoned by other residents because of its changed character. In these areas social life assumed a striking resemblance to that which the ethnics had led in their Old World villages. Their native tongue was generally used in public; restaurants, saloons, and stores catered to their tastes and offered additional chances for casual encounters.

Voluntary Associations. Informal social relationships were supplemented by voluntary associations. These were not alien to the peasant immigrants, for they had been introduced in many parts of Europe when, in the course of modernization, the rural community had lost its comprehensive social functions. In the New World such organizations, however, had even to assume functions which, in the Old Country, had been the responsibility of the extended kinship group, the church, or the state. Mutual benefit societies, which had been organized during the preparatory stage and whose original purpose had been to provide a measure of social security, now expanded their scope to include convivial gatherings and recreational activities such as had been offered by Old World village inns. Eventually, the entire social life of the ethnic group outside the family became focused on what has been popularly called "the Society" (or a set of similar voluntary associations). These "societies" were particularly needed in America where the state has long been reluctant to undertake subsidiary functions and where the disestablished churches themselves often assumed the character of voluntary associations.

In point of fact, the ethnic "societies" were instrumental in the establishment of "national" parishes and denominational schools in which the mother tongue of the ethnics was at least partly used. The significance of parish and parish school for ethnic subcommunities has been discussed at length in earlier chapters. The necessity to take care of and to support churches and schools strengthened the sense of common purpose and solidarity among the members of the "society" who represented the active core of the ethnic subcommunity. The proliferation of voluntary associations—in a large parish there might be as many as seventy associations having an average of ten officers or committee members—provided a chance to attain a position of prestige for almost every active community member. Overlapping club membership intensified the network of communication and interaction encompassing the entire local group.

Supraterritorial Organizations. As the number of ethnic subcommunities increased, alliances of local associations were organized for the whole of the United States. Because we have not yet had occasion to deal with this type of ethnic institution, an explanation is appropriate here. Although voluntary associations and other institutions of a basically voluntary character, such as church or parish school, mainly served economic and "cultural" interests on the local level, supraterritorial federations were deliberately created by ethnic leaders primarily for political reasons.

By way of example we shall single out the Polish alliances. A first attempt was made to assemble delegates from various parishes to discuss common problems. It failed mainly because local interests were too different to offer many opportunities for common action. Of lasting success, however, was the Polish National Alliance, founded in 1880, which reflected the spread of risorgimento nationalism in Europe. Polish peasants coming from premodern agrarian sections of Europe had not yet been affected by the national movement which had already taken hold of the upper classes and above all of the educated middle classes. Immigrants belonging to these strata were mainly responsible for spreading nationalist ideas of the parent society to the Polish communities in America. When they organized the Polish National Association, they conceived of the Poles in America as the "Fourth Province" of Poland, with the responsibility of contributing to the reunion of the three other "provinces" in Russia, Prussia, and Austria into a single nation-state.

As a reaction to liberal and anticlerical tendencies in the Polish National Alliance, priests and other Catholic leaders founded the Polish Roman Catholic Union. Its purpose was less the creation of a *Polonia Americana* than the preservation of Polish traditions, which had always been also Catholic traditions; this to forestall the Americanization of the Poles in America, which was thought to lead inevitably to their secularization. The Alliance of Polish Socialists, finally, was considered a branch of socialism in Poland rather than a federation of Polish communities in America. Its avowed goal was the liberation of Poland and the return of all Poles living in exile. Although the intellectual level of its members was high, it had no great appeal to the masses of American Poles. For these had come to consider themselves permanent residents in America rather than temporary exiles; moreover, improving economic conditions reduced their interest in the socialist point of view.

Another institution of a supraterritorial scope was the foreign-language press. It was either directly supported by the supraterritorial organizations, or its publishers and editors played a leading role in them. It served local ethnic groups as a bulletin and clearing center of information about Polish activities throughout the United States. By facilitating communications between the several ethnic communities and between scattered Poles who would otherwise have lost contact with their fellow countrymen, the press strengthened ethnic solidarity, aided the formation of a Polish-American public opinion, and initiated common actions in the entire Polish subsociety in America. In addition, it provided an important channel through which news from the parent society reached the ethnic group. Like the ethnic school, it promoted literacy, helped to preserve the native language and cultural heritage, mediated ideas of nationalism, and generated national consciousness and pride. Although the foreign-language press helped to create a measure of ethnic particularism in America, it also contributed to the adjustment of ethnics to the host society by interpreting its culture and by familiarizing the ethnics with new developments in a manner that could readily be understood by them.

FACTORS INVOLVED IN GROUP FORMATION

In turning to an examination of the factors involved in the formation of secondary ethnic groups, we are once again confronted with the questions: Why do ethnics from one country prefer to associate with each other, and why do they eventually tend to flock in particular neighborhoods and districts of American cities? It is best to begin with an analysis of the sociopsychological needs of immigrants. By and large, people tend to satisfy their affiliative needs by associating with those available in a given situation who are most familiar to them in terms of language and culture. This permits the most intimate relationships and the most vivid sentiments of solidarity, which is particularly true in situations that engender anxiety (Schachter, 1959). Such is certainly the case when immigrants arrive in a foreign country either singly or in relatively small bands.

Strangers in general, and uneducated peasants in particular, develop specific psychological needs:

1. On the cognitive level, an unfamiliar and thus unstructured situation, especially if it is felt to threaten survival, creates an immediate and urgent need for information and orientation. This presupposes not only unambiguous means of communication with potential informants and interpreters of the situation but also the likelihood that the informants have an intimate knowledge and understanding of the social and cultural background of the questioner.
2. On the instrumental level, a stranger is usually confronted with numerous and persistent exigencies with which he cannot hope to cope without assistance. Yet in a heterogeneous industrialized urban community, cooperation and mutual aid are rarely extended to complete strangers.
3. The emotional needs of immigrants are perhaps still more important. Many of these cannot be properly satisfied except where relationships of considerable intimacy already exist or can readily be activated. By way of example, we may mention the desire to share new and exciting experiences, to relieve tensions and anxieties, to find comfort and consolation for the profound personal crisis experienced by most immigrants due to culture shock and sudden loss of status (not just high status but any status at all), to offer and receive affection, to find response to the expression of feeling.
4. There is a wide area of expressive behavior that requires collective action: religious, esthetic, recreational.
5. Isolation and a strange environment bring about the compelling need of new social anchorages, status definitions, and social security, which the host society is rarely willing or able to offer immediately.

Migrants to a strange society will tend to seek satisfaction of their needs in a manner that has become familiar to them in the course of their early socialization and enculturation. Consequently, they will make an effort to create a social setting for themselves in which this will be possible. They will try to persuade relatives and acquaintances to join them; failing this, they will look for suitable substitutes among fellow countrymen who, although previously unknown to them, are equipped to understand their needs and to respond to them in familiar ways. Concentration of large numbers in compact settlements is important to them, as this provides opportunities for the establishment of familiar services, agencies, and institutions enabling them to lead as full a communal life as possible, without having to rely on corresponding services and institutions offered by the host society.

The manner in which members of the host society define the situation is as important for the development of interethnic relations as the needs and attitudes of the ethnics themselves. Migrant laborers were socially defined as foreigners and temporary residents. Probably few Americans bothered to give much thought to their ultimate fate; those who did had vague and conflicting notions about the most desirable outcome of the new immigration or the practical measures by which such goals might be accomplished. To employers, the immigrants represented little more than a much needed supply of anonymous labor; to business men, new customers; to native laborers, fellows with whom they would have to cooperate at work as well as compete with for work; to politicians, potential voters; to churchmen, objects of charity and missionary zeal.

When ethnics showed signs of settling permanently in America, the reaction was uneasiness or worse—anxiety and hostility. For the natives with whom the ethnics were in direct contact, no real motivation existed to associate with the newcomers on a more intimate level. Their social needs were already satisfied by their own families, religious congregations, and other local groupings. The addition of strangers could only be felt as disturbing to the "American way of life." The arrival of large masses of immigrants caused discomfort and created the fear of being overwhelmed by them and their strange manners. From the standpoint of any American community, the threats of profound social change, adulteration of traditional values, and social disorganization were undoubtedly real, so that resistance appeared justified. Even differential treatment of people unable to converse freely in the language of the host society or to observe its norms of conduct seemed to be legitimate.

But it often happened that differentiation because of foreign origin, which may have been functional at one time, was retained after the original reasons had lost their validity. It was at this point that differential treatment and discrimination caused peasant immigrants to withdraw as much as possible from association with members of the host society. At first they did not think of their hosts' reactions as being entirely unjustified; for, on the basis of their own cultural standards, they could hardly expect any other treatment. Not before the immigrants and their children had become acquainted with American standards of equality and with the basically liberal creed of American society; and not before—in the process of acculturation—they had accepted these principles as generally valid and applicable also to themselves; indeed, not until they had already lost most of the characteristics that had excused their unequal treatment, were these new Americans in a position to question the legitimacy of differential treatment or to resent the discrimination to which they had fallen victim.

In addition to spontaneous reactions to ethnics on the part of those who were in direct contact with them, ideologies that were widely accepted in the host society also played a major role, particularly among those who determined public policies. Laws providing for selective immigration according to the countries of origin and the system of labor permits have been introduced to America relatively late and in the face of grave misgivings. In the heyday of mass immigration, however, no measures were taken to settle groups of immigrants in one place or to disperse them, to direct them to particular occupations or to prevent them from competing with the natives in others, such as was the case, for instance, in Canada. It was in line with the principles of economic liberalism to keep state interference to a minimum, and to leave such arrangements to the operation of social and economic forces emerging spontaneously within society. Thus, the correction of maladjustments, which were the result of the uncontrolled influx of large masses of immigrants, was long left to the initiative of individual citizens, churches, and voluntary associations. Systematic legal measures to compensate for the gross inequalities that had been allowed to arise among Americans because of ethnicity were not introduced until the New Deal, and even then, only with respect to Indians and blacks.

IDEOLOGIES OF AMERICANIZATION

The ideologies that tried to cope with the problem of interethnic relations arising from conflicting interests have been classified by Milton M. Gordon (1964) as follows: first came the idea that immigrants and their progeny should ultimately conform with the Anglo-Saxon Protestant standards; next came the melting-pot concept; and finally, the doctrine of cultural pluralism. Although these ideologies have been evolved at different times—the transition from old to new immigration corresponding to the gradual replacement of the first by the second concept—different sections of American society and official policies have always been prone to waver uneasily between all three of them.

The transition from the preparatory to the formative stage corresponds to a redefinition of the situation by both ethnics and host society. Immigrants were no longer viewed as foreigners and temporary residents but as citizens or at least prospective citizens. Although the accent may have differed concerning the ultimate outcome, in both cases their integration into the mainstream of American life was recognized as the most pressing task. Yet the hosts, while clamoring for rapid and complete assimilation of ethnics, excluded them from full and direct participation in American society. The ethnics, animated by the nationalism emerging in their parent societies, countered by voluntary withdrawal, and made an attempt to provide—in the familiar setting of segregated communities—for their human needs, which had greatly increased with the shift from temporary residence to permanent settlement. As the setting which was familiar to them was the Old World peasant community, they tried to reconstruct its pattern in the subcommunities of American industrial cities. Because complete isolation and self-sufficiency was not feasible in a modern society, such groups, however, remained segmental in that they satisfied social needs mainly on the level of *commensalitas* and *connubium*. The situation is made very transparent in the following analysis offered by W. I. Thomas and F. Znaniecki:

> The local Polish American group does not pretend to cut its members off from their wider social environment, to concentrate all their interests within any territorially limited Polish colony. On the contrary, it seems to endorse in the form of social recognition any activities by which its members participate in American economic, political or intellectual life. . . . But it presupposes that each member personally appreciates most and is most dependent upon the recognition he gets from his Polish milieu, and particularly that he desires social response exclusively from Poles. He is never permitted to put into his relations with Americans the same warmth and immediacy of social feelings as in his relations with Poles; the former are expected to be entirely impersonal, institutional . . , whereas all purely personal contacts must be limited to his own *gens*. This distinction can be best expressed by saying that the only primary-group connections a Pole is supposed to maintain are those which his racial group offers, whereas his relations with racially different social elements must belong exclusively to the secondary-group type . . . the American Pole is permitted to take whatever part he desires in American life provided he does it as a Pole, and the only forms of participation which are socially condemned are those which tend to incorporate him into American primary groups and to draw him away from his Polish *gens*— that is, marriage, personal friendship and all kinds of intercourse implying direct personal solidarity (Thomas, Znaniecki, 1958, pp. 1584 f).

Gordon, taking his cue from Cooley's concept of the primary group, makes a distinction between primary relationships "which are personal, intimate, emotionally affective, and which bring into play the whole personality," and secondary relationships "which are impersonal, formal, and segmentalized, and tend not to come very close to the core of personality" (Gordon, 1964, p. 32). In applying these concepts to ethnic group behavior, he states that:

> . . . within the ethnic group there develops a network of organizations and informal social relationships which permits and encourages the members of the ethnic group to remain within the confines of the group for all of their primary relationships and some of their secondary relationships throughout all the stages of the life cycle of the individual members (Gordon, 1964, p. 34).

He adds:

> Economic and occupational activities, based as they are on impersonal market relationships, defy ethnic enclosure in the United States more than any institution except the political or governmental, but even here a considerable degree of ethnic closure is by no means a rarity (Gordon, 1964, p. 35).

Once we realize that an ethnic group is not a separate society that happens to be geographically located like an enclave in the territory of another society but an integral part of the host society, unable to survive apart from it, the difference between the essential segmentality of the ethnic group and the potential comprehensiveness of the host society becomes intelligible. The ethnics are members of the host society by virtue of their membership in the ethnic group; they participate in the host society directly in some dimensions, and indirectly in other dimensions, as indicated by Gordon and before him by Thomas and Znaniecki, through the mediation of the ethnic group, which is simply a particular subsystem of the overall social system.

THE ETHNIC SUBCULTURE

The processes of ethnic group formation also have their cultural and institutional implications. In forming subgroups, ethnics develop a culture pattern that is neither identical with that of the parent nor of the host society, but is a new "secondary" growth. This is meant when sociologists speak of an ethnic "subculture" in the sense of a typical variety of the host culture. Gordon describes such a subculture as consisting of the culture of the host society "blended with or refracted through the particular cultural heritage of the ethnic group" (Gordon, 1964, p. 38). It "parallels the larger society in that it provides for a network of groups and institutions extending throughout the individual's entire life cycle" (Gordon, 1964, p. 39).

This characterization seems adequate enough for ethnic subgroups already in existence for a considerable period, but not for ethnic groups in their formative stage. The culture complex that a migrant has internalized during the process of early enculturation in his parent society is not changed simply by his transfer into a host society having a different culture. In order to actualize the internalized culture of the parent society, the immigrant needs a suitable social environment, that is, people who are able to interact in accordance with the same cultural norms. This is the most important incentive of secondary ethnic-group formation. Yet the reconstruction of a familiar setting, in which primary ethnic groups such as the Mennonites may succeed to a remarkable degree, is not possible when immigrants are also forced to interact directly with members of the host society in terms of their culture. Both the individual ethnic and the ethnic group are therefore compelled to adjust their traditional culture to the culture of the host society.

This may be achieved in several ways: (1) by adopting the components of the culture of the host society vital to their survival and/or prosperity in the novel situation; (2) by imitating adjustive behavior patterns adopted in analogous situations by other ethnic groups; (3) by inventing original culture patterns suitable to master the unique situation in which they find themselves. In addition, an ethnic group may also make adjustments to the parent society, which may have developed new culture patterns since the migrants left. Depending on the degree of contact and communication between parent society and ethnic group, some of the new components of the parent culture will subsequently be added to the culture complex of the ethnic group while components of their common traditional culture, which have been abandoned by the parent society, are often religiously preserved by the ethnic group.

Thus, we conclude that Gordon's attempt to treat ethnic subcultures in the same way as subcultures developed on the basis of social class, rural or urban residence, and so on, needs correction. He is probably right in describing subcultures of this kind as modifications of a general theme represented by the culture of the large society, but the same is not true of secondary ethnic groups. Their subculture is not simply a refraction of the culture of the host society through the prism of that of the parent society. Not only the parent but also the host culture, and above all—despite all its seeming conservatism—the ethnic subculture, are constantly changing, at times converging, yet at other times diverging still further.

Ethnic Institutions on the Local Level. Institutions may be considered as constitutive components of culture. The emergence of separate ethnic institutions correlates with the formation of ethnic groups. *Primary ethnic groups start the process of adaptation to the host society with a full set of institutions necessary for their functioning as a viable subsociety; they tend to lose these gradually, first in the political, then in the economic sphere. The formation of secondary ethnic groups, on the other hand, begins with the creation of new institutions of their own.* As ethnics of this type have no chances of achieving political autonomy and/or economic autarchy, their efforts are concentrated on satisfying the more intimate social needs of their members and on establishing social controls with regard to *commensalitas and connubium.* In this way immigrants and their descendants are put in a position to preserve their ethnic identity in the face of the homogenizing pressures exerted by the host society. As the frequency and intimacy of social interaction between ethnics and host society are reduced, and opportunities are increased to confine relationships to members of the ethnic group, social controls that prevent individual ethnics from participating directly in the host society are strengthened. The relative closure and self-sufficiency of sizable groups, however, and their permanency beyond the life span of the founding generation cannot be achieved on a purely personal and informal basis; they require a formal organization.

The Institutional Backbone of the Ethnic Subsociety. Supraterritorial organizations supplement and support ethnic institutions and voluntary associations on the level of the local community. They are particularly important in modern societies with their complex fabric of social relations and the thoroughgoing interdependence of their component parts. In the same way as local communities are integrated into the national society, secondary ethnic groups emerging on the local level are sustained by forming a larger subsocietal unit within the framework of the host society. Ethnics residing in a given locality do not only interact frequently on a personal and intimate basis, they also assemble periodically in one place (the church, the community hall, the lodge). Thus the subcommunity is a matter of direct and vivid personal experience. The identity and solidarity of ethnics dispersed widely throughout the host society, however, cannot grow spontaneously but must be promoted deliberately; for this requires more abstract symbols and complex forms of organization that cannot be conceived by simple peasants, but must be supplied by the educated leaders.

This elite acts as a mediator between local ethnic groups, the host society, and also the parent society. Within the framework of supraterritorial alliances, local leaders and delegates meet periodically for conventions, festivals, and demonstrations which provide opportunities for expressive behavior and the elaboration of common symbols. More important still, such associations offer channels of communication between local groups, initiate collective action, and promote cooperation in matters of common vital interest. The network of communication and interaction provided by the foreign-language press and voluntary associations thus represents the backbone of the ethnic subsociety within the host society.

CONCLUSIONS

In conclusion two highly general propositions may be advanced concerning the formation of secondary ethnic groups:

Proposition 1. Whenever members of a parent society are transferred as individuals into a host society which is not isomorphic with the parent society with regard to essential elements of the social structure, then the individuals transferred will not be able to take their places directly in the host society, and will therefore tend to form a secondary ethnic group.

Proposition 2. Conversely, whenever members of a parent society are transferred as individuals into a host society which is isomorphic with the parent society in regard to essential elements of the social structure, then the individuals transferred will be able to take their places directly in the host society, and thus no secondary ethnic group will be formed.

REFERENCES

Additional publications of a more general nature touching upon the subject matter of this and the following chapters will be found in the Selected Bibliography at the end of the book.

Francis, E. K., "Minority Groups in the United States of America," *Integration. Bulletin International*, XXXI (1956), pp. 54–61.

Gordon, Milton M., *Assimilation in American Life: The Role of Race, Religion and National Origins*. New York: Oxford University Press, 1964, p. 32.

Handlin, Oscar, *Race and Nationality in American Life*. Garden City, N.Y.: Doubleday & Co. 1957.

—— *Immigration as a Factor in American History*. Engelwood Cliffs, N.J.: Prentice-Hall, 1959.

Schachter, Stanley, *The Psychology of Affiliation*. Stanford: Stanford University Press, 1959.

Schermerhorn, R. A., *These Our People: Minorities in American Culture*. Boston: D. C. Heath and Co., 1949.

Thomas, William I., and Florian Znaniecki, *The Polish Peasant in Europe and America* (3rd ed.). New York: Dover Publications, 1958. This book was first published in 1927.

The Maintenance and Dissolution of Secondary Ethnic Groups in the United States

18

The factors supporting maintenance and causing dissolution are, as we have mentioned before, complementary, and for this reason we shall treat them together. Ethnic groups undergo processes of dissolution if they suffer the loss of group members through assimilation and absorption into the host society. The dissolution of an ethnic group does not imply the disappearance of its members. The erstwhile group members are transferred to some other structural component of the host society; their participation in the host society is now direct and no longer mediated through the ethnic group.

When the loss of group members is not balanced by a surplus of births over deaths, by an additional immigration, or by the adoption of new group members, for instance, through intermarriage, an ethnic group may be so weakened that it is unable to continue functioning. One necessary condition for the existence of any societal or subsocietal unit is the maintenance of "a sufficient number and kind of the members at an adequate level of operation" (Levy, 1952, p. 151). Accordingly, the maintenance of an ethnic group depends on its capacity to prevent losses to the host society and to preserve a sufficient number of members to guarantee the group's functioning as a viable subsocietal unit. Since members of a secondary ethnic group (being a segmental group) always participate partially in the ethnic group and partially in the host society, the maintenance/dissolution of the ethnic group also depends on the number and kind of social relationships which it is able to monopolize. *The increase of the area of participation promotes maintenance, its decrease spells dissolution.*

Social Disorganization and Acculturation

Neither social disorganization nor acculturation are, as such, indices of ethnic group dissolution. Most societal units maintain themselves more-or-less in the face of social disorganization. As Thomas and Znaniecki have pointed out, provided that social disorganization has been offset by acculturation to the host society, it generally leads to social change rather than to dissolution. Yet acculturation may contribute to a group's dissolution as well as to its maintenance. The transculturation of individual group members is indeed an important element in their assimilation. But as long as acculturation remains partial and the contrast effect unimpaired, the collective acculturation of an ethnic group may indicate a better adjustment to its situation, and actually improve its chances of survival. The partial transculturation of individual ethnics, on the other hand, is likely to lead to marginality. For a marginal man "lives in two worlds but is not quite at home in either " (Park, 1950, p 51).

The standpoint we are now taking is somewhat different. We are not concerned here with social problems, culture, or the fate of individual ethnics, but with the mechanisms of group maintenance/dissolution. The processes by which individual members are retained or lost by an ethnic group are best expressed in terms of group identification, which is basically a matter of social categorization. Nobody can act as a member of a particular group unless he is so classified by himself and by his associates. As group identification is a social fact, one-sided identification does not suffice. Uncertainty or disagreement concerning the group membership of people interacting with each other in a social context, for instance, in a local community, disturbs the social order because different norms of conduct are applied by the interacting persons. It is true that individuals may be assigned to several groups simultaneously; but some species of group are mutually exclusive. This is particularly true of ethnic or religious groups: One cannot be both a Pole and an Irishman, a Presbyterian and a Catholic. The analytical concept of reference group is apt to clarify a situation that is very typical of ethnics.

The Concept of Reference Group

According to M. Sherif and C. W. Sherif, reference groups are those with which an individual identifies or aspires to identify himself; membership groups are those to which he is assigned by his society (Sherif, 1956, p. 175). From a sociological point of view the terminology is somewhat misleading; for interest is focused on the interaction patterns resulting from the identification of individuals with groups and not on the relations of individuals to groups. The group to which a person actually "belongs" is always the one "with reference" to which he is acting. He is, however, unable to act effectively with reference to a given group unless all those with whom he is interacting recognize his membership in that particular group and respond accordingly. If they assign him to some other group, his social action orientation and actual behavior will be considered by them as contrary to accepted social standards, and they will react in a way unexpected by the individual in question. Accordingly, it is probably better to use the terms "group of individual aspiration" instead of "reference group," and "group of social assignation" instead of "membership group."

As the Sherifs have pointed out, the "reference" group of a person is usually also his actual "membership" group (Sherif 1956, p. 177). In this case the application of the concepts is redundant. They become relevant only when, in a given situation, a realistic chance exists of mistaking one's group identity or of choosing between alternative identities. This situation is typical of ethnics. An immigrant may either identify himself with his parent society or aspire to identification with the host society. This depends largely on his expectations. If he wishes merely to make money and to return home as fast as possible, he is likely to continue identifying himself with his parent society and to be content with being defined by the members of the host society as a foreigner and temporary resident. If, however, he intends to settle permanently, he will be inclined to identify himself with the host society. The desirability of his expected position in the parent society, should he return, and of the position which he hopes to attain in the host society, will influence his intention—either to settle permanently or to return home eventually. Both his assessment of the situation and ultimate intentions are, of course, subject to constant revision, dependent on changing conditions and new personal experience. Whether a migrant succeeds in being socially assigned to the host society will depend primarily on the reaction of the host society, although social controls which the parent society continues to exert upon him will also have their effect.

Multiple Loyalties

Once a secondary ethnic group has been formed, immigrants and their descendants tend to identify themselves first and above all with the ethnic group. But an ethnic group is a subsocietal unit, and thus cannot really compete for members on the same level with either the host or the parent society. Anyone identified with the ethnic group is thereby also identified with either the parent or the host society, or both. Since an ethnic group operates within the host society, one should surmise that it is the host society that is superordinate to the ethnic group and in which the ethnics participate indirectly. But the matter is not so simple: the ethnic group collectively maintains ties with both its parent and its host society, and the multiplicity of loyalties is a fundamental problem of ethnic groups.

In distinction to group identification, the term "loyalty" refers to both the cognitive component of identification and the affective component of solidarity. Furthermore, the concept implies a readiness to fulfill the obligations arising from group membership, particularly in the face of competing obligations. *The specific dilemma of ethnic groups derives from the fact that conflicting demands on the loyalty of ethnics are made by the ethnic group, the host society, and the parent society; and that no recognized authority exists to provide generally valid rules as to which obligations should take precedence.* Thus, there is always a certain ambivalance in the collective identification of an ethnic group with either the parent or the host society; and this may differ in different situations touching different social dimensions.

Moreover, loyalties may shift emphasis. It is more likely that primary ethnic groups are identified with the parent rather than with the host society. But the degree to which secondary ethnic groups are identified with the host society also varies. It tends to increase in the course of time as necessary adjustments are made between the demands raised by the ethnic group upon its members and those raised by the host society. Once a definite division of functions is recognized by both the ethnic group and the host society a labile equilibrium may be reached which is likely to last for some time. Conflicts are then minimized, and ethnics may indeed be said to participate in the host society largely through the mediation of the ethnic group. Thus, Irish ethnic groups in American cities are neither completely Irish nor completely American but, where they still survive today as viable subcommunities, they certainly are far more American than Irish because their loyalties to America are far more intensive and less superficial than to Eire.

Family and School

One of the crucial functions of the family and kinship group is to maintain the identity of any societal unit through more than one generation and to safeguard the continuity of its culture despite constant changes in its personnel. The maintenance of an ethnic group is directly affected by changes in the structure of interlacing family and kinship relations. As long as the ethnic family is able to keep up the patriarchical and authoritarian character typical of European peasants, it will act as a transfer point of traditional values and norms. Accordingly, the enculturation of each new generation will follow the pattern of the parent society. As the contacts of children with the host society multiply, mainly through the public (rather than ethnic) school and through peers and playmates, conflicts are bound to arise. If the children are made aware of their lowly class position and of the opportunities for advancement offered by the host society to those who conform with its cultural standards, they begin to reject their own group of assignation and to question the authority of their parents. Instead, they attempt to orient their social actions toward the group of aspiration, only to find themselves rejected by it. Stranded between ethnic group and host society, they stumble into the fate of the marginal man.

The school is meant to continue and supplement the socializing functions of the family. Yet the cultural standards imparted by the school are not always those transmitted by the family; they may sometimes even be in conflict with each other. In the case of peasant immigrants to America, this was not only true of the public but also of the ethnic school above the most elementary level. Generally, *the modern school is a transfer point of national rather than folk culture*. The language of instruction is never the mother tongue of peasants but the literary language, which has been created and used by the elite; the literature taught at school is confined to those writings in the national language that have been canonized by intellectual leaders as a prime vehicle of national values; and history is mostly written to provide ideological support for national sentiments and ambitions. Thus the ethnic school is largely an instrument through which processes of nationalization in the parent society are extended to ethnic groups abroad. At a time when the most pressing problem for illiterate peasants is their adjustment to the national culture of the host society, the propagation of another national culture among their children only increases their dilemma.

Education in the public schools prepares ethnic children more realistically for their future life by acquainting them with the standards of the society in which they will eventually have to make their way. However, it also brings them into conflict with ethnic traditions and tends to weaken parental authority and the social controls that are of greatest importance during the formative years. American ideas of freedom and equality, in particular, are apt to support juvenile tendencies to rebel against the authoritarian proclivities of their elders. In this way, the public school is likely to alienate filial ethnics from parental traditions without necessarily succeeding in complete transculturation. The result for the young is inadequate socialization, inner conflict, often disregard for authority and social rules of any kind, and—once more—marginality. Thus, neither the ethnic nor the public schools have acted as a conservative force but rather as an instrument of social change. *Wherever the ethnic school enrolled all or most of the children of a particular ethnic group, however, it prepared the way for collective change and transculturation, and thereby acted, by helping to maintain the ethnic group, as a cushion to culture shock and as an agent of integration into the host society.*

RELIGION

The role of religion in the maintenance/dissolution of ethnic groups has been dealt with above in connection with ethnicity on the community level and with primary ethnic groups. Only a few words need be added here. Insofar as religion is concerned with the belief in fundamental meanings, value standards, and norms of conduct, it has the same integrative functions for the social system as any other *Weltanschauung*. Accordingly, the maintenance of an ethnic group need not be impaired if it collectively exchanges one religious affiliation for another, or even a religion for a secularized national ideology. For it is the fact that meanings, values, and norms are held in common, not their specific content, which has an integrative effect on the group.

Partial acculturation to the host society does not, in itself, bring about the dissolution of an ethnic group as long as the components of the host culture are collectively accepted; the new patterns appear as an integral part of the culture of the subgroup in exactly the same way as the traditional patterns. The situation is quite different when members of an ethnic group are split on the question of their *Weltanschauung,* which provides the basic interpretations of reality and legitimizes the value standards from which the norms of social conduct are derived. This happens, for example, when some members cling to a traditional religion while others accept another religion or embrace novel ideologies, such as nationalism or socialism. In this case, instead of reinforcing resistance against assimilation, religion contributes to the loss of the contrast effect in a very important dimension and adds to the forces of group dissolution.

REFERENCES

Levy, Marion J., Jr, *The Structure of Society*. Princeton: Princeton University Press, 1952.
Park, Robert E., *Race and Culture*. Glencoe, Ill.: The Free Press, 1950.
Sherif, M., and C. W. Sherif, *An Outline of Social Psychology (rev. ed)*. New York: Harper & Bros., 1956.

European Parallels
19

The study of secondary ethnic groups in industrialized Europe—all but one of Polish origin—will indicate the significance of some additional variables, which has not yet been properly revealed. While some of the migrants under scrutiny were as in previous cases peasants, the parent society of others had already undergone the change from an agrarian to a more industrial type. Other factors to be considered include the relative accessibility of the parent society for European ethnics and their greater familiarity with the institutions of the host society prior to migration. The case of the Poles in Great Britain will shed further light on the role of collective transfer, class composition, and national ideology. In the last two cases, it will be shown that under specified conditions, even migrations of ethnically related populations may lead to the formation of groups resembling secondary ethnic groups. Finally, we shall see that deliberate government interference with the free movement of migrants and with the social forces arising spontaneously within the host society are apt to significantly modify the behavior of ethnics, which we should expect if the isomorphism theorem advanced earlier is correct.

THE POLES IN BELGIUM

The first wave of Polish immigrants reached Belgium shortly after World War I.[1] It was still part of the secular tide that has brought millions of peasants from the agrarian sections of Eastern and Southern Europe to the industrial centers of America and Western Europe. The second wave arrived after World War II under entirely different circumstances. They had been deported as forced laborers or had fled Communist Poland; moreover, they were not peasants, but came from a country which, by then, had caught up with the modernizing trends of the Western nations.

---

[1]The following case studies have been adapted with the permission of the publishers from R. Clémens, G. Vosse-Smal, and P. Minon, *L'assimilation culturelle des immigrants en Belgique: Italiens et Polonais dans la région liégeoise*. Liége: Imprimerie H. Vaillant-Carmanne, 1953.

La Brouck. Belgium's Poles are concentrated in the industrial areas of the French-speaking section of the country. The situation in the industrial settlement of La Brouck—with a total population of over 1500 and a foreign population of 1300, of which 900 were Poles—resembles in many respects that in the American communities studied in Section A. The Poles live almost completely isolated from the host society in segregated neighborhoods and settlements. In the beginning they had to accept work shunned by the natives; Polish ethnicity thus became identified with the lowest ranks of the status scale, and this social categorization has persisted throughout the years.

Social advancement can be achieved only by leaving the Polish settlements and, as far as second-generation Poles are concerned, by gaining a better education and by changing the occupation of the father. As soon as they try to raise themselves above the level conceded to them by the host society, they become a target of discrimination. The natives are quite ready to associate with them at work but refuse to have any more intimate contacts. As many as 14.8 percent (18.5 percent of first-generation Poles) are rated as highly unassimilated, 9.3 percent as highly assimilated; more than half the Polish population are rated in the two lowest categories of a five-point assimilation scale, slightly more than a quarter in the two highest categories. Because of the relatively high proportion of young, single Poles, mostly of the second generation, the frequency of intermarriage is relatively high. In a total of 5392 marriages contracted by Poles, 34 percent of the girls and 38 percent of the males have married Belgians.

Verviers. Among the Polish textile workers of Verviers, Polish ethnicity was not originally associated with low status, so that later immigrants of the laboring class did not encounter the same kind of prejudice as in La Brouck. A number of Poles from upper-class families had been trained before the war in professional schools, and some of them had attained high positions in industry as owners, managers, and white-collar employees. When Polish laborers arrived after World War II, their social prestige was immediately higher than among the metal workers of La Brouck. In both ethnic communities, however, the language of common intercourse remained almost exclusively Polish. In a sample of fifty-four, only twenty Poles spoke French fluently, an equal number spoke virtually none. Occasionally, a knowledge of literary French or the Walloon dialect was brought into the families by schoolchildren or by intermarriage. The Polish language was taught in evening classes organized by the Warsaw Government, which also provided the teachers and paid their salaries.

CONCLUSIONS

It would appear that, unlike in America, the Poles in Belgium identified themselves directly with the parent society; the ethnic group was socially defined not as a Polish sub-community of the Belgium host society but as a colony of resident foreigners. Because the distance between Belgium and Poland is not as forbidding as it used to be between Poland and America, and travelling to and fro is more frequent, the fiction could be kept up more readily that residence abroad was merely a temporary expedient to save sufficient money to return home under more favorable conditions. The Poles who came after World War I thought of themselves as foreigners temporarily residing in Belgium, and had therefore no desire to adjust to the host society more than was necessary to make a living. Accordingly, the overwhelming majority neither acquired nor aspired to Belgian citizenship. The Poles who came after World War II, on the other hand, were under no illusions about the feasibility of an early return to Poland, but their ultimate destination was North America or Australia, not Belgium, which they considered only as a stepping-stone. Thus they, like the earlier immigrants, refused to become absorbed into the host society, and most of their social needs continued to be satisfied within the secondary ethnic group.

THE POLES IN THE RUHR VALLEY

The Poles in the coal district of Westphalia exhibit greater deviations from the American type case.[2] Though roughly contemporary with the great East–West migration of peasants in search of work in mines and mills, this particular movement did not cross state boundaries nor did it occur for purely economic reasons. It was rather the result of Bismarck's policy to Germanize the eastern provinces of Prussia, and to provide the new industries in her western provinces with laborers recruited from among German citizens rather than aliens. The same type of peasant was involved in this migration as in the American and the Belgian cases and, despite their common German citizenship, the same ethnic differentiation existed between them and their hosts. In much the same way as were the Irish immigrants to the United States, the Poles who migrated to the Ruhr valley were already acquainted with the institutions, culture, and, to some extent, with the speech of the host society because the Poles in Germany were compelled to attend German public schools and to serve in the Prussian army. They had also been more subject to the modernizing influences of industrial society than had the majority of Poles who had come to America from less modernized agrarian countries farther east, such as Austria and Russia.

Between 1861 and 1890, the number of Poles in all the western provinces of Prussia rose from a handful to 18,000; and by 1910, the figure was 280,000. Of the Polish laborers, 77 percent were employed in mining, the remainder in

---

[2]The following case study has been adapted from W. Brepohl, *Industrievolk im Wandel von der agraren zur industriellen Daseinsform, dargestellt am Ruhrgebiet*. Tübingen: J. C. B. Mohr, Paul Siebeck, 1957.

seasonal construction work. The migration of the Poles to the Ruhr valley involved entire kinship and locality groups who were accommodated in compact settlements. In this way, they continued to partake in the traditional community life without major disruptions and without any need to seek close association with their German compatriots. As in America, the "Polish Society"— along with the authoritarian family—played a decisive role, not only in sustaining group life and solidarity, but also in preserving Polish culture and language. The first Polish club was founded in 1877; nine years later a supraterritorial alliance of Polish associations was organized. The system of Polish institutions in the Ruhr valley was hardly less elaborate than in America. In many places the Polish subcommunities were nearly self-sufficient; in some localities, even the majority of the population was Polish.

In other respects, however, the situation was very different from that in America. Because of the liaison between church and state in Prussia and the authoritarian character of both, the "Polish Society" was in no position to force the hand of Catholic bishops nor to take the initiative in the establishment of national parishes and minority schools. The most they could achieve was the training of Polish-speaking priests and their assignment to regular parishes with a large proportion of Poles, so that some of the services could be held in their tongue. Nationalism also had a more direct influence upon the Polish laborers in the Ruhr valley than it did in America. Polish newspapers warned against membership in German clubs as tantamount to Germanization; national leaders worked for the preservation of Polish speech and culture. On the pretext that the national struggle was also a religious one, they were able to mobilize the deeply religious Poles for political purposes. National sentiments were intensified when the Prussian government struck back by prohibiting the use of the Polish language in public meetings.

Eventually, however, compulsory attendance at German public schools by Polish children, together with security requirements forcing every miner to acquire a full command of the German language, broke down the language barrier and thereby the main bulwark against acculturation and assimilation. With the resurrection of Poland as an independent nation-state at the end of World War I, the way was open for a return of the Poles from the coal district of Western Germany to their own fatherland, on much more favorable terms than ever before. Simultaneously, the Polish organizations in Germany lost their drive and *raison d'être*. What was left of the Polish ethnic group in the Rhur valley became thereafter integrated into the main stream of German life and was rapidly absorbed by the host society.

The case of the Ruhr Poles shows that migration from an agrarian to an industrial section of one and the same nation-state may have effects quite similar to international migrations, and that divergences from the American prototype are mainly due to greater initial familiarity with the institutions of the host society, greater proximity of the parent society and direct government interference.

THE POLES IN GREAT BRITAIN

The Poles in Great Britain, to be discussed next, represent a borderline case which, because of its theoretical significance, will have to be presented at some greater length.[3] We have indicated earlier that before and after World War I, conditions in Europe were analogous to the situation of the new immigration in the United States. The population transfers since 1933, however, ushered in a new type of migration which also made its mark upon America; the general character of this Third Immigration will be discussed later in this chapter.

Polish immigration to Great Britain before World War II has been so small that it can be ignored. The number of Polish-born residents (other than Polish Jews) rose between 1939 and 1949 from 4,500 to 157,000. This was not due to the voluntary immigration of laborers as in previous cases, but to the unsettling effect of the war. The main contingent of Polish residents was supplied by the Polish Armed Forces in Exile; 249,000 Polish soldiers were under British command in December 1945; of these 105,000 returned to Poland and 21,000 emigrated to other countries; the remainder were allowed to stay in, or come to, Great Britain after being enrolled in the Polish Resettlement Corps. In addition to former military personnel, 33,000 of their relatives and 30,000 nonrelated displaced persons of Polish origin were admitted to the United Kingdom as permanent residents.

SOCIAL STRUCTURE

The demographic composition of the recent Polish migrants was far less homogeneous than that of the Polish immigrants to America, Belgium, or the Ruhr valley. Nor was it a true cross-section of the population from which it originated (as were the German expellees whose case will be investigated later). As many as three-quarters of the adult Poles were males, an unusually high proportion of them between the ages of eighteen and fifty-nine. About 11 percent were children under eighteen. It appears that the rural classes were underrepresented, the middle and upper urban classes overrepresented. One sample of approximately 100,000 veterans included 165 university professors and lecturers; nearly 1,000 elementary and high school teachers; more than 1,000 graduates of institutes of technology; nearly 1,500 lawyers, judges, state attorneys, and so on; 790 physicians and dentists; 300 chemists; 585 journalists, authors, artists, and so on; 70 clergymen; 2,500 civil servants; and 1,800 clerks in private businesses. Despite efforts made by the British authorities to have

---

[3]The following case study has been adapted with the permission of the publishers from Jerzy Zubrzycki, *Polish Immigrants in Britain: A Study of Adjustment*. The Hague: Martinus Nijhoff, 1956.

them take up agricultural work, no more than 10 percent of the Poles in the United Kingdom were so employed. Compared with a total of 79 percent manual workers, the figures given for those who worked in government services and professions or were studying (in each case 2,000) were under the circumstances rather high.

The large proportion of educated urbanites, particularly intellectuals and professionals, among the immigrants is significant, for these classes are generally prone to adjust more quickly and more successfully to life in a foreign country. They also belong to the most modernized section of their parent society. Modernization, urbanization, and better education not only add to the general knowledge of foreign peoples and languages and to the aptitude to enter into secondary relations with strangers almost at once, but they also increase the similarity between different national societies regarding their universalistic, affectively neutral, and performance-oriented value orientation. Thus, a relatively high degree of isomorphism between the parent and the host society of the British Poles should, according to our theory, have diminished the likelihood that ethnic groups be formed. Since they did show a tendency to form an ethnic group and a certain unwillingness to assimilate, we must assume that disturbing factors have interfered.

Definition of the Situation. First, there was a significant difference between former army personnel and regular immigrants. Initially, the Poles in Great Britain were not defined as immigrants in any sense but as members of an allied army destined to return home after the cessation of hostilities. It was only after the war that they were granted domicile. *This change of legal status was tantamount to a redefinition of the social situation by government action,* which the people at large were expected to accept. The relationship between host society and ethnics underwent accordingly several transformations.

It is doubtful if prior to the summer of 1940, the British had any conception of the Poles beyond a vague notion of Poland being a land of counts and peasants in picturesque folk costumes. When the first Polish military contingent arrived after the fall of France, the overall impression was favorable. This attitude changed after the Russian entry into the war (1941–42) on the side of the Allies, whereas the Poles continued to regard Russia as their arch-enemy. Public resentment increased when it was announced that no Pole who had served under British command would be forced to return to Poland. The Poles in England were now presented as endangering full employment, increasing the housing shortage, and consuming scarce food supplies. Rumors sprang up that they were living in luxury in their army camps and that they were menacing British womanhood while the men were absent fighting the war. On the other hand, Polish admiration for Great Britain cooled off considerably after the failure of the Warsaw uprising in 1944 and after the Yalta conference, during which one half of Poland's prewar territory was ceded to Russia.

After the Polish Resettlement Act was passed in 1947, ill feelings gradually began to disappear. This was largely due to improvements in the economic situation, which brought an increasing sense of security to the Poles as well as the British, and to the efforts of the British authorities to give the Poles a fair deal. The scene seemed set for the absorption of the Poles into the host society. Actually, however, they began to form an ethnic group instead of taking their place directly in the host society as, judging from their background, they could easily have done. What had happened?

Government Interference. One reason was, no doubt, government planning and action. The Polish Resettlement Act, providing for the organization of the Polish Resettlement Corps, was meant to prepare the Poles for life in the United Kingdom where they were now expected to remain for an indefinite time. They were placed in camps or hostels; moreover, special hospitals, schools, and government agencies were established. Although this was done with the best intention of facilitating their absorption, it had the same effect as the spontaneous resistance against foreigners on the part of the host society, which we have observed in America or Belgium. Not only were the Poles concentrated in segregated locality groups, but their differential treatment actually emphasized their ethnic distinctiveness.

The Resettlement Corps was really the civilian version of the erstwhile Polish Army in Exile. Accordingly, the formation of the ethnic group did not result from the transfer of individual immigrants into a heteromorphic host society but from the transformation of a social unit that was already present in the United Kingdom. Obviously, an army is not a viable subsociety. It depends on some global society for support—the national society from which it has been recruited to fight for its political aims, on an enemy society in times of occupation, or even on an allied society having a moral obligation. Yet an army does develop a particular kind of identification and solidarity whose importance increases when it is cut off from its home base. Temporarily, at least, it may then operate like a societal unit satisfying at least the emotional needs of its members on the level of *commensalitas*. The cohesion and solidarity of the former Polish army was revived in the Polish Resettlement Corps with the result that a kind of primary ethnic group, consisting of veterans, came into being, which for a while remained the nucleus of the wider secondary ethnic group comprising all the Poles in the United Kingdom.

Ethnic Institutions. The vestiges of military discipline and organization did not suffice to meet the social needs of the Poles, who had to adjust to the British host society but had no realistic chance to develop a viable subsociety conforming to the primary type. Accordingly, their subsequent behavior followed the pattern of secondary ethnic groups which, as we know, is characterized by a proliferation of separate ethnic institutions and organizations. This trend was supported by the Roman Catholic Church, which permitted the establishment of Polish parishes. Of these, twenty-eight were placed under a Polish bishop, another fifty-nine were under the jurisdiction of an English bishop to whom a Polish advisor was assigned. As many of the Polish clergy had shared the fate of their flock in the army or in labor and concentration camps, and also because of the traditional ties between the Polish people and the Catholic church, religion was able to make a significant contribution to the maintenance of the ethnic group.

In contrast to America, voluntary associations were organized from the top down rather than from the bottom up; for, unlike peasants, to whom the local community is the most important group of orientation, modern urbanites are more accustomed to think in terms of a larger societal context. Thus, the Polish Combattants' Association, founded in 1945, became the most important ethnic organization, in many respects resembling the supraterritorial "Society" in America. Its avowed aim was to maintain the identity and solidarity of what was conceived as the "Polish community in exile." It worked for the preservation and enrichment of Polish culture, and encouraged the establishment of Polish subcommunities which, as far as circumstances permitted, were to be self-contained and independent of the host society. These efforts led to the creation of such Polish agencies as a consular service, a financial and a legal assistance bureau, an employment bureau, a library, and a program of adult education and of weekend studies for Polish children attending public schools. Clubs and workshops, which provided employment for Poles, were at the same time meant to increase available funds.

Social cohesion, particularly on a supraterritorial basis, was also encouraged by a host of newspapers, magazines, and bulletins. Without the press, the Polish ethnic group would probably have lost contact with a great many of its members during the period of resettlement and dispersal of demobilized soldiers. The Polish-language press provided information about employment opportunities and about the various Polish organizations and welfare agencies available to individuals. Advertisements by Polish-owned businesses increased cooperation within the group, which lessened its economic dependence on the host society. The press assisted the Poles in their adjustment to the new environment, and prepared them to share eventually in the political, social, and intellectual life of the host society.

After a period of ten years, the Poles in Britain were for the most part still living in hostels, segregated housing estates, self-contained rural communities, or quasi-ghettos in the big cities. By preference, they spent their leisure time in Polish homes or clubs and read Polish newspapers and books; they often even worked in special gangs under the supervision of a Polish foreman. Although the Polish work gangs had been introduced originally because of language difficulties and to decrease the danger of violent aggression on the part of the native laborers, the pattern was later retained by the Poles as emotionally most satisfactory.

A certain amount of assimilation nevertheless was taking place. This trend primarily affected young men with a relatively good command of the English language who were highly mobile and adaptable to the new culture and new social roles. Intermarriage speeded up the naturalization of individual Poles, thus preparing for formal acceptance by the British people. Opportunities to obtain the better paid employment usually reserved for British subjects were also open to them. Naturalization, on the other hand, evoked ostracism on the part of the more conservative members of the Polish community, and thus intensified the tendency to withdraw completely from association with fellow-Poles. In summing up the situation, Jerzy Zubrzycki speaks of "cultural pluralism," both as a program and as an actual state of affairs. By this he understands a type of adjustment, combining accommodation to the institutional framework of the host society with the maintenance of social distinctness and cultural separateness (Zubrzycki, 1956, pp. 191 ff.).

THE FORMATION OF QUASI-ETHNIC GROUPS

According to our theory, it is not the contents of a culture but its structural differences that bring about the formation of secondary ethnic groups. If this be so, one would have to conclude that the transfer of a large population from one section of a national territory to another should also give rise to secondary ethnic groups. Offhand, this seems preposterous. It would be tantamount to saying that if large numbers of Americans were to move from California to Massachusetts, they would tend to form a "Californian ethnic group" in Massachusetts. The argument, however, misses the point. For the theory stipulates as a necessary (though not sufficient) precondition to the formation of secondary ethnic groups that parent and host society be heteromorphic with regard to constitutive elements of the social structure. Something similar to ethnic group formation has actually been observed among native Americans, whenever isomorphism was ostensibly lacking. Everyone recalls Steinbeck's story of the trek which, during the years of drought and depression, brought Americans from "backward" to economically developed areas of the country. Social differentiation and segregation were hardly less severe than if these "Okies" had come from another country or continent. If the evidence offered in the *Grapes of Wrath* is rejected as being mere fiction, we may turn to empirical studies of "hillbillies" who, after World War I, had moved to northern cities (cf. Griffin, 1965; Killian, 1953). These native Americans of the oldest Anglo-Saxon and Protestant stock, after having been transferred from a premodern and agrarian section to a modernized and industrialized section of one country, suffered the same kind of discrimination and formed the same kind of segregated groups as foreign peasant immigrants.

POPULATION TRANSFERS AFTER WORLD WAR II

Two European case studies are presented below to throw additional light on the problem under scrutiny. Both deal with population transfers that have occurred in Europe in the wake of World War II. These transfers involved so many people and were carried out in such a short time that they may be regarded as a huge "natural experiment." After the defeat of Germany, as will be recalled, millions of Germans were expelled from Eastern and South-Eastern Europe, and were forced to seek refuge in what was left of Germany. German territory east of the Oder-Neisse was ceded to Poland in order to compensate her for Eastern Poland, which was annexed to Russia. Eventually, Germany was divided into the Federal and the Democratic Republic, thus causing additional numbers of Germans to move from east to west. The Poles resettled the Western territories, from which the Germans had been driven out, with those Poles who were forced to leave Eastern Poland (officially called "repatriates") and with Polish emigrants returning from abroad after the liberation (called "re-emigrants"). We shall adopt the official designations without debating their appropriateness.

THE GERMAN EXPELLEES

The following statistics should suffice to indicate the magnitude of the population shifts since World War II. In 1955, roughly one-fourth of the West German population (50.2 millions) had immigrated within the previous ten years. No less than 11¼ million of them were German-speaking, two-thirds having been expelled from their countries of origin under the Potsdam Treaty, while the remainder were refugees from Eastern Germany. The total number of German expellees included 8,868,000 in West Germany, and 3,833,000 in East Germany. An additional half a million were received by Austria and other Western countries. About two million Germans remained in countries behind the Iron Curtain other than East Germany, while over four million (not counting military personnel) perished, mostly after the surrender.

There are very definite indications that, for some time, the German expellees did show a tendency to form a kind of ethnic group, at least a distinctive social unit within the German rump society in the Federal Republic. They were not accepted on equal terms by the natives but differentiated as a separate group of aliens. On the other hand, expellees coming from the same region (such as East Prussia, Silesia, Czechoslovakia) tended to congregate for mutual aid and sentimental reasons. A great variety of refugee organizations and institutions, special interest groups and agencies, even a political party were established to serve their needs. Yet after a few years they became so rapidly absorbed by the

West German population that for all practical purposes the dividing lines lost their social significance.

GOVERNMENT IINTERFERENCE

When we try to determine the factors contributing to group formation and dissolution in this particular case, we discover, as much as in the case of the Poles in Great Britain, that certain conditions specified by our theorems concerning secondary ethnic-group formation were lacking: free mobility of individuals, a market economy, and a minimum of government interference. The population transfer enforced by the enemy took place under emergency conditions and extreme emotional stress. The social fabric in the interior of Germany was shaken, political power was in the hands of the armies of occupation, and the prime concern of the local authorities was to provide a bare minimum of food and shelter for natives and new arrivals alike. Those expelled and driven across the borders had to be organized into transports, which were then distributed throughout the country wherever a place for them could be found. After food and shelter, employment also had to be secured. All this was achieved largely by means of deliberate organization rather than by individual enterprise, though the latter also made a significant contribution.

Governmental measures, which hastened integration, were primarily the monetary reform and the so-called *Lastenausgleich*. Once the old currency had been devalued by a stroke of the pen, savings were frozen, and each German was awarded an equal amount of cash to start from scratch. In this way, economic differences between expellees and natives were partly eliminated. Moreover, special tax measures were put into effect so that the losses in property suffered by expellees were counterbalanced by the contributions of those who had been spared major damages. In time, however, the same laws tended to perpetuate the social category of expellees by making them beneficiaries of special rights, even after the social distinctions had, for all practical purposes, been forgotten.

GROUP FORMATION

Government planning and economic measures have also been largely responsible for the ecological concentration of the expellees and for their visible differentiation as a separate category of citizens. This, together with specific experiences and interests not shared with their hosts, as well as the reactions of the natives, created a situation apt to promote the formation of subcommunities and separate social groups among the expellees. The trying circumstances of the initial contact caused marked tensions between the destitute migrants and the natives who were forced to share with them their meagre resources in addition to their private dwellings, 2.2 million of which had been destroyed during the war.

The expellees were inclined to resent the relatively more favorable circumstances of their hosts and to feel exploited when employed to replace the foreigners who had been released from forced labor by the Allies. Of all the heavy losses they had suffered, that of social status and prestige was the most aggravating, since it seemed to be caused by the ill will of the natives. The host society succumbed to the usual reactions of an established population toward the intrusion of a large body of strangers. All told, natives and expellees were not only confronted with different problems, they also defined a situation shared in common in two different ways. Thus, the scene was set for a hardening of divisions, segregation, and the emergence of collective defense mechanisms along the lines of secondary ethnic groups.

Once the expellees had reached safety in Western Germany they tried to reestablish contacts with their relatives and friends. The first reaction was to reunite family groups and strengthen family bonds. Occasionally, transports from one town or region had been directed to the same place in Western Germany. Local concentrations of fellow-countrymen came into existence, others joined them as soon as traveling again became feasible. By and large, however, former social ties were not revived with any convincing consistency, with the exception of family and economic affiliations.

At an early stage, refugee employers seeking to reestablish their businesses and industries in Western Germany tried to assemble their former employees with the help of the authorities, mass communication, and the grapevine. In many cases, entire factories were moved to localities where a labor pool of expellees had already formed. Attempts to bring industries and labor together resulted in a secondary migration of considerable size. A striking example may be seen in the revival of the Gablonz glass industry, a multimillion-dollar export business. This branch is characterized by a subtle division of labor between a variety of small or middle-sized home industries, which require skills and attitudes developed through several generations. To bring them together, a whole new settlement, with a population of 9,000 (in 1956), was created on the grounds of a former army ordinance plant in Bavaria.

The most delicate problems of adjustment occurred in rural areas where, according to census figures for 1950, two-thirds of the expellees were living. Of these, more than 10 percent were regular commuters. As economic conditions and the acute housing shortage improved, they moved in increasing numbers to the cities. Accordingly, a disproportionate share of unemployable and less-active elements was left stranded in the villages. Among these people there were many signs of isolation, frustration, strife, exploitation, and human misery. Yet these problems had more often than not the character of individual maladjustment rather than of group cleavages; for scattered distribution, differences in regional background and a certain inertia fed by hopelessness prevented concerted action among rural expellees.

Relatively few former farm-owners were resettled as farmers; repeatedly, no suitable applicants could be found when the opportunity occurred. But those who were so established found adjustment no more difficult than their urban counterparts. In big cities, on the other hand, adjustment was achieved more rapidly and easily, though at the cost of more intimate human relationships. Most expellees failed to show any particular desire to associate with strangers just because they hailed from their native land. Visiting was confined mainly to relatives or old friends. The mass meetings of expellee organizations, however, were generally very popular because they offered opportunities for renewing old acquaintances rather than for making new ones.

GROUP DISSOLUTION

Although separate refugee institutions, such as voluntary associations, press, and political parties, survived a quarter of a century, attracting even a younger generation not only raised but often born in Western Germany, the maintenance of a viable social group has been only temporary. Several factors have contributed to this failure. No doubt, the improved economic conditions eased the competition between natives and expellees so that less attention was paid to differences of origin. The expellees were offered opportunities of advancement so that status differences were obliterated, which had been typical for them in the beginning. Most of all, common speech and a shared national culture removed any serious obstacles to communication and mutual understanding.

Both the immigrant and the host population had a comparatively high educational standard; they had attended the same type of national schools in which the same values and norms of a modern, industrial and national society had been transmitted. Moreover, a national ideology—strongly propagated, though by no means invented, by the rulers of the Third Reich—according to which all those speaking German as their mother tongue belonged to one nation to be united in one nation-state, had taken firm root among both groups. It was this ideology that ultimately prevented leaders on both sides from treating the expellees as a separate societal unit rather than as an integral part of the German people. The leaders have consistently worked for their direct integration into the society of Western Germany which, since the breakdown following the war, has reconstituted itself within the reduced political boundaries forced upon it. Ever since the hope that the expellees would be allowed to return in a body to their native lands had to be abandoned, it has been their leaders who have stressed the common interest in solving the expellee problem, in rectifying the wrongs suffered collectively by all Germans, and in effecting the absorption of the expellees into the host society.

THE POLES IN THE WESTERN TERRITORIES

The relations that have developed between the Poles native to the Western Territories and the Polish repatriates who have been settled there since World War II, offer a striking parallel to the relations between the native population of

Western Germany and the German expellees. The subject of our analysis (cf. Nowakowsky, 1964) is an industrial community in the Silesian county of Oppel in the fifties and early sixties. Following the expulsion of the Germans and a rapid industrialization, the population of the town increased since the outbreak of the war from 8,000 (half of whom had been Germans) to 30,000. About nine-tenths of the present population are of peasant origin. Because its original social structure had been destroyed, the community was at first somewhat amorphous. Its population included: (1) Poles native to Silesia who had lived under German cultural influences for many centuries; (2) uneducated Polish settlers from central Poland; (3) repatriates from (former) Eastern Poland with a variety of social backgrounds; (4) re-emigrants from France, Belgium, and other countries who had adopted "some elements of the culture of everyday life" from their respective foreign environments.

GROUP FORMATION

In the early postwar period, considerable antagonism existed between these groups. In particular, the native Silesians were heavily criticized by the newcomers from Western and Central Poland who apparently considered themselves to be the only true representatives of Polish culture untainted by German influence. These also took the view that they should be compensated for the losses they had suffered at the hands of the Germans. As a result, the native Poles began to shut themselves off from the new arrivals and to form a segregated group. Both natives and repatriates, on the other hand, "reproached the settlers from Central Poland with not wanting to settle down but with only being interested in short-term material gains." Thus, in the Western Territories of Poland, just as in Western Germany, large-scale population shifts created cleavages and led to the formation of distinctive subgroups among people who were of the same general ethnic origin.

GROUP DISSOLUTION

In Poland again, as in Germany, the fact that all were identified with one national society eventually brought about a rapprochement and a leveling of social distinctions; this was particularly true of the younger generation, who had few memories of their countries of origin and of the social positions that their families had held before the Communist revolution. According to Nowakowsky

> There is no doubt that the inhabitants of the town . . . now form a single community with integration well advanced and even complete between certain groups . . . the differences in culture, customs, in attitudes to work, school, church, and so on, which were at first so stressed by each group have now either disappeared or people are no longer conscious of them (Nowakowsky, 1964, p. 71).

The disappearance of differences is also indicated by the growing number of intermarriages and by intensified contact and interaction in everyday life, in school, and in various organizations. Social differentiation is no longer based on origin or descent but rather on income, education, and social prestige.

REFERENCES

Brepohl, Wilhelm, *Industrievolk im Wandel von der agraren zur industriellen Daseinsform, dargestellt am Ruhrgebiet*. Tübingen: J. C. B. Mohr, Paul Siebeck, 1957.

Clémens, R., G. Vosse-Smal and P. Minon, *L'assimilation culturelle des immigrants en Belgique; Italiens et Polonais dans la région liégeoise*. Travaux du Séminaire de Sociologie de la Faculté de Droit de Liége, III. Liége: Imprimerie H. Vaillant-Carmanne, 1953.

Francis, E. K., "The German Expellees in the Federal Republic of Germany," *Year Book 1957 of the American Philosophical Society*. Philadelphia: The American Philosophical Society, 1958, pp. 303–310.

Griffin, Roscoe, "Newcomers from the Southern Mountains," in Arnold M. Roşe and Caroline B. Rose (eds.), *Minority Problems: A Textbook on Intergroup Relations*. New York: Harper & Row, 1965, pp. 55–61.

Jolles, H., *Zur Soziologie der Heimatvertriebenen*. Köln: Kiepenheuer & Witsch, 1965.

Killian, Lewis M., "The Adjustment of Southern White Migrants to Northern Urban Norms," *Social Problems*, XXXII (1953), pp. 66–69.

Nowakowsky, Stefan, "Egalisation Tendencies and the New Social Hierarchy in an Industrial-Urban Community in the Western Territories," *Polish Sociological Bulletin*, II (1964), pp. 68–83.

Zubrzycki, Jerzy, *Polish Immigrants in Britain: A Study of Adjustment*. The Hague: Martinus Nijhoff, 1956.

CONCLUSIONS TO SECTION C

We are now prepared to specify the general propositions advanced at the end of Chapter 17.

1. Both propositions hold true insofar as the host society conforms to the modern type. If the parent society is also of the modern type, it may be considered to be isomorphic with the host society; if the parent society is of the agrarian type, however, we may speak of lack of isomorphism. A society that is in the process of modernization may also comprise sections that still conform more to the agrarian type; accordingly, when we refer to either parent or host society, attention must be paid primarily to conditions on the subsocietal level. In addition to the particular section of the parent society from which the transferees are recruited, their initial demographic composition must be considered. The upper and middle classes are more likely than the lower classes, the educated more than the rural folk, to meet the requirements of a modern society, and thus to be able to take their place directly in an urban and industrial host society. Moreover, the young and unmarried submit more easily to transculturation than older couples.

2. The transfer of individuals from parent to host society most commonly takes place by way of long-distance migration, either from one country to another or from one to another region of the same country; the change of state jurisdiction, as such, makes no difference, although it decreases the probability that the transferees will be familiar with the institutions of the host society prior to their transfer. A redefinition of a person's status in a specific country from transient foreigner to permanent resident may have the same effect as migration. It is also likely that transfer by way of annexation has similar effects if the annexed territory is highly industrialized and urbanized.

3. The condition that members of the parent society be "transferred as individuals" does not exclude either the transfer of family groups or of small bands or chain migration. Its opposite is collective transfer, which implies that viable societal units are being bodily transferred together with their property and institutions or, upon arrival, are permitted to reconstitute themselves as a viable subsociety after their traditional pattern. Whilst collective transfer may result in the formation of primary ethnic groups, individual transfer is likely to result in the formation of secondary ethnic groups.

4. As long as migrants are socially defined as temporary residents, expected to live and work in the receiving country without settling down permanently, their transfer into the host society is not completed. We cannot speak of their being transferred from parent to host society before they define themselves, and are defined by their associates, as permanent residents ready to be fully integrated into the host society. The formation of a secondary ethnic group thus depends on the social definition of the situation. Citizenship and naturalization tend to signalize the intention of the transferees to take up permanent residence, and to become integrated into the host society, as well as their acceptance as regular members on the part of the host society. Refusal to take out citizenship papers as soon as the legal requirements are met, or failure to grant them within a reasonable time, may be taken as an index of reduced participation or membership status in the host society.

5. Differences in the ethnic origin and the specific culture content of the host and parent societies have no significant influence upon secondary ethnic group formation. Minor modifications are expected to occur because of the initial familiarity of the transferees with the language, culture, and specific institutions, especially religious and legal institutions, of the host society. The image of a particular ethnic group, which initial contacts have induced in the host society, may influence the latter's relations to later immigrants of the same and even of other ethnic origin.

6. Ideas of nationalism, which have either been embraced by the transferees prior to their arrival or which have been transmitted from the parent

society by later immigrants, the press and other publications, or the school tend to increase their awareness of identity and sense of solidarity, and thus promote the likelihood of the formation and maintenance of a secondary ethnic group.

7. The shorter the distance between releasing and receiving country and the more intense the communications are, the greater is the probability that the transferees define themselves as temporary residents, and that they are influenced by the national ideology of the parent society.

8. The behavior of transferees is predictable only under the conditions of free mobility, a free market economy, and a minimum of government interference. Limitations to the free movement of people and goods as well as deliberate planning and political action must be treated as disturbing factors modifying the behavior of the transferees and their hosts, which is to be expected according to our theory of ethnic group formation. Government interference with the free operation of an industrial economy and with the mobility of labor may be the result of politcal exigencies brought about by wars or revolutions. Mass movements of expellees and refugees, or the necessity to care for displaced persons and armies, create problems whose solution cannot be left to spontaneous socioeconomic forces alone, but require direction by public authorities.

Yet there are other reasons that may, as we know, promote state direction for instance, an economic depression or an upsurge of nativism due to a real or believed threat to national integrity. The difference between the new immigration in America, which has its parallels in Europe, and the more recent type of population transfers since the Depression is primarily related to government interference, not only with immigration and settlement in the receiving countries but also with the stability and safety of certain population segments in the countries of origin. Accordingly, the general pattern indicated by our theory has to be modified for this most recent type of migration. Under these conditions, whenever large groups of transferees are subjected to special regulations and treatment by the authorities, the probability increases that they will form separate ethnic or pseudoethnic groups, even if they would otherwise be able to take their place directly in the host society.

In turning to the problem of the maintenance/dissolution of secondary ethnic groups we offer the following general propositions:

1. An ethnic group maintains itself to the extent that it prevents the loss of individual members through assimilation to, and absorption by, the host society.

2. Ethnics are likely to continue their participation in the ethnic group to the extent that it offers them satisfaction of their felt needs. The most pressing needs pertain to primary relations in the sphere of *commensalitas* and

connubium. The maintenance of an ethnic group depends, then, on its ability to create a social environment in which members can find full satisfaction of their cognitive, instrumental, emotional, and expressive needs without having recourse to the host society. The chances for maintenance are increased if the opportunities of communication, face-to-face interaction, and primary relationships are numerous.

3. The wider the area of participation in the ethnic group becomes as compared with the area of participation in the host society, the greater is the likelihood of group maintenance. This is especially true if participation is extended to secondary relations.

4. An ethnic group is likely to maintain itself beyond the life-span of the founding generation if informal social controls are supplemented through formal controls, and the enculturation of children takes place to the exclusion of influences on the part of the host society. Accordingly, the chances that an ethnic group may maintain itself are increased whenever separate institutions and organizations are at its disposal through which social controls can be exerted, enculturation accomplished, and contacts with the host society reduced.

5. Similarity between the traditional culture of the ethnic group and the host culture increases the chances and rate of assimilation of individual members (and accordingly of group dissolution). Although the transculturation of individual members is likely to lead to their leaving the ethnic group, collective acculturation, that is, the acceptance of some traits of the host culture by the ethnic group as a whole, tends to contribute to group maintenance.

We can conclude, therefore, that *secondary ethnic groups function as social mechanisms through which ethnics, unable to take their place directly in the host society, are nevertheless integrated into it. Although ethnic groups impede or delay assimilation, they are functional from the standpoint of both the host society and the personality development of ethnics. Their formation and maintenance is, however, dysfunctional with regard to those ethnics who would otherwise be able to take their place directly in the host society.* The integration of ethnics into the host society without the mediation of ethnic groups will be treated in Section D.

D. Ethnic Categories

INTRODUCTION

In Sections B and C we studied the problem of how ethnics are integrated collectively into the host society. We concluded that if it is true that ethnic groups are structural components of the host society, it follows that their members participate in the host society, albeit indirectly. We also indicated that because ethnic groups are formed and maintained only under specified conditions, not all ethnics participate in ethnic groups. It follows that a society may also comprise isolated ethnics. Moreover, even after an ethnic group has been formed, it is not necessarily joined by all ethnics of the same origin. Finally, some ethnics may leave their ethnic group in order to become directly integrated in the host society. In the present context the concept of *integration refers to the process by which any new addition to a society becomes part of it without disrupting its basic structure.* Immigrants may be viewed as "additions" whose integration in to the host society is likely to pose "ethnic problems."

The first topic of this section concerns the integration of ethnics into the host society without the mediation of a particular ethnic group. As long as ethnicity remains at all a factor in social action orientation, ethnics are assigned to an ethnic category. As we recall, the concept of social category refers to aggregates of social statuses whose occupants do not interact specifically with each other but are simply differentiated by socially relevant criteria, such as sex, age, marital status, income, or ethnicity. Social categorization implies status assignment. Social rewards are distributed among the members of a society in accordance with their status. As we have found in Chapter 12, ethnic status tends to modulate the operation of all other status categories. In other words, general rules governing the distribution of social rewards among the regular members of the host society are modified in a typical manner. For example, a Polish-American is viewed and treated differently from an "unhyphenated" American, that is, one without an ethnic qualification.

Individual ethnics who have become fully integrated into the host society may be said to have been absorbed by it. By implication, *we understand by the absorption of an ethnic group its dissolution through the loss of members to the host society, followed by a complete integration of individual ethnics into the host society.* The sociopsychological processes leading to the absorption of ethnics are called "assimilation." They have been studied most thoroughly in recent years during a period which may be described as the third immigration. *The first or "old" immigration was characterized by the transfer from one agrarian to another agrarian society, the second or "new" immigration by the transfer from an agrarian to an industrial society.* The new immigration, in particular, as we have seen in Section C, has been responsible for the emergence of secondary ethnic groups because of the lack of isomorphism between parent and host society. *The third immigration, which is still going on, is characterized by the transfer from one industrial to another industrial society.* Because of the isomorphism between parent and host societies, no secondary ethnic groups are formed (except when disturbing factors, such as government actions, interfere with the operation of spontaneous social forces as was illustrated in Chapter 19), but ethnics must at once find their niche in the host society directly and individually. Accordingly, assimilation (and the factors impeding or facilitating it) becomes the most pressing problem for their integration.

Most authors mention discrimination as being among the main obstacles to the assimilation of ethnics; in fact, there is a widespread tendency to treat prejudice and discrimination as "the key concepts involved in the study of intergroup relations" (Simpson, Yinger, 1953, p. 13). Accordingly, any discussion on assimilation must also consider discrimination and prejudice. An attempt to fit these concepts into a general theory of interethnic relations will be made in Chapter 21.

The last chapter of this section reverts to a theme that has been repeatedly mentioned in earlier sections, which touches upon the problem of social change. For *social change* refers not only to global societies as a whole but also to their structural components. It *consists primarily of the change from one type of social structure to another rather than the complete disappearance of social units and their populations*. The formation of secondary ethnic groups involves, as we have seen, the transformation of an ethnic category, or at least part of it, into a distinctive subgroup of the host society. The dissolution of a secondary ethnic group also involves a change of social type, namely, its transformation into a social category. The formation and maintenance of an ethnic group is facilitated to the extent to which the assimilation of its members into the host society is impeded. Conversely, the dissolution of an ethnic group is promoted if the chances of individual members to be assimilated are increased. We have also found that a primary ethnic group, or part of it, may be transformed into a secondary ethnic group, as for instance, in the case of the New Mexican Hispanos.

The following paradigm indicates the conceivable types of transformation processes pertinent to the problem of interethnic relations.

Some of these transformation processes have been discussed in earlier chapters, especially, type *a* in Chapter 16. The transformation of a secondary into a primary ethnic group (type *b*) does not seem a realistic possibility under the conditions of modern society. No suitable case studies could be found that would have permitted a closer analysis of type *e* (the attempts made in Chapters 17, 18, and 19 are only of a general nature). This lack of adequate empirical

PROCESSES OF SOCIAL CHANGE

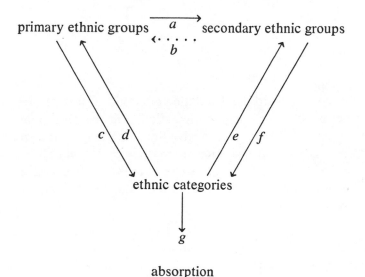

absorption

information is probably because sociologists have paid greater attention to the existence of ethnic groups than to their nonexistence. Transformation processes of type *g* are the topic of Chapters 20 and 21. The transformation of an ethnic category into an ethnic group has been studied in Section B. There we found that people who are categorized on account of religion and who are organized in sectarian congregations, like the Mennonites and Mormons, may under certain conditions be transformed into primary ethnic groups; their case may be considered as approaching type *d*. In Chapter 22 we shall deal with an analogous process conforming to type *f*. We shall show how people who, as slaves, had been assigned to the lowest status category of a society, have been transformed into a secondary ethnic group.

R E F E R E N C E

Simpson, G. E., and J. Milton Yinger, *Racial and Cultural Minorities: An Analysis of Prejudice and Discrimination.* New York: Harper & Bros., 1953.

Assimilation

20

Assimilation works toward the dissolution of ethnic groups, the irrelevance of ethnic categories for social action orientation, and the absorption of ethnics into the host society. It may be conceived of as an asymptotic process in the course of which ethnic categorization approaches zero. Once all restrictions on the membership of ethnics in the host society are lifted and charter membership assigned to them, differentiation on account of ethnicity becomes irrelevant for social action orientation.

DEFINITION OF ASSIMILATION

Ethnics may be said to be assimilated to the extent to which (1) they identify, and are identified by their associates, with the host society; (2) they habitually think, feel, and behave in the same way as charter members are expected to think, feel, and behave in analogous situations; and (3) they participate in the host society on all levels without being excluded from access to any social rewards, positions, occupations, organizations, facilities, institutions, or other components of the social structure by virtue of their ethnicity. We conclude that ethnics may be said to be assimilated if they are assigned social status on equal terms with charter members.

So far, we have considered assimilation under a structural aspect. When viewed as a process, it signifies degrees on a continuum between nonmembership and full membership. An immigrant is initially defined as a complete stranger whose presence requires a minimum of social interaction, when not enough is known about him to calculate his social behavior. Once an ethnic has acquired the necessary social skills and has learned enough of the host culture to participate in ever-wider areas of social interaction, he is assigned the status of "foreigner," which may be terminal.

254

ACCOMMODATION

Unless a foreigner aspires to regular membership in the host society (for instance, if a Pole wants to be recognized as an American, not merely as a Pole residing in America), accommodation suffices. The term has been defined by E. W. Burgess as:

> The process of making social adjustments to conflict situations by maintaining social distance between groups and persons which might otherwise come into conflict.

Immigrants, he adds,

> . . . become accommodated by formal and external arrangements without fully participating in the cultural heritage and common purposes of the host society (Burgess, 1949, pp. 403 ff.).

Accommodation is required of foreigners on the level of *commercium* and secondary relationships rather than of *commensalitas* and primary relationships. This does not imply identification with the host society but only that minimum of loyalty that is to be expected of "guests."

Foreigners may be satisfied with their status and never intend to become regular members, even if they remain in the country permanently, often for generations. Nor may the host society show any great interest in absorbing them, although in a modern national society large colonies of foreigners are usually felt to be an abnormity and a potential threat. By and large, foreigners living permanently in a modern society are eventually expected to become absorbed into the national core of the host society; they are considered as members on trial who should make a sustained effort to conform to the prevailing value standards and norms of conduct.

ASPECTS OF ASSIMILATION

On our continuum between nonmembership and full membership, accommodation represents the first stage; all the subsequent stages are summarily covered by the term *"assimilation."* It refers to a syndrome of processes occurring in several dimensions of the complex fabric of a modern society by which an accommodated foreigner is gradually transformed into a partially integrated ethnic with a limited or qualified member status, and by which he may finally be absorbed as a regular member on an equal footing with natives. Like other social processes, assimilation must be viewed both from the standpoint of the individual and that of his social environment; more specifically, from that of the individual ethnic and of the host society. On one side we have the aspirations of individual ethnics, on the other the expectations of the host society. Both are at the bottom of those problematical situations that turn "foreigners" into "ethnics."

The necessary (though not sufficient) condition for the acceptance of an ethnic by the host society, its degree as well as its rate, is the *transculturation* of the ethnic.[1] Unless an ethnic has internalized the culture of the host society, he is unable to function properly and to fulfill the expectations that the host society has of its charter members. The processes of transculturation through which ethnics are integrated into the host society parallel the processes of enculturation by which children are integrated into the parental society. The difference between the socialization and enculturation of native children and the resocialization and transculturation of foreigners and their children is this: Once socialized and enculturated in relation to one particular society and its specific culture, a person need never again undergo the same elementary processes; he is now able to learn new sociocultural patterns by reference to those that he has already internalized. For example, speech and the art of symbolic expression is learned only once during the process of acquiring one's mother tongue. Any new languages can then be learned, at least to a large extent, by "translating" one set of speech facilities and verbal symbols into another.

IMPLICATIONS OF ASSIMILATION

When trying to explain phenomena of assimilation, we shall do well to distinguish between (1) the implications of the concept; (2) the factors influencing the process; and (3) the indices used in measuring its degree and rate. For analytical purposes, the "implications" must be treated as dependent variables, the "factors" as independent variables. Yet those dependent variables that can be observed directly and measured may be used in empirical research as indices of assimilation. If we fail to follow these methodological precepts, we are likely to confuse the *explanandum* with the *explanans;* that is, we might use as an explanation what is already implied in the definition.

---

[1]Cultural anthropologists, who are interested in culture change rather than in intrasocietal relations between people having different cultures, often use the word "acculturation" in a wider sense, emphasizing the two-way processes involved in culture contact between entire societal units (cf. the definition offered by Redfield et al. 1946, p. 149): "Acculturation comprehends those phenomena which result when groups of individuals having different cultures come into continuous first-hand contact, with subsequent changes in the original culture patterns of either or both groups."

For the present purpose the term "transculturation" seems preferable when we are interested in those processes of acculturation that affect ethnics in their relations to the host society, although, in other places, we have used "acculturation" in much the same sense when there was no danger of unintended connotations.

In the following paragraphs we shall take a critical view of some of the variables that sociologists have considered as indicating assimilation. For example, Gordon (1964, Chap. 3, part. pp. 68 ff.; see also Eisenstadt, 1954, pp. 11 ff.; Glazer, 1956; Borris, 1959), distinguishes (1) "cultural assimulation" whenever ethnics have adopted the culture patterns of the host society; (2) "structural" assimilation when they have entered fully into its social structure; (3) "marital" assimilation when they have intermarried "fully" with natives; (4) "identificational" assimilation when migrants have developed a sense of peoplehood based exclusively on the host society; (5) "civic" assimilation when the migrants do not cause any value or power conflict by raising political demands; and last, when there is an absence of prejudice and discrimination, he speaks of (6) "attitude-receptional" and (7) "behavior-receptional" assimilation.

Proportionate Distribution. The widespread opinion that the assimilation of ethnics implies their proportionate distribution throughout the social structure may serve as a convenient statistical standard for measuring the degree of assimilation, but it raises the question whether this really ever happens in a modern society. *The notion that occupational positions should be distributed in proportion to all conceivable social categories has, we suspect, a definite ideological tinge.* Equal chances of obtaining such positions could be assumed to exist only in a free market economy under conditions of unrestricted spatial mobility, if social positions are assigned exclusively on account of personal accomplishment, and if individual abilities are distributed at random throughout all components of the population (ethnic or otherwise). Even in an open society, this model is barely approximated. Many factors other than ethnicity may cause significant skews in the statistical distribution of social rewards (such as regional differences, differences in the age-sex distribution, in health, and many others). Moreover, even in an ethnically homogeneous population, family connections and descent will always play a role in status assignment.

It is well known that with regard to occupational distribution ethnics in America differ in a typical manner from natives as well as among themselves (cf. Hutchinson, 1959). It would be rash to assume, however, that such differences are entirely, or even predominantly, due to ethnic categorization or outright discrimination. Many other subpopulations (for instance, females, older age groups, believers in a certain religion, some occupational groups, different regional sections) would more likely than not display similar deviances from the statistical average for the total population.

Club Membership. What is true of occupational distribution is equally true of membership in clubs or other organizations. The fact that a particular ethnic category is not represented in proportion to its size cannot be considered as lack of assimilation. In this case a group of native Americans who are under-represented in a particular country club would also have to be considered only as partially assimilated. There are many reasons apart from ethnicity that may account for nonmembership: People may not be affluent enough to participate in club activities or to reciprocate favors received from other members, or they may be merely disinterested. Thus we conclude that proportionate distribution of ethnics in the occupations or voluntary associations cannot serve as a safe index of assimilation.

"Mixing of Blood." The assumption that assimilation implies large-scale intermarriage, eventually resulting in a complete "mixing of blood," is founded on similar suppositions. First, a distinction should be made between "intermarriage" and "interbreeding." The one directs attention to the legitimacy of reproductive unions, the other refers to reproductive unions regardless of whether they are casual or permanent, licit or illicit. Obviously, the social effects will differ widely. The question of relative numbers would have to be raised in either case. How many unions are required for "large-scale" intermarriage? How many generations are involved? Does assimilation imply that one parent, two grandparents, and so on, be natives? Should collateral kin also be considered? Such a genetic arithmetic seems to miss the point. All that can possibly be asserted is this: *Absorption cannot be said to be completed unless reproductive unions among the total population, including both ethnics and natives, have taken place at random during several generations so that conspicuous racial distinctions can no more serve as symbols of ethnicity.*

Identification. With regard to identification with the host society as a necessary condition of assimilation, a few more remarks are suggested. We have already indicated that an ethnic cannot be considered assimilated unless the host society is his group of both aspiration and assignation. Yet the national society is not the only, though perhaps the most comprehensive, reference group with which a person may identify. Moreover, *any kind of social identification should not be assumed to be a constant frame of mind: it becomes intermittently salient whenever a person is called upon to make a realistic choice between different reference groups.* Native Americans, for instance, orient their social actions toward the American nation only in exceptional circumstances. As another example, the reference group "French-Canadians" is activated only when there is a challenge requiring that they be distinguished from Anglo-Canadians, Old-Country English, or Americans.

A third instance: In a study of German expellees in a Bavarian town, which he calls Hausen, H. Treinen (1963, 1965) discovered that expellees and native Bavarians identify themselves in different situations with different societal units, and that the manner of categorization is not the same for natives and expellees, even if the latter may well be considered assimilated. Both groups answer affirmatively when asked whether they regard themselves as Hauseners or as Germans. But the expellees hesitate to identify themselves as Bavarians, and prefer to say they are Sudeten Germans, Silesians, Transsylvanians, and so on, according to their respective countries of origin. Generally, the question whether ethnics are to be identified with the host society, the parent society, or an ethnic group arises only in controversial situations. This may be the case when competing claims on their loyalty are made, or when they are individually excluded from social rewards to which they actually aspire.

Levels of Assimilation. The processes of assimilation do not take place simultaneously or at the same rate in all social dimensions. In particular, a distinction should be made between the associational and cultural level. *Although complete assimilation implies not only free association with charter members of the host society but also the internalization of basic understandings, value standards, and norms of conduct, the social and cultural aspects may vary to some extent independently.* Even ethnicity apart, charter members may merely accommodate to some aspects of the shared culture. For instance, a Buddhist living in a Christian society may refrain from physical labor on Sunday so as not to hurt the feelings of his associates, or to avoid open conflict with them, although he neither believes that Sunday is the Lord's Day nor that God should be honored on this particular day by abstaining from servile work. But items of an alien culture may be adopted for various reasons, and social interaction with its original carriers need not be intensified simultaneously, nor conformity with their behavioral patterns perceptibly increased.

Thus, when it comes to analyzing the factors involved in assimilation, it is indeed useful to make a distinction between transculturation and resocialization; between sharing essential elements of the normative culture and associating, without any reference being made to ethnicity, in the sphere of *commercium* and secondary relations and also in that of *commensalitas*. The salient point is not the perfection of associational equality or cultural uniformity, which cannot be expected even from charter members of a modern society, but the lack of ethnic differentiation. In short, *anything that cannot reasonably be expected of charter members cannot be considered a requisite of assimilation.*

INTERMARRIAGE AND ASSIMILATION

The strategic role of marital relations and of the family in assimilation calls for a more careful analysis. Three aspects must be distinguished: (1) the role of the family in individual adjustment; (2) its significance in determining membership in a society and in assigning social positions within its structure; and (3) its function in tracing descent.

For our purpose, the following processes of individual adjustment, which normally occur within the family, are of special interest: (1) the child is enculturated into the particular subculture, which is adhered to by his family of orientation; (2) for adults, the family of procreation is the setting in which two persons become adjusted to each other who have not only disparate dispositions and experiences but who differ also, to a greater or lesser extent, with regard to their respective cultural or subcultural backgrounds; and (3) where bilateral kinship ties are strong, every new marriage also necessitates an adjustment between the kin groups of both partners. The greater the differences in the cultural background of the spouses, the more difficult will be the enculturation of the children and the mutual adjustment of the adults.

The enculturating role of the family throws a light upon the significance of intermarriage in the process of assimilation. Let us consider a typical situation. An ethnic who marries a native will be exposed to the culture of the host society not only through his spouse but also through their children who, in part at least, are directly enculturated into the host society through peer group and school. No general rule can be established as to whether the parent culture of the one or of the other spouse will be more important in shaping the personalities of the family members. Still one may surmise that an ethnic will be transculturated to the host society more easily in a mixed family than when both parents are of the same ethnic background.

Status Assignment. One of the most important social functions of the family is status assignment for all its members. In modern society, the initial status of children and the basic status of wives are commonly assigned according to the status of the male head and principal provider. The stranger as much as the outcast, who has lost social standing in his society, are typically people who do not belong to an identifiable family. They, and also those who have voluntarily emancipated themselves from all kinship ties, must rely on individual accomplishment and merit to gain a position in society and share in its rewards. Although the stranger has no definite social status, the ethnic shares the (usually inferior) status of his group or category. Again intermarriage may affect his status, and that of his children, in several ways.

Among the upper classes, where the extended family group plays a considerable role, status may depend not so much on the occupation of the head of nuclear families but on the collective wealth, power, and prestige of the extended kinship group. Admission to an extended family is highly selective, but this is less so because of ethnicity than because of other criteria, such as prestige. Moreover, within a high-prestige extended family the chances are that the low-prestige husband of the female member will be identified with her family and assigned a corresponding status. Apart from such cases of male hypergamy, because of the prevailing patrilocal and patrilinear character of the family, the offspring of mixed marriages in which the wife is an ethnic are likely to be assigned the status of the native father, except where strong prejudices exist against mating. Thus, if the mother is Jewish or black, the native status of children derived from that of the father may be questioned.

Symbolic Function. Ethnic descent is in part determined on the basis of what is known of a person's genealogy. If such evidence is not forthcoming, indirect indicators of descent must be relied upon. Surnames, for instance, are institutionalized means of ascertaining ethnic origin.[2] In a similar manner heritable biosomatic characteristics may serve as symbols of descent. Yet, to become socially relevant, racial distinctions must be perceived as relevant; and this happens only when there are other reasons making it desirable to differentiate people who incidentally possess distinctive biosomatic marks permitting ready identification. If such reasons do not exist, or have ceased to exist, the somatic differences themselves are not perceived, or they are brushed aside with no more than passing curiosity.

Yet it is true that shifts in the relative frequencies of biosomatic traits as a result of interbreeding may reduce their discriminatory power. Racial characteristics that once served to distinguish populations of different ethnic origin may not be generally perceived when intermarriage has become so common that the proportion in which people are descended from the one or other original stock is no longer of any great practical interest. We may summarize that interbreeding is likely to assist assimilation if conspicuous racial characteristics, which have served to differentiate between the original components of a population, are thereby redistributed throughout the population in such a way that it becomes hazardous to continue using them as marks of ethnic origin, or if assimilation on other levels has gone so far that the social relevance of, and accordingly interest in, external characteristics are lost, which otherwise could be used to establish certain typical combinations of genealogical lines with reasonable accuracy.

REFERENCES

Borris, W. D., *The Cultural Integration of Immigrants*. Paris: UNESCO, 1959.

Burgess, E. W., "Accommodation," *Encyclopedia of the Social Sciences,* Vols. I-II. New York: The Macmillan Company, 1949.

Eisenstadt, S. N., *The Absorption of Immigrants*. London: Routledge and Kegan Paul, 1954.

Glazer, Nathan, "Integration of American Immigrants," *Law and Contemporary Problems,* XXI (1956), pp. 256-269.

---

[2] In familistic societies, agnomens are rather elaborate so as to indicate not only the genealogy and place of origin of an otherwise unknown person but also his position within the family structure. Together these provide sufficient information to establish his membership in a particular society as well as his overall rank and social status.

Gordon, Milton M., *Assimilation in American Life: The Role of Race, Religion and National Origins*. New York: Oxford University Press, 1964, pp. 68 ff.

Hutchinson, E. P., *Immigrants and Their Children, 1850–1950*. New York: John Wiley & Sons, 1956.

Redfield, Robert, Ralph Linton, and Melville G. Herskovits, "Memorandum for the Study of Acculturation," *American Anthropologist*, XLVIII (1946).

Treinen, Heiner, Differentielle Eingliederung—Eine soziologische Analyse der "Flüchtlinge" in einer oberbayerischen Marktgemeinde. Munich doctoral dissertation, 1963.

——— " 'Symbolische Ortsbezogenheit'; Eine soziologische Untersuchung zum Heimatproblem," *Kölner Zeitschrift für Soziologie und Soziaphyschologie*, XVII (1965), pp. 73–98, 254–297.

Prejudice and Discrimination

21

Our attempt to separate "implications" and "factors" has not only amplified and specified our initial definition of assimilation; it has also revealed some of the conditions that are likely to affect the process of assimilation either positively or negatively. This leads us directly to the problem of prejudice and discrimination. Our task is complicated because little agreement exists among social scientists, and still less among the general public, as to the meaning of either word. One may rightly ask whether this is not largely due to ethnocentric interests in practical issues whose relevance for a general theory of interethnic relations is rather limited. Both words are loaded, yet the moral disapproval implied by them appears to be valid only in a "democratic" social order. Moreover, the principles of democracy admit a wide range of interpretations. Frequently, the ameliorative impulse interferes with the mental discipline required of a scholar; hazy and ambigous concepts serve crusaders and special interest groups better than the scientist who needs precise definitions to arrive at valid insights and generalizations.

PREJUDICE

Analytical concepts acquire their precise meaning only within the framework of a particular theory (cf. Northrop, 1947, pp. 102–118). It is therefore our first task to present definitions that are in line with the theoretical intentions of this book. R. M. Williams, Jr., who follows Gunnar Myrdal closely, remarks that "prejudice is a broad concept having no clear meaning until we give meaning to it" (1964, p. 28). He then proceeds to provide such a meaning. When we adjust his original wording (in a 1947 publication[1]) to the language we have been using

---

[1] Williams defines prejudice as "a common (shared) attitude of hostile nature toward a social group, whose manifestations conflict with some aspects of the basic value framework of the society in which they occur" (p. 42). Another aspect is emphasized, for example, by Vickery, Opler, 1948, pp. 419–428, who define prejudice as a generalization existing prior to the situation in which it is

throughout this volume, we arrive at the following preliminary definition: Prejudice on account of ethnicity is a shared, hostile attitude toward an ethnic category or group whose manifestations in overt action conflict with the normative culture of the host society. Yet prejudice implies more: it has a cognitive as well as an emotional and practical dimension; and it need not involve hostility. This can easily be understood if we recall that in its origin, "prejudice" is a legal term referring to the anticipation of a judicial decision without due process. If an opinion is formed about the facts of a case before an investigation according to the proper procedural rules has been undertaken, the resulting verdict is said to have been prejudiced. Prejudice is a "prejudgment" insofar as preconceived opinions have been assumed to be true before having been put to the prescribed test.

Prejudice expresses itself in several ways. Opinions that are either voiced publicly or that can be elicited by proper stimulation and asking are one aspect. Opinions about ethnic categories and groups may be said to be prejudiced (1) if they include erroneous beliefs about attributes of such categories (groups) that have relevance for social action; (2) if they include (negative or positive) value judgments of such categories (groups), which are invalid in the light of accepted value standards or which are based on erroneous beliefs about relevant facts; and (3) if they result in "discrimination," that is, in actual behavior that is contrary to accepted social or moral norms.

It is, of course, unreasonable to expect people to put all their generalized opinions of ethnic categories (groups) to a scientific test; but one can rightfully expect that they reconsider their preconceived notions, and, if necessary, change them, once they are challenged on the basis of new information. Accordingly, the concept of ethnic prejudice refers first to opinions on controversial issues concerning ethnic categories (groups), which are upheld in the face of strong evidence to the contrary. Moreover, value judgments, which at one time had been perfectly acceptable, may turn into prejudiced judgment if the normative culture of the host society changes; or opinions that are legitimate in the host society may be considered prejudiced when viewed under the value standards of some other society. Yet "prejudice" does not refer only to opinions.

Years before "prejudice" became a widely accepted sociological term,[2] its use was criticized by Robert E. Park. If defined broadly, he wrote in 1928, prejudice "has its source and origin in the very nature of men and their relation

---

involved, directed toward people, groups, or social institutions, which is accepted and defended as a guide to action in spite of its discrepancies with the objective facts. See also Blalock, 1967, who deals with interethnic relations primarily in terms of discrimination; the ninety-seven theoretical propositions presented in this important work overlap only slightly with those arrived at in the present treatise.

[2] Even the first edition of the *Encyclopedia of Social Sciences,* published in 1931–35, did not yet include an article on prejudice.

to one another" (Park, 1950, p. 231). He also reminded his readers that social categorization is fundamental to social structure:

> Where there is substantial agreement as to the categories, as there is bound to be in every stable society, there the status of every individual is defined by the class in which, by tradition or general consensus, he happens to find himself (Park, 1950, p. 232).

Park clearly realized that ethnic categories are of the same stuff as social classes. Every effort to improve the status of a social category, he insisted, is bound to arouse prejudice; ethnic as much as class prejudices are an expression of the resistance of the social order to change.[3]

The situation is quite different if distinctions based on class or ethnicity are part of an established order so that each class or ethnic group

> accepts the definition imposed upon it as if it were a part of the order of nature. Under such circumstances each subgroup . . . maintains its own norms of conduct, and each expects . . . that every individual will live up to the standards of its own group. So far as this normal expectancy is maintained, good-will will exist (Park, 1950, p. 234).

In addition, Park pointed out that any situation in which people of different ethnic background meet is one of vague apprehension tinged with curiosity. When we are confronted with strangers whose behavior cannot be calculated, "anything approaching intimacy may leave us with a vague sense of insecurity," causing antipathies that "seem to constitute the most irrational and . . . invincible elements in racial prejudice" (Park, 1950, p. 238). In an earlier essay, Park traced prejudice to competition and explained that it "is a spontaneous defense reaction the practical effect of which is to restrict free competition between races" (Park, 1917, p. 227).

Similar to Park, Williams admits that much of what is commonly called "prejudice" is an "inevitable and universal feature of social life" (Williams, 1947, p. 36); for men always classify their fellows in various ways and react to others according to their assignment to social categories (Williams, 1964, p. 17). Therefore, prejudice can hardly be considered as a kind of mental epidemic as, for instance, Th. W. Adorno and his associates in the California research project on prejudice seem to have implied (Adorno et al. 1950).

Stereotypes. Another term frequently used in the same sense as "prejudice" is stereotype," which Williams considers as a variety of prejudice and one of its "most common manifestations" (Williams, 1964, pp. 24, 36). It would seem to

---

[3]"Race prejudice . . . is merely an elementary expression of conservatism" (Park, 1950, p. 233).

us, however, that it is little more than a suggestive simile, which draws attention to the rigidity of opinions about ethnic categories (groups) threatening the stability of the social order or vested interests. But social differentiation always involves typing; social categories, in fact, are types of persons. Park was correct in commenting on Lippman's remark that the public thinks in stereotypes: "There is . . . no other way in which the public can think" (Park, 1950, p. 232). As A. W. Gouldner has pointed out, by typing people in accordance with culturally prescribed social categories they are assigned their social identities (Gouldner, 1957, p. 283 as cited by Williams, 1964, p. 36). Moreover, the types used in this process "provide a means of securing high predictability and great economy of attention and effort in social interaction" (Williams, 1964, p. 354).

It is only primary and small-group relations that make personalization possible. One can appreciate the longing—widespread in modern society—for a return of the happy days spent in the family and other primary groups when one was recognized and responded to as a flesh-and-blood human being and not as an abstract item in a category. But prejudice, like sin, is likely to be always with us. To the extent to which primary relations are replaced by secondary relations in urbanized and industrialized society, the necessity of social categorizing increases, and the more inflexible and "impervious to new evidence" stereotyped opinions tend to become. According to Milton Rokeach (1960, esp. pp. 347–365), a closed belief system is the consequence of a threat. The greater the threat, the more rigid the belief system will become, the more intense also the supporting affects, and the more punitive the social sanctions against disbelief will be.

IDEOLOGICAL IMPLICATIONS OF PREJUDICE

No useful purpose will be served by calling "prejudiced" all those who have unreflected opinions about ethnic categories and groups; who attribute to them qualities which they do not possess or which are not equally true of all its members; or who respond to them emotionally. For we all do this in everyday life, and cannot help doing so. We have seen earlier that such preconscious, nonrational, spontaneous judgments and reactions may conceivably contain much practical wisdom (though the generalizations implied in them appear unjustified). They may be quite appropriate as a guideline to social action. They may be positive as well as negative, friendly as well as hostile. They prove indispensable in our relations with persons about whom we do not know enough to safely calculate their individual behavior. Like every probability calculus, however, it fails to predict what any individual included in a category will do precisely; he may prove to be an exception. Such generalizations are, therefore, never able to do justice to a person who is always unique; as wholesale prejudgments they are always false in their application to the individual case. Accordingly, the term "prejudice" should be confined to those attitudes and opinions that persist after the truth of beliefs, the legitimacy of calculations, the virtue of emotions, have been challenged, calling for a rational reexamination.

Several factors may put the stamp of prejudice on attitudes and opinions. Gunnar Myrdal defined prejudice as "the whole complex of valuations and beliefs . . . which are contrary to the equalitarian ideals of the American Creed." He also wrote of the "American Dilemma" (Myrdal, 1944, p. 52 n), which arises from inconsistencies in this social myth.[4] Although prejudice does conflict with the egalitarian ideal, other, more traditionalistic, ideas are also included in the American myth. Real cultures never correspond to the ideal type of a perfectly consistent (or "integrated") system of understandings, values, and norms, just as real markets never correspond to the model of a free market economy. Particularly in the multidimensional culture of a pluralistic society, one has to reckon not only with unintegrated items (or "congeries" in the sense of P. A. Sorokin) but also with inner contradictions.

The American myth, for instance, supports not only the egalitarian views of "liberals" but also those of "conservatives" upholding the "American way of life," which definitely does not exclude marked inequalities in the distribution of social rewards. Finally, societies and their cultures are subject to change so that an opinion that was perfectly legitimate at one time may acquire the quality of prejudice at a later date. This has also happened in America where shifts in the hierarchy of values have caused a stronger accent to be put on equality— equality not only for white, Protestant, Anglo-Saxon natives, but also for foreigners and ethnics who deviate from the American standard. Social mobility has led to controversies over the principles by which social rewards are to be distributed; arguments supporting the existing status system have been labeled "prejudiced." Does the fact that traditional ways of thinking have been seriously challenged by public opinion suffice to impart to them the character of prejudice?

Prejudice as a Disposition to Act

There is, however, still another side to the problem of prejudice, which concerns the use of the concept in social science more directly. Attitudes are treated as predispositions to respond to a certain stimulus in a definite way (Simpson, Yinger, 1953, p. 13). Many believe that if attitudes are known, actual behavior can be predicted. Insofar as opinions are verbalized attitudes, prejudiced attitudes may be ascertained by registering or eliciting opinions. Accordingly, if a person expresses prejudiced opinions, he may also be expected

---

[4]By "social myth" we mean those fundamental beliefs or assumptions shared by members of a society, which provide the ultimate legitimation of the social norms regulating the differential distribution of power, prestige, and other social rewards. As a rule, the social myth of a society has its roots in a religious interpretation of human existence, in a "philosophy," a social doctrine, a political creed that is considered to be self-evident. What is commonly called "democracy" constitutes, in its broad outlines, such a social myth.

to discriminate. This leads to the conclusion that by reducing prejudice, we may hope to reduce discrimination. The great importance generally attached in applied social science to studies on prejudice is largely based on these assumptions.

Unfortunately, there is no constant relationship between opinions, attitudes, and discrimination.[5] Moreover, privately held opinions, as much as attitudes compounded to diffuse emotions which have not yet jelled into definite judgments of fact or value, must be inferred from overt social behavior, and this also includes publicly expressed opinions. Finally, prejudices may not only be a motive of discrimination but also a rationalization of discriminatory practices. From the viewpoint of scientific method, discrimination, as a datum which can be observed directly and intersubjectively, takes precedence over prejudice. In this case, we may most conveniently define prejudice as an attitude that is likely to be associated with discrimination (either as a cause or an effect).

DISCRIMINATION

Although prejudice is not altogether irrelevant to the study of interethnic relations, the macrosociological approach chosen by us suggests that greater attention be paid to discriminatory behavior (including publicly voiced prejudiced opinions) rather than to beliefs, value judgments, and emotions, however prejudiced and untenable these may be. The question of how discrimination may be reduced, possibly by manipulating prejudiced attitudes and opinions, is not our immediate concern; though, by finding out what discrimination is and how it works we may hope to discover ways and means of changing such behavior patterns.

As we have suggested earlier, a major difficulty in defining discrimination as well as prejudice derives from the fact that both involve value judgments whose *general* validity is questionable. The crucial problem therefore is this: Which value standards should be applied to determine the legitimacy of social categorization or differential treatment on account of ethnicity? Once a definite answer is found, we should then be able to define prejudice and discrimination materially. *Formally, however, prejudice can be defined as the illegitimate categorization, and discrimination as the illegitimate differential treatment, of people under the aspect of ethnic descent.*

We have repeatedly pointed out that the legitimation of social patterns is of crucial importance in action orientation and, accordingly, in the actual course of events. The stability of a social order depends largely on the consensus of all concerned as to the unquestionable validity of a shared normative culture

---

[5]For an excellent critical discussion of the assumptions underlying research on prejudice and discrimination, see Blumer, 1958.

through which social expectations are properly legitimized. We also know, however, that such unanimity is frequently lacking, particularly in a modern pluralistic society; not only are basic norms occasionally challenged by some subgroups within society, but even a generally accepted social myth allows for widely diverging interpretations that give rise to ideological controversies and social conflicts. Within the compass of our present undertaking, we cannot venture to solve these fundamental problems of normative social science in general terms.

If we reduce them to the special field of interethnic relations in modern society, we are confronted with a situation which may be simplified (and thereby made intellectually manageable) as follows: There are rules governing the distribution of social rewards according to criteria that are legitimized by value standards constitutive of "democratic" society. They imply social categorization as well as differential treatment. The value standards of democracy may be assumed to be accepted, at least implicitly and tacitly, by all members of a modern society—natives, foreigners, and ethnics. They are epitomized, though not exhausted, by laws and judicial practices; in the United States primarily by the Constitution and the decisions of the Supreme Court. Though vague, not without inherent ambiguities, and subject to gradual change, these democratic standards still permit a rational judgment as to whether the actual distribution of social rewards and the criteria used in social categorization and differential treatment conform with accepted principles; that is, whether they are legitimate.

FUNCTIONAL DIFFERENTIATION

Viewed in this way, it is hardly reasonable to challenge the differential treatment of foreigners on moral grounds. Being a foreigner means that identification is clearly with the parent and not with the host society. The universalistic and diffuse norms of any society, which govern the distribution of social rewards, apply to members only, that is, to those identified with it. Foreigners are admitted on the, at least tacit, assumption that relations with their hosts will be governed by particularistic norms specified by the terms of their admission. Thus, participation in the host society is, on principle, contractual and valid "until further notice." The host society does not assume any comprehensive responsibility for the satisfaction of their basic social needs; nor does it expect undivided loyalty from them. In this case, we should therefore speak of functional differentiation rather than of discrimination.

The situation is different when a newcomer is expected to settle permanently in a modern state. Although he is not a member upon arrival, he is a prospective member supposed to acquire, in due course, all the qualifications necessary for regular membership. Whereas the hosts expect him to comply with the conditions under which he has been admitted as a prospective member, the ethnic in turn expects that, upon assuming his obligations, he will be granted all the benefits the host society has to offer to its charter members in accordance with generally accepted "universalistic" rules. We conclude that *under certain conditions the differential treatment of ethnics may be not only functional but also legitimate, and that this is, as a rule, recognized by both the natives and the ethnics themselves*. In all such cases, it would serve no useful purpose to speak of discrimination.

Illegitimate Differentiation

The concept of (ethnic) discrimination should be confined to the illegitimate differentiation between members of a "democratic" society due solely to ethnicity. There is no doubt that such differential treatment is discriminatory if it is obviously contrary to the social myth of a society. (Think, for example, of the "American Dilemma.")

But this is not the only instance when we may properly speak of discrimination. First, there is always a gap between ideals and reality, between norms and actual behavior. This discrepancy is usually forgotten or regarded with indulgence as long as actual conditions are not challenged by those suffering disabilities, or by their self-appointed advocates. Moreover, some implications of the social myth with regard to the proper treatment of ethnics may not be so obvious as to be always recognized, even by those who are actually put at a disadvantage by a faulty interpretation of the rules governing the distribution of social rewards. The Marxian notion of false conscience refers to this phenomenon. Again, we cannot speak of discrimination unless public conscience is made aware of the error and aroused to question the legitimacy of differential treatment based on it. Any kind of class struggle, and ethnic conflict is one of its forms, involves the awareness of those who are at a disadvantage with regard to the distribution of social rewards that the criteria that are actually applied in social differentiation do not conform with the general norms accepted by a given society (or at least with one of their plausible interpretations).

Finally, judgments concerning the legitimacy of institutionalized behavior patterns are not alone a matter of logical deduction from general principles. For when, in moral as much as in legal reasoning, general principles are applied to particular cases, the factual situation must also be taken into consideration. Accordingly, errors concerning the facts that are relevant to the case may lead as often to faulty conclusions as errors in the interpretation of principles. Thus, new insight in the factual situation may actually render illegitimate behavior which up to that point, though erroneously but still justifiably, had been considered in keeping with both principles and facts.[6]

---

[6]This shows that science does supplement and improve upon practical common-sense knowledge in determining the legitimacy of social behavior. Although the correct interpretation of principles is the concern of the moralist and the normative social sciences, it is the task of the sociologist and

DEFINITION OF DISCRIMINATION

It is hardly possible to indicate with finality when a particular instance of differential treatment should be considered discriminatory. This depends on many factors that are not only subject to change but also often open to doubt and controversy. We have mentioned misrepresentation of generally accepted principles and its consequence for actual behavior, factual errors, awareness of such erroneous interpretations of principles or inadequate information concerning relevant facts, differences in the definition of the situation by the parties involved. Moreover, no practical issue arises unless one party actually challenges the legitimacy of social differentiation in a particular case. Since so many variables are involved, it would seem best to define discrimination in negative terms. *If ethnics actually aspire to a particular right or benefit that is usually granted to charter members of the host society, and if they meet all the requirements to be expected of charter members in analogous situations in accordance with the generally accepted rules governing the distribution of social rewards in the host society, but are nevertheless prevented from competing with other aspirants on equal terms, we may say that these ethnics are discriminated against.*

DISCRIMINATION AND ASSIMILATION

The aspirations of ethnics to a regular status in the host society and to the full enjoyment of social rewards are correlated with their increasing knowledge of the rules governing the distribution of social rewards in the host society. For as they internalize these rules in the process of transculturation, they are made aware of the opportunities offered to charter members as well as of the conditions of full membership. When they experience discrimination; that is, when contrary to these rules, rewards are withheld in spite of their having met the conditions of admission, they are likely to lower their level of aspiration. This indicates an intrinsic nexus between discrimination and assimilation which, as we recall, implies the aspiration of ethnics to regular membership and the concommittant enjoyment of social rewards. Another nexus exists on the acceptance side of the assimilation process. In point of fact, discrimination means the nonacceptance of ethnics as regular members on the part of the host society. Transculturation, finally, is both the cause and effect of aspirations as well as the condition of acceptance. It therefore cannot be treated as a particular

---

the empirical social sciences to provide more accurate knowledge concerning the relevant facts. We can, therefore, understand very well why the topic of discrimination looms so large both in the normative and empirical social sciences concerned with interethnic relations. Despite a casual disclaimer, even Blalock's (1967) overriding concern appears to be a practical or moral one, whereby what we have called the "democratic" value system is taken for granted.

factor facilitating assimilation instead of as a constitutive component of the assimilation process itself.

Earlier we indicated that assimilation proceeds at different rates on different levels; it is more easily accomplished on the level of *commercium* than of *commensalitas* or *connubium*. As the most vital and immediate concern of immigrants is with the attainment of a favorable occupational status and the rewards that go with it, their motivation to acquire the necessary skills (including social skills) is strongest. The acquisition of required skills is part of the transculturation process. Because association on the level of *commercium* is limited, resistance on the part of the natives against acceptance is more easily overcome than on the other levels, where association is more intimate and comprehensive. This is reflected in the observation repeatedly made in empirical studies that discrimination is most intense and resistant to change with regard to marrying ethnics as compared to working together with them. Although increased competition may also increase occupational discrimination, discrimination on the level of *commensalitas* (which also includes admission to certain neighborhoods or voluntary associations), still more on the level of *connubium,* is more consistent and persistent; its illegitimacy is also the last to be generally recognized. At the same time, the kind of pervasive transculturation that is required for association on the level of *commensalitas* and *connubium* is more difficult to achieve (and takes more time) than association on the level of *commercium,* where instrumentality is the primary concern.

THE DYNAMICS OF DISCRIMINATION

Let us now return to a problem which we have mentioned in passing. The assessment of certain types of differential treatment due to ethnicity as illegitimate or discriminatory is far from being constant. But value standards, particularly their public acceptance are unlikely to change at random. Although we need not subscribe to the Marxian theory that the ideological superstructure is merely a reflection of the economic substructure and the class interests that follow from it, we have already become convinced, especially when discussing nationalism, that the acceptance of ideas and collective interests are at least functionally interdependent. Thus, we may assume that the late emergence of egalitarian principles in the area of interethnic relations and the concomittant expansion of the scope of discrimination are somehow related to changing conditions in industrial society. Equality before the law or equal voting rights have hardly been questioned in modern democracy. Differentiation due to ethnicity in this sphere has been widely, if not generally, considered discriminatory; although we know that, even here, attempts have been frequent to make differentiation appear legitimate by all sorts of spurious argument and illicit subterfuge, as in the case of American Negroes or Indians. The same, perhaps with some delay, is true of differentiation in the occupational and economic sphere, for instance, with regard to the principle of equal pay for equal work.

Restrictions on immigration and naturalization have been common, yet once ethnics had been admitted to potential regular membership, their differential treatment has relatively soon been recognized as illegitimate, although countless attempts have been made to rationalize this. It was, however, relatively late that "democratic" (or better, egalitarian) principles were expanded to broader spheres of social life, such as club membership or intermarriage. The ideological changes that have taken place in this respect cannot be ascribed simply to the gradual refinement of the moral conscience or to a self-generated improvement of philosophical insight.

"Open" and "Closed" Societies

Without exhausting the theme, we shall confine ourselves to a few pertinent remarks by way of illustration. *Whenever vital (mainly economic or military) interests are such that a society is liable to gain through population increase, the immigration and rapid integration of foreigners are encouraged.* In an industrial society with an expanding economy, integration is most commonly initiated by granting foreigners regular membership on merit. By "merit" we understand a person's proved ability to perform adequately the role-set assigned to him, or the probability that he will actually do so. If there is an urgent demand for a population increase, the conditions of acceptance are likely to be reduced and the "openness" of the host society and its opportunities for upward mobility will be increased. Thus we may conclude that economic interests that are typical of a modern society in the process of industrialization or industrial expansion will tend to broaden the dimensions in which ethnic differentiation should be considered discriminatory. Such a society will approach the type of an "open society," tending to stamp as illegitimate any kind of social action orientation that takes ethnicity into consideration, and to fight discrimination so defined as contrary not only to moral values but to common interests.

Yet the situation is liable to change when economic conditions become less favorable and competition for available opportunities stiffens, or when a conflict with the parent society of a particular ethnic group (category) throws doubt upon their unconditional loyalty to the host society. In such cases there is a tendency to reduce mobility and to stablilize the social structure. *An effective contribution to closure is made by reemphasizing ethnicity as a criterion of status assignment, and by giving it greater weight than merit.* Simultaneously, fewer instances and fewer levels of ethnic differentiation are likely to be socially defined as acts of discrimination.

Special Interest Groups

What is true of the collective interests of a global society is also true of special interest groups within a society. Not all of them are equally liable to discriminate or are equally sensitive to the illegitimacy of ethnic differentiation.

This is reflected in marked differences in the interpretation of the common social myth. By way of simplification, we may distinguish between "conservative" and "liberal" ideologies. The conservatives tend to resist social change and to uphold ideologically the inviolability of tradition ("the American way of life"!) because of their interest in keeping the gains already made. As incumbents they perceive as an imminent threat the acceptance of ethnics who are likely to compete for available rewards and to initiate changes in the normative culture of society. Conservatives, therefore, are also opposed to removing handicaps from ethnics and are reluctant to define them as discriminatory. Liberals, on the other hand, are those who expect social change to improve general conditions and also their particular chances of advancement. Accordingly, they tend to disregard inherited status and to stress individual merit. They are liable to advocate the acceptance of ethnics on easy terms and to define more instances of ethnic differentiation as illegitimate. The argument of discrimination also serves them as an intellectual and moral weapon to further their own interests.

While both conservative and liberal tendencies are ever-present in modern society, *the dominance of liberalism seems to be associated with economic prosperity and expansion, that of conservatism with times of recession or stagnation*. If, after a period of liberal treatment, the trend is reversed, ethnics tend to define the renewed intensification of ethnic differentiation as particularly discriminatory. The situation is aggravated when ethnics who are moving toward assimilation have no ethnic subgroup to fall back upon and to cushion the shock, either because none have been formed or because they have been dissolved. This may even lead to a genuine regression in their identification with, and participation in, the host society, a process which can be properly called "dissimilation." In contrast to the enforcement of dissimilation by the host society, severely disappointed and frustrated ethnic groups may themselves withdraw from the host society by ceasing to identify with it, thereby initiating their own dissimilation. This has, for instance, happened in the case of the American Negroes and the Black Power Movement. In fact, the spread of any kind of ethnic nationalism on either part—the hosts or the ethnics—is apt to be accompanied by processes of dissimilation.

The competition and influence of ethnics does not equally affect the interests of all segments of the host society. This depends largely on the occupational and class composition of the ethnic population, which may not be the same for ethnics of different origin. The lower classes are likely to be opposed to the acceptance of ethnic laborers on equal terms, while the increase of middle-class ethnics will be felt as a threat by professionals or businessmen. *As immigrants in a particular social category increase, acceptance is likely to change to rejection, depending on the potential or perceived threat to the interests of the incumbents.*

Secondary and Symbolic Discrimination

Two subtypes of discrimination deserve brief mention.

1. The initial discrimination of ethnics, resulting in their exclusion from many social rewards for which they are already qualified, also deprives their children of opportunities to acquire the additional social skills needed for their full participation in the host society. The children of charter members are socialized and enculturated not only through public facilities of formal education, but through their families and other primary groups, as well as many other casual associations. All this is denied to ethnic children who must be partially resocialized and transculturated before they are able to participate fully in the host society. To make up for their real disabilities, it is not enough to provide them with a formal education equal to that of native children. Allowance must also be made for their initial handicap, by offering remedial training and special opportunities of associating freely with their native peers. The failure to do so may be considered an instance of secondary discrimination.

2. Even if ethnics have become assimilated to such an extent that they are indistinguishable from charter members, they may still be exposed to discrimination when their origin is inadvertently discovered. Let us take the example of a job applicant who thinks, feels, and acts like a native in every respect, and whose qualifications for the job are beyond doubt. He may still be rejected, if it becomes known that he is, say, of Jewish extraction. *Whenever a person has become indistinguishable from natives in all respects and only the knowledge or assumption of ethnic descent makes him unacceptable to the natives, we may speak of "symbolic discrimination."* It is particularly aggravating when people have completely ceased to identify with the ancestral group, and have become otherwise fully accepted as equals by their native associates.[7]

---

[7]An analysis of a number of sociopsychological studies (Kent, 1953; Weinstock, 1964; Johnston, 1965; Price, 1963; Taft, 1961, 1963, 1965; and numerous other articles by the Australian research group), which has not been included in this volume because it did not fit into a macrosociological treatise, has revealed that prejudice and discrimination are not the prime obstacles to assimilation as they have often been thought to be. They tend to retard assimilation only in combination with other, particularly personality, factors such as emotional instability. The evaluation of ethnic differentiation as illegitimate by the ethnics themselves is but one factor in shaping their aspirations. Unfavorable attitudes and actions are apparently often not even perceived by ethnics as illegitimate, and are of relatively minor importance for their integration into the host society.

Other findings of immediate interest concern situational factors which affect the integration of ethnics belonging to the third immigration. The degree to which the culture of the parent society differs from that of the host society is likely to influence the time required by ethnics for transculturation. The length of time during which an ethnic is exposed to formal education in the receiving country also tends to improve the rate of transculturation. Yet the exposure to the culture of the

REFERENCES

Adorno, Theodor W., et al., *The Authoritarian Personality*. New York: Harper & Bros., 1950.

Blalock, Hubert M., Jr., *Toward a Theory of Minority Group Relations*. New York: John Wiley & Sons, 1967.

Blumer, Herbert, "Research on Racial Relations: United States of America," *International Social Science Bulletin*, X (1958), pp. 403–447.

Gouldner, Alvin W., "Cosmopolitans and Locals: Toward an Analysis of Latent Social Roles, I," *Adminstrative Science Quarterly*, II (1957).

Johnston, Ruth, *Immigrant Assimilation: A Study of Polish People in Western Australia*. Perth: Peterson Brohenska, 1965.

Kent, Donald P., *The Refugee Intellectual*. New York: Columbia University Press, 1953.

Myrdal, Gunnar, *An American Dilemma: The Negro Problem and Modern Democracy*. New York: Harper & Bros., 1944.

Northrop, F. S. C., *The Logic of the Sciences and the Humanities*. New York: The Macmillan Company, 1947.

Park, Robert Ezra, "The Bases of Race Prejudice," in: *Race and Culture: The Collected Papers of R. E. Park*. eds. E. C. Hughes et al., Vol. I. Glencoe, Ill.: The Free Press, 1950.

———, "Introduction" to J. F. Steiner, *The Japanese Invasion*. Chicago: McClurg, 1917, in: *Race and Culture: The Collected Papers of R. E. Park*, eds. E. C. Hughes et al., Vol. I. Glencoe, Ill.: The Free Press, 1950.

Price, Charles A., *Southern Europeans in Australia*. Melbourne: Oxford University Press, 1963.

Rokeach, Milton, *The Open and Closed Mind: Investigations into the Nature of Belief Systems and Personality Systems*. New York: Basic Books Inc., 1960.

Simpson, G. E., and J. M. Yinger, *Racial and Cultural Minorities: An Analysis of Prejudice and Discrimination*. New York: Harper & Bros., 1953.

Taft, Ronald, "The Assimilation of Dutch Male Immigrants in a Western Australian Community: A Replication of Richardson's Study of British Immigrants," *Human Relations*, XIV (1961), pp. 165–281.

———, "The Assimilation Orientation of Immigrants and Australians," *Human Relations*, XVI (1963), pp. 279–292.

———, *From Stranger to Citizen: A Survey of Studies of Immigrant Assimilation in Western Australia*. London: Tavistock Publications, 1965.

Ronald Taft and A. G. Doczy, "The Assimilation of Intellectual Refugees in Western Australia: With Special Reference to Hungarians," *Research Group for European Migration Problems Bulletin*, IX (1961).

---

host society provided by formal education seems to be less important than the fact that school attendance provides chances of associating with natives on the primary-group level. The same is true of church affiliation and length of residence in the receiving country. A command of the language of the host society will facilitate assimilation to the extent that it approximates the command of language that is expected of natives playing roles corresponding to those assigned to an ethnic or aspired to by him. Economic success and upward mobility increase the likelihood that an ethnic will feel secure and satisfied. This in turn will make him more ready to aspire to identification with the host society and to cut ties with the parent society. Given satisfaction, identification, and opportunity, only time and intelligence seem to be required for maximum transculturation. The chances of assimilation tend to improve with occupational and educational status: Persons in low-grade occupations are more likely to form secondary ethnic groups; higher education, on the other hand, is likely to improve an ethnic's chances of learning new skills as well as understanding a foreign culture and adjusting to existing conditions. Those who are better educated and are lower on dogmatism, mistrust, and anomie are more ready to transculturate so that the chances of association with, and acceptance by, natives are increased.

Vickery, William, and Morris Opler, "A Redefinition of Prejudice for Purposes of Social Science Research," *Human Relations,* I (1948).

Weinstock, S. Alexander, "Some Factors That Retard or Accelerate the Rate of Acculturation—With Specific Reference to Hungarian Immigrants," *Human Relations,* XVII (1964), pp. 321–340. See also S. Alexander Weinstock, "Role Elements: A Link Between Acculturation and Occupational Status," *British Journal of Sociology,* XIV (1963), pp. 144–149.

Williams, Robin M., Jr., *Strangers Next Door: Ethnic Relations in American Communities.* Englewood Cliffs, N.J.: Prentice Hall, 1946.

———, *Social Science Research Council Bulletin,* "The Reduction of Intergroup Tensions," LVII (1947).

From Status Category to Ethnic Group: The Problem of Race

22

The main thesis of this chapter may be summed up as follows: (1) "racial groups" are ethnic groups or categories defined on the basis of marked contrasts in the somatic appearance of the ethnic and host populations; (2) the modern notion of race is a byproduct of slavery and colonialism, which gave rise to racism; (3) racism, just as nationalism, has its roots in a particular historical situation.

Slaves of diverse ethnic origin were integrated into colonial societies as one social category. Assignment to it was made, not only on account of legal status, but also on conspicuous biosomatic differences from charter members of the colonial society. When the colonial society was transformed into a national society and slavery was legally abolished, the inferior status of former slaves and their descendants was upheld by classifying them according to their distinctive biosomatic characteristics. This social redefinition led to the emergence of subgroups in the host society, which conformed with the pattern of secondary ethnic groups. The following discussion will first concern the sociological significance of race. In addition, two cases will be analyzed: the Negroes in the United States and the Cape Coloureds in South Africa, to show how a status category may be transformed into a secondary ethnic group, whereby ethnicity is primarily symbolized by race.

THE CONCEPT OF RACE

Anthropologists, such as Ashley Montague, who are worried about the ambiguity and the vicious abuse of a popular word, are inclined to insist that:

> There is no such a thing as the kind of "race" in which the layman believes. . . . The term "race" takes for granted what should be a matter of inquiry. . . . For the layman,

as for others, the term "race" closes the door on understanding (Montague, 1964, p. 24).

In the past, the expression has been used both in the sense of ethnic category and social class. In the same way as obsolete expressions like "French race" or "English race," the Spanish word *"la raza"* conveys the meaning of "our people": the kinship group, but also the ethnic unit. Although both terms refer to affinity through descent indicated by characteristics shared by a population through many generations, they do not today cover entirely identical phenomena. If we speak of the white race, for instance, we think of a large population divided into many ethnic societies and subsocieties. We would also admit that the same ethnic group may be composed of several racial or subracial elements. Ethnic groups are conceived of as viable social units, but races have a purely taxonomic character. Moreover, "race" emphasizes physical properties and biotic heredity, "ethnic unit" emphasizes cultural characteristics and social heritage. The semantic difference is mainly due to different scientific approaches. Physical anthropologists are interested primarily in biological laws affecting human organisms, including those of genetics; social scientists, in human behavior based on mental processes and in human artifacts. Still, the viewpoints are complementary.

Despite difficulties of conceptualization, "race" is not simply a *Leerformel*, but refers in part to biotic facts of human existence, in part to "real" factors in social action orientation. The distribution of typical somatic features among ethnic units is a matter of experience, as is their transmission from generation to generation. Moreover, somatic characteristics serve fairly well as a means of distinguishing phenotypically ethnic units from each other, or of recognizing genotypically the ethnic descent of populations. What then is to be understood by "race" in the context of sociology? And in what way should the concept of race be distinguished from that of ethnie? It will be best to approach the matter naively.

When the need arises to differentiate between members of one's own group—the "in-group"—and nonmembers to apply the proper rules of conduct in a given situation, we rely primarily on sense perception: Nonmembers look different, they act differently, they sound different, they even smell different. Similar differences can be recognized between the members of various out-groups with whom we come into contact. More often than not it is not isolated properties but combinations of them that are used in real-life situations to distinguish members of different groups (remember Atrisco!). It is also common experience that people related to each other through procreation tend to look alike.

We do not need to be trained biologists to know that descent can frequently be ascertained with the help of typical features amenable to sense perception. This finds its expression in the belief that many qualities of human beings, including mental dispositions and aptitudes, are innate. It is only recently that popular notions about the mysteries of "blood" have been disproved by natural science. Nevertheless, the belief in the heritability and constancy of typical ethnic characteristics serves a useful purpose for the business of getting along in society, however unscientific, irrational, and even absurd such common-sense explanations may be. We should not be surprised if popular theories of this kind still reflect scientific attitudes that have long been discarded; for there is always a feedback of science, though with a certain delay, which often makes for quaint incongruities.

THE CONTRIBUTION OF SCIENCE

The concept of race is primarily a device for classifying human populations with regard to typical combinations of somatic properties transmitted from one generation to the next. Such classifications, however rough, permit us to estimate the degree of consanguinity of various ethnic units as well as the ethnic descent of individuals and populations. They are of greater importance to social scientists than to natural scientists. The latter are apt to point out that the criteria used by anthropologists for the classification of "races" have been chosen because they could be measured easily, but that typical combinations of them do not exhibit regular geographical patterns and are less stable through generations than was at one time believed. The information that physical anthropologists are able to offer social scientists concerned with the problem of race may be synthesized in the following remarks.

No constant relationship has as yet been proven to exist between the "race" and the "mentality" of individuals or groups. Intelligence, inventiveness, artistic reativity, emotional exuberance, sexual voluptuousness, and so on, are too complex to be linked to the kind of unit traits that are genetically transmitted from generation to generation. It is unlikely that the genes controlling the various unit traits, which together provide the biotic basis of mental qualities or dispositions, should vary simultaneously. Moreover, social environment and social heritage are known to have such an overriding effect upon the development of the personality that whatever influence the physical environment and the genetic composition may have, it is liable to be changed past recognition by social and cultural factors.

This, however, is not to deny that particular populations that are racially distinct from their social environment occasionally show typical mental and cultural differences. Thus, the achievements of Negro children in American schools have been found to be inferior as a whole to those of white children. But this can be explained much more readily by historical, cultural, and social factors than by innate race-linked dispositions. For, given the same favorable environment, Negroes do no worse in school than whites, while white children under the same unfavorable conditions approach the level of Negro children (cf. Klineberg, 1940, pp. 297–303). There is even something to be said for the popular belief that the typical "character" or "mentality" of various ethnic groups differs in accordance with their racial composition.

THE SOCIAL FUNCTION OF RACIAL DIFFERENTIATION

Let us take a delicate example, one that has been the occasion of many fierce controversies and most inhuman practices: that of the Jews in Eastern Europe. Scholars insist that there is nothing like a homogeneous Jewish race. Nevertheless, the typical frequencies of certain racial characteristics among Jews and Poles, for instance, though they admittedly concern very minor and minute details of the physical appearance, seem to be so different that many, if not most, Jews as well as Poles have an uncanny aptitude for singling out Jews from Gentiles even without being able to give a precise reason why. Of course, they will not be in a position to recognize every single Jew or to avoid many mistakes. Still, they have a better than even chance to make a correct distinction. This would be far less easy in a Mediterranean population or in a highly mixed population like the American, although even here some people seem to achieve striking hits.[1]

It is in this sense that the Jews in Poland may be considered an ethnic group having distinctive racial characteristics and at the same time some conspicuous mental traits in common, such as a high business acumen or intellectual talents, as compared with their Polish neighbors. It is also quite conceivable that typical "Jewish" features could have served as a fairly reliable clue for expecting from a person an exceptionally acute mind or a better-than-average business sense. Obviously, there is no causal nexus between a "Jewish" nose and a disposition for sharp business practices. Most Jews in the world have neither such a nose (which is more typical of Armenians) nor are they necessarily successful businessmen. Moreover, Jews in other environments appear to have quite different mentalities; and these again may change with changing conditions. When Eastern Jews were transferred to Israel, for instance, they lost their "typically Jewish" characteristics after an astoundingly short time.

We come to the following conclusions: Although it is never "race" that is invariably associated with certain mental and cultural characteristics, it is nevertheless quite possible that in a given population at a given time certain body featues are empirically associated with definite mental qualities. Moreover, biotic distinctions of the human organism, which are distributed with typical frequency among ethnic groups in direct contact with each other, and which are relatively constant through several generations, do have an influence upon human behavior for very practical reasons. Together with other

---

[1]An experiment undertaken by Lund and Berg (1946) has shown that Jewish and Christian students in America are able to identify each other from sight with a much better than chance accuracy (cf. Blumer, 1958, pp. 422 ff.).

clues they serve as fairly reliable guides for the differentiation of ethnic groups and the recognition of ethnic descent in a given situation. Occasionally, they can even tell something about the typical behavior to be expected of groups and individuals. They are also to some extent "hereditary," although this has to do much less with genetic heredity and natural selection than with cultural heredity and social differentiation.

Yet popular beliefs in the heredity and invariable association of definite physical and mental characteristics of ethnic units, which at one time may have had some basis in observable fact, tend to persist after they have completely lost their validity. That is, mental characteristics are ascribed to persons purely on the ground of certain racial features although the nexus has disappeared which, at one time, may actually have existed in the ethnic group from which they are descended; or although the persons in question have nothing to do with the ethnic group of which the nexus may be typical. This, of course, is the quintessence of racial discrimination. There is, furthermore, a tendency to lump strangers together as if they belonged to one ethnic unit when they are distinguished from the host society by striking or unusual physical features. Finally, race theories and popular explanations of race-linked social and cultural phenomena not only influence the perception of racial features, they also influence the significance attached to them and accordingly, the social behavior toward individuals and groups displaying such features.

RACE AS STATUS CRITERION

Originally, "status" was a legal term indicating the degree of freedom that was granted by law to categories of persons. According to Roman law, whence our notion is derived, there are three types of status: (1) *status libertatis,* referring to the distinction between freeman and bondsman; (2) *status civitatis,* distinguishing citizen from alien *(peregrinus);* and (3) *status familiae,* setting apart the head of a family *(paterfamilias)* from members under his authority.

The status of servitude involved complete lack of freedom. Fundamentally, a slave, legally defined as chattel, is therefore subject to his master's will without any restrictions and he may neither invoke the protection of the courts nor enter a valid contract, including a marriage contract. Servile status may be inherited or acquired on account of seizure, sale, or punishment. Servitude may be for life or temporary; it may also be terminated by escape, ransom, an act of grace by the master *(manumissio)*, or public law *(emancipatio)*. Whilst the marriage of a slave with a freeman is as invalid as with another slave, the children issuing from sexual unions with slaves are, as a rule, assigned servile rather than free status even if the partner is a freeman. *Hereditary slavery tends to lead to the emergence of a self-propagating slave population, socially assigned to the same status category at the bottom of the scale.*

COLONIALISM, SLAVERY, AND RACE

In social differentiation of any kind, external characteristics are utilized that are readily discernible and, at the same time, have a high discriminatory power. Now, modern colonialism has frequently solved its labor problem by enslaving autochthones or by importing slaves from other continents (cf. Davis, 1966). In both cases, biosomatic differences between colonizers and slaves were likely to be conspicuous. Accordingly, race became a reliable criterion for recognizing slaves; race and servile status became so closely associated as to be practically indistinguishable. In colonial America, for instance, "Negro" meant primarily "slave," and every slave could be assumed to be of African descent. As a rule, however, the actual ethnic origin of slaves is either not known or forgotten. Accordingly, there is a tendency to assume an ethnic affinity for all those exposing roughly similar racial features which distinguish them from freemen.

We may hypothesize that this tends to lead to a redefinition of the total slave population in ethnic terms, including their descendants as well as freedmen. The social definition is likely to continue after the legal abolition of slavery. All those exhibiting racial characteristics that were originally associated with servile status are consequently treated in very much the same way as a genuine ethnic category. Like immigrants, they are assigned an ethnic status modifying the distribution of social rewards. From what we have learned in the course of our discussion, it is obvious that those assigned to the status of servitude, as much as those assigned to a particular ethnic category, form an integral part of the host society; for both slavery and ethnicity, including fictitious ethnicity based on racial distinctions, are elements of the social structure of the host society. Accordingly, the transformation of the status category "slaves" into a group is likely to follow the same general "laws" as the formation of secondary ethnic groups. The analysis of the two following case studies will show whether the hypothesis is tenable.

The American Negroes

The Negroes in the United States have been chosen as a type case for two reasons. They are, as Charles Wagley and Marvin Harris write, "perhaps one of the most highly publicized and thoroughly studied minority groups in the world" (Wagley, Harris, 1958, p. 19). Moreover, their case offers an opportunity to investigate the contributions of all three factors commonly involved in ethnic-group formation of this type—colonialism, slavery, and race ideology. Due to the availability of a formidable and in part excellent literature on the subject, we can restrict our presentation to the most essential facts relevant to our problem.

SLAVERY

It might be well to recall some of the historical facts of Negro slavery. It has been estimated that in the course of time altogether 50 million slaves have been shipped from various parts of sub-Saharan Africa, where they had been kidnapped by raiders, mostly Arab or native, or sold into slavery by their own kin or rulers. A conservative estimate would put the number of slaves who were imported to what is today the United States of America at close on 700,000. The first "Negers"—as they were called at the time (whence the derogatory word "niggers")—are reported to have been sold in Virginia one year before the landing of the Mayflower. By 1860, the number of slaves had increased to 4,400,000, and that of free Negroes to almost half a million.

In early days, Negroes were treated much like indentured servants of English descent, and like them, were able to earn their freedom after some years of servitude. The distinctive features of Negro slavery were partially developed through social custom but primarily through legal measures known as "Black Codes." Unless proved otherwise, any man displaying Negroid features came to be looked upon as a slave (or at least tainted through descent with the marks of slavery), although some of the free Negroes had never been slaves. By 1750, slavery had been institutionalized in all the colonies; by 1861, it had been abolished in all states north of the Mason-Dixon line. Actual social conditions, however, differed widely. Masters who owned a few slaves were often on friendly terms with them. In towns and cities, slaves even had their own businesses, and were only obliged to pay a stipulated sum to their masters. Free Negroes occasionally kept their own slaves, and were even rather respected members of the community.

The Plantation. The bulk of the slave population, however, was concentrated in the South and in the hands of a relatively small clique of plantation owners. Thus, the plantation became the most important single force in shaping the social pattern typical of American Negroes before the Civil War. In many respects it resembled a feudal or semifeudal estate in Europe. As the system has been characterized in Part II, no detailed description is required. In the American South the overwhelming majority of manual workers were Negro slaves who were socially differentiated among themselves. Servants were treated as members of the master's household and had the highest prestige among the slaves. Below them was a slave middle class which had relatively little contact with whites. The lowest rank consisted of farm hands and laborers who had practically no direct contact with the host society.

There were many opportunities for plantation Negroes to associate with other Negroes, and for higher ranking Negroes to associate with whites, sometimes on fairly intimate terms, for instance, as nurses. Interaction beyond the plantation was more restricted. There was some visiting between neighboring plantations, and Negro slaves also performed errands for their masters. The grapevine provided a means of long-distance communication, and the slave trade and markets added more opportunities for social interaction. Although the law and the policy of the slaveholders restricted both mobility and association among Negroes, a network of social relations gradually came into being, tying the Negro population of America together in a kind of subsociety with a peculiar subculture and structure of its own.

Interbreeding. There was also much interbreeding with whites. The law provided that the offspring of mixed unions would have the mother's status. Generally, the mother was a Negro slave whose children inherited her status. A white master who had children with a slave woman, could avoid the legal downgrading by releasing her from servitude and marrying her. Later laws, however, prohibited intermarriages altogether. From here it is but a short step to the ruling that all those who had "but one drop of Negro blood in their veins" should be considered Negroes and thus presumed to be slaves or descended from slaves. In this way, intermarriage was rendered ineffective as a road to assimilation and absorption, leaving subterfuge, mimicry, and "passing" as the only channels of social mobility.

THE EFFECTS OF EMANCIPATION

The situation changed after the abolition of slavery. Essentially, emancipation means removal of legal disabilities. Neither the emancipation of Jews nor that of peasants, serfs, and slaves has, as such, implied social equality. With legal status differences gone, the real struggle for social equality was to begin. In Europe, after the common status of citizen was instituted, class differences and new forms of social differentiation emerged. Seen in this light, the numerous and diverse measures taken by whites to keep the Negro "in his place" were an attempt to restore traditional inequality in the distribution of social rewards, and thereby to preserve by new means the old order shaken by emancipation. The main difference between the old and the new system of distributing social rewards was a moral one. What was once legitimate and legal now ran contrary to the universalistic rule that those who were equally free and of one legal status must not be discriminated against.

The period of Reconstruction brought not only the removal of legal disabilities but also greater spatial mobility, freer association, and participation in many social activities hitherto barred to Negroes. The reaction on the part of the whites consisted of diverse attempts to restore the color line and to reaffirm the servile status of the Negroes. In the Southern states legal and paralegal measures (the "New Black Codes") served this end. More pervasive and effective still were private covenants, a far stricter etiquette in white—Negro relations, and violence and terror of the kind organized by the Ku Klux Klan.

There are many levels and degrees of servitude. Although slavery is the most radical and inclusive kind, the type introduced as a substitute for slavery was perhaps less stringent or inescapable but more arbitrary and incalculable. In its effect, however, the new servitude was far more cruel and painful; it also was more repulsive to moral sensitivities precisely because it involved the violation of both the law and the moral code by devious and fraudulent means.

Expansion of the Negro Subsociety

Several other factors contributed to the further development of the Negro subsociety, to its expansion in scope, density, and intensity of interaction, and to its solidarity. While the opportunities of association within the ethnic group became freer, the barriers against association with whites were now stricter than before. As the social structure of the Negro subsociety became more differentiated and complex, social interdependence also increased. As in all ethnic groups, its maintenance was further supported by the proliferation of separate institutions, organizations, and voluntary associations. Among the Negroes, churches, the first of which date back to the last quarter of the eighteenth century, played the most decisive role. The segregated public school had a similar effect. The inferior status imposed upon all Negroes, even those who by their education and skills qualified for higher positions and prestige, created strong common interests. This provided an opportunity for leaders to propagate a kind of class consciousness which, combined with awareness of "race" or ethnicity, symbolized by conspicuous biosomatic differences, strengthened solidarity and a sense of common purpose. White ideologies of race were reinterpreted so as to provide powerful social myths and a further stimulus for collective indentification and concerted action.[2]

CONCLUSIONS

In conclusion we shall now compare the type of secondary ethnic group represented by the American Negroes with that discussed in Section C. Like immigrants, the Negro slaves were transferred individually to the American

---

[2]In keeping with its paradigmatic purpose, this brief outline stresses the common features of slavery as it has developed in Europe's colonies rather than the distinguishing features of slavery in the United States. Ever since Tannenbaum (1947) has raised the question, there has been much speculation as to why the treatment of African slaves and their descendants has differed ostensibly

society. Yet they did not originate in one definite parent society but in many unrelated tribal societies. Moreover, dissociation from their separate parent societies went so far that these could not realistically serve as reference groups. Thus, the Negroes acted, and were reacted to socially, not with reference to any particular parent society but to a generalized and fictitious ethnic unit or "race." Because they were gradually transformed into a segregated, segmental, and self-recruiting subsociety, race assumed the function of ethnicity in two ways: Phenotypically, it served as a means of recognizing membership in the ethnic group, genotypically, as a proof of common descent. When they were finally incorporated as citizens into the American nation, whose normative culture excludes descent as a legitimate criterion for assigning social status, the Negroes suffered the fate of national minorities.

A secondary ethnic subgroup is normally related to a definite host society and a definite parent society, both serving individual ethnics as reference groups. Yet for the American Negroes there did not exist any one parent society with which all of them could identify realistically, except at a much later period when Pan-Africanism and the emergence of the new African nations suggested a new kind of ethnic solidarity. This solidarity has found its expression in Negro movements, most recently in the Black Power movement, whose ideology conforms to ethnic nationalism. Furthermore, inescapable and inheritable biosomatic attributes excluded any chance of making people forget differences in origin; ethnic dividing lines tended to be fixed indefinitely, obstructing assimilation on most noncultural levels. The social controls and the near hysteria with which intermarriage was resisted reflect the desire to close this only feasible road to absorption, and to block hypergamy and upward mobility. Finally, ethnicity remained firmly linked to an inferior status, which actually derived from the legal institution of slavery. In all other respects, however, "racial" groups of this kind follow the same general pattern as do secondary ethnic subgroups.

The Coloureds of South Africa

Superficially, one might be inclined to compare the Negroes of the United States with the "Negroes" of South Africa.[3] But the situation of the Bantu-speaking peoples of South Africa resembles that of the Indians in the United States,

---

in various colonies, particularly those established by Protestants and Catholics. Recently Schermerhorn (1970) has taken up the argument. To clarify his point he has slanted his analysis of the case of the Negro in North America in a somewhat different direction than has been done in the present context without, however, rendering invalid—we believe—our own attempt at a more generalizing interpretation.

[3]The data on which this interpretation is based have been adapted, with the permission of the publishers, mainly from S. P. Cilliers, *The Coloured of South Africa: A Factual Survey*. Cape Town: Banier, 1963.

while the situation of the American Negroes compares with that of the so-called Cape Coloureds. The reader should keep in mind that the South African term "Coloureds" means something different from what at one time had been understood by "colored" in the United States (which was a polite euphemism for black). We shall therefore retain the different spelling.

According to census figures for 1960, the South African population of 15,982,664 consisted of 10,907,789 (68.25 percent) "Bantu," that is, Negroid Africans; 3,880,492 (19.33 percent) "Whites" (including Afrikaners); 477,125 (3 percent) Asiatics (mostly from India); and 1,509,258 (9.44 percent) Coloureds. The census, however, classifies all those as Coloureds who cannot be classified as members of the other three census categories, including not only the Cape Coloureds but also more recent mixtures between them and Negroid Africans. In 1960, almost 90 percent of the people classified as Coloureds lived in the Cape Province, 29 percent alone in the Western Cape, and 25 percent in the Metropolitan area of Cape Town.

The basic population elements from which the Cape Coloureds are descended include aborigines, slaves, and Europeans. Yet the social pattern was set mainly by the aboriginal Hottentots who were first drawn into the orbit of the emerging colonial society. Like the Bushmen they belong to the Khoi-San-speaking peoples. With their light yellow complexion, wide cheekbones, small stature, peppercorn hair, and the pronounced buttocks of their women they cannot easily be mistaken for the Bantu-speaking Negroids who arrived many centuries later in this part of Africa. The resistance of the Hottentots, who were nomadic pastoralists, to the Dutch arriving in 1652 was remarkably weak. After their tribal organization had been destroyed and their herds taken away by European settlers, they quite readily entered the service of white farmers. Because the Cape autochthones, although excellent herdsmen, were unfit for strenuous and sustained work, slaves were imported to meet the urgent demand for farm labor. The Bushmen, also autochthones of the Cape (and beyond it of Southern and Central Africa), were very primitive hunters who were looked down upon as little better than wild animals. In the struggle for hunting grounds, Bushmen were usually killed, but their children were taken alive and distributed among farmers who kept them in virtual slavery. Moreover, the Bushmen mated freely with Hottentots.

SLAVERY

The first slaves came from West Africa, but the majority were imported from Mozambique and Madagascar, India, Ceylon, and above all from the Dutch East Indies. Considerable miscegenation took place between slaves and Hottentot women, as the sex ratio among the slaves was 6:1 as late as 1708. The Dutch settlers, on the other hand, were interbreeding with both autochthones and imported slaves. By the second half of the eighteenth century the "Bastards," as the Hottentot-half-breeds were called, had become a separate ethnic unit much like, for instance, the Métis of Manitoba. And within two decades after the introduction of slaves to the Cape, fully three-quarters of the children born of slave mothers had white fathers. Additional European blood was infused into the Coloured population by sailors, soldiers, and visitors from many lands. This mixture of diverse ethnic elements with their manifold Caucasian, Khoi-San, and Negroid biosomatic heritage fell victim to the same type of social categorization as the American slaves, although they were racially much more heterogeneous than the Negroes. While not all of them were slaves, the slave element represented the core of the Coloured population. Cilliers describes the historical situation as follows:

> The white settlers almost from the beginning distinguished and later differentiated between themselves and the nonwhites. Originally this distinction was not so much associated with color or race but rather sprang up from distinction between Christians and heathens. Added to this was the obvious difference in culture and standard of civilization. So strong was this basic distinction that an embargo was very soon put on indiscriminate assimilation with nonwhites, and conversion to the Christian faith became a condition for acceptability. In due course, however, this basis of differentiation came more and more to be identified with the more perceptible features of race and color. In time, race and color was not only accepted as the symbol of difference but also became the criterion of differentiation and discrimination (Cilliers, 1963, p. 11).

TRANSFORMATION OF A SOCIAL CATEGORY INTO AN ETHNIC GROUP

This pattern was upheld because, by the eighteenth century, the Coloured population had been integrated into the colonial society as a distinctive status category at the bottom of the scale. As was the case with the American Negroes, the color line prevented any upward mobility of the Cape Coloureds due to merit or hypergamy. Even after slavery was abolished in 1834, they remained a distinctive social category associated with both racial features and low rank.

Just as did the American Negroes, and for the same reasons, the Cape Coloureds assumed the character of an ethnic group with a social structure of its own. They also accepted the ideology of the Europeans, according to which racial features were causally related to cultural retardation. Because the Khoi-San-speaking peoples (as much as some of the slaves) were lightly pigmented, frizzy hair rather than skin color became the principal symbol of nonwhite descent. The highest social status within the ethnic group of Coloureds was accorded to persons with straight hair, while those with peppercorn hair held the lowest rank. Within the Coloured group vertical mobility was possible on the basis of accomplishment, such as education, property, moral standard, or informal association.

The factors that contributed most to the emergence of the ethnic group include the fact that by the end of the eighteenth century, sexual unions between whites and Coloureds became tabu, and half-breed children were no longer absorbed into white society. Yet the Coloureds had become not only completely Christianized but also largely transculturated in most other respects. They had no common language other than Afrikaans; they shared the same normative culture with the Boers; and they identified fully with South African colonial society. Despite the legal and informal discrimination they have suffered, and which has even increased, the Cape Coloureds have not been affected by the Pan-African nationalism which has made progress among the Bantu-speaking population of South Africa. They are well aware that in the life-and-death struggle between white and black, their lot is inseparably linked to that of the whites. The Boers, on the other hand, much like the Americans in the South, have put up an ever-stiffening resistance against assimilation of the Cape Coloureds who were losing their distinctive cultural characteristics. This requires some further explanations.

After the Cape Colony had become permanently British in 1806, opposition to the social pattern established by the Dutch settlers and their descendants gained momentum. The latter

> . . . came to identify British rule with championship of the nonwhites to the detriment of their own interests. Inevitably, this also led to the hardening of attitudes towards nonwhites who were the subjects of the dispute. Although the nonwhites generally, and especially the Coloureds, were to reap material, political, and spiritual benefits from this struggle, the bitterness produced by this struggle had flavoured the attitudes of the majority of the whites towards them ever since (Cilliers, 1963, p. 12).

In reading these remarks, who would not be reminded of white-Negro relations during the Civil War? From 1836 until 1910, whites and Coloureds enjoyed identical civil rights. The year of 1836 witnessed the great exodus of the Boers from the Cape Province. Among those who stayed behind, alienation from the Coloureds and resistance against social equality grew. In 1857, the Dutch Reformed Church decided to separate church facilities. Although few Coloureds had followed the Boers on their treck, the constitutions of the two Boer republics explicitly excluded them from civil rights. This pattern was maintained after union, and finally imposed also upon the two other provinces, including the Cape Province.

DETERIORATION OF SOCIAL STATUS

As the power and position of the Afrikaaners improved in the Union of South Africa, the situation of the Coloureds progressively deteriorated. Ever since 1861, they have been excluded from government schools. Eventually, two completely separate systems of education were developed for whites and Coloureds. Even the curriculum for Coloureds was different, assumedly in keeping with their proper needs. A further step in their segregation from South African society is marked by the legislation of 1924, for the protection of white labour against competition by nonwhite labour. By this Act, Coloureds were excluded from certain occupations and from training for certain vocations. Moreover, their wages were fixed at a lower rate than those for white employees in comparable positions. In 1951, their civil rights were severely curtailed, and even the Cape Province, where political equality had always prevailed, was forced to accept the pattern set by the Transvaal and the Orange Free State.

APARTHEID

The final break came with the enforcement of the Apartheid policy when Coloureds, in the same way as Bantu, were physically removed from white neighborhoods. True enough, the separate districts (called "locations") set up for the Coloureds have not the same appearance of an internment camp as the Bantu locations, complete with barbed-wire fences and guards at the gates. It is also true that simultaneously with the gradual removal of the Coloureds from white areas, which was accompanied by the compulsory sale of their homes and other great hardships, slums were cleared and schools as well as other public services and facilities were improved. Still, the Coloureds are sharply segregated from the white community of which they have been an integral part for centuries, and all opportunities for more intimate contacts and *commensalitas* are reduced to a minimum. Intermarriage and sexual unions are prosecuted by law and severely punished. Thus, the Coloureds of South Africa are becoming more and more a completely separate and segregated ethnic society, supposed to eventually form a multiethnic commonwealth together with the Afrikaaner national society and the different Bantu societies a-building in the "Bantustan" reservations.

CONCLUSIONS

The preceding discussions add to our knowledge of the role played by ideology in assimilation. While the ideology of democratism provides a legitimation of aspirations at full membership, nonacceptance is legitimized by the ideology of racism. In a postcolonial society the inclusion of egalitarian principles in the normative culture of the emerging nation challenges the legitimacy of a social structure based on slavery. When legal support is withdrawn after the abolition of slavery, the stability of the social structure is threatened. Those who have a vital interest in the maintenance of the existing order tend to substitute legal provisions by other means, thereby preventing the acceptance of former slaves and their descendants on equal terms. These include primarily measures to hinder the acquisition of skills necessary to achieve higher status, economic and political power, intimate association with natives, and intermarriage. Separate educational facilities serve the dual purpose of minimizing association and of lowering the chances of acquiring skills, while contributing to enculturation with regard to basic norms of the society.

The ideology of racism provides relief for the "normative dissonance" ensuing from the contradiction between the prevailing system of distributing social rewards and the social myth. Although its egalitarian principles are not questioned outright, they are supplemented by the tenets of racism in such a way that actual practice has the appearance of being legitimate. In other words, racism relieves the bad conscience of the incumbents and supplies them with a justification of discriminatory behavior. The victims, on the other hand, tend to accept the racial hetero-stereotypes as their self-image in the same way as they adopt other items of the normative culture. Because they have been acculturated to, and identify with, the national society, they have internalized social definitions and do not challenge the social rules governing the distribution of social rewards as long as these, on the basis of shared understandings about race, appear to be in tune with democratic principles.

The ideology of racism has been applied also to situations not related to slavery. For instance, the Jews in Germany were redefined in racial terms to impose irrevocable disabilities upon them. By the Nuremberg race laws they were declared to be nonmembers of the national society to whom the general rules for distributing social rewards should not apply. In this way their dissimilation was initiated. Similarly, the apartheid policy of South Africa is meant to promote the dissimilation of partly assimilated populations which are distinguished by conspicuous biosomatic differences from the population identified with the nation.

Elsewhere in colonial Africa the race ideology has also served to separate the autochthones from the settlers, and to prevent their intimate association with and acceptance by the settlers. On the other hand, partial transculturation was fostered by missionaries and other educators; it led to the acceptance of the race concept by the autochthones themselves along with other items of European culture. In Part IV it will be shown how the ideology of racism turns against its originators when conclusions are drawn from it that make plausible the illegitimacy of their supremacy and the birthright of the native "race" to a whole continent.

REFERENCES

Aptheker, Herbert, *American Negro Slave Revolts*. New York: Columbia University Press, 1943.
Banton, Michael, *Race Relations*. London: Tavistock Publications, 1967.
Blumer, Herbert, "Research on Racial Relations—United States of America," *International Social Science Bulletin*, X (1958).
Brotz, Howard, *The Black Jews of Harlem: Negro Nationalism and Dilemmas of Negro Leadership*. Glencoe, Ill.: The Free Press, 1964.
Carstens, Peter, *The Social Structure of a Cape Coloured Reserve*. New York: Oxford University Press, 1967.

Cilliers, S. P., *The Coloureds of South Africa: A Factual Survey*. Cape Town: Banier, 1963.

Davie, Maurice R., *Negroes in the American Society*. New York: McGraw-Hill, 1949.

Davis, David Brion, *The Problem of Slavery in Western Culture*. Ithaca, N.Y.: Cornell University Press, 1966.

Dickie-Clark, H. F., *The Marginal Situation: A Sociological Study of a Coloured Group*. London: Routledge & Kegan Paul, 1966.

Essien-Udom. E. U., *Black Nationalism: A Search for Identity in America*. Chicago: University of Chicago Press, 1962.

Francis, Emerich, *Ethnos und Demos: Soziologische Beiträge zur Volkstheorie*. Berlin: Duncker & Humblot, 1965.

Hocking, George W., Jr., *Race, Culture and Evolution: Essay in the History of Anthropology*. New York: The Free Press of Glencoe, 1968.

Jourdan, Winthrop D. *White over Black: American Attitudes Toward the Negro, 1550–1820*. Chapel Hill, N.C.: University of North Carolina Press, 1968.

Klineberg, Otto, *Social Psychology*. New York: Henry Holt and Co., 1940, pp. 297–303.

Lund, Frederick, and Wilner C. Berg, "Indentifiability of Nationality Characteristics." *Journal of Psychology*, XXIV (1946), pp. 77–83.

Marais, J. S., *The Cape Coloured People, 1652–1937*. Johannesburg: Witwatersrand University Press, 1957.

Mead, Margaret, et al., eds., *Science and the Concept of Race,* New York: Columbia University Press, 1968.

Montague, Ashley, *The Concept of Race,* Glencoe, Ill.: Free Press, 1964.

Myrdal, Gunnar, *An American Dilemma: The Negro Problem and Modern Democracy*. New York: Harper & Bros., 1944.

Rose, Arnold, *The Negro in America*. New York: Harper & Bros., 1948.

Schermerhorn, R. E., *Comparative Ethnic Relations: A Framework for Theory and Research*. New York: Random House, 1970, pp. 199–217.

Tannenbaum, Frank, *Slave and Citizen: The Negro in the Americas*. New York: Alfred A. Knopf, 1947.

UNESCO, *Four Statements on the Race Question*. Paris: UNESCO, 1969.

Van den Berghe, Pierre L., *South Africa: A Study in Conflict*. Middletown, Conn.: Wesleyan University Press, 1965.

——, *Race and Racism: A Comparative Perspective*. New York: John Wiley & Sons, 1967.

Wagley, Charles, and Marvin Harris, *Minorities in the New World: Six Case Studies*. New York: Columbia University Press, 1958.

Williams, Robin M., Jr., *Strangers Next Door: Ethnic Relations in American Communities*. Englewood Cliffs, N.J.: Prentice-Hall, 1964.

The Integration
of Ethnics into
Modern Society

23

The central topic of Part III was the integration of ethnic components into a modern society. In summing up the results, we shall concentrate on the conceptual scheme with which we were able to detect basic regularities in interethnic relations. Since the problems of the empirical social sciences cannot be solved by a purely deductive method, the precision of analytical concepts can only be achieved step by step.

In the beginning we were compelled to operate with common-sense notions and conventional terminologies. Particularly in presenting case studies culled from the available literature, we adopted, as far as possible, the language of their authors. Whenever we found that different words had been used to convey closely related meanings we proceeded to streamline the nomenclature. We continued to confine ourselves to conventional terms in order to preserve the cumulative effect of social research. Eventually, however, a point was reached when the consistency of the theory could only be achieved by dropping terms that had proved redundant, by redefining traditional concepts, and even by introducing new ones. In addition, we strove to reduce the final definitions of key concepts to those essentials that are relevant to the problem in hand. Although they are not exhaustive, they are at least free of connotations and equivocations. If the meanings given by us to certain expressions seem far removed from their common-sense meanings, the reader should keep in mind that analytical concepts assume their precise meanings only within the framework of the theory in which they occur. It is not a shortcoming of sociological theory that it cannot pinpoint exactly the empirical referents of many conventional terms, such as "nation" or "democracy"; for these—more often than not—are not only vague but also loaded with ideological assumptions that contradict established facts.

294

In order to increase the transparency of the system of interdependent concepts that we have adopted, we shall now reverse the procedure by which we arrived at the final definitions of key terms. Accordingly, we shall first summarize our findings about direct integration of individual ethnics and then proceed to the problems involved in the indirect integration of ethnic collectivities. This requires a final definition of "integration" that avoids the assumption that ethnics cannot be said to be fully integrated into the host society unless they have become indistinguishable from charter members. In this case we would also have to accept the practical implication that societal integrity can frequently be realized only at the cost of extreme human suffering, including forced assimilation, violent expulsion, or genocide.

The term "integration" in its widest sense, we suggested, indicates the fact that all components of a social structure, individuals as well as groups, are assigned a definite status according to general principles that have unquestioned validity in a given culture. In its transitive sense the term refers to the processes by which components of the social structure are assigned a status in such a way that no major social problems arise to threaten the social order. Since in Part III our primary concern was with the structural integration of new additions to a modern society, *"integration of ethnics" refers in this context to the processes by which the practical problems involved in the status assignment of ethnics are minimized*. Thus, ethnics may be said to have been integrated to the extent that they function properly within the social order of the host society.

In the course of our investigation we felt compelled to give a strict, if narrow, meaning to the term "social structure." The concept that we adopted refers primarily to the differential distribution of social rewards among the members of a society according to social categories with which they are identified. When a person has been identified with a particular social category, he may be said to have been assigned a social status. Strictly speaking, the status system of a society applies to members only. *Membership in a society necessarily implies the assignment of a definite status; lack of status precludes membership*. There are, however, degrees of membership in a society. Regular or charter members enjoy full membership; that is, the accepted system of distributing social rewards applies to them without any restrictions.

New additions to a society include (1) children born to regular members who are at once assigned full membership, and (2) foreigners who are not identified with the host society, and thus excluded from the normal system of distributing social rewards. In time, however, resident foreigners may be granted membership, first qualified and eventually perhaps full membership. Their integration proceeds as the limited status assigned to them is replaced by a more comprehensive one, until finally it becomes indistinguishable from the status of full members or "natives." When this is accomplished, the erstwhile foreigners have been absorbed in the host society. We have pointed out that membership of a society is based on reciprocity of identification. *When the group of aspiration does not coincide with the group of assignation, the resulting lack of complementarity renders the social calculus ineffective, which promotes social interaction in large and complex societies and thus leads to problematical situations disturbing the social order.*

The rules governing the distribution of social rewards and the criteria according to which the members of a society are assigned social status are embodied in its normative culture. The cultural norms that determine the social structure differ with the general type of society. They also affect interethnic relations; for these concern the relationship between components of the social structure that are categorized by ethnicity and are accordingly subject to differential treatment in the distribution of social rewards. We have been able to demonstrate that, in modern societies, ethnicity tends to create specific problems that are not known to agrarian societies politically organized in power structures of the empire type. We have furthermore shown that these problems are directly connected with the partly antithetical processes of nationalization and industrialization.

As a rule, the national core of a modern society is socially defined as constituting a major ethnic unit from which foreigners are characteristically excluded. Ethnic differentiation, however, remains unproblematical as long as ethnically heterogeneous population elements are socially defined as foreigners and thus not identified with the host society. The situation is radically different when the transferees define themselves, and are defined by their associates, as permanent residents who, sooner or later, are to be integrated into the host society. It is only then that we may describe them as ethnics. For the term *"ethnics"* refers to *elements included in the population of a nation-state which differ ethnically from the national core, and which are assigned a qualified membership status in the national society.*

As we have seen, ethnic differentiation modulates the operation of the rules governing the distribution of social rewards according to general status criteria. Ethnic problems arise when those who are put at a disadvantage in the distribution of social rewards become aware that the general rules and criteria are, in their case, violated and replaced by particular norms that are not legitimized by the basic ideology (that is, by beliefs, understandings, value standards, and norms of conduct more-or-less common to modern societies). A number of people who are identified with a particular ethnic unit other than the national core of the host society, and who suffer differential treatment because of this, form an *ethnic category.* By *"ethnic groups,"* on the other hand, we understand subgroups of a national society formed by ethnics whose differential treatment in the distribution of social rewards creates specific social problems.

Let us now consider some typical processes of social change involved in the integration of ethnics. The simplest case is the *transformation of individual ethnics into full members*. This occurs when ethnic differences become socially irrelevant because they are either forgotten or are neglected in the distribution of social rewards.[1] These processes are referred to as direct integration ending in absorption. As we have seen, direct integration is primarily a matter of assimilation. By *"assimilation"* we *understand the processes by which an individual is assigned increasing degrees of membership status in the host society until he becomes indistinguishable from charter members with regard to the distribution of social rewards*. For analytical purposes we have distinguished four interdependent aspects of assimilation: aspiration, acceptance, transculturation, and association. Assimilation progresses to the extent to which ethnics aspire to full membership, and to which they are accepted as full members of the host society by their associates.

Full membership implies (1) that ethnics identify themselves, and are identified by their associates, exclusively with the host society, and that they share a sense of solidarity with charter members of the host society; and (2) that they are assigned social status in accordance with the general rules governing the distribution of social rewards among the charter members of the host society. The assimilation of ethnics requires furthermore (3) that they share with the charter members the essential elements of the culture, and that they have acquired the skills and qualifications that are expected of charter members in analogous situations; and (4) that no restrictions because of ethnic differences are imposed upon their factual association with charter members in the sphere of both primary and secondary relations. The processes of assimilation on the level of aspiration, acceptance, culture, and association tend to proceed at different rates, and tend to have been achieved to different degrees at any one time; they may diverge or converge. These differences give rise to typical problems of integration, which are resolved as the processes of assimilation converge.

Our discussions have revealed that under certain conditions, individual transferees to the host society are inclined to associate with their own kind in order to satisfy basic social needs that are not met by the host society. Once the ethnics have become sufficiently transculturated and integrated in the host society on the level of *commercium* to aspire to the enjoyment of social rewards offered by the host society to its charter members but are rejected (that

---

[1]The initial transformation of foreigners into ethnics can be disregarded. The analytical distinction between foreigners and ethnics has been introduced to draw attention to the fact that not all foreigners present in a given state population pose ethnic problems; for instance, travelers, tourists, and visitors, but also businessmen and professionals who remain identified with their parent society, having the status of guests in the host society. To some extent, this is true even of transient laborers unless they appear on the scene in great numbers or show a tendency to stay for a considerable length of time approaching permanent settlement. In this case they are likely to assume the character of true ethnics. In this transitory category, we find at present the millions of foreign laborers in many industrial countries of Western Europe, notably the Federal Republic of Germany. Immigrants, on the other hand, are frequently considered as prospective members of the host society, and thus from the outset, are put in the position of ethnics.

is, not accepted on equal terms), such preferential associations of a more casual kind tend to become institutionalized and permanent. *When a set of institutions has emerged that is specific to a particular category of people, we say that these people form a subgroup in a society.* The social participation of ethnics is typically segmental; for they participate in the host society directly in some dimensions but through the mediation of secondary ethnic groups in all the others.

Secondary ethnic subgroups are maintained to the extent to which the loss of members to the host society through assimilation can be prevented. *The maintenance of an ethnic group depends on its ability to satisfy the cognitive, instrumental, emotional, and expressive needs of its members without having recourse to the host society.* The chances of maintenance will be increased, (1) if the area of participation in the ethnic group is widened, simultaneously reducing the association of the ethnics with members of the host society; and (2) if the effectiveness of social controls is increased through separate institutions and organizations, particularly those bearing upon the enculturation of the children.

Ethnics may become collectively integrated into the host society through the mediation of the secondary ethnic group to which they belong. Such indirect integration occurs whenever both the ethnic group and the host society have become adjusted to each other so that major conflicts or disturbances of the social order are avoided. But ethnics who have dissociated themselves from their ethnic group are likely to be still socially identified with it and to be treated accordingly. The same is true of ethnics when their ethnic group has been completely dissolved. In this case, the ethnic group has been transformed into a social category. The direct integration of such ethnics into the host society takes place in the same manner as the integration of ethnics who have never formed an ethnic group or have never attached themselves to one.

Primary ethnic groups emerge, as we recall, when a population, which differs ethnically from the national core of the host society, has been transferred collectively from the parent society, and when it is put in a position to reconstitute itself as a viable subsociety of the host society. As compared with secondary ethnic groups, a primary ethnic group has the advantage of starting with a more-or-less comprehensive set of separate institutions, which tend to monopolize social controls over its members at all levels. Members of a primary ethnic group are mainly concerned with its maintenance, which depends on the strength of separate institutions and on the preservation of distinctive characteristics, including language. They do not clamor for equal treatment with the majority of the host society, but for the recognition of their separate collective identity.

Thus, the situation of primary ethnic groups is quite different from that of secondary ethnic groups. The latter are formed and maintained to compensate for deprivations suffered by individual members because of their unequal treatment by the host society. To this end, separate institutions that exercise partial social controls over the group members, mainly in the sphere of primary relations, are created and upheld on a more limited scale. Members of secondary ethnic groups are not so much concerned with the preservation of their separate collective identity as with the enjoyment of social rewards on equal terms with the natives. They are also more inclined to assimilate to the host society, unless prevented to do so by their rejection on the part of the natives, and also by social controls that their own group is exercising. These, however, tend to be more feeble than those exercised by primary ethnic groups through the more comprehensive institutions at their disposal.

When the presence of a primary ethnic group is no longer felt to constitute a major problem, it may be said to have become *indirectly* integrated into the host society. This depends largely on the willingness of the host society to take political, legal, and administrative measures for the protection of its distinctive characteristics, of its separate institutions, and of its specific social structure. The removal of disabilities, economic advancement, and the toleration of cultural or somatic marks of distinction, which do not jeopardize the proper functioning of democratic government or industrial economy, help to promote the assimilation of individual ethnics, their integration into the status system of the host society, and the dissolution of secondary ethnic groups.

In the case of primary ethnic groups, however, provisions for the prevention of discrimination are likely to have the opposite effect. Characteristics by which their members may be readily distinguished from the natives are all the more demonstratively emphasized and even new ones deliberately added, thereby contributing to group maintenance. The transculturation of individual ethnics increases their chances of becoming assimilated and tends to promote the dissolution of ethnic groups. This is more common in the case of secondary ethnic groups than of primary ethnic groups, which are more likely to accept parts of the host culture collectively. Such collective transculturation, however, facilitates the accommodation of a primary ethnic group to the existing situation, and thus increases its chances of maintaining itself in an alien environment.

The outright dissolution of primary ethnic groups is less common than their transformation into secondary ethnic groups. This occurs not only because of the gradual loss of separate institutions, but especially because of the modernization of the economy. It is precisely when the host society has been generous in granting protection against the loss of their demographic and cultural substance that primary ethnic groups are inclined to give up their resistance against economic change, thereby exposing themselves to the processes that transform them into secondary ethnic groups.

The distinction that we have made between primary and secondary ethnic groups has a direct bearing upon the postcolonial situation, which will be the topic of Part IV. For nation-building in former colonies is typically confronted with the problem of integrating not only tribal societies, which may be considered primary ethnic groups, but also secondary ethnic groups, which have emerged among the ethnically diverse population of detribalized migrants to the modernized sections of colonial society and the new urban centers.

REFERENCE

Bundesanstalt für Arbeit, *Ausländische Arbeitnehmer: Beschäftigung, Anwerbung, Vermittlung–Erfahrungsbericht 1971*. Nürnberg: Bundesanstalt für Arbeit, 1972.

ETHNIC RELATIONS IN COLONIAL SITUATIONS IV

INTRODUCTION

The theories presented in the main body of this treatise have been developed on the basis of the history and sociology of the Western World. In this last part we shall extend their scope to the "Third World," sometimes also called "Poor World," "undeveloped countries," or "new nations." None of the current labels, which have been invented for political rather than theoretical purposes, is sufficiently precise to delimit the empirical referent of an analytical concept. Viewed under the aspect of interethnic relations, it appears promising to reduce the meaning of "Third World" to situations that are typical of colonialism and its aftermath. Unfortunately, the term is no less opaque than the others. M. I. Bonn (1932), for instance, defined "colonialism" as the "transfer of political, economic, and cultural institutions from one society to another."[1] In this broad sense the term covers a great variety of measures designed to carry out expansionist power policies, to exploit the natural and human resources of distant countries, and to interfere with autochthonous cultures. It is equally applicable to what some mean by Capitalistic Imperialism and what others describe as Communist Imperialism.

When we turn to etymology for a suitable starting point, we find that the word "colony" has two basic meanings. One refers to the permanent settlement of foreigners in places that are not contiguous to their home base, usually

---

[1] Bonn (1932) was also the first who introduced the term "decolonization" to describe the counter-movement that he saw gathering momentum after empire-building by the European powers had come to an end. For a further discussion, see also Albertini, 1966, pp. 28 ff.

to agricultural settlements on virgin soil, whereby the settlers in this case generally retain their allegiance to the parent society. A second meaning of "colony" refers to a transoceanic possession or a dependency of a colonizing political unit or "metropolitan country," whereby the autochthones are not fully incorporated in the metropolitan society. The second meaning is of more immediate interest here. It allows us to conceive of colonization as a process of social change culminating in a colonial situation (cf. Francis, 1968; Balandier, 1966). What then are the situations that are typical of colonies?

THE COLONIAL SITUATION

1. A territory becomes a colony when a metropolitan society extends social control over the alien populations of a foreign country. There is, however, a significant difference between the simple annexation of a contiguous territory and colonization. When, for instance, a nation-state annexes a contiguous territory together with its population, the annexed territory is identified with the national territory, and its population becomes an integral part of the state population. There is also a tendency to "nationalize" the annexed population, that is, to integrate it into the national society. Not so in the case of a colony. Typically, the colony is a distant, usually transoceanic, territory. Even if the legal fiction is upheld that the colony is a province of the metropolitan country, it is not treated in the same way as other administrative districts of the colonizing country. The colony remains clearly separated from the metropolis, not only geographically but in many other respects as well.

2. It is widely accepted that the most outstanding feature of colonialism is economic exploitation by the metropolis. Occasionally, metropolitan control over a colonial country is confined to the economy without involving outright annexation. More often than not, economic exploitation antecedes political domination and economic controls remain untouched (or may even increase) after a colony has been politically emancipated from its metropolis. Typically, however, a colony is subjected to the sovereign rule of a metropolitan country, and the economies of both the metropolis and the colony are treated as one unit to be protected against outside interference. Nevertheless, they form very distinctive subeconomies having separate functions, one being clearly subordinate to the other.

   There is also a significant difference between the functions allotted to a colonial territory and to other territories that have been annexed by a modern state. In this respect we can distinguish two different subtypes of colonies. In the case of "settlement colonies," as they have been called by R. Maunier (1949, vol. I, p. 19), the primary aim is the direct exploitation of natural resources through migrants from the metropolis. In the extreme case, the autochthonous population is destroyed or at least pushed back into segregated reservations and prevented from further interference with the new settler society emerging in the colony. Typical examples are the United States, Australia, or Argentina.

The other type has been called by Maunier "exploitation colonies." Here the autochthonous population is, to a greater or lesser extent, left in the possession of the natural resources, but is compelled to give up a good part of their produce to the colonizers, either by way of ordinary market transactions or by other means approaching violence and fraud.

In the beginning, there may be little interference with the native economy on the part of the metropolis and its colonial representatives. Yet economic control tends to increase significantly as the industrialization of the metropolis increases the need for colonial raw materials, and pressures are applied to modernize the colonial economy in order to make it more productive. Enforced modernization tends to destroy the economic and social system of the autochtonous societies, which are characteristically of the agrarian and subsistence type.

A third type of colonial exploitation is that of the native labor force; once the autochthones have been deprived of their land and other natural resources, they are bound through various kinds of servitude (including slavery). In this case much more than in the first two, the autochthonous population becomes integrated into the colonial society, which is entirely dominated by the metropolitan settlers. We shall return to this situation later. It should be remembered, however, that in the same colonial territory, different types of economic exploitation may coexist, giving rise to a variety of colonial situations in different sections and regions of the colony.

3. A colony is characteristically subjected to the sovereign rule of a metropolitan country. Whatever the formal constitution of a colony may be, defense and external affairs are always the sole responsibility of the metropolis. Laws are enacted and imposed by the metropolitan legislative; civil administration is carried out, or at least strictly supervised, by metropolitan representatives; law courts are instituted and regulated by the metropolis. Colonization always involves the imposition of institutions by the metropolis and, consequently, interference with native institutions. Yet the colonial situation precludes the simple transfer of metropolitan institutions. Even if a colony is formally declared a province of the metropolitan country, the colonial administration remains different and needs a specialized personnel. In their application to the colony, metropolitan laws are suspended or modified, and special colonial laws are enacted (often different laws for different sections of the colonial population). This differentiation is suggested not only by the aims of colonial policy but also by the problems arising from the great distance between metropolis and colony; these are partly of a technological nature, partly due to great geographical differences, and especially because of the

typical heteromorphism between the metropolitan society and the autochthonous societies in the colony.

4. It is not our task to put forward a theory of colonialism. Of more immediate significance for the task at hand is the analysis of the social structure of a colonial population. A fundamental factor determining it is space. Colonization involves surmounting considerable distances. The metropolitan and the autochthonous populations of a colony are bound to differ greatly both culturally and physically. Unfamiliarity and lack of isomorphism will be extreme. This fact has a definite bearing on interethnic relations. As we recall, the notion of shared ethnicity is based both on a contrast effect and the assumption of common descent. When close contact is established between extremely distant populations, an expansion of the fundamental assumption of common descent takes place beyond the limits of the ethnie. This point is worth examining.

Ethnic differences, as we have found, are recognized and symbolized in various ways. Among European peoples, language most widely serves the purpose. In colonial situations, where the problem is how to differentiate between very distant populations—the metropolitan society and its migrant offshoots on the one hand, and a variety of autochthonous peoples in the colony on the other—the contrast is most readily symbolized by marked somatic differences which, from this point of view, have the advantage of being indelible and, without exception transmitted from one generation to the other. Although, the phenotype cannot be mistaken, differences in the genotype also serve as infallible indices for the absence of biological kinship.

Accordingly, in a colonial situation race tends to supersede ethnicity. In its characteristic function of differentiating between heterogeneous populations, race tends to take precedence over shared ethnicity. To the white colonizers, for instance, whether the autochthones were Sioux or Hurons was of far less significance than the fact that they were Indians. And in their struggle with the Europeans, it was relatively unimportant to the Indians whether the settlers were of English, Dutch, or German origin. *We can hypothesize that the more vital the confrontation with the autochthones becomes, the more likely it is that the saliency of race increases while the saliency of ethnicity decreases; or the more the problem of the aborigines loses its strategic importance in the colony, the more likely it is that greater attention will be paid to ethnic differences among the settlers themselves.*

The most fundamental distinction within a colonial population is that between the metropolitans and the autochthones. In order to uphold economic exploitation and political domination of one population element by the other, a generalized status is assigned to either one of them on the basis of obvious racial differences. Race does not serve only as a criterion for the differential distribution of social, especially economic, rewards, but also as a legitimation of their permanency.

The same is true in the political sphere. This will become clear when we compare the colonial situation with the situation that arises when a nation-state annexes a contiguous territory. In the latter case, as we have seen earlier, there is marked tendency to integrate the annexed population into the national society by way of nationalization. In a colony, on the other hand, national homogenization may perhaps occasionally be visualized for some distant future; typically, however, colonial policy goes in the opposite direction by obstructing the absorption of autochthones into the national society of the metropolis. In one case social barriers are broken down, in the other the color bar is institutionalized. Here the population is homogenized, there segmentalized. One set of laws are valid for all on the one hand, whilst privileges, exemptions, and diversification of law are usual on the other. Generally, in one case the differential treatment of the autochthones is regarded as justified or at least inevitable; in the other it runs contrary to standards of national unity, and is accepted at best as a temporary expedient.

Accordingly, metropolis and colony are not integrated into a single political unit based upon a homogeneous population having one law, one culture, one economy, and one social structure. There are always two distinctive political units, the unified nation-state and its colonial appendix. The metropolis is sovereign; the colony does not share its sovereignty. Its autochthonous population is excluded from the nation. The government of the colony is not dependent on the collective will of its people but subject ultimately to the collective will of the metropolitan nation.

5. Among the population elements that may become salient in colonial social structures other than the autochthones, the following deserve mentioning: There is a difference between metropolitans who serve as temporary representatives of the metropolis and migrants from the metropolis who settle permanently in the colony. Such settlers have a tendency to form a distinctive subsociety of the metropolitan society. Colonial societies of settlers may even become alienated from the metropolitan society and may eventually struggle for national independence, as did the United States and many others.

Exogenous additions to the colonial population result either from the annexation of new territories contiguous to the colony or from immigration. Racial and cultural similarities or differences usually determine whether, and to what extent, later additions are identified with the metropolitans and settlers or the autochthones. Sometimes they are assigned an intermediate status. In the course of colonization, endogenous additions to the basic population elements of a colony also emerge, particularly half-breeds and detribalized autochthones who have become integrated into the colonial society as a lower stratum.

6. Colonization has been instrumental in spreading so-called Western Civilization all over the globe, destroying or profoundly changing the autochthonous cultures. From the beginning colonization was combined with, and even in part motivated by, the missionary effort to "Christianize," later to "humanize" and "civilize," and more recently to "modernize." As much as nationalization, colonization involves the transculturation of the autochthones, be it through schools, mass communication, or indoctrination. For it is only through education that the autochthones are fitted to function properly in the political and economic system imposed upon the colony by the metropolis. Education in the colonies tends to be highly selective in order to safeguard economic exploitation and the dominance of the metropolitans in the emerging colonial social structure. In the colonies the term "modern culture" assumes a more definite meaning than in other contexts. Earlier we decided to define it with reference to the adjustment of culture to the economy. In a colonial situation, by contrast, "modern culture" can be defined with reference to acculturation. From the standpoint of the metropolitans, their own culture is felt to be superior to the manifold traditional cultures of those they colonize. If education is successful, however, the values it inculcates must be recognized as higher by those who are to become "educated" and "civilized." Modern culture points to the future, traditional culture to the past. The dominant culture is by definition modern; the recessive, traditional. A culture is dominant not only because its carriers have the power to impose it; those who become civilized must also consent, must accept civilization as a valid guide to their social actions. Thus, colonization involves the cultural modernization of the autochthones inasmuch as the value orientation of their social actions is in accordance with the cultural values and norms of the colonizers.

DEFINITIONS OF KEY CONCEPTS

We are now prepared to present definitions of some key terms required for the analysis of interethnic relations in colonial and postcolonial situations.

We speak of a *colony* if the metropolitan society exercises social control over the population of a distant territory, interfering significantly with its social system, without integrating it into the metropolitan social system.

By *colonization* we understand the processes of social change through which an approximation to the ideal type of a colony (as defined above) is being achieved.

By *decolonization* we understand the processes of social change through which a colony is transformed into a modern nation-state independent of its (former) metropolis. This does not imply, however, that nation-building inevitably and necessarily follows from the decomposition of a given colonial pattern. On the contrary, it is our contention that unless certain conditions are met, different arrangements are more suitable to solve the human problems resulting from colonization. Yet the model of the nation-state has so far been widely accepted, at least as the short-range aim of decolonization.

STAGES OF COLONIZATION/DECOLONIZATION

When we view colonization and decolonization as processes of social change, we are also able to distinguish typical stages. It should be pointed out that many historical situations that are often considered colonial are of no further concern to us by virtue of the definition proposed above. These include, for instance, sporadic contacts through travelers, explorers, traders, and so on. But also more permanent establishments, such as trading posts, mission stations, military bases, and the like, even the search for luxuries (spices, furs, or precious metals) carried out by organized and armed companies of merchant adventurers—all these must be treated as intersocietal and international relationships without any specific reference to colonies (although they may lead to their establishment).

Of more immediate interest to us are the processes that characterize the transition from a precolonial to a colonial stage, especially how intersocietal relations between metropolitans and autochthones are changed, existing social structures transformed, and new ones created. By making a clear distinction between a transitional period, a full-fledged colonial period, and a postcolonial period, we are enabled to discover striking parallels between the processes involved in the emergence of the old European nations (which we have discussed in Part II) and the emergence of new nations in former colonies.

For this purpose it is also necessary to distinguish several aspects or moments of decolonization. The process does not begin with political emancipation but is set in motion during the preceding colonial period.[2] Nor does it end with the formal release from colonial rule and international recognition of sovereignty. Even if the original colonial power can be successfully prevented from continuing to exploit the colony economically, to influence it culturally, and indirectly to dominate it politically; it may be replaced in this respect by some other metropolitan country. More typical and frequently more enduring

---

[2]A method for studying secular change in concrete societies has been suggested by Francis, 1961, 1965.

than "neocolonialism" in the economic sphere is the problem of accomplishing cultural emancipation in a former colony.

Interethnic relations in colonial situations concern the relationship between colony and metropolis in addition to that between the different population elements within the colony. Here we should distinguish between colonies in which the settler population is the dominant element (settlement colonies) and others in which relatively small numbers of metropolitan representatives are confronted with a vast majority of autochthones organized in a great variety of tribes (exploitation colonies).

By and large, the course of colonization also determines the way in which decolonization may be achieved.[3] During the precolonial period the relations between the metropolitans and the various autochthonous peoples are typically confined to *commercium*. To the autochthones the metropolitans are simply emissaries of a foreign power. Even when individual autochthones take up temporary service with the metropolitans, they remain aliens who come one day and return the next to their own communities, much like foreign laborers in the European countries. They are in no way integrated in the social structure of the metropolitan host society and its colonial branch. This type of intersocietal rather than intrasocietal relationship may persist through the period of colonization as far as remote tribes and large parts of the rural hinterland are concerned.

THE COLONIAL SOCIETY

A new situation arises when superficial contacts are replaced by more intensive interaction and cooperation between the colonizers and ever-widening sections of the autochthonous population. At this stage more of the autochthones are drawn into the social structure of the metropolitans. At the height of colonial development, a new colonial society emerges that is different from both the metropolitan society and the autochthonous societies in the colony. Decolonization concerns primarily the relationship between the new society formed in the course of colonization and the metropolis, independence from which signalizes the emergence of a new nation. The core of the national society in former colonies is represented by the colonial society; the manner in which nationalization in a colony may be achieved depends largely on the composition of this colonial society. For the present purpose it will suffice to distinguish four typical cases:

1. The colonial society is formed by the settlers. Relationship with the autochthonous tribal societies is similar to that described for the precolonial period. They interact with each other as independent societal units through representatives. When the settlers separate from the metropolis

---

[3]For an empirical analysis of the phases of decolonization, see Binder-Krauthoff, 1970.

to establish a sovereign nation, the remnants of the autochthonous population remain excluded from the new nation. This has happened, for instance, in the United States with regard to the Indian tribes.

2. The other extreme is represented by exploitation colonies where there is no significant settler element. In this case a new colonial society tends to emerge under the impact of modernization induced by the metropolitans. Under the direct influence of metropolitan representatives and relatively small numbers of settlers, the autochthones who move into the colonial centers, such as cities, mines, plantations, and so on, are directly integrated into the emerging colonial society. Not all of them cut off ties with their several tribal societies; they do communicate with their kinsfolk and return periodically to their communities. These lie in the tribal hinterland where the influence of the metropolitans is more indirect and remote. In the tribal section of the colony the modernizing influences of the metropolis primarily affect the chiefs who, with their kinsfolk and staff, are educated and "civilized" at least to the extent that they are able to serve as a mediating elite linking the tribesmen to the colonial society.

Thus we have two links between the emerging colonial society and the tribal hinterland: the tribal elite on the upper level, the autochthonous masses living within the colonial society and commuting to the hinterland on the lower level. Yet tribesmen living in colonial centers tend to become detribalized, having no reference group other than the colonial society itself. Such underprivileged masses tend to be transformed into a genuine proletariat, thus indicating the emergence of a typically modern class structure in the colonial centers, a class structure along racial lines that is reflected in the differential distribution of social rewards. Among the modernized and usually urbanized masses of autochthones a new elite also emerges, the so-called *évolués,* who carry the main burden of nationalization. In exploitation colonies nation-building is therefore characterized by both emancipation from the metropolis and exclusion of the metropolitans from the new nation. Between these two extremes a variety of intermediary situations is conceivable.

3. One typcial intermediary case is this: The settler population develops a complex colonial society, but also includes large numbers of autochthones into its status system. Apart from the remnants of the autochthonous tribes, which in this case remain outside the colonial society, many of the autochthones as well as half-breeds are completely integrated into the colonial society as its lowest stratum. When such a colony succeeds in emancipating itself from the metropolis, the ethnically and racially heterogeneous population forming the colonial society are transformed into the new nation.

Type 1 mentioned above is of no further interest to us at this point; for interethnic relations after emancipation do not differ significantly from those in metropolitan societies. In fact, a postcolonial nation of this type may itself become a colonial metropolis. Such situations have been treated extensively in Part III. Examples of the other two types, 2 and 3, mentioned above will be found in the following pages.

On principle, a sociological theory of interethnic relations should enable us to understand and explain relevant phenomena in any society, Western and non-Western, and at all times, present, past, or future. The *comprehensive theory* presented in this volume has been developed mainly on the basis of the study of the so-called Western societies and high cultures. Applicability to novel situations, however, is the crucial test of any sociological theory. We now want to know whether our generalizations go far enough to provide us with concepts and theorems that are also useful for the analysis of colonial and postcolonial situations in which advanced Western societies meet with less-developed societies.

PLAN OF PART IV

In the first chapter on sub-Saharan Africa, an attempt is made to analyze colonial situations bearing upon nation-building in exploitation colonies. The chapter on Mexico, on the other hand, offers an opportunity of surveying the full course of colonial development in a settlement colony where several population elements, including metropolitans and autochthones, have been combined into a new national society, and where a considerable degree of political and cultural emancipation has been achieved.

The chapter on South Africa is likely to prove controversial. For at this point we shall, however briefly, go beyond the general design of this treatise. So far we have confined ourselves to the development of a theory of interethnic relations by analyzing empirical evidence; at the same time, we have also employed the conceptual scheme and empirical generalizations thus attained to understand particular cases, and in retrospect to explain the actual course that events have taken. This will remain our procedure when we analyze a different type of settlement colony which, in South Africa, has given rise to a new Afrikaner nation on the basis of strict segregation from both its autochthonous and half-breed population. In the last part of the chapter, however, we shall have an opportunity to analyze actual policies, the outcome of which at the time of this writing remains unknown. Despite the criticism levelled against positivism by Neo-Marxists, Marx and Comte have assigned an essentially practical function to social science, namely, the task of improving the human condition. At this late stage of our deliberations it is out of the question to adequately deal with the much-debated problem of how theory relates to practice. Still, we should take up the challenge, at least within a modest scope. At the end of Chapter 26 we shall therefore make an attempt to indicate by way of an example what claim to practical usefulness our essay in the theory of interethnic relations may possibly have.

REFERENCES

Albertini, Rudolf von, *Dekolonisation: Die Diskussion über Verwaltung und Zukunft der Kolonien, 1919–1960*. Köln: Westdeutscher Verlag, 1966.

Balandier, George, "The Colonial Situation: A Theoretical Approach," in Immanuel Wallerstein (ed.), *Social Change: The Colonial Situation*. New York: John Wiley & Sons, 1966, pp. 34–61.

Binder-Krauthoff, Kristine, *Phasen der Entkolonialisierung: Eine Analyse kolonalpolitischer Relikte in Afrika* (Munich doctoral dissertation). Berlin: Duncker und Humblot, 1970.

Bonn, M. J., "Imperialism," *Encyclopedia of the Social Sciences,* 1st ed., 1932.

Francis, E. K., "Prolegomena to a Theory of Social Change," *Kyklos,* XIV (1961), Fasc. 2, pp. 213–233.

———, *Wissenschaftliche Grundlagen soziologischen Denkens*. Bern: Francke Verlag, 1965, pp. 132–135.

———, "The Ethnic Factor in Nation-Building," *Social Forces,* XLVI (1968), pp. 343–344.

Gossett, Thomas F., *Race: The History of an Idea in America*. Dallas: Southern Methodist University Press, 1963.

Maunier, R., *The Sociology of Colonies: An Introduction to the Study of Race Contact*. London: Routledge and Kegan Paul, 1949.

Nation-Building and Tribalism in Sub-Saharan Africa

24

Our understanding of decolonization implies the assumption that its eventual outcome is the transofrmation of a colony into a nation. The notion of neocolonialism notwithstanding, which is more germane to political rhetoric than to sociological theory, the domination and exploitation of one country by another is not strictly confined to colonial or postcolonial situations. Even so, the parallelism, which we have suggested as existing between decolonization and nationalization (understood as the process of social change asymptotically approaching the ideal type of a sovereign nation) appears to be most conspicuous in settlement colonies, especially those in which a numerous and dominant settler population has succeeded in eliminating the autochthones from the emerging national society.

As will be shown in the next chapter, a similar, if more complex, situation can also be observed in settlement colonies in which a considerable autochthonous population has been integrated into the emerging national society. Less obvious are the similarities between nation-building in exploitation colonies and in the Old World. The reference to Europe, however, requires some specification. As we have seen, the modern nation as a historical type is linked to Western Europe while the realization of the idea in the former empires of Eastern Europe has been beset with particular problems, which in many respects recall the situation in (former) exploitation colonies. If we tried to explain this by conjecturing that the power structure in exploitation colonies is generally more "imperial" in character than in settlement colonies, we would probably stretch the point too far. Still, let us see how far the lessons learned earlier, particularly in Part II, can aid us in understanding the basic difficulties that tend to arise in former exploitation colonies with regard to nation-building and the relationship between the modern national core and the variety of traditional tribal societies present within the state territory. We shall confine ourselves to conditions in sub-Saharan Africa.

DECOLONIZATION IN EXPLOITATION COLONIES

Decolonization implies preparing the population of a colony for self-determination.[1] As the colonial society forms the nucleus of the emerging nation, it becomes the main focus of decolonization. In exploitation colonies, sectionalized along racial lines, decolonization concerns more specifically the autochthones who have been integrated into the colonial society. A comparison with nationalization in European countries suggests significant analogies.

In both cases the territory and the personnel of the nation-to-be are pre-determined by an "alien" will. Even if the metropolitan government represents the "general will" of the metropolitan nation, it exercises precisely the same kind of despotic rule in the colony as did the absolute monarchs of the *ancien régime*. It also plays the same role in preforming the nation. Colonialism means intensified communication and an improved infrastructure throughout the territory, rational administration, and a set of common institutions whose key positions are manned by emissaries of the central power and their local collaborators. Experiences of this kind tend to create an awareness of common destiny, even a sense of identity, although different sections of the colonial population are affected in varying degrees. Thus, under the impact of colonialism a new "colonial society" tends to be formed out of the mobilized (activated) elements of the traditional tribal societies.

DEMOTIC TRENDS

During the colonial period the nation emerging from colonial society tends to conform for several reasons with the principles of demotic nationalism. First, this is the type of nationalism current in the Western countries who were most influential in the colonies. Furthermore, according to the prevailing system of international relations, the modern state represents the predominant unit of action. Finally, the international status of a state depends, *ceteris paribus,* on the efficiency of its organization.

The initial aims of African nationalism were liberation and Africanization. This involved gaining international recognition of the colony as a sovereign state and then replacing aliens by Africans in key positions of the existing institutions. But national movements require popular support, a national elite needs a constituency, and a nation-state implies a nation. Thus, to the national elite, the *évolués,* fell the task of activating the population of a given colony, of making them aware of their own political relevance, of arousing in them a sense of common purpose, and of organizing them into political action groups. This

---

[1]The following propositions are adapted from Francis, 1965 and 1968.

was a comparatively straightforward proposition as long as colonial domination provided a common enemy and liberation from it a common goal, and insofar as primarily urban masses were concerned.

The processes of nationalization do not end when a colony is pronounced a sovereign nation. As we have seen, the modernization of ever-wider sections of the state population and their integration into the national core have remained a problem also for the nations of Europe. The ideal of an all-pervading demotic identity and solidarity has hardly been fully realized anywhere, and counter-movements promoted by ethnic nationalism have remained a latent threat. In most instances, "plural" nations now prevail which do not conform to the classical model of the monolithic nation-state, although this model has remained the mainstay of political ideology and legal theory. Even sociology draws from it the inspiration for its traditional concept of society as a closed or "boundary-maintaining" system.

ETHNIC PROBLEMS

Once a colony has been emancipated politically, there still remains the formidable task of integrating the tribal population into the new nation. If the aims of demotic nationalism are to be realized, modernization of the rural hinterland must also take place in order to weaken tribal authority, break down traditional social structures, and incorporate mobilized tribal members directly into a homogenized national society. "Tribalism" thus becomes the main challenge to nation-building. It is not confined to the resistance of politically organized tribes and their chiefs to pressures exerted by nontribal "educated" elites and the central national government, but has a definitely ethnic root.

Just as rural migrants to European and American cities were drawn together by a new awareness of ethnic affinity and have formed segregated ethnic communities, so too have linguistic and cultural affinities assumed a hitherto unrealized social significance among the members of different African tribes gathering in urban centers. The experience of rapid social change due to colonialism, not only in urban centers but also in the tribal hinterland, led to a general restlessness and dissatisfaction, vague expectations, and a readiness to accept new ideas and novel types of social organization. This orientation was provided by local leaders and action groups who interpreted a common situation in terms of common ethnicity. To become activated, however, an ethnic society needs not only leadership but also some kind of organization through which it can express itself; for example, a trade union, a political party, a church, or a "tribal association" *(association des originaires)*.

TRIBALISM

The term "tribalism" refers as much to the new ethnic structures emerging in urban centers as to the traditional tribal societies. Tribalist ideology aims not simply at the revival of past patterns of social organization but, at least in part, at their reconstruction in the setting of a nation-state and at their adaptation to modern conditions. In this respect, African tribalism offers parallels to the restorative and ethnic types of nationalism which we have met in Europe. It, too, finds occasional expression in regionalistic and secessionist counter-movements against the homogenizing and centralistic tendencies of demotic nationalism. Thus, the ethnic factor becomes relevant to African politics in several different ways.

First, in the struggle for supremacy within a given nation-state, opposing leaders and action groups canvas for popular support to the ethnic society to which they themselves belong. Their appeal to ethnic solidarity is apt to release powerful moral and emotional forces for goals that need not have any particular relevance to specifically ethnic interests. Such goals may bear upon pure power aspirations, upon economic reforms, or upon the realization of a variety of cultural values that concern the totality of the nation-state. What counts is that they are rationalized and legitimized in ethnic terms.

Some of the most important national movements and parties in contemporary Africa lean heavily on one powerful ethnic society or on a coalition of smaller ones, even if their political concepts and programs eventually involve overcoming their ethnic differences and building a homogeneous national society. Accordingly, ethnicity is temporarily utilized in preparing mobilized tribal folk for direct participation in the demotic nation. Ethnic groupings and *associations des originaires* serve as intermediary powers fulfilling functions that su-praethnic organizations, such as parties, trade unions, or the demotically oriented institutions of the nation-state, cannot as yet effectively undertake. While, within the framework of demotic nationalism, the nucleus of the emerging nation is formed by colonial society, it is the strong politically organized tribes, the extended ethnic societies, and their formal organizations that must in other cases be visualized as the foundation of a nation. Promotors of ethnic nationalism use the ethnic factor as a subsidiary or temporary expedient, but especially as the principal vehicle of nation-building. Sometimes a native kingdom or a feudal structure still in existence, or even just memories of some former political unit, provide ethnic nationalism with rallying points and impressive symbols, and give occasion for typically restorative tendencies and interpretations.

PAN-AFRICANISM

Finally, Pan-Africanism (cf. Legum, 1962) calls for our attention. Among its numerous varieties, what may be called more correctly "Pan-Melanism" is of particular interest. It stresses the essential oneness of all those descended from the autochthonous peoples of sub-Saharan Africa, as manifested by common racial features, which distinguish them from all other populations in significant contact with them. Pan-Africanism actually antedates other types of African nationalism. It developed under the impact of the American Negro movement, American Negro churches, and the messianic mission assigned by American leaders to the whole black race. The notion that race was a relevant criterion for social differentiation originated, however, among the Europeans. The distinction between black and white as significant social categories was learned by both sub-Saharan Africans and American Negroes through the incessant and grim experience of social differentiation and discrimination along racial lines. They have accepted it for the purpose of self-identification in order to cope with the situations imposed upon them by the Europeans and their colonial kin. Race has become a social reality because people actually orient their social actions in accordance with racial criteria.

In this respect, Pan-Africanism (as much as Pan-Slavism or Pan-Germanism) bears a close resemblance to ethnic nationalism. Just as an ethnic society draws together several tribal and subtribal units into a larger whole, race assumes the character of a superethnie, which embraces all the ethnic societies of sub-Saharan Africa and paves the way for a national union on a continental scale. Pan-Africanism is a variety of ethnic nationalism that recommends itself to nationalist leaders and action groups as a remedy for the difficulties with which demotic nation-building has to cope and as an antidote against the disruptive forces of tribalism. The idea of the whole African race as a single ethnie with a legitimate claim to solidarity and eventually to political union also has particular appeal in view of the technological and economic developments that require the integration of very large territories.

In the last section of this chapter we shall deal with the regional conflicts that tend to arise within the heterogeneous population of a colony, once the initial aim of political emancipation has been achieved. Latent antagonism among the autochthonous population, which had been checked in the common struggle against the metropolitans, now flare up, and overt conflicts tend to be symbolized in terms of competing nationalisms. The parties vying with each other for dominance are likely to define the new nation, the supposed common goal, according to different criteria, which are in keeping with their own particular economic interests and power aspirations. Nigeria proves to be particularly instructive in this respect.

THE EMERGENCE OF A NEW NATION: NIGERIA

The territorial boundaries of Nigeria, like other countries of sub-Saharan Africa, were drawn up by the colonial powers without regard to geographical distribution. The northern frontier between Nigeria and Niger splits the Hausa tribe; the western frontier between Nigeria and Dahomey separates the Yoruba tribes, whilst the eastern frontier divides various tribes between Nigeria and the Cameroons. Within Nigeria itself there are several ethnically diverse groups, some of whom had nothing in common with each other before colonization.

THE PRECOLONIAL HERITAGE

In precolonial days what came to be known as the Northern Region of Nigeria coincided (with the exception of Bornu and the pagan tribes of the Jos plateau) with an area dominated by Fulani empire-builders. The Western Region (except for a few small Delta groups as well as Ibo and Ijau minorities) was organized into sizeable political units by the Yoruba. The Eastern Region was occupied by many acephalous tribes mainly of Ibo- and Ibibio-speaking peoples. Let us study the precolonial situation in each region more closely.

The Fulani are found from the upper Nile to the Senegal. Following a *jihad* (religious war) that had started in 1802 under the leadership of Sheik Othman dan Fodio, they established themselves as the leading political power in northern Nigeria. After having infiltrated the autochthonous kingdoms, they spread their religion and authority over the Hausa-speaking peoples. Yet, as a result of intermarriage with the Hausa, the Fulani lost most of their distinguishing somatic characteristics; the majority of them also assumed the Hausa language. Subsequently, the Fulani- and Hausa-speaking peoples fused into a number of semiindependent emirates governed by a Fulani aristocracy that recognizes the religious leadership of the Sultan of Sokoto.

The third largest group in the North are the Kanuri-speaking peoples who are located in the Chad area. Like the Hausa the Kanuri had been Muslims long before the Fulani invasion, but unlike the Hausa they were able to repulse the invaders and to strengthen their own kingdom of Bornu.

A fourth group, which was predominantly Moslem before the Fulani *jihad,* are the Nupe. Although their political unity was broken up by the Fulani and later by the British, they retained their identity, which was supported by a common historical tradition, a common culture and language, and a sense of shared ethnicity, symbolized by the king of Nupe.

The Tiv are the fifth of the so-called Big Five. Although non-Moslem and acephalous, their sense of unity is based on the uniformity of their language and racial characteristics, their common culture, and their belief in a common origin.

The Big Five constitute about 65 percent of the population of the North. The remaining 35 percent is made up of the so-called pagan tribes, some of whom were organized into scattered village communities. Others formed loose confederacies for war purposes or were organized into tribal societies. These people of the Middle Belt, who had been caught between Arabic and European cultural influences, later became the source of separatist movements in the Northern Region (cf. Schwarz, 1965; Seibel, 1968; Antonello et al., 1961).

In contrast to the Northern Region, the peoples of the Eastern Region, including the Ibo, Ibibio, Efik, the Ijaw, and some smaller language groups, were acephalous. Among the Ibo and Ibibio the basic social unit was a single extended family or a kinship group. The largest unit was the village community, while the lineages and clans cut across the boundaries of the villages.

The Ibo, the second largest ethnie in Nigeria, was divided into thirty major divisions, sixty clans, and about five hundred village communities. Despite this apparent fragmentation there seems to have existed a strong underlying unity in religious, cultural, and economic matters (Dike, 1965, pp. 24–46). Although there are many similarities in the social structures of the Ibo and Ibibio peoples, they belong to different branches of the large Niger-Congo linguistic family. Similarly, there are marked differences between the Ibibio and the Efik. Although both speak basically the same language, the Effik claim an independent origin and strongly resent any identification with the Ibibio. The nine smaller groups remained until recently politically inarticulate, and identified themselves with none of the major ethnic units.

The political organization of the Western Region may be described as midway between that of the North and the East. In contrast to the Fulani-Hausa, the Yoruba peoples failed to organize themselves into a system of imperial power structures yet, unlike the East, they formed larger tribal societies. These included the kingdom of Oyo, which came into open confrontation with the Fulani, and the kingdom of Benin, which reached the peak of its power in the fifteenth and the sixteenth centuries.

Before the British occupation, the Yoruba tribes were constantly warring against each other. Several war camps developed into towns, among them Ibadan. By 1956, about half the population of Yorubaland was living in urban centers. Despite political differences, fragmentation, and tensions produced in former times by the slave trade and intertribal wars, a comparatively strong sense of shared ethnicity has persisted among the Yoruba, which is based on the belief in a common origin and on widespread intermarriage. Their seven major tribes also respected the Oni of Ife as the head of their common cult.

FROM COLONY TO NATION

Within less than half a century this incongruous land mass with its ethnic mosaic was welded together into something like a demotic unit by a colonial system of political domination and economic exploitation, which in its social consequences was not so very different from the impact of absolutism discussed in Part II. The new nation was preformed by the conjuncture of several factors: Colonial statecraft managed to establish internal peace, impose a common system of centralized administration, and maintain law and order. By this as well as by the introduction of a common monetary system and the building of roads, railways, and harbors, free trade and traffic were introduced and intensified throughout the whole territory. Since the vital trade with the metropolis was possible only over the coastal routes, all goods coming from the interior, especially from the Northern Region, were directed through the South. The export trade also stimulated the commercialization of the agriculture and the concentration of landed property in the hands of a small group of autochthones.

Increased demand for labor and the lure of the new opportunities for economic and social advancement led to large-scale migrations from the rural hinterland to the urban centers. In time, however, the number of job seekers exceeded the vacancies, causing serious unemployment. The migrants therefore depended for subsistence on their already established relatives and kinfolk. Voluntary associations were organized whose original purpose was to assist their members in the performance of tribal ceremonies. Eventually, they developed into interest and pressure groups, which helped fellow tribesmen to obtain employment, licenses, or capital to set up trade. Later, supraterritorial tribal associations came into existence, which exerted a strong influence also on their regions of origin where they contributed to the establishment and maintenance of schools as well as the improvement of the infrastructure.

The first association of this kind was introduced by the Ibo as early as 1928. The Yoruba and Hausa followed suit to counteract their growing influence.

Although in the beginning these associations were nonpolitical, they soon became a platform for the new educated elite who used them as a training ground and power base for their later political careers. The spatial mobility initiated by colonialism was, however, not confined to rural–urban migration. Of equal importance were population shifts across regional boundaries. Ever-increasing numbers of Yoruba and Ibo invaded the Northern Region; the spread of Ibo into Yorubaland began even earlier. The consequences of these developments for nation-building and interethnic relations will be discussed at a later point.

Although all this meant modernization of the social structure, the advancement of Western education was probably the most important single factor paving the way for the nationalization of Nigeria's heterogeneous population. Both bureaucracy and business were in great need of trained technicians, clerical staff, instructors, and so on, which in an exploitation colony, could not be met by metropolitan immigrants and settlers. The Christian missions, which had a monopoly on Western-style education, supplied the cadre of professionals, army officers, civil servants, and employees who, together with modernized farmers, urban traders, and craftsmen, became the nucleus of a new autochthonous society identified with the common concerns of the entire colony, or at least one of its major subdivisions, rather than the particularistic interests of their tribal parent societies. The mobilized autochthones, who were quite ready to submit to transculturation and modernization, were also most directly exposed to racial discrimination. The pay for autochthonous employees was much lower than for their metropolitan colleagues; their chances of advancement were severely restricted. Businessmen were unable to obtain bank credit on equitable terms and to compete with the overwhelming strength of European companies. Moreover, it was the policy of the colonial administration to exclude educated Africans from higher civil service and army careers.

In addition to differences in economic development, the rate in which mission work and education progressed in the different regions assumed strategic importance in the emergence of national movements. As a rule, areas of high civilization are most resistant to cultural colonization and modernization. In Nigeria, the Northern Region was of this type: Islamic learning had been well established before the arrival of Christian missionaries and European colonizers. In contrast to the Hausa peoples, the Yoruba, part of whom had also become Mohammedanized but had resisted Fulani domination, displayed a vivid interest in Western education and cultural values; soon they were even surpassed by the Ibo. The educational superiority of the South over the North was supported by the British tendency to concentrate schools where their economic interests were greatest.

The educational gap between the North and the South gave the Southerners—especially the Ibo—a monopoly on recruitment into the colonial economy and administration. They occupied most of the positions open to autochthones in the civil service and on the executive level in business enterprises. Even in the Northern Region, 82 percent of such positions were occupied by Southerners, mainly Ibo. It is therefore no coincidence that on the eve of independence no more than 1 percent of the civil servants in the Lagos ministeries were Northerners. The differential economic, political, and educational development of the three regions was reflected in the national movements that emerged in the colonial period. Owing to their leading position, the Southerners were the first to organize themselves against colonial domination. Comparable nationalist sentiments, however, did not appear in the Northern Region before the late 1940s (cf. Schwarz, 1965, p. 15; see also Seibel, 1968; Antonello et al., 1961).

NATIONAL MOVEMENTS

At the eve of political emancipation the national movement that was directed primarily against colonial exploitation and domination had already split along ethnic lines (cf. Coleman, 1958). A demotic type of nationalism was propagated by Azikiwe, an Ibo, and the National Council of Nigeria and the Cameroons (NCNC). It was supported by the United Native African Church whose principal function was to provide a myth for Azikiwe's leadership and to awaken a consciousness of race. Nigerian nationalism was perceived as the heart-piece of a Pan-African crusade that was to lead the children of Africa out of their centuries-old slavery. The followers of Azikiwe, who eventually became Prime Minister of the Federal Government, included, in addition to his fellow tribesmen in the Eastern Region, Ibo migrants especially in Yorubaland, and also educated leaders of urban organizations (especially the labor movement) and of the smaller tribes who felt threatened by Yoruba dominance in the Western Region and by Hausa-Fulani rule in the Northern Region. Faced with strong opposition and even the danger of secession on the part of the other regions, Azikiwe, himself a proponent of a centralized unitarian state, agreed to a subdivision of the whole country into administrative units along ethnic lines, to assure himself of the support of the smaller tribes found in each of the three major regions.

In the West, Awolowo and the Yoruba Action Group advocated an ethnic type of nationalism. The old Yoruba families, a growing bourgeois upper and middle class, as well as intellectuals tended to stabilize their dominant position by cultivating historical traditions and stressing regional autonomy. Awolowo, who had become Prime Minister of the Western Region in 1957, was later sentenced for high treason.

The Northern Region has preserved the agrarian character of traditional feudal structures; it also suffered least from direct metropolitan influences. The native educated middle class, which was relatively small, found ample openings in the autonomous administration of the region and were thus ready to identify with the ruling upper class. Since the colonial power had the least occasion to interfere with still viable autochthonous power and social structures, and since the metropolitan element remained altogether in the background, no serious race problems or frictions arose in the North. A "national" reaction made itself felt against the masses of autochthonous migrants from the South and the movement of social reform promoted by them through the Northern Elements Progressive Union. Northern nationalism found its expression in the Northern Peoples Congress (NPC) under the leadership of Balewa, who became the first President of the Federation, later assassinated in an army uprising instigated by Ibo officers. The national movement among the Hausa-Fulani was directed as much against the economic and political preponderance of the South in the colony as against the competition by the educationally and otherwise better equipped Yoruba and Ibo intruders, who threatened to monopolize the modern economic and administrative sectors of colonial society in the region. The national leaders were able to count on broad popular support: the native craftsman hated the Ibo trader who sold his goods more cheaply in the market; the camel-rider could not compete with the Ibo chauffeur who transported passengers faster and at a lower price; the coran teacher was afraid of losing his pupils to the new schools manned by Southerners; and the traditional ruler resented the Ibo administrative officers who challenged his authority, which the NPC promised to support, declaring that "we want to help our natural rulers in the proper discharge of their duties" (Coleman, 1958, p. 358).

During the early stage of decolonization, which started while Nigeria was still under British rule, the Hausa-Fulani even more than the Yoruba leaders supported a strong regional autonomy. Their "nationalism," which emerged mainly as a reaction against the national movements among their competitors, had a highly conservative, even restorative character. Unlike the Southerners, however, the Northerners opposed an early release from colonial rule under which they felt better protected against Southern ambitions. In 1956, the Sadauna of Sokota, the most influential of the traditional chiefs, expressed the general feeling among his group by declaring that the North was not yet ready for such a step and did not intend to accept the invitation to commit suicide. By gaining time, they hoped to catch up with the South and thus to be better able to stand their ground, should Nigeria become a nation-state within its present territory. In the ethnically mixed Middle Belt, which was included in the Northern Region, the United Middle Belt Congress represented the diffuse interests of the population, but Awolowo and Azikiwe commanded a considerable following there.

If we pause to apply what we have learned in Part II to a colonial situation, the suggestion seems not altogether farfetched that Nigeria on the verge of nationhood had the makings of a multiethnic nation-state on the pattern of Austria before her dismemberment under Allied auspices. Hausa-Fulani nationalism is remindful of the states-rights movement among the Bohemian estates. The demotic nationalism of the Ibo, on the other hand, is to some extent comparable with that of the Germans in Cisleithanian Austria. The Yoruba, and at later stages, the other major ethnic units that were dominant in each of the regions carved out for political and administrative purposes, bear a certain resemblance to the "historical nations," the other tribes with the "small nationalities" of the Dual Monarchy. Although the national problems and their reasons were similar, the actual course of action did not follow the model of a multiethnic nation-state. Whether the tragedy of Biafra could have been avoided in this way is difficult to say. But it might be useful to ponder the alternatives, now that political unity has been preserved without really solving the problems of nation-building in a country exhibiting such a deepseated ethnic heterogeneity.

When Nigeria was finally recognized as a sovereign nation, after protracted negotiations it had been endowed with a federal system of government that was tied together so loosely that the individual regions became the real centers of political power, economically independent of the central government at Lagos. After 1958, however, new developments threatened the very foundations of the Federation: (1) regional deficits became acute; with the exception perhaps of the Eastern Region where oil deposits were an important resource, the regions became more and more dependent on the central government for their revenue;

(2) except with permission from the central government no regional government was to take foreign loans; (3) the army was controlled by the central government, which also (4) held a monopoly over Nigeria's international politics.

THE POSTCOLONIAL POWER STRUGGLE

Notwithstanding the gradually increasing power of the central government, and with it the growing political preponderance of the Northerners, the regional governments continued to nurture the feeling of regional or ethnic consciousness. The term "foreign" was applied to migrants from other regions (Kaden, 1968, p. 138), and in the recruitment to administrative offices, the regions practiced an ethnocentric policy. The North, especially, discriminated against the Southerners, and reserved job openings for Northerners even if they were less qualified than Southerners.

The Ibo remained, however, the dominant group in the national army. About three-fourths of the commissioned and noncommissioned officers were recruited from among them (Kaden, 1968, p. 105). It was therefore feared that the Ibo might achieve through the army what they had failed to accomplish through politics. The events of 1962 and 1965 prepared the ground for the seizure of power by Ibo army officers. In 1962, Awolowo and thirty others from the West were charged with treason.

In 1964 a general strike, which was originally organized for higher wages as recommended by the Morgan Commission, soon broadened into an attack on the central government and its administrative machinery. The establishment was criticized as being corrupt, ostentatious, and inefficient.

In the same year trouble brewed over the census report. Out of a total population of about 55.6 million, almost 30 million were claimed to have come from the Northern Region. Since the seats in the Federal House were to be allocated in proportion to the population of the regions, the preponderance of the Northern Region came as a shock to the Southerners who had hoped that a new count would end Northern superiority. The split among the Southern politicians over the issue of the census report broke the southern front against the North and led to their doom in the general elections that took place in 1964/65 (Schwarz, 1965, p. 187). Despite the troubles that preceded them and the dozens of petitions that asked for their nullification, Balewa and his coalition went ahead to form the federal government.

The final event, which triggered the army take-over, was the riot that followed elections in the Western Region in November 1965. The first proclamation issued by General Ironsi read in part as follows:

> The former Regions are abolished into a number of territorial areas called provinces. Nigeria ceased to be what is described as a federation. It now becomes simply the Republic of Nigeria (Fed. Min. of Information, 1966).

The Ibo hegemony was, however, short-lived. The countercoup six months later and the massacre of the Ibo in the North led to their attempt at secession under the name of Biafra on May 30, 1967, and to the civil war in which the Northern and Western Regions were united against the Eastern Region.

CONCLUSIONS

The foregoing survey has traced the process of nation-building in a colonial/ postcolonial situation. The foundations of present-day Nigeria were laid by the British colonial power. Colonialism, however, did not encounter a political vacuum. There were diverse societal units, ranging from the Fulani-Hausa imperial structures in the North and the sizeable kingdoms of the Yoruba in the West to the small acephalous tribes in the Middle Belt and the Eastern Region. These differences in societal organization and cultural as well as linguistic diversities kept the various peoples of the colony apart before the British intrusion.

It was the colonial economy and administration that initiated closer contact and cooperation between the regions. Yet the demographic effects of urbanization counteracted efforts to integrate the whole population into one societal unit. Migrants were led to organize themselves into tribal associations rather than to identify with the ethnically diverse natives of their new environment. Furthermore, the concentration of Western schools in the South favored the Southerns—especially the Ibo—as it gave them a relative monopoly of higher positions in the colonial economy and administration. These disparities as well as regional and ethnic segregation became the sources of conflict that have since accompanied nation-building in Nigeria. However, so long as the colonial power existed as a common enemy, the regional or ethnic conflicts were kept in check by the concerted struggle against the metropolis.

Insofar as the colonial power determined the boundaries of Nigeria and served as a check on interregional and intertribal conflicts, colonialism performed a function analogous to that of the absolute state in Western Europe. Because nationalism was introduced by a small elite of autochthones with a Western education before demotic unity could be accomplished by colonial statecraft, nation-building in Nigeria was to encounter problems similar to those that had existed in the imperial power structures of Central and Eastern Europe. As soon as the common enemy was removed, hitherto latent conflicts became overt in the form of competing nationalisms propagated by the various political parties. The Federal Constitution attempted to solve the national problem of Nigeria along the lines of a multiethnic nation-state. The relative autonomy granted to the regions actually increased differences and led to demands of boundary revisions in order to protect subregional and ethnic interests.

The case of Nigeria sharpens the argument that conditions created by the colonial system, whose example was followed by the postcolonial government, do not, in themselves, necessarily lead to the formation and maintenance of a unitarian nation-state. The alternative of a multiethnic nation-state would require constitutional adjustments and/or a balance of internal power to check effectively latent conflicts. Though we have not included in our general discussion the functions of the army in postcolonial nation-building, it seems permissible to conclude that the role of the military regime in Nigeria is akin to Bonapartism. In both cases physical violence or threat of force are adopted to prevent secession and to mold the population into the demotic union originally visualized by civilian leaders.

AN AMPLIFICATION OF THE GENERAL THEORY

With the insights gained from the preceding analysis, several supplementary propositions to our general theory of interethnic relations may be suggested. The following statement seems to be of the widest applicability: The saliency of the ethnic factor tends to increase,

1. the lesser the degree of social mobilization;
2. the less evenly opportunities and levels of education are distributed over the ethnic subunits of the state population; and
3. the less evenly key positions in national institutions are manned by members of the different ethnic units included in the nation-state.

Underprivileged areas are likely to support ideologies that are based on regional nationalism, so as to decrease their weak position in the colonial and postcolonial situation.

If one ethnic group occupies an intermediate or strong position in the national system, this group is more likely to identify with an ideology calculated to maintain the total system as a demotic nation.

If there is a disequilibrium in the development of the total structure of the nation—if, for instance, one regional center loses its political power in favor of another regional center, or if, through constitutional changes, a new division of the provinces causes disparity in the machinery of the central government or tends to weaken it—latent conflicts are likely to develop into manifest conflicts and to find expression in ethnic feuds.

The role of elites in nation-building can be specified as follows:

Tribal elites, having a stake in the preservation of the status quo, are most likely to uphold ethnic values and to legitimize their authority in ethnic terms when challenged by nontribal elites and by the institutions of the nation-state. To the extent that they resist modernization they also reject nationalism.

Nontribal (educated) elites are likely to split over the issue of what role ethnicity should play in nation-building.

1. Political leaders who identify with an existing state, and who seek to maintain political control, are most likely to embrace demotic nationalism, and to reject tribalism or other forms of ethnic nationalism.
2. Some leaders seek modernization within the framework of traditional ethnic societies. They try to replace the tribal elite, but seek legitimation of their own authority in ethnic terms. Their nationalism is likely to assume ethnic, restorative, regionalistic, or even secessionist forms.
3. A third type of educated leader tries to strike a balance between demotic and ethnic nationalism. His immediate goal is the transformation of the state population into a demotic nation. In this, and in his attempt to harness tribal and ethnic forces for the purpose of gaining wide popular support, he leans heavily toward revolutionary concepts and methods. To meet the difficulties inherent in nation-building, he tends to set ulterior goals in keeping with the Pan-African type of ethnic nationalism.

A ruling or dominant elite is less likely to legitimize its claim to power in ethnic terms than an elite in opposition, (1) unless one ethnic unit is clearly identified with the state, and strong enough in numbers and resources to maintain ascendency over other ethnic units included in the state; or (2) unless the state population is ethnically homogeneous. As a rule, this homogeneity can be achieved only if the colonial stage has lasted long enough to assure the homogenizing effect of bureaucratic administration. The solidarity of a demotic nation can be strengthened by subsequently reinterpreting it in ethnic terms.

An elite in opposition is more likely to legitimize its claim to power in ethnic terms, (1) if one ethnic unit is disproportionately represented in the ruling elite; (2) if a disadvantaged section of the state population can clearly be distinguished from the dominant section by using ethnic criteria; and (3) if the elite in opposition can identify with an elite formerly ruling a territory that has lost its political independence and has been submerged in the nation-state.

An educated elite, identified with a particular ethnic unit, is likely to oppose the centralizing and homogenizing tendencies of the ruling national elite on ethnic grounds, if the tribal elite identified with the same ethnic unit admits members of the educated elite to key positions in subnational (regional) institutions and to the ranks of the tribal elite itself.

Finally, concerning intersocietal relations the following can be said: If a state or several states, within their present boundaries and with their present ethnic composition, lack viability or are threatened from the outside, political leaders will be inclined to advocate a change of state boundaries. The ethnic factor may then be activated in two ways: (1) if an ethnic territory is divided among several states, and if the ethnic unit appears to be more privileged in one of them than in others, leaders may favor a change of state boundaries according to ethnic criteria so as to assure a maximum of advantages to all parts of the ethnic unit; and (2) if inside and outside pressures suggest the cooperation, federation, or amalgamation of several existing states, legitimation is likely to be sought in terms of an ethnic nationalism along the lines of Pan-Africanism or Pan-Arabism.[2]

REFERENCES

Additional titles will be found in the Selected Bibliography at the end of the book.

Antonello, Paolo, Bettina Decke, Franz J. T. Lee and Herbert Schmelz, *Nigeria gegen Biafra?* Berlin: Verlag Klaus Wagenbach, 1961.

Apter, David E., *The Political Kingdom of Uganda: A Study in Bureaucratic Nationalism.* Princeton, N.J.: Princeton University Press, 1961.

Balandier, George, "Les mythes politiques de Colonisation et décolonisation en Afrique," *Cahiers Internationaux de Sociologie*, XXXIII (1962), pp. 85–86.

Bühl, Walter L., *Evolution und Revolution, Konstruktionsprinzipien einer Theorie des Gesellschaftswandels angesichts der Dritten Welt: Eine wissenssoziologische und wissenschafts-theoretische Kritik der symmetrischen Soziologie.* München: Wilhelm Goldmann Verlag, 1970.

Carter, G. M. (ed.), *National Unity and Regionalism in Eight African States.* Ithaca, N.Y.: Cornell University Press, 1966.

Coleman, James S., *Nigeria: Background to Nationalism.* Berkeley: University of California Press, 1958.

———, and Carl G. Rosberg, Jr. (eds.), *Political Parties and National Integration in Tropical Africa.* Berkeley: University of California Press, 1964.

Dike, K. Onwuka, *Trade and Politics in the Niger Delta, 1830–1885.* Oxford: Clarendon Press, 1956, pp. 24–46.

Diop, Abdoulaye Bara, *Société Toucouleur et Migration: Enquéte sur L'immigration Toucouleur à Dakar* Dakar: IFAN, 1965.

Fallers, Lloyd, "Ideology and Culture in Uganda Nationalism," *American Anthropologist*, LXIII (1963), pp. 677–686.

Federal Ministry of Information, Press Release No. F 610, Lagos, May 24, 1966.

Francis, E. K., "Dreimal Nationalitätenstaat," in Francis, *Ethnos und Demos.* Berlin: Duncker & Humblot, 1965, pp. 178–194.

———, "The Ethnic Factor in Nation-Building," *Social Forces*, XLVI (1968), pp. 337–346.

---

[2]An analysis of community studies, not included in this volume, has revealed that in sub-Saharan Africa, ethnic solidarity and the organization of migrants from rural to urban areas serve to strengthen their social, economic, and political positions. Migrants are thereby aided in their adaptation to the urban environment. Insofar as this threatens the higher status of other groups, interethnic conflict is likely to arise. Secondary ethnic groups are not simply replicas of some tribal parent society but novel products of colonial/postcolonial situations, occasionally combining people of different tribal origin, in other instances, dividing members of the same tribe. Because of their position as aliens and the widespread tendency to close the labor market against foreigners, migrants across international boundary lines are likely to organize themselves into groups according to their country of origin, rather than along tribal lines.

Hodgkin, Thomas L., *Nationalism in Colonial Africa*. New York: New York University Press, 1956.

————, "A Note on the Language of African Nationalism," *St. Anthony's Papers*, X (1961), pp. 22–40.

————, "The Idea of Freedom in African National Movements," in David Bidney (ed.), *The Concept of Freedom in Anthropology*. Den Haag: Mouton & Co., 1963.

Kaden, Wolfgang, *Das Nigerianische Experiment; Demokratie und Nationale Integration in einem Entwicklungsland*. Hannover: Verlag für Literatur und Zeitgeschehen, 1968, p. 138.

Kohn, Hans, and Wallace Sokolsky, *African Nationalism in the Twentieth Century*. New York: D. van Nostrand Company, 1965.

Kuper, Hilda (ed.), *Urbanization and Migration in West Africa*. Berkeley: University of California Press, 1965.

Kuper, Leo, and M. G. Smith (eds.), *Pluralism in Africa*. Berkeley: University of California Press, 1969.

Legum, Colin, *Pan Africanism*. New York: Frederick A. Praeger, 1962.

Lewis, W. S. (ed.), *French-Speaking Africa: The Search for Identity*. New York: Walker Co., 1965.

Little, Kenneth, *West African Urbanization: A Study of Voluntary Associations in Social Change*. Cambridge: Cambridge University Press, 1965.

Lloyd, Peter C. (ed.), *The New Elites in Tropical Africa*. London: Oxford University Press, 1966.

————, A. L. Mabogunje and B. Awe (eds.). *The City of Ibadan: A Symposium on its Structure and Development*. Ibadan: Cambridge University Press and Institute of African Studies, 1967.

Mazrui, Ali A., *Toward a Pax Africana: A Study of Ideology and Ambition*. Chicago: University of Chicago Press, 1967.

Parkin, David J., *Neighbours and Nationals in an African City Ward*. London: Routledge & Kegan Paul Ltd., 1969a.

————, "Tribe as Fact and Fiction in an East African City," in P. H. Gulliver, (ed.), *Tradition and Transition in East Africa: Studies of the Tribal Element in the Modern Era*. London: Routledge & Kegan Paul Ltd., 1969b.

Perham, Magery, *The Colonial Reckoning*. London: Collins Sons & Co., 1961; New York: Alfred A. Knopf, 1962.

Rotberg, R. R., "African Nationalism: Concept or Confusion?", *Journal of Modern African Studies*, IV (1967), pp. 33–46.

Schwarz, Frederick A. O., Jr., *Nigeria, the Tribes, the Nation or the Race: The Politics of Independence*. Cambridge: M.I.T. Press, 1965.

Seibel, Hans Dieter, Industriearbeit und Kulturwandel in Nigeria. Köln: Westdeutscher Verlag, 1968.

Shepherd, George W., Jr., *The Politics of African Nationalism: Challenge to American Policy*. New York: Frederick A. Praeger, 1962.

Wallerstein, Immanuel, "Ethnicity and National Integration," *Cahiers d'Etudes Africaines, I* (1960), pp. 129–139.

————, "The Search for National Identity in West Africa," in Werner J. Cahnmann and Alvin Boskoff (eds.), *Sociology and History,* New York: The Free Press, 1964, pp. 303–313.

Ziegler, Jean, *Sociologie de la nouvelle Afrique*. Paris: Gallimard, 1964.

The Transformation of a Colony into a New Nation: Mexico

25

No particular colony can be said to represent one ideal type throughout its history. Nevertheless, in the process of colonization and decolonization typical situations can be distinguished, which tend to be repetitive. The analysis of the Mexican case is revealing for several reasons.[1]

1. The long colonial and postcolonial history of Mexico offers an opportunity to isolate typical situations and to analyze typical changes in the relationship between metropolis and colony, and to analyze the relationship between several strong ethnic elements in the (former) colonial territory.
2. Modernization in the metropolis initiated similar trends in the colonial polity and economy, which, in turn, have led to significant changes in the colonial social structure, particularly as regards the relationship between metropolitans and autochthones.
3. Mexico, by and large, conforms to the type of settlement colony. Yet the colonial society from which the new nation emerged was neither formed by the settler population alone, as in the United States, nor by the autochthonous population alone, as in most of sub-Saharan Africa. Instead, a new ethnic society emerged as a result of the integration into the colonial settler society of a numerically strong and occasionally dominant "Mestizo" population. This endogenous addition to the colonial population is not simply derived from interbreeding and racial hybridization between

---

[1]The following interpretation is based mainly on Wolf, 1953, as well as on data which have been adapted with the permission of the publishers from Charles Wagley and Marvin Harris, "The Indians in Mexico," in: Wagley and Harris, *Minorities in the New World: Six Case Studies*. New York: Columbia University Press, 1958, pp. 48–87.

settlers and autochthones, but has also been recruited directly from acculturated descendants of aboriginal tribes, although subsequent intermarriages have largely rendered the actual racial origin of different population
elements socially irrelevant.

4. When turning to the processes of decolonization we find that they are so
closely linked to nation-building in Mexico that decolonization there may
be treated as identical with nationalization. It has been suggested that
Mexico became a nation-state before a Mexican nation had come into
existence. As a matter of fact, colonization continued and economic
exploitation, if anything, increased for some time after Mexico had
achieved political emancipation.

5. Mexico has been more successful than many other former colonies in
integrating ethnically heterogeneous elements of her population into the
new national society, and in creating a national culture of her own.

THE FEUDAL PERIOD

New Spain was at first not considered a colony (the word itself does not
appear in the documents before the eighteenth century), but it was treated as an
integral part of the empire in the same way as were the several kingdoms of the
Iberian Peninsula. The *conquistadores* were, for all practical purposes, military entrepreneurs who, by leave of their king and with the blessing of their
church, meant to establish strongholds of feudal domination and exploitation
on another continent. They acted like medieval lords living by the produce and
labor of a native peasantry, extracting precious minerals, exacting tributes and
taxes, profiting from the trade with the metropolis (especially the sale of silver),
and eventually expanding their wealth and power through further military and
diplomatic exploits. The feudalism of the American kingdoms, however, ran
counter to the policy of the Spanish Crown, which had just set out to remodel
its metropolitan possessions on the pattern of a modern centralized and
bureaucratic state.

The introduction of the *encomienda* was an attempt to regularize the relations that had developed in early days between the metropolitans and the
autochthones. It was a typically feudal institution by which the *conquistadores*
were rewarded for their services and enabled to carry out their obligations as
vassals of the king of Castile. An *encomendero* was given the right to collect
tribute in a certain territory, but he did not thereby acquire any property rights
nor was he entitled to exercise jurisdiction over the autochthones; for the latter
were, on principle, considered vassals of the king to whose overlordship they
had submitted. Accordingly, they had retained the natural right to their property and personal freedom as long as they did not forfeit it through stubborn
resistence to their Christian king. Yet lawlessness in the conquered territories,
and the inability or unwillingness of the authorities to curb abuses, led to
large-scale expropriation and enslavement of the Indians.

CURBING FEUDALISM

It seems to be generally true that responsible metropolitan authorities are much more anxious than are their countrymen stationed in occupied territories to uphold the rights of natives and to observe the obligations of international treaties concluded with them. But when the central government is weak, the migrants tend to infringe ruthlessly upon the life, freedom, and property of autochthonous peoples. On the other hand, attempts of the metropolis to protect the natives and to restore law and order in the relations between them and the settlers have occasionally been responsible for rebellion against, and even secession from, the metropolis on the part of the settlers. Such was the case, for instance, of the South-African Boers and the British in a major part of North America.

Protection of the Indians. The aims of the central government were in the main threefold:

1. As in the Peninsula, overall policies supported the general trend toward the modernization of feudal structures.
2. The crimes perpetrated against the autochthones, which had become known through the reports of missionaries such as Fray Bartolomé de las Casas, were to be checked and remedied in accordance with contemporary ideas of natural law, human dignity, and responsible government.
3. At the same time, however, not only metropolitan needs for precious metals and other raw materials had to be met, but the economic subsistence of the overseas kingdom had to be safeguarded in order to consolidate Spanish rule and to stabilize economic and social conditions.

The Spanish authorities repeatedly issued orders that no one should lay hands on the person of an Indian, enslave or sell him abroad, or cause him any bodily harm or damage his property. The failure of Spain to abolish slavery in the Americas was mainly caused by the pressing need for an adequate labor supply, which could not yet be met by a large-scale immigration from Europe, whereas the expedient of importing African slaves, adopted in other settlement colonies, proved impractical for several reasons (cf. Beltrán, 1946). In a country with a large indigenous population which was only in part subdued and pacified, there were too many opportunities for Negro slaves to escape and mingle with the autochthones or to organize themselves into bands and communities of their own. Moreover, Negroes constituted a danger for the internal order, as they were apt to prey upon the Indian villages, rape their women, and commit other acts of violence.

Towards the middle of the sixteenth century, it was decreed that the Indian communities should no longer pay their tribute to the *encomenderos* in form of labor service but in kind or money. Yet the economy still depended on Indian labor. Although it was the official policy to integrate the autochthones into the colonial economy as free wage earners, their reluctance to do so on a voluntary basis led to a system of forced wage labor. The permanent serfdom that ensued enabled the Spanish aristocracy to exploit the land granted to them by the Crown as a reward for past merits. Eventually these *mercedes* were managed according to the manorial model, with Indians constituting a peasantry tied to the soil.

Racial Segregation. The ruthless manner in which the legal system of *repartimentos* and serfdom was handled continued to threaten the survival of the autochthonous peoples. The policy introduced by the authorities was not only meant to save the Indians from extermination but also to subject the Spaniards to more effective controls. Best known among these measures are the reservations established by religious orders where, under the paternal care of missionaries, Indians were organized in self-governing communities and isolated from the Spaniards.

Of much greater importance for interethnic relations, however, was the general segregation of the metropolitan from the autochthonous population. For this purpose all Spaniards were compelled to live in urban centers designed according to the model of Mediterranean country towns (cf. Lopez Casero, 1967). In contrast, the Indians who populated the rural areas were resettled in the so-called *reducciones,* that is, in village communities that were put under their own elected authorities but still controlled by the colonial administration. The agriculture of the autochthones was organized in such a way as to allow them to fulfill their obligations as regards tribute payments; at the same time measures were taken to prevent the *encomenderos* from expanding their landholdings and power at the Indians' cost. Each Indian community was alloted communal land *(ejido)* which could be sold only by special permission; but the individual Indian was forbidden to own land privately. Spaniards as well as Mestizos were neither allowed to reside on *ejido* land nor to use it for their own purpose, as for example, for the establishment of textile mills.

Similar measures were taken with regard to the autochthones who were recruited for labor service in the urban centers. These were forced to live in segregated quarters and to wear a special costume composed of both Spanish and traditional elements. As were the rural Indians, they were subject to special laws that exempted them from military service and the payment of ordinary taxes; but they had to surrender their share of the tribute, which was exacted from their native communities collectively. They also were forbidden to carry arms or to ride on horseback.

Economic Change. Ruthless exploitation and infectious diseases introduced by the Europeans led to a sharp decline in the aboriginal population. Lack of native labor reduced the productivity of the mines, and the depression in

Europe during the seventeenth century decreased the trade between metropolis and colony. Simultaneously, immigration from the metropolis increased. Although opinions are divided, it seems likely that as a consequence of changed economic conditions, the settlers tended to take advantage of rising prices for agricultural produce. Thus, they switched to the production of foodstuffs (for the colonial markets) and textiles, which the metropolis no longer supplied. The demand for land on the part of the Spaniards, including those who had so far been propertyless, grew considerably. The need was met not only through purchase but also through land grants from the Crown *(mercedes)* and frequently by fraudulent means at the cost of Indian *ejidos*.

The agricultural economy that emerged was based on the *hacienda* system. Although there were many variations, particularly relating to the size of property, number of laborers, capital investment, output, and so on, the economy displayed common features, which signaled the transition to commercialized farming and to a modern type of colonial exploitation. The *haziendero* was no longer a feudal lord or a settler working a moderate land grant with the help of native or slave labor, but a landowner working for maximum profit. The substantial latifundia, which became an outstanding feature of modern Mexican agriculture, are reminiscent of the landed estates found in many parts of the world, including Eastern Europe and the southern United States. Their proprietors managed them at the highest possible profit in order to obtain the luxury goods that would provide them with the comfort and prestige deemed appropriate to their upper-class standing, and which could only be purchased abroad.

Characteristically, a plantation (or a stock ranch) was not only an economic unit tied to national as well as international markets, but internally, for the greater part, it was self-supporting. It was also an administrative unit at the lowest level, with its own police force and jail, as well as an ecclesiastical unit, all under the ultimate control of the estate owner. The absentee landlords lived most of the time in the urban centers of the colony or even abroad, and appeared on rare occasions, such as harvest or fiesta time, in order to demonstrate their paternalistic authority.

The *peónes* (laborers) were recruited from among the Indian and Mestizo population. Although nominally free wage earners, the Indians, especially those who had lost their communal lands, were, for all practical purposes, forced to seek work with Spanish farmers for minimal wages. The permanent labor force of a farm—numbering anything from one hundred to several thousand—was prevented from leaving by various devices. Some were *medieres* (sharecroppers) who, in return for a parcel of poor land, implements, and animals, owed half of the harvest to the landowner. More effective still was a system of debt bondage, which resulted from the fact that the sale of all necessities of life that the *peónes* could buy with their small income was monopolized by the store owned and operated by the *haziendero*. As long as a *peón* was indebted to the *tienda,* he was forbidden to leave the farm; he was returned by the police if he tried to do so and, if he resisted, put into the army.

A Dual Social Structure

This brief outline of economic and administrative developments indicates the basic dualism of the social structure. One section of the colonial population included the autochthonous peoples and their descendants, the other was dominated by the metropolitans and settlers. Both sections maintained their essentially agrarian character throughout the colonial period; but whereas one was characterized by a subsistence economy, in the other a money economy gradually replaced feudal forms of exploitation. The one section remained underdeveloped, uneducated, disfranchised, while in the other the settlers had abundant opportunity to acquire wealth, power, education, and a refined culture. In the autochthonous sector the basic social unit was the local community, closely knit together by collective property, religious ritual (particularly the cult of the patron saint as the successor to local deity), and a largely autonomous administration patterned after Spanish models. Few organized relations existed between the Indian settlements, as they were directly subordinated to Spanish provincial or regional administrative units.

The other section was both segregated from and superimposed upon the autochthonous section. It included not only the metropolitan and settler population which was originally relatively small, but also a growing portion of the autochthonous population, as well as the half-breed offspring of the two basic elements. The latter were integrated as its lowest stratum into the colonial society, which emerged mainly in the urban centers, but gradually expanded to include rural and mining areas.

The two sections were bound together by a centralized administration in which the functions of state and church were interlocking. It was manned by a small elite concentrated in the capital city and larger regional centers, who provided the mediating link between the metropolis and the colony. The settler core of the colonial society, on the other hand, was linked to the autochthonous section at the top by the dominant elite and, informally, at the bottom through detribalized additions to the marginal laboring class.

Ethnic and Racial Differentiation

The preceding discussion should help us to understand the social structure as it had developed in New Spain at the end of the colonial period, and the role that ethnicity played in forming the colonial society from which the new nation emerged. The autochthonous population of the territory had been divided into a great number of ethnic societies, speaking different languages, having different cultures, and lacking any sense of common identity. The situation changed when all the autochthones—regardless of their particular ethnic origin, station in life, or occupation—were summarily classified by the Spanish authorities as belonging to one social category with a status differing radically from that of the metropolitans. The legally sanctioned status differences between the two basic population elements involved two particularistic sets of rights and duties as well as a different habitat, different economic activities, a different way of life, and preferential marriage within each category. The separation was further supported for pastoral reasons. On principle, the Catholic church, unlike some Protestant churches, does not tolerate any differentiation between the baptized faithful on account of status or descent. Nevertheless, expediency suggested that those who spoke different languages and observed different ways of life be cared for in parishes of their own, and ministered to by priests who were familiar with and sympathetic to their cultures.

In the beginning the dividing line between metropolitans and autochthones was clear-cut and unambiguous. The legal and administrative measures introduced by the Spanish authorities recognized existing differences rather than created them. Somatic distinctions played a minor part in the Spanish possessions as compared, for instance, with sub-Saharan Africa. For both the metropolitan and autochthonous population included a wide range of subracial variations which overlapped in part. While Spaniards of the Mediterranean subtype were often quite dark, many Indians were rather lightly pigmented and displayed few mongoloid features. Spaniards, far from being repelled by the Indian phenotype, were apt to notice the dignity of their bearing and particularly the beauty of their women. Attitudes formed from early experiences with strangers are likely to draw selective attention to external characteristics which seem to support such attitudes. In their early contacts with Indians and their cultures the Spaniards had been impressed with many traits that they themselves valued highly.

New endogenous additions to the basic population elements were a result of both interbreeding and transculturation. The growth of the Mestizo population was brought about by a combination of factors: the conquerors had raped the women; the slaves and serfs were sexually exploited by their masters; the absence of any physical aversion and the general lack of white women in the early period also help to explain it. More than the biological phenotype resulting from miscegenation, which was often ambiguous, cultural factors played a decisive role in the social differentiation between Spaniards and Mestizos. In a caste society like the Spanish, in which the distribution of social rewards is based primarily on inherited status, genealogies and the proof of legitimate birth assumed major importance. This had nothing to do with the kind of racism that developed during the nineteenth century in the wake of biological science and Social Darwinism.

The problem here was not interbreeding or the belief in the inferiority of people displaying distinctive somatic traits, but marriage taboos and the legitimation of bastards. In medieval Spain *limpieza de sangre* (purity of blood) had assumed a particular meaning during the struggle with the Moors. Whoever

could prove legitimate descent from an unadulterated line of Christian ancestors was thought to be firmly grounded in the faith, while baptized descendants
of Mohammedans or Jews were looked upon with suspicion. This distrust of
aliens not only strengthened the superior prestige of "pure-blood" Spaniards,
but also led to discriminatory laws and practices. Thus, persons of mixed blood
were excluded from certain occupations and public functions, and were limited
in their right to acquire certain types of property.

Although interracial mating was not tabood in Mexico, Spaniards of the
upper class nevertheless refused to marry Indian girls; for, like marriage with a
white woman of lowly birth, it would have been considered a blot on a noble
name and family tradition. Among low-class Spaniards, on the other hand, legal
marriage with a first-generation Mestizo girl carried no particular social stigma
and was a common practice; their legitimate offspring was considered to be
Spanish. Male Mestizos, however, unless legitimized by their Spanish fathers,
had difficulties in finding a Spanish mate and were forced to content themselves
with Mestizo or Indian spouses. The general rule was that legitimate children
were assigned to the social rank of their fathers, while the offspring of illicit
unions followed the status of the mother. Accordingly, hypergamy was open
even to pure-blood Indian girls but not to males of Indian or mixed descent who
were compelled to marry into the lower strata.

Designations that merely indicated descent eventually came to symbolize
social rank. Thus, an "Indio" was one who spoke a native language rather than
Spanish; who upheld cultural traditions that deviated from the Spanish standard; who hailed from a rural rather than an urban settlement; who, typically,
earned his living with his own hands; and who also was readily recognizable by
external characteristics such as dress and, possibly, somatic appearance.

The word "Mestizo," on the other hand, originally referred to persons of
mixed European and Indian descent, who combined the stigma of illicit birth
with a low-class occupation. These shared the uncertain status of marginal man
rather than any particular status that would have been assigned to a whole
category by law or by custom. The identification of the Mestizos with the
Spaniards rather than with the Indios was favored by the official policy to
exclude not only Spaniards but also Mestizos (and Negroes) from settling in
Indian villages. As urban dwellers the Mestizos, unlike the rural Indians, had a
much better chance of observing and imitating Spanish customs. They also
were exempted from the payment of tribute and from wearing Indian dress.

The Ladinos were a further population element, which eventually merged
with the Mestizos. They consisted of pure-blood Indians who had become
separated from their communities, settled in Spanish towns and mingled there
with the lowest classes, assuming their speech and culture. As the Ladinos
tended to mate with and marry Mestizos and even poor whites, the lowest
stratum of the Spanish-speaking colonial society eventually consisted largely of
a mixed population. The words "Mestizo" and "Ladino" came to be used interchangeably to describe a man of low standing, and presumably of Indian or

part-Indian descent, who spoke Spanish, dressed like a Spaniard, followed a Spanish way of life, and above all was not enrolled in the official Indian register.

To sum up: It is not race in the sense of actual genealogy or obvious phenotype that divided the Mexican population into three major ethnic categories, but social dividing lines, which emerged from history, came to be symbolized in racial terms. The categories of major significance included: (1) descendants of the autochthonous population who had preserved their speech and way of life, who lived in rural settlements of their own, and who were registered in the Indian tax role; (2) acculturated Indians and part-Indians, who were distinguished by low occupational, educational, and prestige status; and (3) the Creole elite of the colonial society, whose status, occupation, and way of life were taken as prima facie evidence of pure metropolitan descent.

Colonial Language Policy

The integration of the autochthones and their descendants into the colonial society was also influenced by the language policy of church and state. During the early days of missionary activities native languages, in particular, the Nahuatl spoken by the Aztecs, were used as lingua franca and as the language of instruction. This changed when, with the extension of church activities, not enough priests with an adequate command of the native language were available. Moreover, modernization encouraged the spread of literacy and of a literary language suitable to mediate appropriate ideas and skills.

In the eighteenth century the statecraft of Absolutism and the moral ideas of Enlightenment encouraged a language policy aiming at outright transculturation of the aboriginal population. It was thought that the common use of one national language would not only facilitate the manifold administrative tasks of the modern state, but it would help to unify its population and activate a sense of common identity and solidarity: in our case, strengthen Spanish rule in the Americas. It was also expected that in this way the tremendous inequality in economic opportunities would be overcome, the productivity of the Indians enhanced, and their integration into the modernizing economy of empire and colony accomplished.

Before the emancipation of the colony, however, the success of these policies remained moderate. By the end of the eighteenth century, about 30 percent of Mexico's total population was counted as Mestizo or Ladino, compared with 60 percent of unacculturated tribal Indians.

Cradle of a New Nation

The modern society of New Spain, which was eventually to be transformed into the new Mexican nation, emerged on the pioneering fringe of colonial society. In the mining district of the North, neither Spanish feudalism nor

Indian "high civilization" had left vestiges strong enough to resist social change. Innovations were all the more readily accepted by the numerous immigrants from other parts of Mexico; these were attracted as much by the opportunities offered by an expanding regional economy as by the fact that they could thereby shake off social burdens and controls under which they had suffered in their native communities.

A case in point is that of the Bajio, the general area of Guanajuato and Querétaro, where the expansion and modernization of the mining industry, producing for international markets, stimulated agriculture and livestock farming on land hitherto little utilized. The new farms and ranches supplied local markets with foodstuffs, and a growing textile industry with wool. Two big highways crossing the Bajio stimulated the development of urban commerce, which catered primarily to the monopolistic company stores maintained by mine, factory, and farm owners for their employees.

Neither state nor church were able to stem the tide that threatened to destroy the established order or to control the stirrings of a new social order, which found an outlet in lawlessness and armed self-help, thus repeating the pattern of the American "Wild West," whose main features were importations from (formerly Mexican) Texas. The rapid growth of a modern economy and the lack of an efficient administration paved the way for a new society in which the ethnic factor tended to recede into the background. The mottled crowd of mobile individuals drawn from various regions and segments of colonial society, Spanish and Indian, urban and rural, Mestizo and even Negro and Mulatto, was attracted by economic opportunities as much as by the prospect of freeing themselves from discrimination that, in the older parts of the country, inherited status had imposed upon them.

Here individual achievement, stamina, enterprise, courage, or just physical strength now promised not only a higher standard of living but also a chance of advancement in prestige and new opportunities for self-expression. Wherever they managed to develop a collective will and to organize common action or even to rise in armed rebellion, the masses of miners, farmhands, and cowboys were able to force employers and authorities to yield to their demands. Their position was further strengthened by the fact that the Spanish colonial army was organized into regional units officered by members of the local upper class. The cavalry, recruited from among the cowboys, and the special regiments formed by mine workers played a major role in a chain of regional revolts against the central government, which marks Mexican history.

In a pioneer society actual descent is rarely common knowledge, and individual achievement is bound to count more than ancestral background in the differential distribution of social rewards. Thus, the migrants to the Bajio and other northern mining districts were able to emancipate themselves from the traditional mechanism of status assignment, from legal restrictions on the choice of occupation, and from other measures maintaining dividing lines between classes, ethnic groups, and races. Even Indians, once they were able to escape registration and the head tax, had little difficulty in merging with the new class of free laborers who, in time, developed a characteristic subculture of colonial Spain. The modernization of the economy, the impoverishment of the rural masses, the neutralization of the ethnic factor, and the rise of a self-asserting laboring class—all contributed to the revolution that set off the process of decolonization in New Spain.

THE NATIONAL REVOLUTION

Nation-building in Mexico has been marked by a series of violent uprisings, civil wars, and radical socioeconomic changes that can truly be called revolutionary. The first revolution resulted in national independence, while during the second, the middle and lower classes were integrated into the national society.

The National Revolution that culminated in secession must be seen against the background of the numerous insurrections by military *juntas* throughout the Spanish colonies, which followed the weakening of the metropolis during the Napoleonic era. The first Mexican revolution, which lasted from 1810 to 1823, was mainly the work of two opposing social forces. The divergent economic interests and political aims had their roots in the colonial period. As we recall, the autochthonous section was ecologically, occupationally, and culturally separated from the mainstream of the colonial society, which was dominated by a *criollo* upper class of landowners, businessmen, professionals, army officers, and civil servants. The lower classes were represented by the mine workers, the *campesinos* (farmhands and cowboys), as well as a growing urban proletariat.

The Mestizo and Ladino population, occasionally supported by Indio communities, were the first to rebel. Prominent among their leaders were members of the lower clergy, educated in the spirit of Enlightenment and steeped in the ideas of the French Revolution. Their chief concern was the improvement of the lamentable conditions in which they found the common people. Best known among them is Miguèl Hidalgo y Costilla, a Creole priest, who was later executed. He was succeeded by a Mestizo priest, José Maria Morelos, who went so far as to proclaim an independent republic that was to bring the abolition of slavery and the equality of all races before the law.

Once the rebellion had been put down, the Creole establishment joined forces with the remnants of the populist movement. The ideas of liberalism, democratism, and nationalism, at the time current in Europe, provided the colonial elite with an ideology to legitimize their struggle against political domination, economic exploitation, and taxation by the metropolis. As was to be expected, the contrast between the *criollos,* who, as natives, claimed birth right to New Spain, and the *gachupines,* that is, Spaniards born in the Peninsula, who enjoyed superior power and prestige in the colony, was expressed in quasi-ethnic terms in much the same way as was the distinction between autochthones and metropolitans in sub-Saharan Africa; of this we spoke in the preceding chapter. There are also similarities between present-day efforts towards "Africanization" and the replacement of *gachupines* in key positions and their partial expulsion after secession.

Although the new men in power had agreed in principle to equality of race, the abolition of discriminatory laws, and land reforms in favor of the underprivileged, they saw to it that private property, including the vast latifundia of the church, was left untouched. At the same time the living conditions of the laboring people in mining, agriculture, and industry remained unchanged or even worsened.

NATIONALISM

Colonialism did not end with political emancipation. If anything, the processes of colonization were speeded up in the period following independence; they reached a climax during the regime of Porfirio Diaz, whose presidency lasted, with a short interruption, from 1876 to 1911. When the trade monopoly, taxes, and revenues by which Spain had sapped the wealth of the colony for her own benefit became a thing of the past, other colonial powers took over the role of the metropolis. First came England, which had sparked off and supported the liberation movements in all Latin America, later France, and finally the United States.

Foreign aid and investments brought Mexico on the road to modernization, but by the same means made it increasingly dependent on international markets and foreign capital. The export of raw materials was intensified, monocultures were introduced, industrialization that concentrated mainly on the processing of finished products imported from abroad was stepped up. Shortly before the second or "social" revolution, which followed a century of neocolonialism, more than half of Mexico's oil reserves and three-fourths of other mineral resources, vast livestock ranches, as well as cotton and rubber plantations were owned and controlled by foreign, mostly American, interests. One-seventh of the entire surface of the country was in the hands of foreign companies.

Together with colonial exploitation went massive political interference with internal affairs and even military intervention. Examples of this are the annexation of Texas and the Southwest by the United States about the middle of the century. These interventions were followed by the operation of a French expeditionary force during and after the Mexican civil war (1857–60), and the abortive attempt by Napoleon III to install the Hapsburg Maximilian as emperor. In 1914, United States Marines landed at Vera Cruz, and in 1917,

General Pershing led a punitive expedition against the revolutionary troups of Pancho Villa. No wonder that xenophobia became an essential ingredient of Mexican nationalism.

Economic and political developments since 1823 particularly benefited an upper-class bourgeoisie and, to a lesser extent, a rising middle class. The broad Mestizo and Indian masses, on the other hand, suffered more than they gained from economic expansion to which they themselves made a substantial contribution by working for extremely low wages; between 1792 and 1908, wages remained practically unchanged while prices rose sharply; prices of the most common foodstuffs rose up to 700 percent. Despite the progress made by commerce and industry, Mexico remained a predominantly agrarian country. Her central problem was the social and economic conditions among the impoverished landless *peónes* as well as in the Indian communities whose property was threatened by ruthless speculation. This was also the main issue in the civil war. The attempts of the liberal, anticlerical government of Benito Juarez, a Mestizo, to turn Mexico into a country of small and medium family farms by partitioning large ecclesiastical estates, brought some relief. Yet the land reform was hampered by internal strife and foreign interference. Eventually, the progressive trend of economic and social policies was reversed under President Diaz who, disregarding the need of the landless *peónes,* favored commercial farming and ranching on a large scale.

THE INDIAN QUESTION

In the vagaries of Mexican agricultural politics, the Indian question held a prominent place. The Indians had achieved full citizenship and legal equality as an immediate consequence of the establishment of a republican government. Yet the equality that pleased the doctrinaire cut both ways; for it also removed the privileges that had been granted them by the Spanish Crown for their own protection. Corporate ownership of land had been most important for the preservation of their communal life. When, in the middle of the century, laws that had been originally directed against the church were passed prohibiting corporate property, communal Indian land was also transferred into the private ownership of individual villagers. As a consequence, it could now be sold in the open market, and most of it was finally turned over to large property owners, including foreign companies, while the dispossessed Indians were forced to work, alongside with the Mestizo *peónes,* as common laborers bound in debt bondage to their master.

Two opposing ideologies had a similar effect on Indian policy: on the one hand, the liberal ideas of individualism, human equality, and civil rights regardless of origin and inherited status; on the other hand, Social Darwinism, which affected public opinion on the innate difference of races. Both ideologies had no use for particularistic measures to protect communities of autochthones from destruction; for these hindered the general economic progress. The impression that Indians were not worth special consideration was supported by the fact that individual tribesmen, having lost the use of common land, were forced to merge with the Mestizo proletariat (cf. Whetten, 1948, p. 89).[2] Thus the epithet "Indio" assumed the significance of an uncouth, barbarous person—a *peón* of the lowest human quality.

> . . . it was believed that the Indian was destined to adapt or to disappear in the competition of the "survival of the fittest." The poverty and illiteracy of the Indians was taken as proof of their racial inferiority, and they were considered a burden to society" (Wagley, Harris, 1958, p. 61).

Nevertheless, 41 percent of the Indian villages managed, by one subterfuge or another, to keep their communal property intact and to elude the threat to their very survival. This was probably in part because once the size of an estate had reached the point of diminishing returns, its owner often allowed Indian settlements to survive on its fringes, thereby securing for himself an adequate and cheap supply of seasonal labor.

As we intend to analyze interethnic relations for the entire period from 1823 to 1940 at the end of the chapter, we shall only note at this point that in 1910, despite progressive proletarization and latinization, 30 percent of Mexico's population was still counted as "pure Indians" as against 43 percent "Mestizos" and 20 percent "pure Whites."

The Social Revolution

The social revolution, whose violent phase of revolts and civil war was followed by a no less revolutionary period of radical change, was brought about by the explosive mixture of socioeconomic developments that had culminated towards the end of the Diaz regime. Among the most important factors are the following: (1) economic modernization, especially the spread of commercialized farming, industrialization, and urbanization; (2) neocolonialism; (3) the impoverishment of the rural masses and the loss of *ejido* land by Indian communities; (4) the dissatisfaction among a growing middle class and urban proletariat; (5) the ambitions of army officers and regional military leaders; and (6) the general disappointment arising from the failure to redeem the promises of earlier revolutions.

Accordingly, the social forces that took an active part in the ensuing struggle included the mine workers, farmhands, and cowboys, among whom Francisco (Pancho) Villa recruited his revolutionary army in the North; as well as the Indians, plantation workers, Mestizo *peones,* and small peasants in the South

---

[2]According to Whetten, on the eve of the second revolution, 90 percent of the villages in the Central Mesa had no land whatsoever; 95 percent of the heads of rural families in all but five states had no rural property of their own, and nearly half the rural population was bound to debt slavery.

who followed Emiliano Zapata, himself an Indian. Large numbers of Yaqui-Indians fought under Alvaro Obregón, who had first supported President Carranza (basically a man of the middle classes), but later opposed and succeeded him. When Villa and Zapata marched against Mexico City, the "Red Battalions" organized among the laborers made common cause with Carranza and Obregón, as they had been promised more favorable labor laws.

By 1917, the central government had lost control over large parts of the country, which had become the domaine of civil war generals, guerilla leaders, and even bandits. A telling document, which sums up the more pressing grievances for whose redress the revolutionaries were fighting, was an open letter addressed to Carranza by Zapata, who describes himself as a

> ... peasant knowing the necessities of the humble people to whom I belong as a revolutionary . . . who has had an opportunity to know the national soul . . . with its miseries and hopes. In the agrarian reform, *haziendas* have been given or rented to (your) favorite generals; the old landlords have been replaced in not a few cases by modern landholders dressed in *charro* costumes, military hats and with pistols at their belts; the people have been mocked in their hopes. The *ejidos* have not been returned to the village . . . nor have lands been distributed to the workers, the poor peasants and those truly in need (Whetten, 1948, pp. 122 ff.).[3]

This time, unlike in 1823, the revolution had not been fought in vain. Plutarco Calles (president between 1924 and 1928, but also the leading figure under his successors) improved conditions among the urban proletariat. The agrarian reform, promoted with the greatest determination and success by President Lazaro Cárdenas (1934–40), had the most far-reaching impact upon interethnic relations. Between 1915 and 1945, over 30 million hectar, or 23 percent of the total agricultural land, were repartitioned and turned into collective property, called *ejido* land (as a reminder of a colonial institution which had, however, a somewhat different character). Mexico's modern *ejido* system is reminiscent of the solidaristic type of village settlement once widespread among European peasants. The land gained by partitioning large estates subsequently becomes public property, portions of which are transfered to villages and agricultural cooperatives. While wood- and wastelands remain indivisible for common use, cultivated *ejido* land is allowed to be portioned out among individual heads of families. Although it is inheritable by succeeding generations, it may not be mortgaged, sold, or otherwise disposed of.

The Agrarian Reform and the Indian Question

The principal beneficiaries of the reform have been the masses of Mestizo *peónes*. Yet the Indians have also been strongly affected by it. The collective property of land, which some of their villages had managed to keep intact

---

[3]By 1940, about 47 percent of the cultivated land was divided among 1,600,000 *ejidatarios*. The holdings averaged about 4.4 hectar and were individually cultivated.

through the preceding century, was now confirmed and even expanded. Although other Indian villages were allowed to retrieve land lost to the *hazienderos,* these had, as a rule, not been able to preserve their communal life. They had become acculturated and had merged with the Mestizo population. And all the Indians living on new-style *ejido* land were subject to much more direct state control than under the colonial *ejido* system and exposed to outside influences.

Coupled with the agrarian reform, strenuous efforts were made to spread and improve education in rural areas. This aspect had been neglected during the earlier period, for the upper classes had a strong interest in keeping the laboring masses illiterate and culturally separated, the better to be dominated and exploited with impunity. There was a pressing need for teachers who were both motivated and trained to serve in rural areas. Thus, as a first step in rural education, the Bureau of Public Education, founded in 1921, sent missionaries into the rural communities to promote the cooperative building of schools and to recruit suitable teachers on the spot. The schools, called "Homes of the People," were supposed to educate the whole community, children and adults alike, and to promote community projects. In this way the Mexican peasantry were gradually enabled to take their place in a modern society, and to benefit from its economic and social opportunities. Simultaneously, the state-controlled system of public education contributed substantially to the homogenization of the state population.

Both the improvement of rural education and the fact that, legally, Indian communal property is being treated in the same way as all the other *ejido* land held by Mestizos or detribalized Indians, have brought into prominence the peculiar situation of those Indians who so far had escaped detribalization. Opinions were, and still are, divided as to whether they should be treated on equal terms with other depressed rural masses, particularly the Mestizos, or whether measures should be taken to cope with their special needs. The *Indigenistas,* partly inspired and actively aided by American anthropologists,

> . . . insisted that there were Indians with individual needs other than those of the general rural population, whose heritage merited a cherished notch in the Mexico of the future (Ramón Eduardo Ruiz, cited in Wagley, Harris, 1958, p. 62).

These, it was thought, would have a chance to survive as viable ethnic units only if special legal and administrative measures, special agencies, and special methods of education were provided for them. The assimilationists, on the other hand, looked forward to a rapid absorption of the remaining Indians into the mass of the Mexican population. As the most effective means to this end, they considered *castellanización,* that is, making them linguistically Spaniards.

Denouncing the pseudoscientific doctrines of Social Darwinism, both schools of thought have been firmly convinced that present conditions were to be accounted for, not by an innate racial inferiority, but by environmental factors.

> To transform the environment . . . the reformers gave the peasants land and schools. In them, they saw the key to the future of the rural scene, for both gave the peasants the means for survival (Ruiz, cited by Wagley, Harris, 1958, p. 61).

Actual policies have labored between opposing ideologies ever since; in the long run, the net effect of rural education and the land reform has been to hasten the Indians along the road to becoming Mestizos, rather than to restore their traditional ethnic integrity. The breakdown of ethnic isolation, acculturation and urbanization, and bilingualism and marginality have tended to transform the still-existing Indian communities into primary ethnic groups operating within the new national society of Mexico.

THE CHANGING SOCIAL STRUCTURE

The creation of a modern nation-state had been the explicit purpose of the National Revolution. In the cauldron of a social revolution, it took a century for a national society to come into being. Nation-building in postcolonial situations, as we have said, is closely associated with the course that decolonization takes. In our analysis of interethnic relations, it is important that we follow the relative position of the ethnic components of the colonial population during this process. We have seen how modern economic trends changed Mexico's social structure; it is now our task to analyze how social change influenced ethnic differentiation and interethnic relations. We shall later investigate how structural factors have affected the formation of the new Mexican nation and the particular character it was to assume.

In 1823, at the eve of the revolution, a twofold division expressed in terms of race cut deeply through the colonial population. One line separated the autochthonous ("tribal") sector from the colonial society which itself was bisected into an upper metropolitan and a lower Mestizo layer. Nevertheless, the three sectors were not entirely rigid: there was a moderate upward mobility from the Mestizo to the settler sector and, to a still lesser degree, a downward mobility of "poor whites" into the Mestizo sector. The largest mobility, however, was from the autochthonous to the Mestizo sector. The colonial society had preserved its general character of a status society, but the first traces of a transition made themselves felt on its pioneering fringe.

POSTCOLONIAL DEVELOPMENTS

When we turn to postcolonial developments, two stages must be distinguished, one immediately following political emancipation from the metropolis in 1823, the other lasting from about 1910 to 1940. During the first of the two periods, modern trends of commercialized agriculture and (to a smaller degree) industrialization were colored by stepped-up colonization. Economic modernization was accompanied by a political liberalization. Both contributed to reducing the gap between the autochthonous sector and the settler society (which was heir to the colonial society), and thus led to the merging of increasing numbers of autochthones with the lower Mestizo masses. The more the settler society assumed the character of a modern class society, the more intensified the rural-urban cleavage as well as the vertical differentiation of its social structure became. To the Creole upper and Mestizo lower classes were now added new middle-class elements containing a larger Mestizo contingent than the upper class. Compared with other sectors of the society, mobility among the rural Mestizo masses, with which the detribalized autochthones tended to merge, was relatively reduced.

Despite the social cleavages just described, and despite diverging regional interests that threatened the unity of the state—the concentration of economic and political power in the hands of a mediating elite, a strong central government with its army, the increase of means of transportation and communication, and the growing independence and intertwining of economic interests—all these factors, which made great strides, especially under the Diaz regime, worked towards demotic unity in a manner reminiscent of the preformation of modern nations in Europe under absolutism.

The core of the nation-to-be, however, was confined to the upper and, to some extent, to the rising middle classes of the settler society to which the principles and benefits of "democratism" were extended, while the vast majority of the lower Mestizo and Indian masses remained, for all practical purposes, excluded from the emerging national society. It was not until the revolutionary period that both the lower urban classes and the rural masses were gradually integrated into the demotic core, and the new Mexican nation began to take shape. Shared revolutionary experiences in which violence, always a powerful factor in the processes of radical change, paved the way for sentiments of solidarity, which superseded the regional, class, and ethnic dividing lines.

DEMOTIC UNIFICATION

During the revolution, ever-wider sections of the state population became politically mobilized and articulate, and they also began to actively determine their own political destiny. At first political participation meant joining revolutionary armies and their generals. After strong presidents like Obregón, Calles, and Cárdenas had succeeded in wresting power from revolutionary generals and guerilla leaders, disbanding their troops or integrating them into the national army, and strengthening the authority of the central government, sectionalized solidarities gave way to identification with the nation and to political participation through the civil channels provided by democratism. When Calles founded the Partido Nacional Revolucionario in 1928/29, it was a loose aggregate of regional power groups. After Cárdenas took over, the Partido Nacional Institutional combined the pillars of the new society: trade unions, farmers' federations, the army, and a heterogeneous public sector, while the reorganized boards of commerce and of industry acted as mediators between a government based on the party and business. Thus, party and government had become strong links between almost all sectors of society, a democratic representation and symbol of national unity.

At the same time, the homogenization of the population, with the exception of the remaining Indian communities, was promoted through increased mobility and communication as well as the impact of public education. Alphabetism supported the influence of the mass media which, together with the schools, were instrumental in spreading a uniform culture and a national ideology. What tied the rural masses most closely to the nation, however, was the distribution of land, which gave them a stake in the country and a sense of common purpose.

In Search of National Identity

The Republic of Mexico was aided in its search for national identity by a long historical continuity, which was not even broken by territorial losses in the far South nor through secession in the North brought about by subversion and conquest. The insistent struggle against metropolitan domination, colonial exploitation, and foreign intervention united all Mexicans regardless of status or race, and impressed on their minds societal boundaries. But the fact that the country shared its lingua franca and basic culture with Spain and her other former colonies posed problems regarding national identification.

In the face of social cleavages inherited from the colonial past which, though with different accents, continued through the first postcolonial period, an impulse stronger than a sense of separateness was required to transform the Mexican society into a new nation. Yet tangible proof was needed for the legitimacy of the universalistic claim to authority and loyalty advanced by the central government. And the validity of race as a criterion for the distribution of social rewards had to be reevaluated. The most important contribution to solving the problem of legitimacy was made when the central authorities honored the demands of the revolutionary masses for land and social justice, and when they took effective steps to fulfill their hopes for relief from discrimination and oppression.

In the demotic nation, which received its final shape during the second revolution and subsequent radical reforms, the center of gravity had definitely shifted from the Creole upper class to the middle and lower classes which, in varying degrees, comprised Mestizo and Ladino elements. The recognition of the lower classes as full members of the national society necessarily implied an upgrading of Mestizo and even Indio descent. Ethnicity expressed in terms of race assumed a new meaning.

Earlier, as we have seen, race had served to legitimize and stabilize the existing system of distributing social rewards unequally among conquerors and conquered, elite and masses, propertied and propertyless classes. When the balance of power was reversed by the revolution, racial differentiation lost its sharp edge. This did not mean that race was completely ignored, but it assumed different functions. Social status was no longer assigned on the basis of somatic appearance, but racial differences were still perceived whenever they happened to coincide with class differences. In this case racial characteristics come to serve the practical purpose of providing indices of status and guidelines for proper conduct. If a Mexican looks like an Indian, he probably will prove to be a member of an Indian community, or else belong to the lowest strata of society. Additional characteristics, such as speech, dress, or birthplace, help specify his social position still more narrowly. If, on the other hand, a man is known to belong to the upper classes, traces of Indian descent in his appearance will not lower his status.

NATIONAL IDEOLOGY

Descent and race have also played a strategic role in national ideology. Earlier we found that national movements have a tendency to reinterpret demotic unity in ethnic terms in order to provide added legitimacy and sentimental support. Such attempts to intensify a sense of identity and sentiments of solidarity as well as to underline the birthright to the country are widely reflected in national literatures (cf. Tömmel, 1971). In former settlement colonies efforts to legitimize national identity and to arouse national sentiments by recourse to both shared ethnicity and autochthony are usually confronted with particular problems. In Mexico, the unequal distribution of somatic traits remained an unquestionable reminder of the basic ethnic division among the state population, while autochthony was least attributable precisely to the most dominant population element, the Creoles. Nevertheless, ethnic nationalism did have its representatives among Mexican intellectuals during the first postcolonial period. For instance, Heriberto Frias, in a novel published in 1892, described the aborigines as the ethnic foundation of the nation. About the same time, Andrés Molina Enriquez, drawing attention to the local isolation of the Indians, represented the Mestizos as the true core of the Mexican nation.

Once more the social revolution made a definite contribution to the ethnic interpretation and to the vigor of the new nation. The struggle of the rural masses against the large property owners permitted a new definition of the situation: The Mestizo had successfully risen against both foreigners and Creoles, the former metropolitans. This together with the increased weight of the *peónes* suggested that the Mestizo element be viewed as the genuine national core representing the vast majority of the people.

As did the romanticists of Europe, Mexican leaders began to take a positive interest in the lore and history of the common folk. Yet, unlike the European scene, the colonial past of Mexico involved an intrinsic contradiction between ethnic revival and the exigencies of a modern nation; for ethnic traditions that were truly aboriginal to the country meant Indian traditions, while the background of the emerging modern society was culturally Spanish. It was therefore the Mestizos (whose numbers were constantly increased by latinized Indians leaving their communities) who were a purely native product linked not only to the Indian and colonial past, but also clearly differentiated from the Spanish parent society. Eventually, a rich symbolism of Mexican nationhood, which combined such heterogeneous elements as the Aztec heroes, Hidalgo and Zapata, or the Reforma Agraria, was codified by the intelligentsia and propagated by the state as a potent national myth.

CONCLUSIONS

With regard to the formation of nations and the role of national movements and ideologies, the preceding account of nation-building in a former settlement colony with a substantial autochthonous and still larger half-breed population seems to confirm the general insights gained in Part II. The analysis suggests, however, that the role of revolutions, the common experience of war and violence as a factor stimulating sentiments of solidarity, and the army as a political power deserve greater attention than has so far been given; for in this book we have laid the main emphasis on evolutionary processes of change intrinsic to a given social structure rather than to sudden mutations. As far as the role of race is concerned, however, the Mexican case suggests a few additions to the theory presented so far:

1. Whenever racial and status differences in a given population coincide, race is likely to have a greater social significance and to be more readily perceived than where similar racial mixtures are found indiscriminately among all segments of the social structure.
2. Regarding the relationship that exists between class struggle and saliency of ethnicity, Colby and van den Berghe have advanced an interesting hypothesis which we are inclined to adopt as a whole. They write:

> The paternalistic type of group relations is typically found in preindustrial societies with little social or geographical mobility, a clear-cut division of labor along group lines, and a wide gap in wealth, education and/or culture between

dominant and subjugated groups. Intergroup relations are of the master—servant variety with benevolent despotism on the part of the dominant group and submissive accommodation on the part of the subjugated group. Such relations are generally intimate, but inequality of status is strictly enforced. Urbanization and industrialization undermine this paternalistic system which then tends to evolve towards the competitive type of group relations if the racial or ethnic line remains rigid. The economic and social rise of the subjugated group is then perceived as a threat to the dominant group. The lower group ceases to be accommodated and is viewed by the dominant group as . . . dangerous rather than . . . inferior but lovable so long as it remains in its place. Whenever the ethnic or racial line become fluid, however, the competitive stage may be by-passed to the extent that group distinctions become obliterated through acculturation and miscegenation (Colby, van den Berghe, 1961, pp. 788 ff.).

3. In a stable agrarian society where hopes for social change appear unrealistic and the balance of mutual accommodation between ethnically diverse populations, each having a different social status, has been maintained through a period of time, there is no struggle for status advancement, and thus no occasion to symbolize and legitimize it in ethnic terms.

4. The dynamism of modernization, on the other hand, makes social advancement a tangible goal. Whenever status divisions run along ethnic lines, there is a tendency to express status competition and class conflict in ethnic terms.[4]

5. Ethnicity once more tends to lose its saliency as soon as mobility on account of urbanization and industrialization obliterates marked ethnic differences between social classes, and a plausible national ideology is able to promote a common sense of identity and solidarity.

REFERENCES

Beltrán, Gonzale Aguirre, *La Población Negra de Mexico, 1519–1810*. Mexico: Ediciones Fuente Cultural, 1946.

———, *El Processo de Aculturación*. Mexico: Universidad Nacional Autónoma de Mexico, 1957.

Beyhant, Gustavo, *Süd- und Mittelamerika II*. Fischer Weltgeschichte, vol. 23. Frankfurt/Main: S. Fischer Verlag, 1965.

Cline, Howard, *Mexico: Revolution to Evolution. 1940–1960*, New York: Oxford University Press, 1963.

Colby, B. N., and P. L. Van den Berghe, "Ethnic Relations in Southeastern Mexico," *American Anthropologist*, LXIII (1961), pp. 788–789.

———, *Ethnic Relations in the Chiappas Highlands*. Sante Fé: Museum of New Mexico Press, 1966.

De la Fuente, Julio, *Relaciones Interéthnicas*. Mexico: Instituto Nacional Indigenista, 1955.

Hayner, Norman S., *New Patterns in Old Mexico*. New Haven, Conn.: College and University Press, 1966.

---

[4]Accordingly, whether ethnic and racial factors become salient seems to depend largely on whether a society (or a section of it) conforms more to the agrarian or to the industrial type.

Harris, Marvin, *Patterns of Race in the Americas*. New York: Walker and Co., 1964.

Konetzka, R., *Süd- und Mittelamerika I*. Fischer Weltgeschichte, vol. 22. Frankfurt/Main: S. Fischer Verlag, 1965.

Lieuwen, Edwin, *Mexican Militarism, 1910–1940*. Albuquerque, N.M.: University of New Mexico Press, 1968.

Lopez Casero, Francisco, *Die differenzierte Agrargemeinde als Primärgruppe: Sozialstruktur und Interaktionsprozesse eines spanischen Pueblo*, unpublished Munich doctoral dissertation, 1967.

Markov, Walter (ed.,), *Lateinamerika zwischen Emanzipation und Imperialismus*. Berlin: Akademie Verlag, 1961.

Ramos, Samuel, *Profile of Man and Culture in Mexico*. New York: McGraw-Hill, 1963.

Rosenblat, Angel, *La Población Indigena y el Mestizaje en América* (2 vols.). Buenos Aires: Editorial Nova, 1954.

Simpson, Eyler N., *The Ejido: Mexico's Way Out*. Durham, N.C.: University of North Carolina Press, 1937.

Tömmel, Sieglinde, *Nation und Nationalliteratur: Eine soziologische Analyse des Verhältnisses von Nationalliteratur und Nationwerdung, dargestellt am Beispiel der in den Jahren 1830–1840 in französischer und niederländischer Sprache geschriebenen Belletristik Belgiens*, unpublished Munich doctoral dissertation, 1971.

Turner, Frederick C., *The Dynamic of Mexican Nationalism*. Chapel Hill, N.C.: The University of North Carolina Press, 1968.

Van den Berghe, Pierre L., "Mexico," in Van den Berghe, *Race and Racism: A Comparative Perspective*. New York: John Wiley & Sons, 1967, pp. 42–58.

Wagley, Charles, and Marvin Harris, "The Indians in Mexico," in: Wagley and Harris, *Minorities in the New World: Six Case Studies*. New York: Columbia University Press, 1958, pp. 48–87.

Whetten, Nathan L., *Rural Mexico*. Chicago: Chicago University Press, 1948.

Whitaker, A. P., and D. C. Jordan, *Nationalism in Contemporary Latin America*. New York: The Free Press of Glencoe, 1966.

Wolf, Eric, "La Formación de la Nación: Un Ensayo de Formulación," *Ciencias Sociales* (Union Panamericana), IV (1953), pp. 50–61, 98–111, 146–170.

Racial Segregation and Nationalization: South Africa

26

The central themes of the present chapter are: (1) nation-building in a settlement colony in the presence of a large and potentially powerful autochthonous population, combined with (2) racial segregation, and (3) internal colonialism. The last point requires an explanatory note. Our earlier definition of colonization referred to the relationship between a metropolitan society and a "distant" territory. In the case of South Africa we shall see that it is the settler nation itself which, playing the role of the metropolis, dominates the autochtones politically, exploits them economically, and interferes with their internal conditions without integrating them into the "metropolitan" social system. On previous occasions we found that the coexistence of state jurisdiction, state territory and, national society, typical of the nation-state, exist neither in imperial power structures nor in multiethnic nation-states. Internal colonialism, as we shall call the situation exemplified by South Africa, represents another deviation from the classical model. It is not unique and has existed, for instance, during certain stages of Russian and United States history.

Let us turn to a brief historical survey. The colonization of the southern tip of the African continent was not inspired by any intention to exploit its natural or human resources; it was merely instrumental to trade interests in East Asia. Cape Colony was established in 1652. All the Dutch East Indies Company had bargained for was "a cabbage patch on the way to India" and a protected harbor. What they had on their hands by the time the British took over at the turn of the eighteenth century was a considerable colonial territory inhabited by 16,000 settlers, 17,000 slaves, as well as 20,000 autochthones and half-breeds. The extension of the colony, which continued after the British occupation, had mainly economic reasons. Because the demand for fresh vegetables and meat was greater than could be satisfied by small-scale horticulture or peaceful barter with the autochthones, it was decided to expand agriculture and stock-raising. These activities were carried out either by the Company through its own servants, or increasingly through free settlers. Economic necessity also led to the encouragement of immigration and the occupation of land that the autochthones considered their property, and with which they had no intention of parting.

EARLY INTERETHNIC RELATIONS

Although it was in the interest of the Company to avoid conflict with the Hottentot tribes, relations grew increasingly hostile on account of the territorial and economic expansion. Mutual cattle raiding became common. The autochthones, deprived of land and cattle, helped the Dutch solve the labor problem. Upon entering the colonial society they were assigned a status of servitude. They were not alone in this class, which also included slaves imported from abroad and half-breeds. Thus, in keeping with metropolitan traditions of the time, the Dutch established a rigid status society whose stability was safeguarded by blocking social mobility. Most important was the differentiation between freemen and bondsmen which, by and large, conformed to the distinction between settlers and strangers as well as between Christians and heathens. It was only when transculturation and Christianization reduced the discriminatory power of ethnic and religious differences that inheritable somatic traits assumed major significance as the chief criterion for social differentiation.

ROOTS OF RACISM

After what has been said elsewhere about the role of race in the distribution of social rewards, we can limit ourselves to a few remarks about specific developments in Cape Colony under the Dutch regime. Quite apart from humanitarian or religious motives, the Christianization and education of the servile population served as a means of domestication. The more the slaves became acculturated to their masters, the more important ethnic origin, symbolized by racial characteristics, became for status assignment. The role played by race in status assignment was very similar in South Africa, Mexico, and the United States. In each case *race was not the cause of social differentiation but a means to uphold an existing system of distributing social rewards between masters and servants under changing conditions.* With insignificant exceptions, the original Hottentot and Bushmen population of Cape Colony, together with the slave and half-breed population, were integrated into the colonial society as a social category. Servile status was assigned on the basis of heritable somatic characteristics which distinguished them from the settler population; all those assigned to this status tended to merge and were eventually transformed into the ethnic subgroup of the Cape Coloureds (cf. Part III, Chap. 22).

Thus interethnic relations between the autochthones and the Dutch developed on two levels. On the intersocietal level, the relationship was one of commerce and of conflict between separate societal units which differed greatly with regard to their social structure, way of life, religion, language, and also physical appearance. The autochthones who were transferred into the settler society either by annexation or voluntary or involuntary migration were in no position to challenge the dictates of the Company and the social order upheld by it. Their inclusion in the host society remained segmental and was confined mainly to the level of *commercium*.

MIGRATIONS

The most important factor in the territorial extension of the colony was the uncontrollable migrations of the Dutch pioneers in search of new pastures. This unorganized trekking beyond the official borders of Cape Colony reminds one of the relentless westward encroachment by American pioneers upon territories that lay beyond the original jurisdiction of their government and were the recognized homeland of the aboriginal Indians. In both instances the extension was spearheaded by herdsmen rather than by farmers. In both instances the ensuing clashes with the autochthones ran contrary to official policies. The governments were forced by the pioneers to extend the political boundaries and to get involved in conflicts with the autochthones.

The pioneers were guided by blind self-interest; they neither cared for the life and property of the weaker nor for international treaties guaranteeing the rights of the latter. They were further guided by a craving for individual freedom and opposed to any coercion by lawful authorities. A strong sense of independence among the Trek Boers obstructed almost any kind of social organization that transcended the bonds of the kinship group and the partiarchal family. Conditions on the pioneering fringe, whether in the Mexican Bajio, the American West, or South Africa, played an important role in the foundation of the new nations. The exploits and sufferings of the pioneers in a hostile environment later provided the heroic myth upon which national identity was to be founded.

When one speaks of interethnic relations in South Africa, one thinks just and foremost of Boers and Bantu, Yet the word "Boer" is incorrectly applied to the entire Dutch-speaking population of South Africa; and the Bantu-speaking tribes, whose origin and social organization have been described in Part I, were neither the only nor the first autochthonous people whom the settlers met. Thus, the development of interethnic relations is not one unilinear process beginning with the first encounters with Hottentots and Bushmen at the Cape and leading up to the Apartheid policy embraced by the new Afrikaner nation. The Bushmen and Hottentots had nothing in common with the black Africans, neither linguistically, culturally, nor racially. With insignificant exceptions, Bushmen and Hottentots have been integrated into the Cape's Coloured population, and form an ethnic subgroup of the national society. The bulk of the Bantu-speaking people, on the other hand, have preserved their ethnic identity:

they have not been transformed into a subgroup of the settler society, but have remained a separate autochthonous population with their own culture and social structure. The difference in racial attitudes that still exists between the Cape and the former Boer Republics may have something to do with the different type of autochthones the settlers encountered. Today, South Africa is one entity, and the local differences are of minor importance when it comes to the relationship between the white national society and the Bantu, who are in the throes of a national awakening, comparable to the Risorgimento in nineteenth century Europe.

The Trek of the Boers. In their migrations, the Trek Boers finally encountered Bantu-speaking tribes which, as we recall, were for the most part highly complex power structures with large populations and a considerable military potential. They could not be coerced into submission and servility as easily as could the more primitive Khoisan-speaking peoples. That, in itself, constituted a serious threat to the Dutch colony. The authorities tried in vain to control the Boer migrations and to keep them within boundaries that could be effectively policed. In 1778, the Boer and Bantu migrants confronted each other across the Great Fish River. Although raids across this border continued, it was not till 1836, the year of the Great Trek, that the deadlock was finally broken, and the boundaries of white occupation were pushed farther north again.

As early as 1806 (the year the British took over Cape Colony), trekking had become a firmly entrenched institution and a part of the folk traditions of the Dutch settlers. The Great Trek, however, in the course of which 20,000 Boers (no less than one-fourth of the total Dutch population) left the Cape, was an event of momentous significance both for the development of interethnic relations with the Bantu-speaking Africans and the emergence of the Afrikaner nation. It was, above all, a protest of the original settlers against the new colonial masters, whose policies were dictated by the wish to strengthen the position of the British and to weaken the dominance of the Dutch. The key positions in the colonial administration and the armed forces were taken over by the British. British immigration was encouraged; 5000 settlers arrived from the British Isles in 1820 alone. A knowledge of the English language was made a requisite of holding public office; English teachers and ministers were brought into the country to spread not only the language but also English culture. An attempt was even made to replace Dutch-Roman law by British common law. Although this attempt failed, the central administration was intensified. The British dealt a final blow to the political dominance of the Dutch settlers; they weakened their whole economic system by abolishing the civil and legal disabilities imposed upon the Coloureds and by emancipating the slaves. A large number of the Dutch answered the threat by seeking freedom from British interference and control, and by restoring beyond the frontiers of the Colony the traditional master-servant relations with the autochthones.

The British administration was unable to control the Voortrekkers, who legally remained British subjects, or to enforce its laws concerning the relations with Bantu tribes and the treatment of those autochthones who lived on Boer farms as servants or laborers. The Boers, on the other hand, made repeated attempts to rid themselves of British interference altogether by proclaiming independent republics.

When the Boers left British territory they were neither a distinctive ethnic unit nor a nation. They were pioneer farmers and cattle men of Dutch origin and speech with a common agrarian culture and patriarchal family organization. They had a common religious affiliation to the Dutch Reformed church. They were also united by a sense of ethnic contrast, not only against the autochthones, slaves, half-breeds and Coloureds, but also against the British.

The first Boer republic was created in Natal in 1838. When the British quickly declared Natal a separate British colony to protect their commercial interests in the port of Durban, the Boers moved north and eventually established the republics of Transvaal and Orange Free State, whose independence was recognized by the British in 1852 and 1854, respectively. After three decades of near anarchy, 40,000 Trek Boers were scattered over a territory of 100,000 square miles—without towns or roads and in a perpetual state of war. After the opening of Witwatersrand gold fields in 1886, British economic interest in the Boer territories became so strong that it was decided to bring them under direct political control. The war that Great Britain waged upon the South African Republic (Transvaal) and the Orange Free State between 1899 and 1902 ended with their annexation. In 1910, the two Boer colonies were united with Cape Colony and Natal to form the Union of South Africa.

The gold rush of the 1880s marks the decisive break in Boer history. Mining and, since World War I, manufacturing were to dichotomize South Africa into an agrarian and industrial section, each with its typical ethnic problems and its own methods of coping with them. But before turning to this topic, we must retrace our steps and look at the role played by religion in shaping race attitudes and behavior amongst the Voortrekkers; for it has been primarily the north that has determined racial policies since union, in the face of strong opposition from the British as well as the Cape Afrikaners.

THE ROLE OF RELIGION IN RACISM

Boer society, as we recall, was strictly agrarian and traditionalist. The Trekkers even experienced a certain regression after they had cut ties with the more advanced Dutch society in the Cape as well as in the metropolis; in many respects they had become adjusted to the more primitive pastoral cultures of the autochthones. Their Calvinist religion has been occasionally surmised to have played an important role in the rise of racism in colonial South Africa. The suggestion is intriguing as there are striking differences between race relations in Catholic and Protestant countries (cf. Tannenbaum, 1947). Is there the same parallel between Protestantism and the rise of racism as there is between Protestantism and the rise of capitalism? We have already found that religion may have a variety of functions in interethnic relations: church membership and participation in religious practices may serve as symbols of ethnicity just as language or other external characteristics do; *like any other institution, organized religion may support the maintenance of ethnic groups; like any other ideology, religious interpretation of reality may legitimize the aspirations of ethnic groups, either with regard to the present or the future*.

In colonial situations, Christian religion has apparently made several significant contributions: (1) by differentiating between the baptized and unbaptized, the colonizers could exclude the non-Christians from the system of distributing social rewards within Christian society; (2) at the same time, Christian beliefs introduced a humanitarian component into interethnic relations by upholding the natural rights of the baptized autochthones; and (3) a sense of mission has inspired the expansion of Christianity; whenever possible, autochthones were converted and raised to membership status in the Christian community. Whereas Christian ideology legitimizes the differential treatment of autochthones in a particular case, their domination and exploitation, religious education tends to reduce the distance and heteromorphism between autochthones and colonizers. Although this is true of Christian colonization in general, it does not explain the differences in actual conduct of various Christian colonizers.

The specific role of Calvinism in racism has been investigated by Gerhard Beckers, who makes some cautious suggestions (Beckers, 1969). It certainly cannot be maintained that the fundamental beliefs and practices of Calvinism have a direct connection with the particular type of racism adopted by the Boers. It is, however, likely that sectarian and political Calvinism have inspired and legitimized the Boer view of interracial relations. Sectarianism was indeed widespread among the uneducated Trek Boers who effectively evaded a control by the authorities of the Dutch Reformed church. They sought divine guidance in the Bible and tried to detect God's will in actual events. In this way, they came to identify themselves with the Chosen People in search of the Promised Land. They also inferred from the Bible that their social structure and economy, which closely resembled those of the patriarchs, were ordained by God.

Of course, such interpretations are common to many sectarians; we have also found them amongst the Mormons and Mennonites. More typically Calvinist was, however, the Boers' belief in their divine election, which entitled them to domination over the condemned, who were represented to them by the autochthones. Moreover, the success of the Greak Trek appeared to be a divine confirmation of their election. Becker finds a second root of Boer inspiration in the idea of God's sovereignty and the duty of realizing the divine order on earth through law and authority. This includes the struggle against evil and the heathens and barbarians who are considered to be the epitome of evil; the possibility of domesticating and educating the barbarians and savages is limited by their innate evil nature.

It is at this point that a difference becomes apparent between the race ideology upheld by the Trek Boers and that upheld by the Cape Dutch. In the Cape, the Hottentots and Coloureds were considered capable of becoming gradually integrated into the settler society as equals. The Boers, on the other hand, believed in the irrevocable inequality between Bantu and Boer. They did integrate the autochthones into the settler society as the lowest status category— much in the same way as was done in the Cape—but they insisted that this order of things be upheld forever. If we consider Cape racism as the thesis and Boer racism as the antithesis, then the Apartheid policy adopted more recently by the Afrikaner nationalist government appears as the synthesis between the northern and the southern views. Although Apartheid admits the fundamental equality of Bantu and Boer, it nevertheless enforces their strict segregation and separate development. Of this more will be heard below.

INDUSTRIALIZATION

Industrialization in the Transvaal led to large-scale migrations of ethnically heterogeneous populations to a hitherto homogeneous agrarian area. The immigrants to the Boer republics, mostly English-speaking and of British origin, were called by the Boers *"uitlanders,"* that is, "foreigners." In order to uphold the traditional social order against the challenge of industrialization, the governments of the Transvaal and the Orange Free State put restrictive laws on immigration and the immigrants. The struggle against the British and the experiences of the Boer War were instrumental in promoting Afrikaner nationalism, which was of the ethnic kind that one would expect from an agrarian population. The defeat of the Boers confirmed the dichotomization of the colonial society which included, besides a traditionalistic agrarian section, a rapidly expanding industrial section. Inclusion in the British colonial system reestablished relations between the Cape Dutch and the Boers who had been separated by the Great Trek. Afrikaans, the folk dialect spoken by the Trek Boers, was adopted by the Cape Dutch, but not before the late nineteenth century. A common vernacular and a common religious affiliation, in addition to a consciousness of common origin and differentiation from both the autochthones and the English, combined to create a new ethnic identity and sense of solidarity. Within the political union of South Africa the new Afrikaner nation was emerging, and contrasted with the growing colonial society of the English-speaking newcomers as well as the Bantu.

As regards the latter, some had been transferred into the agrarian settler society where they represented a servile status category of labor tenants and wage laborers, bearing close resemblance to the Hispanos in part of New Mexico and the Negroes in the southern United States. Later, Bantu were transferred into the growing industrial section. If we consider the situation of the Bantu in the Cape colony alone, it was, in many respects, similar to that of other ethnically diverse immigrants to countries in the process of modernization.

THE RESERVATIONS

The territory claimed by South Africa included, in addition to the agrarian and industrial settler sections, a third section made up of a number of reservations set aside for the Bantu. Reservations are a device of colonial policy with which we have already become acquainted. The settler colonies established in eighteenth-century Russia or the Mennonite Reserves in early Manitoba had also served the purpose of internal colonization. In this way, settlers of diverse origin were offered cultural as well as political autonomy and other important exemptions from general laws; they were separated from the native population and left momentarily outside the emerging national society. In Mexico and other Latin American countries, Indian reservations were established to protect defeated autochthones from further depredations by the settlers.

In the British colonies, on the other hand, the reason for establishing reservations was almost the exact opposite, namely, to protect the settlers from raids, plunder, and other disturbances by autochthones who could not be destroyed, expelled, or integrated into the colonial society. *The British type of reservations did not serve the exploitation but the neutralization of colonial populations*. One of the first objectives was the demilitarization of aboriginal tribes, the suppression of tribal wars and raids, and the abolition of slavery and ritual murder: in short, the elimination of possible sources of disturbance. To avoid conflict with the settlers, the latter were prevented from acquiring titles of land within the reservation, and their dealing with the autochthones was strictly controlled. Migration was regulated, and educational and missionary activities were supervised. As long as the autochthones caused no trouble, they were allowed to maintain their tribal organization.

Yet the colonial policy of breaking their potential power of resistance and of domesticating them sufficiently to reconcile them to their segregated existence amidst a settler society, involved considerable interference with the internal conditions in the reservations. A system of indirect rule was adopted. It was similar to that applied in protectorates and exploitation colonies where at least the fiction of the native chiefs' authority was upheld. The appointment of commissioners and magistrates, added to the requirement that chiefs and headmen be confirmed in their position by colonial authorities, undermined the status of traditional chiefs and frequently made them puppets of the colonial government. To sum up our brief outline, it may be said that a *reservation*

*resembles a colony within a colony, or a colonial enclave within a modern
state.*

In South Africa the great number and potential power of the Bantu who were
excluded from the settler society made their territorial segregation and con-
finement to separate reservations imperative, but, at the same time, highly
problematical; alone the economic interdependence of the settler society and
the reservation Africans worked against any total territorial separation for the
following reasons: The reservations were the nearest and most readily available
labor pool for the expanding industrial economy (although black migrant workers were also recruited from other British and from Portuguese colonies). Their
population, due to pacification and medical care, was on the increase. The land
that was left them after the white settlers had appropriated two-thirds of the
most fertile tracts was inefficiently farmed, disastrously eroded and incapable
of supporting them. The Bantu were thus dependent on cash income obtained
in the settler economy outside the reservations. This mutual economic dependence steadily increased over the years, greatly aggravating the conflict situation between the three principal ethnic components of the colonial population.

The conflict is reflected in a twofold power struggle. The mechanisms of
democratic government were only available to cope with the conflict between
the emerging Afrikaner nation and the British colonial society. The English
had, and still have, economic supremacy in the industrial section. They also
have greater control of the mass media. The Afrikaners are still dominant in the
agrarian sector and, because of their numerical superiority, greater natural
increase and adherence to one political party, they determine racial policies and
the character of interethnic relations.

ECONOMY AND POLITY

Political and economic dominance not only follow ethnic dividing lines, but
economy and polity also work at cross-purposes. Afrikaner politics are guided
by a national myth exalting a romanticized agrarian past that was based on a
rugged pioneer individualism; a myth, as we have seen, that provides legitimation, often still in religious terms, for a paternalistic rule over the autochthones
based on the assumption of the innate inequality of races. This belief has also
inspired a legislation that puts severe restrictions upon the migration of laborers; it excludes all but the white settlers from higher occupations and sets the
wage level for identical work many times higher for the whites; it limits the
educational facilities and opportunities of 80 percent of the country's population, thereby stopping any social mobility and preventing competition for social
rewards on equal terms.

Such measures are directly opposed to the mechanisms of a modern
economy; they hinder the development not only in the industrial sector but also

restrict agricultural productivity. We saw in Part III that modernization tends to promote the meeting of heterogeneous populations in addition to contributing towards their cultural homogenization and towards a status assignment on the basis of accomplishment. In contrast, South African policy insists on inherited ethnic status as the sole criterion for the distribution of social rewards; this forces a modern economy to operate under conditions of an obsolete status society and prevents the most efficient utilization of the country's resources.

SOCIAL STRUCTURE

Within the borders of South Africa there exists a national society of settlers (politically organized in a modern state) and a colonial population of autochthones who are dominated and exploited by the settler society. The coexistence of a metropolis and a colonial economy within the same state territory is reflected in the social structure. The population is divided by law into four racial categories, which are at the same time status categories: the "Whites" include the European settlers, amounting to nearly 20 percent of the total population; and the "Bantu" autochthones (approximately 70 percent); the "Coloured" including the Hottentots (approximately 9 percent); and the "Asiatics," mostly East Indian (approximately 3 percent). Only the Whites enjoy full citizenship and the right to landownership, free movement (outside the reservations), participation in voluntary associations and labor unions, the free choice of occupation and schooling, and many other rights which, outside South Africa and other colonial countries, are rarely challenged. The Whites have a monopoly on skilled jobs, the higher grades of clerical work, and almost all occupations that command higher remuneration and carry greater prestige. All these rights are, in various degrees, denied to the other racial groups. At the lowest end of the social scale are the Bantu, next come the Indians. The Coloureds, who in earlier days had been a political pawn in the power struggle between the Cape Dutch and the British and had enjoyed the same rights as the Whites in the Cape Colony, now share, in a mitigated form, the many disabilities imposed upon the Bantu. The criteria used in assigning a person to one status category are a combination of somatic appearance, known ancestry, association, and reputation. The official classification and the discriminatory laws based on it have helped to legalize the development of four separate status systems that interlock only on the level of *commercium*.

When we turn to interethnic relations in the 1960s, the basic issue is Apart-. heid. It is more than a new name for traditional policies and existing laws. It is a further attempt to consolidate the castelike social structure and the system of economic exploitation and political domination. Apartheid is also a reaction to changing conditions that require the adaptation of government policies and the principles of societal organization; it is a guideline and legitimation of those policies. Among the factors of social change, which have contributed to the frame of mind epitomized by Apartheid, the following deserve mention:

1. The progress of industrialization has greatly increased the economic interdependence of White and Bantu. In the wake of urbanization there has occurred a concentration of Bantu in urban centers, situated in the White sections of the country, so that Bantu contacts with the settler society and culture have multiplied.
2. In addition, the spread of education and mass communication has accelerated the selective transculturation (Westernization) of the Bantu. The partial acceptance and internalization of so-called Western standards has made them increasingly aware of the discriminatory character of actual practices.
3. The emergence of an educated Bantu middle class has provided them with a mediating elite who—unlike the traditional chiefs—has learned to identify themselves with South African society rather than with a particular tribal society from which they have become emancipated. The acceptance of Western ideas has also taught the Bantu to conceive of South Africa as a modern nation-state in the making and of its total state population as a potential demotic nation.
4. Changes in the international political climate have favored the trend toward decolonization and the reduction of discrimination in the distribution of social rewards, adding moral support to the Bantu's claim for emancipation from colonial rule and for equality with the Whites.
5. A still more serious challenge derives from the growing appeal of Communism and Pan-Africanism, not only among the educated, but also among the urban Bantu masses. As we have explained earlier, the doctrine of Pan-Africanism can be viewed as a type of ethnic nationalism, for it treats all black people as one ethnie defined in the same racial terms that had been originally introduced by the colonizers. Apart from promoting solidarity transcending tribal and territorial units and suggesting a more powerful economic and political union, Pan-Africanism also makes legitimate the demand that, by virtue of birthright, African sovereignty should be reestablished in the whole of the sub-Saharan continent.

Among the Bantu both demotic and ethnic nationalism aim at the reversal of existing power relationships in South Africa. The democratic principle of "one man, one vote" would guarantee a Bantu majority rule. If, subsequently, with the help of the homogenizing institutions at their command, the Bantu were to become the core of a new South African nation, the Whites would be reduced to an ethnic subgroup and a national minority. If, further, the principles of Pan-Africanism were to be wholly adopted, the settlers would be altogether excluded from the national society; they would become foreigners, making discrimination and even their expulsion appear legitimate.

APARTHEID

Apartheid is the answer to the threat implied in these developments, not only to the Whites' political and economic supremacy, but to their cultural tradition and, conceivably, to their very survival. Two aspects should be distinguished, which may be termed "little" and "big" Apartheid. "Little" Apartheid is an attempt to regulate race relations within the White districts. Its workings are especially visible in the industrial, urban centers. Ordinances include (1) a set of measures aiming to enforce the strict limitation of social relations between White and Bantu to the level of *commercium;* (2) a second set of measures enforces the urban segregation of the Bantu to residential quarters well outside the cities, and places these compounds, like the reservations, under the authority of the "colonial administration," and (3) a third type of measure legalizes discrimination and emphasizes the inequality in the distribution of social rewards. Taken together, these measures uphold economic exploitation and eliminate competition; they force South African Bantu (in the same way as migrant laborers from other African countries) to return periodically to their native reservations, and prevent their permanent settlement in the metropolitan section; and they are intended to keep Bantu from raising their level of aspiration and from making any collective effort to improve their lot.

In a modern society, a system that permanently assigns the majority of the state population to low status on the basis of race, cannot escape being considered obsolete, even by its beneficiaries and advocates. Thus, in order to legitimize the system, an effort is made to reinterpret the social status of the Bantu who work and live in the metropolitan section, as that of foreigners. In this way, they are excluded from the national society by definition, and exempted from its system of distributing social rewards. From this viewpoint "big" Apartheid appears to be a vital supplement to "little" Apartheid; for it helps to make this interpretation plausible and the policy based on it workable. "Big" Apartheid, however, is also an attempt to help solve the problems of an equally obsolete colonialism.

The main features of "big" Apartheid may be summarized as follows:

1. The creation of Bantustans is meant to provide homelands for the entire Bantu-speaking population of South Africa.
2. For this purpose they are divided into ethnic units that could eventually grow into new nations. But the classification that uses linguistic and ethnological criteria is only partly based on the traditional tribal divisions, and each Bantustan includes several tribal societies that have little in common. The Bantu living in urban locations or otherwise scattered in the metropolitan section are expected to identify with one of the Bantustans according to their ethnic origin.

3. The Bantustans are granted regional autonomy under a (modified) parliamentary system. Although the autonomous government is allowed a fairly wide competence in internal affairs, its decisions are subject to approval and manipulation by the metropolitan administration.
4. The economic base of the Bantustans is to remain agriculture, together with the export of manpower to the metropolis. The establishment of industries is planned in the settler section along the borders of the Bantustans to secure employment for migrant laborers without endangering "little" Apartheid.
5. Further Westernization of the Bantu is presented as contrary to their own interests, while the preservation and revival of (innocuous) tribal cultures is encouraged.

ANALYSIS OF POLICY

The following attempt to discuss South African race policies critically confronts the sociologist with certain theoretical problems that cannot be treated here at length. It will suffice to remind the reader of two major difficulties: one concerns the nature of his subject matter; the other concerns limitations intrinsic to his chosen method, which cannot be abandoned without foregoing the advantages that an exact empirical science has to offer in its attempt to improve upon common knowledge. In its classical version, applied sociology claims to be in a position to reduce the risk involved in chosing appropriate means to given ends. Thus, in assessing actual policies and suggesting alternatives, the sociologist tries to estimate their relative chances of success as well as their costs and unintended by-products. This involves prediction based on theory. Yet propositions of the kind advanced in this volume are valid only if the tacitly assumed marginal conditions do not change significantly.

In an earlier version of this chapter we had suggested that the Apartheid policy, by its inner dynamism (even contrary to the intentions of its originators and advocates), may have consequences that would provide a workable solution to the race problem in South Africa. In this we relied on the theoretical insights gained in Parts II and III regarding nation-building and the integration of ethnically heterogeneous populations contained in a modern state. At the same time, however, we excluded *expressis verbis* speculations on the possibility of armed interventions, guerilla warfare, economic crises, and other factors not covered by our theory. Yet it was precisely the significant changes in some of these marginal conditions, as well as in others we had not specified, that invalidated earlier conclusions.[1] It should nevertheless be possible to assert that, in the light of our theory, certain policies are likely to fail.

---

[1] A summary of this earlier version was presented in a paper entitled, "South Africa—A Maverick View," to the 1974 meetings of the American Sociological Association at Montreal. There I

Policy-making concerns not only means but also ends. Yet political goals are more often implied than spelled out, they tend to shift incessantly, and they are frequently incompatible with each other. Even social scientists criticizing actual policies are prone to pretend that the ultimate ends are common knowledge and, for all practical purposes, self-evident. Yet without making goals explicit, they cannot adequately consider appropriate means. We cannot enter into a serious discussion as to what ultimate state of affairs would be most desirable for South Africa. Sociologists are neither prophets nor moral preceptors. Yet we hope to find acceptance when, in general terms, we take as a measuring rod for assessing South African policies the resolution of conflicts pertaining to interethnic relations at the least cost in human suffering which appear to be realistically feasible.

Our analysis has shown that the doctrine and policy of Apartheid should be viewed as an attempt to adapt to changing conditions a system of internal colonialism in which the emerging Afrikaner nation has replaced Great Britain as the metropolis. Settler domination and the exploitation of the autochthones are, if anything, consolidated rather than mitigated. Observers are generally agreed that a policy of internal colonialism is not only obsolete and contrary to the prevailing moral climate in which the ideas of liberty and equality take precedence over traditional principles of an established order, but that rigid adherence to this policy courts disaster. As van den Berghe (1967, p. 110) remarked, "Three million people cannot indefinitely repress the frustration and fury of thirteen million people who live in their midst. A South Africa divided against itself awaits its impending doom."

The more radical advocates of a different policy are inspired by the ideas of Pan Africanism, according to which (by virtue of birthright) African self-government should be reestablished as much in South Africa as in other parts of the sub-Saharan continent. The racial argument is supported by an appeal to democratic doctrine, both of which have been adopted from the colonizers and

---

argued that a more radical and more consistent policy of separation may conceivably contribute to decolonization, provided the following changes were made:

a. Resolute modernization of the economy and industrialization would contribute to nation-building in each of the Bantustans.
b. Extended Bantustan autonomy in fiscal and economic affairs would offer a tangible basis for common interests. The expansion of an autonomous educational system could help to develop a common culture and national ideology, thereby contributing to the formation of a national core in the Bantustans.
c. If the South African government were to adopt a policy of enlightened etatism instead of an obsolete colonialism, there would be hope for future nation-building in the Bantustans. The outcome may be at first a federation of a white and several black nation-states; ultimately an alliance of Bantustans would be likely to lead to secession without necessarily undoing economic interdependence.

When a South African colleague attending the session remarked afterwards that this interpretation would have been acceptable at the time when the actual research had been undertaken, even as late as five years ago, but that intervening events, including the collapse of the Portuguese colonial empire, had made the conclusions untenable, the entire argument had to be eliminated from the manuscript.

turned against them. If the principle of "one man, one vote" were realized in South Africa, an African majority could be expected to reverse existing power relations along racial lines. It would then appear not only feasible but legitimate to treat the settlers as foreigners, even to repatriate them in the same way as, for instance, after World War II, millions of East Germans had been expelled from territories to which Poles or Czechs claimed an original birthright.

Yet whoever contemplates alternative policies to resolve the conflict, short of a violent overthrow of the present power structure by inside and/or outside forces, will have to consider the situation of the settler population. Social scientists who wish to contribute to practical politics that would be germane to their profession, should not allow moral indignation to interfere with a realistic assessment of the possibilities to restructure a given politically organized society in a more acceptable manner. It is difficult to see how any radically different policy could be implemented without taking into account vital interests of the Whites, particularly the Afrikaners. One cannot expect a majority of them to be willing to accept any arrangement that would threaten their collective survival as a nation. Unlike the French settlers in Algiers, for instance, they cannot be repatriated since they have literally no homeland to go to. Their reclassification as expatriates—as imposed, for example, on the English settlers in Kenya—could hardly offer a solution to them because they have no other fatherland to look to for emotional anchorage and protection.

Another alternative, supported especially by English-speaking settlers, more moderate Bantu leaders, Indians, and Coloureds, amounts to the transformation of the entire country into a modern nation-state according to the tenets of demotic nationalism. In Part II, it has been shown that the self-constitution of a nation, which would embrace the entire population included in a given political power structure, presupposes the demotic homogenization of a viable national core representing a majority. Moreover, the preformation of a nation is unlikely to be achieved except through the "alien will" of a despotic government—an absolute state, a military regime, a totalitarian government, or a colonial metropolis. In South Africa, British colonial rule has failed to initiate the emergence of a colonial society integrating whites and blacks. Instead, the principles of racism have helped to institutionalize the separation between the settler society and the Bantu masses who have remained divided into several tribal societies. It is this colonial heritage of racial separation that made the political union of British colonies, even after the gradual emancipation from colonial rule, an unsuitable foundation of a modern nation-state. The presence of a relatively large settler nation wielding political as well as considerable economic power is likely to aggravate the difficulties with which nation-building elsewhere in sub-Saharan Africa has been confronted, causing much bloodshed and human suffering without, as yet, resolving the ethnic conflict. Even after the challenge of the common enemy were removed in one way or another, there would be no guarantee for a lasting community of purpose among the Africans of widely differing ethnic origin and traditions.

If, therefore, South Africa were to be proclaimed a unitary nation-state, its government—presumably dominated by an African majority—would be faced with the formidable task of building from scratch a new nation embracing all its ethnic and racial components. It is unlikely that it could undo separation with the stroke of a pen, or transform the entire population into one national society simply by outlawing discrimination. Even its gradual reduction would have to be met by corresponding measures enforcing national homogenization. This could hardly be accomplished alone by the mechanisms of democratic government or by the voluntary agreement of those concerned. On the contrary, it would call for dictatorial powers and violent means, whose eventual success would still remain doubtful. At this point, we must rest our case and return for the last time to matters of principle.

REFERENCES

Beckers, Gerhard, *Religiöse Faktoren in der Entwicklung der südafrikanischen Rassenfrage: Ein Beitrag zur Rolle des Kalvinismus in kolonialen Situationen* (Munich doctoral dissertation). Munich: W. Fink, 1969.

Crijns, J., *Race Relations and Race Attitudes in South Africa*. Nijmegen: Janssen, 1959.

De Ridder, J. C., *The Personality of the Urban African in South Africa*. London: Routledge & Kegan Paul, 1961.

Hunter, Monica, *Reaction to Conquest: Effects of Contact with Europeans on the Pondo of South Africa*. London: Oxford University Press, 1936.

Hutt, W. H., *The Economics of the Colour Bar: A Study of the Economic Origins and Consequences of Racial Segregation in South Africa*. London: Deutsch, 1964.

Kiewiet, C. W. de, *A History of South Africa, Social and Economic*. Oxford: Clarendon Press, 1941.

Kuper, Leo, *An African Bourgeoisie; Race and Politics in South Africa*. New Haven: Yale University Press, 1965.

Lewin, Julius, *Politics and Law in South Africa: Essays on Race Relations*. London: Merlin Press, 1963.

MacCrone, Ian Douglas, *Race Attitudes in South Africa: Historical, Experimental and Psychological Studies*. London: Oxford University Press, 1937.

Marquard, Leo, *The Peoples and Policies of South Africa*. London: Oxford University Press, 1952.

Mayer, Philip, *Townsmen and Tribesmen: Conservativism and the Process of Urbanization in a South African City*. Cape Town: Oxford University Press, 1961.

Munger, Edwin S., *Afrikaner and African Nationalism: South African Parallels and Parameters*. London: Oxford University Press, 1967.

Patterson, Sheila, *Colour and Culture in South Africa*. London: Routledge & Kegan Paul, 1957.

Rhoodie, N. J., and H. J. Venter, *Apartheid: A Socio-Historical Exposition of the Origin and Development of the Apartheid Idea*. Amsterdam: De Bussy, 1960.

Sampson, Pienaar and Anthony, *South Africa: Two Views of Separate Development*. London: Oxford University Press, 1960.

Tannenbaum, Frank, *Slave and Citizen: The Negroes in America*. New York: Afred A. Knopf, 1947.

Van den Berghe, Pierre L., *Caneville: The Social Structure of a South African Town*. Middleton, Conn.: Weselyan University Press, 1964.

———, *South Africa: A Study in Conflict* (2nd ed.). Middletown, Conn.: Wesleyan University Press, 1966.

———, "South Africa." in van den Berghe, *Race and Racism: A Comparative Perspective*. New York: John Wiley & Sons, 1967, pp. 96–111.

Van der Horst, Sheila T., "The Effects of Industrialization on Race Relations in South Africa," in: Guy Hunter (ed.), *Industrialization and Race Relations*. New York: Oxford University Press, 1965, pp. 97–140.

Wilson, Monica, and A. Mafeje, *Langa: A Study of Social Groups in an African Township*. Cape Town: Oxford University Press, 1963.

CONCLUSIONS TO PART IV

In Part IV we have tried to apply the lessons learned in the preceding parts to novel situations. Was the effort worthwhile? Has a theory based on past experience proved at all useful for present practice? Can history teach us anything beyond the past? Are the "laws" of sociology sufficiently general, and at the same time meaningful enough, to forestall an undesirable course of events?

In our attempt to apply the insights gained by analyzing the emergence of the nation-state and the problems it has engendered in the industrialized countries of the "First World" to the problems faced by the new nations of the "Third World," we made the assumption that the end of decolonization was nation-building. By this we understood the self-constitution of modern nations in former colonies. Inasmuch as we concentrated on the restructuring of a given territorial population, we neglected exogeneous factors (cf. Part III, pp. 168f.) and changes of international boundary lines. Heuristic devices of this kind are legitimate in the construction of theories as long as one does not forget that concepts and generalizations are not duplicates of "reality," but the means to grasp and control it. Nevertheless, the assumption that nation-building is the central concern of decolonization was not arbitrary. The idea that colonies should be transformed into nation-states is not only uppermost in the minds of the men of affairs fighting colonialism, but also social scientists offering them expert counsel have relied on the notion of nation-building in their attempt to make postcolonial situations intellectually manageable (cf. Mazrui, 1972).

There is probably no other way but to proceed from the known, namely, the experience of the "developed" nations, to the unknown outcome of the struggle against colonialism. But this does not mean that we have to stop there. The progress of science depends on the effort to replace a paradigm (in the sense of Kuhn, 1962) that has proved inadequate to cope with an "anomaly." In the present case we have therefore to ask: Does it make sense to assert that the nation-state (as long as the term is not used as a purely rhetorical device but is given as precise a meaning as possible) can or should be taken as a realistic goal and standard of anticolonial policy? Or should it be replaced by some other model, which as yet is not even in sight?[1]

---

[1]No doubt, there will be objections against the last assertion on the grounds that "Socialism" does already offer an adequate paradigm. For reasons stated in the Preface, we are not in a position to

Before we venture an answer, we propose to discuss a school of thought that has gained stature and prominence in the sixties and early seventies, and whose efforts point in a direction similar to our own. A brief review of the theory of the plural society would also offer an opportunity, hitherto missed, to indicate the place that the theoretical frame of discourse presented in this book may hold in the context of recent developments in comparative ethnic research.

Schermerhorn (1970, pp. 122–128) distinguishes four meanings of pluralism: an ideological, political, cultural, and structural designation. For the first he refers to Wirth's characterization of a "pluralistic minority" as one that "seeks toleration for its differences on the part of the dominant group" (1945, p. 354). Since this is true of all ethnic subgroups of "pluralistic" societies, the notion does not seem to add to what has been discussed at great length in Part III. According to the Tocquevillean tradition,

> Societies are pluralistic insofar as they are *segmented into corporate groups* that frequently, although not necessarily, have different cultures or subcultures, and insofar as their social structure is *compartmentalized into analogous, parallel, noncomplementary but distinguishable sets of institutions* (van den Berghe, 1967, p. 34).

This seems but another way of characterizing modern societies in general.[2] Indeed, several critics of the political concept of pluralism have made precisely this point.[3]

---

pass a definite judgment on the validity of the claim. We do not have sufficient empirical evidence to know precisely how the principles of Marxism-Leninism are actually put into operation. Nor can we rely on unsubstantiated prognostications offered by authentic Communist sources, such as: "In socialism the nations awake to a new, better life, reach perfection. At the same time the socialist nations get closer to each other. . . . The national differences are more and more reduced until the nation . . . becomes obsolete and only the universal communist society exists. . . . The working class proceeds from the existential interests of the nation of one country and from the common interests of the working class of the whole world . . . their patriotism and internationalism are one" (Klaus, Buhr, 1969, pp. 758f; translation by E. K. F.). It would also be rash to take for an accomplished fact the declarations of intention included in the constitutions of Communist countries. The principles found in the liberal constitutions of Western countries sound just as good as long as one ignores the formidable practical problems they entail. In point of fact, constitutions all over the world have a similar ring revealing their common origin in the political philosophy of the Enlightenment. From what we were able to gather from the available literature and conversations with Soviet colleagues, we are not under the impression that Communist countries like Russia or China, which are faced with sizable nationalities and minorities, have as yet succeeded either politically or theoretically in solving the problems involved in interethnic relations.

[2] Modern society has also been characterized as having a "pluralistic" value system. This implies the toleration of a plurality of values which are, at least in part, incompatible and only pragmatically "integrated," although cultural integration is considered a requirement for the proper working of a society. Cultural pluralism seems to have its origin in the idea of religious tolerance, which has played an important role in the making of modern societies. This is reflected in the following definition of religious pluralism: "We say that religious pluralism exists in a community when more than one religious system is considered acceptable, and when the prevailing norms of conduct permit alternatives in the choice of one's religious beliefs and church membership" (Francis, 1955, p. 23n).

[3] A summary of criticisms together with a careful discussion is offered by M. G. Smith (Kuper, Smith, 1969, pp. 418ff.), which relieves us of the necessity to compare terminologies. Although it is irrelevant which language symbols we prefer, the question we wish to raise at this point is whether the employment of the one term "plural society" in several meanings tends to confuse different problems by obscuring significant distinctions.

In addition to political pluralism, Schermerhorn mentions cultural and social, or structural, pluralism, but finds it difficult to distinguish between them. He employs both terms in their broad meaning. According to him, cultural pluralism refers to situations in which

> ethnic groups come into focus when one or more have a language, religion, kinship forms, nationality, tribal affiliation, and/or other traditional norms and values embodied in patterns that set them off from dominant or majority groups (1970, p. 123).[4]

In discussing social, or structural, pluralism Schermerhorn concludes at one point that "it seems best to employ the term heterogeneity as a synonym for pluralism rather than give it a more restricted application" (1970, p. 126), as the pluralists tend to do. In this broad meaning the term "plural society" is also used, for instance, by Barth (1969) as a synonym for "polyethnic society."[5]

Because of frequent shifts and inconsistencies in their position, it is not easy to synthesize the precise teaching of the pluralists. It is not even certain whether they represent a school that has come forth with a new theory, perhaps a germinal paradigm. That they have more in common than a catchall label is borne out by the following facts: (1) their empirical work has been specifically concerned with colonies focusing on three distinctive areas; namely, (former) Dutch East Asia, (former) British Central Africa, and the Caribbean; (2) they have engaged in an intensive discussion of their respective view points on pluralism; and (3) they have cooperated in symposia whose results have been presented in several stimulating publications (INCIDI, 1958; Rubin, 1960a and b; Kuper, Smith, 1969; Despres, 1975).

When comparing their theoretical work with our own undertaking, we find that they have approached the same subject matter from the opposite end. While we, like others, have treated colonial/postcolonial situations[6] as the product of a concrete historical development and as a step in the logical evolution of societal types, they have worked their way back from a profound knowledge of colonial situations to problems of a more general significance, such as are found in advanced industrialized nations.[7] M. G. Smith, the protagonist of the school,

---

[4] Here Schermerhorn repeats the error to which he has fallen victim in his earlier definition of minorities (1959, p. 5). Like many others, he believes that external characteristics, by themselves, including specific cultural and linguistic differences, are responsible for the emergence and maintenance of an ethnic group. But it has never been shown convincingly that a particular language, a sectarian religion, certain biosomatic traits, or any specific moral and legal ideas make all those of whom they are characteristic *ipso facto* a distinctive social group (Francis, 1951, p. 220; see also Part III, pp. 158ff.).

[5] "Polyethnic" is linguistically better than the more common term "multiethnic," which combines a Latin with a Greek radix.

[6] It may be more correct to speak here of postcolonial situations and new nations *as they emerged after World War II*. For the experience on the basis of which current sociological theory has been developed also includes "new nations," such as the United States or Canada, whose problems, however, cannot be treated in an identical fashion.

[7] Like sociological theorists, many pluralists suffer from a certain parochialism. Their references indicate that they are unaware of the work done by Central European historians, political scientists, and jurists on situations that, in more than one respect, bear a resemblance to the ones studied by them (cf. Part II).

has been inclined to treat so many different types of social and political relations as instances of pluralism, particularly in his article, "Pluralism in Precolonial African Societies" (Kuper, Smith, 1969, pp. 91–167), that the word threatens to lose its specific meaning and thereby its usefulness for scientific classification. This oscillating between maximal and minimal definitions is found throughout the debate on pluralism.

This notion of a plural society goes back to Furnivall (1944, 1948), who found it difficult to interpret the colonial situation, which he studied in South East Asia, within the framework of traditional sociology. As M. G. Smith explains this trend of thought, "Societies whose organization and composition . . . [block] their functional or normative integration and [minimize] their internal cohesion," but are held together by external coercion and economic interdependence, "cannot be handled within a theoretical framework designed for functionally integrated societies of tribal or industrial types" (Kuper, Smith, 1969, pp. 419f.). Societies in which (in our terms) inherited group identity and ascribed status serve as the overriding criterion in the differential distribution of social rewards remained the principal interest of the pluralists, who took their cue from Furnivall. But they tended to include in their scheme societies whose pluralistic structure of group relations was based on class, estate, and caste, even on regional and territorial organization or on ecology and economy (Kuper, Smith, 1969, pp. 459, 472; van den Berghe, 1969, p. 68). This is not unexpected once it has been realized that class position as much as ethnicity are aspects of social structure.

Such similarities led to the expansion (and, as we believe, the overexpansion)[8] of the concept, so that it ultimately referred to all modern, complex societies. Yet pluralists have never lost sight of the specific problem that is at the root of the Furnivallian tradition, namely, the "incorporation" of diverse "sections" into a "society" by coercion, instead of their integration by consensus as the classical model required; and "despotic" rule by a metropolis or a settler minority, instead of "democratic" government based on the general will of the governed. We can therefore better understand what the pluralists of the second tradition are driving at by considering the problems with which they have been struggling. This has involved them in a controversy of a more general nature, which has arisen regarding whether the equilibrium model of society should be replaced by the conflict model.

In their latest statement, Kuper and M. G. Smith (1969) return to a more specific meaning of the concept. Smith surmises that few would deny the "unity" or boundaries of plural societies, but he adds that this unity differs with regard to institutional inclusiveness, consensus, cohesion, and functional coherence (p. 433). He distinguishes three levels of pluralism: Cultural pluralism consists of institutional differences without corresponding collective

---

[8]Whereas the overexpansion of concepts leads to meaningless generalizations, overclassification reduces the chance of arriving at any generalization.

segregation (pp. 440, 444); social pluralism "is the condition in which such institutional differentiations coincide with the corporate divisions of a given society into a series of . . . virtually closed social sections" (p. 440); whereas structural pluralism consists of the differential incorporation of collectivities within a society which are segregated as social sections and characterized by institutional divergences (pp. 440, 444). The type of "incorporation" in a society is another dimension in Smith's scheme. "The differential incorporation, that institutes structural pluralism is found only in societies where institutionally diverse collectivities are set apart as corporate social sections of unequal status and resources" (pp. 444ff.). This is obviously the classical model of a plural society in the Furnivallian tradition.

A second type is consociational incorporation, where territorially distinct corporate units hold equivalent or complementary rights and statuses in the "common public domain," which precludes neither institutional nor ethnic differences (pp. 434, 440). Not quite appropriately, as we have seen (pp. 102ff.), Smith mentions Switzerland as a typical instance. This type corresponds with our "multiethnic nation-state" (more correctly, the *"Nationalitätenstaat"* as it had existed in Cisleithanian Austria before 1918; cf. pp. 91ff.). In the third type, which is characterized by uniform incorporation according to Smith, we can readily recognize our demotic nation. According to him, it incorporates individuals as citizens directly and on equal terms into the "public domain." Whereas it proscribes social pluralism, it is consistent with cultural pluralism and ethnic heterogeneity (pp. 435, 440, 444, 447).

Kuper focuses his attention on ethnic and racial pluralism as well as on depluralization; by this he understands approximately the processes that we have described as neutralization of ethnicity and homogenization (Kuper, Smith, 1969, pp. 480, 482, 483, 485). He suggests a distinction between "pluralism," which he considers as typical of all (complex) societies, and "plural society" as one type of society "characterized by both divisive and integrative structures . . . in such a manner that the vertical and divisive cleavages threaten to prevail" (p. 469) over counterbalancing horizontal cleavages across the component ethnic groups (cf. Mitchell, 1960, p. 28). Kuper concentrates on the structural and political aspects of polyethnic societies. In one place he finds it advisable to defend Smith against the suspicion that he may be "dealing with cultural pluralism as a disembodied phenomenon" (Kuper, Smith, 1969, p. 466). But the emphasis put on cultural diversity independently of social heterogeneity or the structural aspect of a plural society is not just a slip of the tongue. The problem lies much deeper being linked to the difficulty many sociologists find in relating "culture" unambiguously to "society."[9]

---

[9]The difficulty seems to spring from the different traditions of the sciences employing the terms. One tradition has its roots in Hegel's (cultural) "objectivations of the spirit"; it makes sense only in the framework of an idealistic philosophy. According to the Hegelian tradition, which some

The crux of the controversy appears to be the meaning of "society." There is a remarkable reticence to commit oneself to the consistent use of the expressions "society," "nation," and "state." Each of them conjures up a welter of conflicting denotations referring to attributes that are neither universal nor obvious. Thus Schermerhorn asserts that "in the modern world" . . . it is most appropriate to define a society as a nation-state" (1970, p. 14). Even some of the contributors to the volume edited by Kuper and Smith (1969) point out the relativity of the concept "society" (H. Kuper); ask how a plural society can be both plural and a society (Mazrui); prefer to speak of a system of differential incorporation and extreme conflict (Davidson); or conclude that the concept of society should be "elastic" enough to take care of different and unfamiliar situations. Similar doubts have been voiced by Morris (1966, 1967), R. T. Smith (1961), Benedict (1962), Banton (1967), and others. The issue is pointedly summed up by Edward Shils: "The constituent *societies* (S₁) on which the new *states* rest are, taken separately, not civil *societies* (S₂), and taken together, they certainly are not a single civil *society* (S₂)" (1963, p. 22; italics and symbols supplied by E. K. F.).

In this statement, "society" is used in accordance with two different traditions of sociological thought for which the designations "Spencerian" and "Hegelian" seem appropriate. S_1 corresponds with the Spencerian tradition to which most Western sociologists are indebted (cf. Kellermann, 1967), whereas S_2 is more in line with an older English usage of the word, the literal translation of which is "*bürgerliche Gesellschaft*"; in the writing of Marx this phrase has assumed the dual meaning of "civil" and "bourgeois" society. Both concepts have been coined to cope with a particular historical situation. When the situation changed, the same word was applied to new situations both in and outside of the Western world, and its meaning expanded. In the Hegelian tradition, "society" in the sense of S_2 refers to one aspect of S_1, namely, that sphere of freedom from government interference that the rising bourgeoisie claimed for their economic activities.

The Spencerian concept of society (S_1), which was adopted by Durkheim and the functionalists but not by Simmel or Max Weber, has been formulated to

contemporary historians and cultural anthropologists also follow without realizing its implications, a (particular) culture is conceived of as a homogeneous phenomenon having an independent objective existence. Sociologists, on the other hand, are primarily interested in the structural aspects of societies, each of which is thought to be endowed with a particular culture or at least typical cultural attributes. According to this sociological tradition, culture is something that a society "has" or brings forth; any particular culture can be recognized and described only with reference to a concrete society. Typical cultural manifestations can not only be shared by different societies, but in a complex society there are also significant differences in the cultures of their diverse components, such as regions or classes. Moreover, at least under modern conditions, cultures tend to change more rapidly than the identities and boundaries of their societal carriers (cf. Part II, pp. 77ff; Francis, 1957, pp. 38ff, 1965, pp. 108–114; Weiss, 1973). An earlier statement by M. G. Smith on "Cultural and Social Pluralism" will be found in Rubin, 1960b. It should be read together with the excellent explication of the issue by Despres (1967, pp. 13–29, 268–278, 285–292), who as an anthropologist is inclined to put the stress on the cultural aspect, together with Smith's comment in the foreword to Despres' book.

take care of the emergent nation-state. This meaning was not known, for instance, to Adam Smith who wrote about the wealth of nations, not of societies. And as late as 1885, the Austrian, Ludwig Gumplowicz, altogether rejected the word in the sense of S_1 because there already existed a perfectly adequate German word for it: *Volk*. Only the fully developed Western nations permitted the conceptualization of society as an integral social system in which state, territory, jurisdiction, economy, culture, and social structure coincided. At this stage of historical development, the distinction between S_1 and S_2 also tended to lose its significance; for by then, bourgeois society (S_2) had taken over the state and was set to absorb the nation (S_1).

By and large, sociologists have been content with the Spencerian concept because their primary concern remained the changes that occurred in Western society in the course of "modernization." As more and more widely divergent situations caught their attention, whatever deviated from the model aroused their irritation and, at least latently, also their moral indignation. The preoccupation with the Spencerian paradigm seems to be responsible also for other professional biases, including the notion that the proper working of a society depends on the "integration" of the total population residing in the territory of a given nation-state, on the homogeneity and consistency of their culture, on democratic government and the consensus of the governed, on the sovereignty of the state and the integrity of its territory, on the incorporation of population elements and collectivities of foreign extraction on equal terms, on the reduction of coercion in favor of the self-regulation of society, and related ideas discussed elsewhere in this volume. It is not our intention to judge the merits of the political philosophy underlying the sociological paradigm of society or its moral quality. The issue here is rather whether the assumed indispensables of a respectable society are really so obvious that they cannot be questioned; more important still, whether they are valid criteria for the analysis of situations, which in the light of an accepted model, are really nonsocieties. From this it would appear that the theory of the plural society is an attempt to take care of an "anomaly," as perceived under the perspective of a traditional paradigm.

In this respect, Lockwood (1970) has made still another point deserving close attention. He reminds us that sociology has concentrated "on the universal constitutive properties of societies in general." Accordingly, it was thought

> that by ignoring the necessary but unimportant, and the important but contingent, lines of division, the theorist is better placed to construct simple general propositions about the structure and functions of those inequalities of power and deference which are present in all societies, and in relation to which the "complicating" features of ethnic, racial, or religious bases of stratification can be introduced at a later stage in the analysis (p. 58).

From this point of view, he adds, "the idea of a plural society merits special attention . . . because it might be regarded as an example of the introduction of concepts into general sociology that have emerged from the study of race relations'' (p. 62).

Once it was realized that colonial/postcolonial situations were anomalous, it was but a short step to discover similar anomalies in Western history. This suggested a general reclassification of societal types, such as van den Berghe's distinction between the "democratic" and "despotic" types of both pluralistic and nonpluralistic societies. His democratic type of pluralistic societies corresponds with M. G. Smith's consociational type, and resembles the *Nationalitätenstaat* that we have described. As examples of despotic pluralistic societies, van den Berghe lists "colonial and slave regimes of Asia, Africa, and the Americas, Tsarist and Stalinist Russia, the Napoleonic Empire, Sudanic empires, Ethiopia." From what has been said in Parts II and IV, it becomes clear that van den Berghe sees one type where we believe to discern two distinctive types, the *Reich* and the colonial/postcolonial situation. Despite significant differences, there are indeed striking similarities.[10] In both cases, the components of these structures are not individuals but collectivities of diverse origin, culture, and history. They are held together neither by a consensus of the governed nor by a shared valued system. They are not coordinated on equal terms nor ruled according to democratic principles. Their cohesion is guaranteed by political devices, and thus ultimately by the exercise of power, although conflicting interests need not manifest themselves in overt "conflict" or violence.

When we try to find a common denominator for both *Reich* and colonial situations (and possible other types not mentioned), it seems to boil down to this: In no way do they resemble modern nations nor can they be properly described as modern states *in sensu stricto*; accordingly, they cannot be handled adequately by a sociology that uses the nation-state as a model of any society. Even after colonies have been emancipated from metropolitan rule and become recognized at law as "states" or "nations," it is doubtful whether many of them constitute national societies, politically organized into modern states. Before the new nations of recent vintage came into existence, Hans Kohn had already pointed out that many "civilized societies" of the past and present bore little resemblance to nations. Would it be possible that during all this time, social scientists should have mistaken the idea of the nation for a faithful description of political reality, and that they had constructed their paradigm of society in accordance with a moral postulate?

The reference to "democratic" and "despotic" societies would seem to imply the ethnocentric assumption that any arrangement that does not conform

---

[10]We also would take exception to describing South Africa as an *Herrenvolk* democracy; for the slur overlooks the fact that most democracies have exhibited similar traits: Surely ancient Athens was a democracy only for its 10,000 full citizens, the patrician cantons of Switzerland were by no means democratic in dealing with their rural hinterland, and the Marxists claim that bourgeois democracies are altogether prone to cement the "despotic" rule of one class over the others.

to the Western image is objectionable, still worse, that it is unworkable and ultimately bound to fail. When Kuper speaks of depluralization as a process by which the salience of racial, ethnic, or other sectional ties is diminished, he, too, visualizes—though with less assurance than hope—the demotic nation as the ultimate end. As a more realistic proximate goal, he thinks of an intermediate phase during which depluralization in the "public domain" would be combined with continued sectionalization in the "private domain." He realizes, however, the instability of a federation combining several collective components on equal terms, and the always present danger of secession and division. From what we have learned in Part II, we are inclined to prognosticate that such a federation is likely to generate new problems that would not be any easier to solve than those involved in the homogenization of the entire population of a given state by way of despotic coercion. We would also not be quite so sure that consociational arrangements necessarily mark a transitory stage of development culminating in the best of all societies resembling our own.

The great merit of the pluralists should be sought in their sensitizing social scientists for the inadequacies of both the principles upon which the nation-state is based, and the sociological theories using the same scheme in interpreting the actual functioning of quite different societal units. They have supplied a wealth of new evidence and perspectives deserving more careful consideration than has been possible in these pages. Our discussion has revealed that there is considerable dovetailing between their findings and our own. Some of the difficulties implied in the theories of the pluralists seem to have to do with the indiscriminate use of the word "society." These difficulties we have tried to avoid (1) by substituting for "society" a set of carefully defined terms including "societal unit," "national society," "national core," "demotic nation," and so on; (2) by clarifying the role of culture in interethnic relations; and, above all, (3) by distinguishing between a political power structure and its societal substratum. For political boundaries can be changed rather quickly by deliberate military and/or diplomatic action, whereas the cohesion of a society, which at one time had been politically organized in one state, may linger on for quite a time after it has been divided or incorporated into another political power structure. This is demonstrated, for instance, by the controversy carried on by spokesmen of Eastern and Western Germany over the continuity and identity of the German nation.

Having said that much, we could content ourselves with the customary ritual of declaring that the theories advanced by us should be considered as being quite tentative, and that much more empirical work would be required to test their validity. Such a commonplace finish, however, would add nothing to the claim, voiced at the beginning of this book, that our theoretical undertaking was supposed to remain within the framework of an empirical science. But there is still some unfinished business that arises from our other claim that, in the last analysis, our purpose was a practical one. Offhand it would seem that neither we nor the pluralists have redeemed the promise.

This, however, could be a shortsighted view of the possible contributions that social science may make to the resolution of practical problems. According to Rex (1959, p. 118), the sociologist who is faced with group conflicts may define his role in two ways. He can take a frankly partisan stand and offer practical advice to those with whom he is personally in sympathy. This, of course, involves the danger that applied social scientists become indistinguishable from *literati,* in the sense of Max Weber, or the mediating intelligentsia, in the sense of Geiger and Mannheim. There is also the danger that social science turns into a political rhetoric, which draws on the prestige that the natural sciences are enjoying because of their technological achievements, to give strength to some political argument and to "prove" what is "known" beforehand to happen. This is countered by the assertion that bourgeois sociologists, whether consciously or not, overtly or under the disguise of objectivity, have nonetheless been using their science as an ideological prop for capitalistic interests.

The alternative mentioned by Rex is more in line with the traditional definition of the sociologist's professional role, which is supposed to consist of the discovery of the principles of social and cultural change to predict what is likely to happen next. This, however, would omit the third, and to our mind the most important, clause in Comte's classical formula: *prévoir pour prévenir.* Even if the sociologist cannot, or does not want to, provide any recipe knowledge, his findings should serve as a *caveat* and food for thought for those who have the power of making political decisions.

Let us see whether any practical conclusions could be drawn from the contents of this volume. We shall confine ourselves to three instances. One is still in the realm of cognition, though with very practical consequences. It concerns the classical case of a plural society, South Africa. The very adoption of the term "society" is likely to suggest that we have to do with an integral whole, the viability of which should be safeguarded by a process of internal restructuring. This definition of the situation would be changed, however, suggesting quite different practical consequences, if one were to accept the viewpoint proposed by us that South Africa is not a society but a political power structure containing several societies—not just "sections," a term that the pluralists prefer without defining it or indicating its status within the framework of general sociological theory. These societies, or to put it more cautiously: societal units, include one emergent settler nation in addition to a number of tribal societies, or what is left of them. This would enable us to question whether a division of the country might not be less costly than the attempt to build one nation.

Since Comte, we have come to believe that increasing differentiation increases interdependence, and that the increasing complexity of society is pre-determined by technological progress and economic development. When we ponder the recent malaise and discontent with progress, perhaps the idea will not seem so unrealistic, as it would have appeared to the generation of Ogburn, that the reduction of complexity may be a realistic alternative to progressive complexity. The question could even be asked whether at one point complexity may not become so unmanageable that its reduction becomes an inescapable evolutionary consequence.[11] This is not to say that a federation of one white and several black societies is the one solution we advocate for South Africa. But the redefinition of the situation would at least enable us to state the conditions under which some sort of consociational arrangement could be expected to materialize, for instance, despotic rule, military intervention, population transfer, dictatorship of the proletariat, or some other device not yet thought of. It would also be an invitation to question the unquestionable in this and similar cases.

Another lesson one could think of concerns the idea that the nation-state should serve as a guideline of practical politics. If we have been correct in maintaining that ever since the conditions that had made possible the rise of the older nation-states are past recovery, and that the principles of demotic nationalism are inapplicable to plural and polyethnic societies, it becomes imperative to think of better principles and novel forms of political organization—a task best left to those who are immediately concerned, know the situation from personal experience, and bear the responsibility. The most pressing problem of the Third World does not appear to be nation-building, but replacing the model of the nation-state and the Spencerian paradigm of society. What seems to be needed are not new nations but viable social structures negating the political relevance that has been attached to shared ethnicity and racial diversity in one particular historical moment.

When thinking of alternatives, the study of different structures that have actually worked in the past should be of major interest. We have spent considerable time analyzing the coordination of ethnic units in tribal societies, in the *Reich,* in the absolute state, and in some historical instances of the consociational type. This was done partly to put into bold relief the essentials of the nation-state. At the same time, however, it was our intention to overcome ethnocentric blocks to new vistas. Obviously, history never repeats itself. But it is only in history that we can detect the elementary social processes, which do return again and again in ever-new combinations, and which show regularities of a general, if not universal, nature. Once we have taken account of

---

[11]The opposite view has been put forth by Banton (1967, p. 292), who suggests that pluralism may be adequate precisely for the increasingly competitive urban society of the future with an automated technology and a highly industrialized system of production. There may indeed be situations in which the limit of complexity has not yet been reached, and therefore pluralistic forms of social organization can yet be expanded without danger. On the other hand, we doubt whether this is true of South Africa.

unique historical conditions, there still remains much to be learned from the intrinsic shortcomings and/or the undeniable advantages of other types of societal organization. There are men of affairs, with a more than ordinary knowledge of both the operation of the Hapsburg *Nationalitätenstaat* and the problems facing the new nations, who believe that today's statesmen and politicians could take a leaf from the book of Austrian administrative law and practice.

Perhaps this does not amount to much. Still if our essay should have provided impulses, however weak, for reconsidering current principles of social and political organization and for getting beyond theories reflecting them, we would feel that our undertaking was not in vain.

REFERENCES

Banton, Michael, *Race Relations*. London: Tavistock Publications, 1967.

Barth, Fredrik (ed.), *Ethnic Groups and Boundaries: The Social Organization of Cultural Difference*. Boston: Little, Brown & Co., 1969.

Benedict, Raymond, "Stratification in Plural Societies," *American Anthropologist*, LXIV (1962), pp. 1235–1246.

Boeke, J. H., *Economics and Economic Policy of Dual Societies*. New York: Institute of Pacific Relations, 1963.

Despres, Leo A., *Cultural Pluralism and Nationalist Politics in British Guiana*. Chicago: Rand McNally and Co., 1967.

———— (ed.), *Ethnicity and Resource Competition in Plural Societies*. The Hague: Mouton and Co. N. V., Publishers, 1975.

Francis, Emerich K., "Minority Groups—A Revision of Concepts," *British Journal of Sociology II*, (1951), pp. 219–230.

————, "Religious Pluralism in a Peasant Community," *Religious Education*, (1955), pp. 23–26.

————, *Wissenschaftliche Grundlagen Soziologischen Denkens*. Bern: Francke Verlag, 1957.

————, *Ethnos und Demos: Soziologische Beiträge zur Volkstheorie*. Berlin: Duncker und Humblot, 1965.

Furnivall, J. S., *Netherlands India: A Study of Plural Economy*. Cambridge: The University Press, 1939.

————, *Colonial Policy and Practice: A Comparative Study of Burma and Netherlands India*. London: Cambridge University Press, 1948.

Hoetink, H., *De Gespleten Samenleving in het Caribisch Gebied*. Assen: Royal Vangorcum Ltd., 1961. English trans.: *The Two Variants in Caribbean Race Relations: A Contribution to the Sociology of Segmented Societies*. New York: Oxford University Press, 1964.

INCIDI (Institut International des Civilisations Différentes), *Ethnic and Culteral Pluralism in Intertropical Countries*. Brussels: INCIDI, 1957.

Kellermann, Paul, *Kritik einer Soziologie der Ordnung: Organismus und System bei Comte, Spencer und Parsons* (Munich doctoral diss.). Freiburg i. Br.: Verlag Rombach und Co., 1967.

Klaus, Georg, and Manfred Buhr (eds.), *Philosophisches Wörterbuch* (6th ed.), vol. 2, art. "Nation." (East) Berlin: das europäische buch, 1969, pp. 755–760.

Kuhn, Thomas S., *The Structure of Scientific Revolutions*. Chicago: University of Chicago Press, 1962.

Kuper, Leo, *An African Bourgeoisie: Race, Class and Politics in South Africa*. New Haven: Yale University Press, 1965.

————, and Michael Garfield Smith (eds.), *Pluralism in Africa*. Berkeley: University of California Press, 1969.

Lockwood, David, "Race, Conflict, and Plural Society," in Sami Zubaida (ed.), *Race and Racialism*. London: Tavistock Publications, 1970.

Mazrui, Ali A., *Cultural Engineering and Nation-Building in East Africa*. Evanston, Ill.: Northwestern University Press, 1972.

Mitchell, J. C., *Tribalism and the Plural Society*. London: Oxford University Press, 1960.

Morris, H. S., "Review of M. G. Smith, *The Plural Society in the British West Indies*," *Man*, n. s. I (1966), pp. 270f.

————, "Some Aspects of the Concept Plural Society," *Man*, n. s. II (1967), pp. 169–184.

Rex, John, "The Plural Society in Sociological Theory," *British Journal of Sociology*, X (1959), pp. 114–124.

Rubin, Vera, (ed.), *Caribbean Studies: A Symposium* (2nd ed.). Seattle: University of Washington Press, 1960a.

————, Social and Cultural Pluralism in the Caribbean, in *Annals of the New York Academy of Sciences*, LXXXIII (1960b), pp. 761–916.

Schermerhorn, Robert A., *Comparative Ethnic Relations: A Framework for Theory and Research*. New York: Random House, 1970.

Shils, Edward, "On the Comparative Study of the New Nations," in Clifford Geertz (ed.), *Old Societies and New States: The Quest for Modernity in Asia and Africa*. New York: Free Press of Glencoe, 1963, pp. 1–26.

Smith, Michael Garfield, *The Plural Society in the British West Indies*. Berkeley: University of California Press, 1965.

Smith, Raymond T., Review of *Social and Cultural Pluralism in the Caribbean*, *American Anthropologist*, LXIII (1961), pp. 155–157.

Van den Berghe, Pierre Louis, *Race and Racism: A Comparative Perspective*. New York: John Wiley & Sons, 1967.

————, "Pluralism and the Polity: A Theoretical Exploration," in Kuper, Smith, 1969, pp. 67–81.

Weiss, Gerald, "A Scientific Concept of Culture," *American Anthropologist*, LXXV (1973), pp. 1376–1413.

Wirth, Louis, "The Problem of Minority Groups," in Ralph Linton (ed.), *The Science of Man in the World Crisis*. New York: Columbia University Press, 1945.

OUTLINE OF
A THEORY

V

INTRODUCTION

The arguments and insights presented in the main body of this book have been derived from the analysis of empirical materials. A welter of relevant problems were discussed as the occasion arose: conclusions were often reached in devious ways. The case method we have chosen for reasons stated in the Preface is apt to obscure the structure of the theory. Therefore, the principal results of our investigation will be once more outlined below in a systematic manner. This should be an added contribution to the consolidation of the conceptual framework, the standardization of terms, and the codification of research carried out under the auspices of several sciences—an effort that seems particularly desirable in a field of knowledge hampered by a lack of cooperation and a Babylonic confusion of tongues. The synopsis should also serve the casual reader as a ready reference for locating those sections that are of immediate interest to him, and for the serious student and expert as a compact survey of essential results, otherwise scattered throughout the text.

The presentation includes definitions, propositions, connecting remarks, and explanatory notes, though not always in their original order. The definitions of concepts, which are printed in italics, represent the final versions often arrived at after experimenting with several tentative formulations. They can only be fully appreciated after studying the arguments offered in the main text. All terms to be defined are placed between quotation marks. By arranging the bare definitions in their logical order the consistency of the conceptual scheme should become apparent. The propositions refer to regularities (or "laws") that have been found to prevail in interethnic relations.

If there seems to exist a certain imbalance between definitions and hypotheses, one must realize that the former do not merely refer to analytical tools for constructing theories, but are meant to describe social reality, primarily its ideological components. The supplementary remarks, which appear as abstracts, are added to aid the reader in understanding the theoretical statements at a glance.

ETHNICITY IN SOCIAL ACTION ORIENTATION

Definition 1. In its most general meaning the term "interethnic relations" refers to social action in which ethnicity is salient.

Definition 2. "Ethnicity" refers to the fact that (1) a relatively large number of people are socially defined as belonging together because of the belief in their being descended from common ancestors; that (2) because of this belief, they have a sense of identity and share sentiments of solidarity.

Shared ethnicity extends genealogical relationships to a wider population whose precise genealogical nexus is unknown or disregarded.

Proposition 1. Shared ethnicity becomes salient in social action orientation (1) if there is a contrast effect between two or more groups of people coexisting in a given social context, and (2) if the contrast can be interpreted in ethnic terms.

Proposition 2. The saliency of shared ethnicity as a principle of societal organization differs with the general type of society. Shared territory may serve a similar function in social organization and in legitimizing a societal unit.[1]

Proposition 3. Where the genealogical principle of social organization is dominant, there is a tendency to define socially a population sharing a common territory in terms of shared ethnicity.

ETHNICITY AND TYPES OF SOCIETY

I. Ethnicity in Acephalous Societies

Definition 3. By "acephalous society" we understand a societal unit lacking distinct and separate political institutions. The exercise of political power is diffused among a variety of subsocietal units performing other functions as well. Societal identity and solidarity may be based (1) on shared territory, (2) on shared ethnicity.

When the synchronic and diachronic identity as well as societal solidarity are derived from the legitimate and religiously sanctioned ownership of, and jurisdiction over, a definite territory, this claim need not be legitimized in terms of shared ethnicity.

---

[1]"Societal unit" is used in preference to "society" whenever certain connotations of the concept of global society do not fit the case in question.—Societal units based primarily on shared religion (such as Islamic societies) have not been treated in this volume.

When the genealogical principle of social organization is dominant so that rights and duties of tribesmen are socially ascribed by virtue of their relative positions in the kinship structure, the tribe represents the widest web of kinship relations within which incest taboos and rules of exogamy are recognized. Insofar as social identification and solidarity are based on the belief in common descent from one mythological ancestor, the tribe is to be considered an ethnic unit. Several tribes may be combined into an ethnie[2] by the belief that they have a still more distant ancestor in common. Members of different tribes are allowed to travel and settle throughout the ethnie.

II. Ethnicity in Politically Organized Societies

Proposition 4. Shared ethnicity may serve to legitimize a political power structure.

A. ETHNICITY IN POLITICALLY ORGANIZED TRIBES

Permanent association and cooperation between ethnically diverse components of a tribal society, which are similar in size and power potential, can be maintained only through political organization leading to the emergence of a societal superstructure over and above the structures based on genealogical or spatial relationships.

Proposition 5. In a society in which genealogical relationships serve as the dominant principle of social organization, political power structures comprising ethnically diverse components tend to be legitimized by expressing societal identity and solidarity symbolically in genealogical and ethnic terms.

B. ETHNICITY IN MULTITRIBAL SOCIETIES

If several ethnically diverse tribes, similar in size and power potential, are to be organized in one political power structure, and if they can no longer be controlled effectively by a pyramidal system of administration and by appeal to genealogical solidarities, demotic organization provides a solution to the problem of strengthening and maintaining societal identity and solidarity, and of legitimizing the political power of the paramount chief.

Definition 4. By "demotic society" we understand a complex and ethnically heterogeneous society that is politically organized in such a way that all its members are linked directly, and without the mediation of subsocietal units, to the central authority through special institutions. Societal identity and solidarity are based neither on genealogical nor on spatial but on political relationships.

The synchronic identity of a preliterate demotic society is based on shared allegiance to the paramount chief. Its diachronic identity is maintained not through the belief in

---

[2]In contrast to "ethnic society" the term "ethnie" refers to a wider social context with somewhat vague boundaries which is defined in ethnic terms. For instance, a Nuer tribe may be considered an ethnic society, while all Nuer tribes form an ethnie.

the common descent of the total population and/or its tribal chiefs, but through the continuity of the kinship unit that supplies succeeding paramount chiefs.

Proposition 6. The principal demotic institutions are military and administrative. They extend to all the members of the demotic society and are under the ultimate control of the paramount chief.

Proposition 7. The demotic principle of societal organization tends to transform the traditional chiefs of tribal subdivisions, who are selected on the basis of genealogical relationships, into administrative officers who are appointed by the paramount chief on the basis of merit.

Proposition 8. Increased spatial and social mobility tend to decrease the saliency of genealogical and ethnic relationships, and to increase the saliency of spatial and political relationships.

Proposition 9. In a demotic society, ethnicity is a potentially disturbing factor; it tends to be neutralized by the homogenizing influence of demotic institutions.

Proposition 10. After the cultural homogenization of its population has been accomplished, a demotic society is likely to be reinterpreted in ethnic terms and thereby to be transformed into a (secondary) ethnic society.

C. ETHNICITY IN EMPIRES[3]

If a complex societal unit has a dual structure of interlocking levels, consisting of a variety of tribal societies[4] ruled by their traditional chiefs[4] on the lower level, and of a superstructure based on centralized military, administrative, judicial, and/or religious institutions under the control of the paramount chief[4] on the upper level, and if the other tribal societies are joined to the dominant tribe (which is under the direct rule of the paramount chief) by virtue of the other tribal chiefs being bound to the paramount chief through contract, personal allegiance, and/or genealogical relationships, the conflict between the claims of the paramount and other tribal chiefs may be resolved in two ways.

1. Whenever the paramount chief succeeds in destroying the independence of the other chiefs, the stage is set for the emergence of a demotic society.
2. Whenever the paramount chief's claim to sovereign rule through demotic institutions is successfully checked by the other chiefs, and a balance of power is struck between the tribes and the political superstructure, an empire is likely to emerge.

---

[3]While tribal societies are typically preliterate and national societies are typically literate, political power structures of the empire-type occur in preliterate, semiliterate and also literate societies. The paradigm used in the present context conforms primarily to a semiliterate society in which the elite are literate but not the common folk.

[4]When speaking of semiliterate or literate societies it is appropriate to substitute "territorial unit" for "tribe," "territorial lord" or "prince" for "tribal chief" and "paramount ruler" or "emperor" for "paramount chief." The word "King" has been avoided because it may stand for a great variety of types of rulers.

In case 1. the members of the tribal components are linked to the paramount ruler and his staff directly through a system of demotic institutions. In case 2. the constituent tribes are linked to the paramount ruler collectively through the mediation of their chiefs. Paramount chief and the other tribal chiefs together with their staffs constitute the elite of the superstructure.

Definition 5. By "empire" we understand a political superstructure, superimposed upon a variety of territorial units whose internal conditions, ethnic traditions, folk cultures, and languages are left undisturbed. These units are linked to the superstructure by virtue of the personal relationships established between their territorial lords and the paramount ruler.

> As the territorial lords are identified with their respective territories, they are, as a rule, of diverse ethnic origins. Accordingly, the elite of the empire are likely to be ethnically heterogeneous, while the population of the constituent territorial units tend to be ethnically homogeneous.
>
> Territorial lords participate at the same time in the superstructure of the empire and in the societal structures of their own territories, whose prime focus of identification and symbol of unity they are. They therefore represent particularistic interests of their own peoples as well as pursuing universalistic interests related to the proper functioning of the superstructure. This is also true of the paramount ruler who, although he is the prime focus of identification and symbol of the entire empire and in control of imperial institutions, is nevertheless a territorial lord.

Proposition 11. Shared ethnicity as a principle of societal organization is irrelevant for the proper operation of an imperial superstructure, but it tends to remain salient in the constituent political units, which may or may not be ethnically homogeneous.

Proposition 12. Regional opposition against centralized political power tends to be expressed and mobilized in ethnic terms. Whenever territorial lords or other power groups seek greater independence from the paramount ruler and imperial institutions, they are likely to activate latent ethnic divisions which are apt to legitimize their claim to freedom and to mobilize wider support for their political designs.

D. ETHNICITY IN THE MODERN STATE

A typical problem of empires is the conflict between the claim of the emperor to supremacy and the emancipatory tendencies of powerful territorial lords. If the paramount ruler manages to win the power struggle with the territorial princes, he becomes a sovereign monarch unhampered by the traditional curbs to his power, and the segmented imperial power structure is transformed into a modern state. If the territorial princes succeed in emancipating themselves from imperial authority and in suppressing similar emancipatory tendencies within their own territorial units, the superstructure is dissolved into independent territorial states, each territorial prince becoming the sovereign ruler over his own territory.

Definition 6. *A modern state is characterized by the continuous exercise of power over the population of a contiguous territory by a central authority through a bureaucratic administration.*

> During a transitional period the state has two centers of power: (1) the prince and his staff, exercising central authority; and (2) the estates, representing traditional powers. The traditional authorities rather than the prince are likely to be of the same ethnic origin as the common people; accordingly, they tend to act as their representatives and advocates vis-a-vis the prince and his staff.

a. Ethnicity and the Absolute State

The transition to the absolute state is marked by an expansion of state functions that require increased financial resources, thus adding to the power of the estates whose corporate consensus is necessary for introducing new taxation. If the conflict between prince and estates is resolved by the prince, reducing the estates to impotence, the stage is set for the emergence of an absolute state.

Definition 7. *By "absolute state" we understand a modern state in which political power is monopolized by the sovereign prince and his staff to the exclusion of the estates.*

Proposition 13. Shared ethnicity as a principle of societal organization is irrelevant for the power operation of the absolute state. The ethnically heterogeneous population becomes integrated into the absolute state through demotic institutions whose homogenizing effect tends to neutralize ethnicity as a potentially divisive force.

Proposition 14. The absolute state tends to initiate the demotic integration of the state population (1) by removing traditional (including ethnic) barriers to statewide mobility, communication, and social interaction; (2) by adopting an official lingua franca; (3) by promoting the free movement of goods, persons, and ideas throughout the state territory; (4) by heightening the barriers against other states through the control of immigration, travel, the traffic of goods, and the flow of ideas across international boundary lines; and (5) by propagating patriotism.

Definition 8. *By "patriotism" we understand a political ideology extolling the state as a supreme value, and promoting the identification of the state population with the state and its institutions, which is supposed to supersede their allegiance to traditional (including ethnic) social subunits.*

Proposition 15. The homogenization and integration of a heterogeneous state population initiated by the absolute state is a precondition for the emergence of a national society within its boundaries.

b. The Role of Ethnicity in Nation-Building

Definition 9. By "nation-building" we understand the social processes contributing to the emergence of national societies.

Definition 10. By "national society" we understand a complex society organized according to the principles of nationalism.

Definition 11. By "nationalism" we understand a political doctrine extolling the nation as a supreme value and representing it as a dominant principle of societal organization.

Definition 12. "Nation" is a political concept serving as a symbol of societal identity and solidarity as well as a legitimation of practical politics. Therefore, the content of the term will be defined differently in accordance with particular interests and policies. The types of nationalism differ according to the meanings given to the word "nation" by different political doctrines and movements.

Definition 13. By "demotic nation" we understand a demotic society (1) which is coextensive with the population of a modern state, and (2) the integration of which is based on democratic government and cultural homogenization.

Proposition 16. A demotic society that is politically organized in a modern state tends to be transformed into a demotic nation when the alien rule of an absolute prince is replaced by the self-determination of the ruled.

> In the language of demotic nationalism, "self-determination" refers to the right of the population of a modern state to democratic self-government. The proper functioning of democratic government requires the integration of the citizens into a viable societal unit which is achieved through the cultural homogenization of the state population.

Proposition 17. In a demotic nation, shared ethnicity is a divisive factor to be neutralized by the imposition and expansion of demotic—especially educational—institutions.

> Demotic nationalism is primarily concerned with the sovereignty of self-governing national societies. Ethnic nationalism is primarily concerned with the ethnic homogeneity of the population of nation-states.
>
> In the language of ethnic nationalism, "national self-determination" refers to the right of an ethnic unit to be politically organized into one nation-state which is identified with it.

Proposition 18. If nation-building takes place according to the principles of demotic nationalism, the state antedates national integration. If nation-building takes place according to the principles of ethnic nationalism, shared ethnicity antedates political organization in a common state.

Definition 14. By "ethnic nation" we understand an ethnic society supposed to be politically organized in a nation-state and exclusively identified with it.

Proposition 19. The principal indicators used to identify a potential ethnic nation and its territory include a common language, culture, and history.

Definition 15. By "nation-state" we understand a modern state identified with a particular nation in whose name ultimate political power is exercised by the central government through a bureaucratic administration.

Proposition 20. New demotic nations emerge when an existing state or major administrative subunit has been transformed into a nation-state, and when its population has been successfully nationalized.

Definition 16. By "nationalization" we understand the general homogenizing processes through which traditional and particularistic identifications and solidarities, including those based on shared ethnicity, are replaced by the nation as the principal focus of societal identification and solidarity, providing legitimacy for political actions.

Proposition 21. The processes of nationalization, set in motion within a given state population, are apt to transform ethnic units that differ from the national core into nationalities and national minorities.

Proposition 22. If the nationalization of its ethnically diverse components has been successful, a demotic nation tends to be reinterpreted as an ethnic society.

Proposition 23. Whatever argument in the armory of nationalism best serves a particular national cause in a given domestic and international situation, it tends to be advanced in order to awaken the national consciousness of a population envisioned as a potential nation, and to legitimize political claims advanced in its name.

Proposition 24. If the demotic integration of a state population has been accomplished by the absolute state, its transformation into a nation-state follows the principles of demotic nationalism.

Proposition 25. If the demotic integration of a state population has not been accomplished previously, and if its ethnic heterogeneity is therefore preserved, demotic nationalism is likely to be adopted to define and legitimize the leading role of the dominant ethnic society in nation-building, while ethnic nationalism is likely to be adopted to express opposition and to promote the cause of other ethnic units included in the state population. Once, however, full sovereignty (or at least limited territorial autonomy) has been achieved by such ethnic units, demotic nationalism is likely to serve their national consolidation.

c. The Origin and Resolution of National Problems

The principles of nationalism, in both their theoretical and practical dimension, are fraught with inconsistencies and contradictions. They are also often unworkable due to particular geographic and especially demographic conditions.

Definition 17. By "national problems" we understand conflict situations between modern states as well as within politically organized societies, which are incidental to efforts to adopt national principles as guidelines to political action.

Proposition 26. National problems tend to originate in the imperfections of the national doctrine and/or in the difficulties encountered in an attempt to apply it to the realities of a given situation.

Proposition 27. National problems are most likely to arise when the ideals of ethnic nationalism serve as guides to political action in countries with an ethnically mixed population.

> The homogenizing pressures exerted by the nation-state on ethnically diverse components of its population tend to call forth an opposition that finds its ideological expression in the principle of nationality.

Definition 18. According to the principle of nationality, ethnic units antedating the formation of a demotically conceived nation-state, or added to the state population by annexation after demotic nation-building has been accomplished, are supposed to have a right to be organized politically in nation-states of their own.

Proposition 28. National problems are most likely to concern claims of ethnic units if not to complete political emancipation at least to territorial autonomy, adequate participation in overall state policy and protection of their substance with regard to personnel and culture.

> National problems are primarily political issues requiring legal and government action. Accordingly, they are usually formulated in terms of "rights of nationalities."
>
> While a nation is sovereign in exercising political power through its state, both internally and externally, the political power exercised by a nationality within an administrative subdivision of the state is limited. A nationality participates collectively in the policy decisions of the central government in all matters concerning the entire population, especially with regard to internal relations between different nationalities and external relations with other nation-states.

Definition 19. "Nationality" refers to an imperfect nation.

Proposition 29. An ethnic unit is transformed into a nationality when the following three conditions are met:

1. Corporate participation in the exercise of state power on equal terms with other nationalities.
2. Relative self-determination in the administration of the territorial subunit identified with the ethnic unit.

3. Protection of its vital interests including its maintenance and advancement, both on the state level and on the level of all its autonomous administrative subdivisions, against whatever nationality threatens domination. This implies, above all, protection against being outvoted by a majority of different ethnic origin.

> In the demotic nation-state there is but one national core to which the state "belongs" in a specific manner; in the multiethnic nation-state there are several nationalities that are formally equal, although—within the limit set by the inalienable rights imputed to the ethnic units in accordance with a mutually acceptable national doctrine—these are free to compete in the struggle for political power and even supremacy.

Proposition 30. There is a tendency to identify the national core of a modern society with a particular ethnic unit.

Definition 20. By a multiethnic nation-state we understand the political integration of imperfect nation-states into one sovereign nation-state. Internal sovereignty is limited on principle; for both the superordinate state and its autonomous subdivisions have but limited and mutually complementary competence.

> The multiethnic nation-state is a form of federal state whereby the boundaries of its components are determined with a view to the ethnic homogeneity of their populations rather than historical, economic, topological, or other considerations.

Proposition 31. Wherever the population is divided into several relatively large ethnic units, the ideology and political principles on which the modern nation-state is based are bound to lead to a clash between national aspirations of the demotic and the ethnic type, unless a balance of power has become firmly established in political traditions and social myth well before the ideas of modern nationalism have captured the public mind.

Proposition 32. The multiethnic nation-state representing a political federation of nationalities cannot achieve more than a labile equilibrium. Apart from international developments, its relative stability depends primarily on the mobile middle classes of the different nationalities.

Proposition 33. The mobile middle classes are likely to support the multiethnic nation-state if they realize that any other alternative would serve their interests to a lesser degree, and if they are unwilling to shoulder the cost of a more radical change.

Proposition 34. The principle of self-determination is likely to be realized when a country is too weak to resist secession and/or dismemberment.

d. National Minorities

Where either the full self-determination of a nation or the limited self-determination of a nationality has been denied to ethnic units, the concept of national minority has been introduced as a residual category.

"Minorities" may be said to be the result of bad conscience. The term reflects the fact that even if the principle of nationality were carried to its logical consequences, a residue of national problems would remain.

The difficulties in defining the concept of national minority reflect the great variety of conflicting interests involved in the issue of minority rights, on the one hand; the diversity of partly contradictory principles employed in legitimizing opposing claims, on the other.

The term "minority" is releated to the democratic principle of majority rule. Minority rights are derived from those human rights and individual freedoms that have been declared fundamental and inalienable, and which have been widely recognized by democratic state constitutions and international consent. The basic meaning of "minority" refers to categories of citizens who are unable to advance their rightful interests because they are bound to be outvoted by the dominant majority.

Definition 21. By "national minority" we understand an ethnic unit or part of it which, contrary to the ambiguous and largely unworkable principle of self-determination, has been denied the right of national autonomy.

Definition 22. "National problems" refers to social problems that arise when ethnic units claim, if not complete political emancipation, at least territorial autonomy, adequate participation in overall state policies, and protection of their substance with regard to personnel and culture.

National problems are strongly influenced by international power politics. Ethnic units are likely to embark upon a course of irredenta only when they are encouraged and backed by a powerful nation-state who claims them as an integral part of its national core. It is rare that territories are reapportioned in accordance with the principle of nationality unless there is a special occasion for doing so, such as wars or peace treaties, and/or unless international constellations are particularly favorable.

The actual content of minority rights is controversial. Short of secession and complete political emancipation it reaches from regional political autonomy to mild forms of cultural autonomy.

"Cultural autonomy" implies that an ethnic group represented by self-appointed agencies should be entrusted by the state with the autonomous management of their schools and cultural affairs. In addition, the state should be responsible for the financial support of separate educational, cultural, and even charitable institutions of the ethnic group, in proportion to its share in the total population.

There are two basic types of minority rights, one concerning the protection of minorities and the other the prevention of discrimination.

Definition 23. "Protection of minorities" refers (1) to the right of ethnic units to the preservation of their substance and to their collective self-development, with the active support either of the state into which they are politically incorporated, or of the state whose national core is of the same ethnic origin; and (2) to the guarantee of such rights through international bodies.

Definition 24. "Prevention of discrimination" refers to the restatement of those universal human rights which—because of the minority position of an ethnic unit—are in a particular danger of being violated under majority rule.

Proposition 35. Ethnic units forming viable subsocieties with a long history of independent existence, which have fallen under the sway of a nation-state not their own, are more likely to aspire to the political recognition of their separate identity within a given state population and to the recognition of particularistic rights (protection of minorities) rather than equality in the enjoyment of universalistic rights (prevention of discrimination).

Proposition 36. Immigrants to a foreign country are less likely to be concerned with the prosperity of the ethnic collectivity than with the individual enjoyment of social rewards on equal terms with the charter members of the host society. They therefore tend to emphasize the prevention of unequal treatment of individuals ("discrimination") rather than the preservation and the advancement ("protection") of collectivities.

III. Interethnic Relations in Modern Society

With the emergence of national societies, specific problematical situations tend to make themselves felt, which in their political and legal aspects, have been called "national problems." When the broad sociological implications are considered, however, it is preferable to refer to "ethnic problems" and to use the wider term "ethnic groups," instead of "national minorities."

When we speak of "interethnic relations in modern society" in this context, we mean intrasocietal processes involving ethnic problems.

Definition 25. "Ethnic problems" refer to social problems that arise due to the partial integration or malintegration of population elements differing ethnically from the national core of a modern society.

Proposition 37. Ethnic problems are likely to arise when those who are put at a disadvantage in the distribution of social rewards become aware that the general rules and criteria accepted in the host society are, in their case, violated and are replaced by particular norms that are not legitimized by the normative culture common to modern societies.

A. BASIC CONCEPTS

Definition 26. By "modern society" we understand a society that is characterized by the processes of nationalization in the political dimension and of industrialization in the economic dimension.

Industrialization and nationalization have partly opposite effects on interethnic relations.

The proper functioning of a modern national society presupposes a reasonably homogeneous state population with a common identity, a sense of solidarity, and a common culture.

Proposition 38. Industrialization tends to increase the ethnic diversity of the population through long-distance migration, and to bring forth an industrial culture that is not tied to any particular national society.

Proposition 39. Nationalization tends to promote the absorption of ethnically diverse populations into the national core, to exclude or reduce the influx of ethnically diverse immigrants, and to prevent the formation of ethnic groups.

Definition 27. "Integration" refers to the social processes by which new additions to a society become part of it without disrupting its basic structure.

New additions to a society include, besides the children of charter members, also transferees from other societies.

Definition 28. By the "transfer" of population elements, we understand a qualitative change of their typical relationships with the societal environment.

Endogeneous transfer occurs when ethnically heterogeneous population elements are socially redefined as belonging to one national society. The exogeneous transfer of ethnically heterogeneous population elements takes place by way of either annexation or long-distance migration.

Definition 29. The integration of a modern society may be said to be accomplished when all the components of its social structure are assigned a definite status according to general principles that have unquestioned validity in that society.

Definition 30. In this context we understand by "social structure" the overall result of the differential distribution of social rewards among the members of a society according to social categories with which they are identified.

Definition 31. "Social status" refers to the rights and duties through which one social category is differentiated from others in a given society.

Definition 32. "Social reward" refers to a benefit with regard to any kind of goods and services (including power or prestige) that a person (or group of persons) gains by participating in a particular society at a particular time.

Definition 33. In this context we understand by "member of a society" a person who has been socially assigned a recognizable social status in that society by virtue of either inheritance, acquisition, or accomplishment. There are degrees of membership in a society.

Definition 34. By "foreigners" we understand strangers physically present in a state territory who—by virtue of their descent from a people identified with another country—are, on principle, excluded from membership in the host society, so that the normal system of distributing social rewards valid in that society does not apply to them.

Proposition 40. As long as population elements that differ ethnically from the national core are socially defined as foreigners, their differential treatment remains relatively unproblematical.

Resident foreigners have a chance of being granted qualified and eventually full membership. Their integration in the host society proceeds as the limited membership status, assigned to them at first, is replaced by an increasingly comprehensive membership status. When the membership status of erstwhile foreigners has become indistinguishable from that of the charter members, they have become absorbed in the host society.

Definition 35. "Social category" refers to aggregates of social statuses whose occupants are differentiated on account of socially relevant criteria (such as sex, age, marital status, income, or ethnicity), but they need not interact specifically with each other.
Definition 36. By "ethnics" we understand individuals who are socially assigned to a particular ethnic category.
Definition 37. "Ethnic category" refers to population elements of a nation-state who differ ethnically from the national core, and who—on account of this—are assigned a qualified membership status in the national society.

Proposition 41. Ethnic categorization tends to modulate the operation of the general rules governing the distribution of social rewards in the host society.
Proposition 42. People assigned to the same social category tend to associate with each other and to form specific status groups. People socially assigned to one category of ethnics tend to form particular ethnic groups.

Definition 38. By "ethnic group" we understand a subgroup of a modern society formed by ethnics whose differential treatment in the distribution of social rewards is causing specific social problems.

Proposition 43. An ethnic group comes into being when a particular ethnic category develops its specific set of institutions.

B. THE INTEGRATION OF ETHNICS INTO MODERN SOCIETY

Definition 39. By "integration of ethnics" we understand the processes by which the practical problems involved in the status assignment of ethnics are minimized.

The integration of ethnics into a modern society may take place either directly through the assimilation of individuals or indirectly through the mediation of ethnic groups.

Definition 40. The direct integration of an individual ethnic through assimilation has been completed when he is being assigned social status on equal terms with the charter members of the host society. Ethnic differentiation has therefore become irrelevant for social action orientation.
Definition 41. The indirect integration of ethnics has been accomplished collectively when an ethnic group and the host society have become so adjusted to

each other that the continued presence of the ethnic group in the host society is no more felt to constitute a social problem by either party.

The processes leading to the absorption of an ethnic group include (1) the dissolution of the ethnic group through the loss of its members, and (2) their individual absorption by the host society.

*Definition 42. By the "absorption" of an individual ethnic, we understand his complete integration in the host society through assimilation. The absorption of ethnics is the ultimate goal of the processes of nationalization (cf. **Definition 16**).*

a. Assimilation

Definition 43. By "assimilation" we understand the processes by which an individual ethnic is assigned increasing degrees of membership status in the host society until he becomes indistinguishable from charter members with regard to the distribution of social rewards.

For analytical purposes we can distinguish four interdependent levels of assimilation: aspiration, acceptance, transculturation, and association:

1. The assimilation of an ethnic progresses to the extent that he aspires to membership and is accepted by the host society.
2. An ethnic cannot be considered to be a full member unless the host society is both his group of aspiration and assignation. Ethnics have been absorbed by the host society (1) when they identify themselves, and are identified by their associates, exclusively with the host society, and (2) when they share a sense of solidarity with the charter members of the host society.
3. The transculturation of ethnics involves (1) their sharing with the charter members of the host society the essential elements of its culture, and (2) their having acquired the skills and qualifications that are expected of charter members in analogous situations.
4. Assimilation progresses to the extent to which restrictions are reduced upon the factual association of ethnics with charter members of the host society because of differences of ethnic origin.

Discrimination of ethnics occurs when they actually aspire to a particular right or benefit usually granted to charter members of the host society, and if they meet the requirements to be expected of charter members in analogous situations (in accordance with the generally accepted rules governing the distribution of social rewards in the host society), but are nevertheless prevented from competing with other aspirants on equal terms.

Definition 44. By "discrimination" we understand the illegitimate differentiation of members of a society in the distribution of social rewards.

Proposition 44. Processes of assimilation on the level of aspiration, acceptance, transculturation, and association tend to proceed at different rates. At any given time, assimilation may have progressed to different degrees on different levels. These differences give rise to typical problems of integration, which are resolved as the processes of assimilation converge.

Proposition 45. Membership of an ethnic group tends to decrease the extent and rate of assimilation of individual ethnics. The latter stages of assimilation are concommitant with the loss of membership of the ethnic group.

Proposition 46. The more effectively individual assimilation is blocked, the greater are the chances that ethnic groups are formed and maintained.

Proposition 47. The dissolution of an ethnic group becomes more likely when the chances are increased for its members to assimilate.

Proposition 48. The chances of an ethnic group to maintain itself are increased whenever separate institutions or organizations are at its disposal through which social controls can be exerted, enculturation accomplished, and contact with the host society reduced.

Proposition 49. The maintenance/dissolution of an ethnic group depends on the number and kind of social relationships that it is able to monopolize. This varies with the type of ethnic group.

b. Formation, Maintenance, and Dissolution of Ethnic Groups

The laws governing the formation, maintenance, and dissolution of ethnic groups differ according to their type.

Members of ethnic groups participate indirectly in the host society by virtue of their direct participation in the ethnic group. They may also participate directly in the host society in some dimensions. In this respect a basic distinction exists between primary and secondary ethnic groups.

Definition 45. By "secondary ethnic groups" we understand subgroups of the host society whose members participate directly in the host society in some dimensions, particularly on the level of commercium, but indirectly through the mediation of the ethnic group in other dimensions, particularly on the level of commensalitas and connubium.

By "connubium" we understand the readiness to establish affinal kinship ties through intermarriage.

By "commensalitas" we understand convivial activities, such as visiting, eating and feasting together, and associating for games and entertainment. Commensalitas also presents the most important opportunity for connubium.

By "commercium" we understand a purely functional cooperation for practical ends as pertaining mainly to the economic sphere.

Proposition 50. When individual ethnics suffer deprivations because of differential treatment in the host society, they tend to form and maintain secondary ethnic groups to compensate for these deprivations. To this end, separate institutions are created and upheld that exercise partial social control over the group members.

Definition 46. *By "primary ethnic groups" we understand viable corporate units which, after their transfer from the parent to the host society, tend to continue to function in the host society as closed subsocieties able to satisfy the basic social needs of their members. Participation of their members in the host society accordingly tends to be indirect in all dimensions.*

Proposition 51. Whereas migration is more likely to lead to the formation of secondary ethnic groups, annexation or collective transfer are more likely to lead to the emergence of primary ethnic groups.

> Annexation or collective transfers are likely to involve viable regional subsocieties. Under modern conditions, migration generally involves individuals or small groups.
> "Collective transfer" implies that viable societal units are being transferred bodily together with their property and institutions and/or, upon arrival, are permitted to reconstitute themselves as a viable subsociety after their traditional pattern.

Proposition 52. Economic factors tend to be of paramount importance in the formation of secondary ethnic groups; political factors in the formation of primary ethnic groups.

Proposition 53a. The formation of secondary ethnic groups begins with the creation of new institutions of their own. As they have no chance of achieving political autonomy and/or economic autarchy, their efforts are concentrated on satisfying the more intimate social needs of their members and on establishing social controls with regard to commensalitas and connubium.

Proposition 53b. Primary ethnic groups start the process of adaptation to the host society with a full set of institutions necessary for their functioning as a viable subsociety. They tend to lose these gradually, first in the political sphere then in the economic sphere.

Proposition 54a. Members of secondary ethnic groups are not so much concerned with the preservation of their separate collective identity as with the enjoyment of social rewards on equal terms with the charter members of the host society (cf. **Proposition 36**).

Proposition 54b. Members of a primary ethnic group are mainly concerned with its maintenance, which depends on the strength of separate institutions and on the preservation of distinctive characteristics. They do not clamor for equal treatment with the majority of the host society, but for the recognition of their separate collective identity (cf. **Proposition 35**).

Proposition 55. Members of a secondary ethnic group are more inclined to assimilate to the host society than are members of a primary ethnic group, unless they are prevented from doing so by lack of acceptance on the part of the natives and/or by social controls that the ethnic group is exercising over its members.

Proposition 56. The social controls exercised by secondary ethnic groups over their members tend to be more feeble than those exercised by primary ethnic groups because of the more comprehensive institutions at their disposal.

Proposition 57. The removal of disabilities, economic advancement, and the toleration of cultural and/or somatic distinction tend to promote the dissolution of secondary ethnic groups. In the case of primary ethnic groups, however, provisions for the prevention of discrimination tend to increase the probability of their maintenance.

Proposition 58. Secondary ethnic groups are likely to be formed and maintained under the following conditions:

1. There must be sufficient opportunities of communication between dispersed ethnics and sufficient freedom of movement to permit the concentration of a relatively large number of them in one locality.
2. Communication with the parent society must be restricted, and the chance of returning home must be limited, so that the ethnics can find satisfaction of their basic needs only within the host society.
3. The economy and institutional framework of the host society must be sufficiently elastic to accommodate considerable numbers of ethnics in one locality, and to permit them to function as a segmental subgroup of the host society.
4. The wider the area of participation in a secondary ethnic group becomes as compared with the area of participation in the host society, the greater is the likelihood of group maintenance. This is especially true if participation in the ethnic group is extended to the level of commercium.
5. The chances that a secondary ethnic group is able to maintain itself are increased whenever separate institutions and organizations through which social controls can be exerted are at its disposal.
6. The spread of the ideas of nationalism among ethnics tends to increase their awareness of identity and sense of solidarity, and thus to increase the likelihood of secondary-ethnic-group formation.

Proposition 59. Differences in the ethnic origin and in the specific culture content of the host and the parent society have no significant influence on secondary ethnic-group formation.

Proposition 60. Whenever members of a parent society are transferred as individuals into a host society that is not isomorphic with the parent society with regard to essential elements of the social structure, then—under the conditions of free mobility—the transferees will not be able to take their place directly in the host society, and will therefore tend to form a secondary ethnic group.

Proposition 61. Whenever members of a parent society are transferred as individuals into a host society that is isomorphic with the parent society with regard to essential elements of the social structure, then—under the condition of free mobility—the individuals transferred will be able to take their place directly in the host society, and thus no secondary ethnic group will be formed.

Proposition 62. Whenever large groups of transferees are being subjected to special regulations by the authorities of the host society, limiting their free mobility, the probability increases that they will form separate ethnic or pseudoethnic groups, even if they would otherwise be able to take their place directly in the host society.

Proposition 63. After a secondary ethnic group has been dissolved by virtue of losing its members to the host society, the former members and/or their descendants still tend to be socially identified with the ethnic group. The dissolution of a secondary ethnic group thus is most likely to lead to its transformation into an ethnic category.

Proposition 64. Provided that the host society is of the modern type, lack of isomorphism most commonly occurs when the parent society is of the agrarian type.

> Migrants to urban industrial sections of a modern society are frequently recruited from rural sections either of their own society or of other modern societies that have preserved a premodern, usually agrarian character, or from foreign countries of the agrarian type.

Proposition 65. The resistance put up by agrarian societies (or agrarian sections of modern societies) against the pressures of nationalization and industrialization that threaten their traditional way of life tends to be expressed in ethnic terms.

Proposition 66. Industrialism tends to weaken ethnic solidarities; agrarianism tends to preserve them, in case of conflict even to strengthen them.

Proposition 67. The chances that transferees are integrated collectively into the host society and that they form a relatively closed and self-sufficient ethnic group increase if their parent society is of the agrarian type.

Proposition 68. Primary ethnic groups tend to emerge and to maintain themselves in a modern society under the following conditions:

1. Parent and host society are sufficiently heteromorphic with regard to essential elements of their structure, so that their respective members can be readily differentiated in ethnic terms.
2. The population transferred from the parent society and/or significant sections of the host society resist the direct integration of the transferees into the host society.
3. The population transferred is sufficiently large and cohesive to be able to reconstitute itself as a relatively closed and viable subsociety of the host society.
4. The host society has the capacity (mainly economic) of accommodating the new addition to its population as a segregated collectivity within its boundaries.

Proposition 69. A primary ethnic group is most likely to emerge and maintain itself if it is of the agrarian type; for in this case, it is in the best position of satisfying basic economic and social needs with a minimum of reliance on the resources of the host society (cf. **Proposition 66**).

Proposition 70. Partial acculturation to the host society need not bring about the dissolution of a primary ethnic group—in fact, it may help to maintain it—as long as the traits of the host culture are accepted collectively.

Proposition 71. Primary ethnic groups are less likely to be dissolved through loss of members than to be transformed into secondary ethnic groups through the gradual loss of separate institutions, and especially through the modernization of the economy.

Proposition 72. When primary ethnic groups are granted generous protection against the loss of their demographic and cultural substance, they are likely to give up resistance against economic change and thereby to expose themselves to those processes that transform them into secondary ethnic groups.

c. Race as a Social Category

The concept of race is a device of classifying human populations exhibiting typical combinations of somatic properties transmitted from one generation to the next. Social differentiation on the basis of race serves to establish genealogical distance between groups of ethnic units and to estimate the ethnic descent of individuals. The ideology of racism represents race as a dominant principle of societal organization. According to it, race takes the place of ethnicity as a criterion in the differential distribution of social rewards.

Definition 46. By "racism" we understand a social doctrine that assumes a constant relationship of social with mental and cultural characteristics, and which provides a legitimization of the discrimination against people exhibiting particular somatic characteristics by postulating their innate inferiority.

Racism has its roots in a particular historical situation. It tends to emerge in modern societies when, in the wake of colonialism, slave trade, and large-scale intercontinental migrations, distant populations, which differ markedly with regard to their genetically transmitted somatic appearance, are brought into close contact with each other.

Definition 47. In a sociological context, "race" refers to a typical combination of genetically transmitted somatic properties on the basis of which human populations in contact with each other are socially differentiated.

Definition 48. By "racial category (group)" we understand an ethnic category (group) that is socially identified on the basis of racial differences from the host society.

Proposition 73. When transferees to the host society, even if they are ethnically heterogeneous, exhibit common racial characteristics that are markedly different from those exhibited by other components of the host society, especially its national core, there is a tendency that they are socially defined as belonging to one racial category.

Proposition 74. If tranferees to the host society, exhibiting common racial characteristics in marked contrast to those of the host society, have the same inherited status of servitude, they are likely to be socially defined as one racial category, especially if their actual ethnic origin is not known.

Proposition 75. Individual ethnics socially assigned to one racial category tend to form racial groups corresponding to the type of secondary ethnic groups.

Proposition 76. Subsocieties that exhibit racial characteristics in marked contrast to those of the host society, and which have been transferred collectively to the host society, tend to form racial groups corresponding to the type of primary ethnic groups.

Proposition 77. As long as miscegenation remains largely blocked, the absorption of racial groups is much less likely than that of other ethnic groups because, in contrast to culturally transmitted characteristics, genetically transmitted characteristics are not subject to deliberate change.

IV. INTERETHNIC RELATIONS IN COLONIAL AND POSTCOLONIAL SITUATIONS

The propositions advanced in sections II and III are, on principle, also applicable to colonial/postcolonial situations. In the following section the correspondence will be specified, and supplementary propositions that apply more typically to colonial/postcolonial situations will be introduced.

A. BASIC CONCEPTS AND PROPOSITIONS

Definition 49. *"Colonial situation" refers to the typical results of colonization.*
Definition 50. *"Postcolonial situation" refers to the typical changes in a colonial situation that occur after a colony has been politically emancipated from the metropolis.*

> A distant (transoceanic) territory is transformed into a colony when a metropolitan country extends political and/or economic control so as to exploit its natural and/or human resources for the benefit of the metropolis, without integrating its autochthonous population into the metropolitan society.

Definition 51. *By "colony" we understand a distant territory over whose inhabitants a metropolitan society exercises social control, interfering significantly with their social system without however integrating them into the metropolitan social system.*
Definition 52a. *By "colonization" we understand the processes of social change approximating the ideal type of a colony.*
Definition 52b. *By "decolonization" we understand the processes of social change by which a colony is transformed into a modern nation-state.*

The processes of colonization/decolonization tend to proceed at different rates in the economic, political and cultural dimension. At one time they may have progressed to different degrees in different dimensions.

Proposition 78. Interethnic relations in colonial/postcolonial situations concern the relationship (1) between the metropolis and the colony, and (2) between the various population elements within the colony.

The important elements of colonial populations include autochtones, metropolitans, half-breeds, detribalized autochthones, and exogenous additions.

Metropolitans either enter a colony as (temporary) representatives of the metropolitan society or establish themselves permanently as settlers.

Definition 54. By "colonial society" we understand the dominant social system that tends to emerge in a colony during the colonial period.

Proposition 79. Interethnic relations in colonial/postcolonial situations differ according to the type of a given colony.

In a settlement colony the settlers seek to deprive the autochthonous societies of their natural resources to exploit these resources directly. In an exploitation colony the metropolitan society, through its representatives, seeks to exploit the natural resources indirectly by compelling the autochthonous societies collectively to yield some of their produce for the benefit of the metropolitan economy.

During the precolonial and the early colonial period, intersocietal relations tend to prevail between the metropolitan society and the autochthonous societies. It is only when a colonial society has been formed that intersocietal relations tend to be replaced by intrasocietal relations between metropolitan representatives, settlers, and autochthones.

Proposition 80. In settlement colonies, the settlers form the colonial society. The autochthonous societies are likely to be destroyed, expelled, or confined to reservations. Detribalized autochthones and/or half-breeds tend to be integrated into the colonial society as the lowest status category of servile labor. **Proposition 81.** In exploitation colonies, metropolitans and detribalized autochthones tend to be integrated into the colonial society. As decolonization progresses, the metropolitans tend to be excluded from the national society emerging from the (former) colonial society.

Different types of exploitation and, accordingly, of colonial situations, may prevail in different regions and sections of one and the same colony.

Colonization involves the (partial) transculturation of the autochthones through education, indoctrination, and mass communication.

Proposition 82. Colonial education serves to adjust the autochthones to the colonial administration, economy, and social structure.

B. RACE AS A PRINCIPLE OF SOCIAL DIFFERENTIATION

Colonies tend to be situated at a great distance from the metropolis. Consequently, metropolitan and autochthonous populations are likely to exhibit marked racial differences.

Proposition 83. The basic differentiation between the metropolitans and the ethnically heterogeneous autochthones in colonies is likely to be symbolized in racial terms.

Proposition 84a. The more vital the confrontation between settlers and autochthones in a (former) settlement colony becomes, the more likely it is that the saliency of race increases and the saliency of ethnicity decreases.

Proposition 84b. The less vital the confrontation becomes, the more likely it is that the saliency of ethnic differentiation among the settlers increases.

Proposition 85. In colonial/postcolonial situations, status assignment according to race serves the metropolitans to uphold and legitimize economic exploitation and political domination.

Proposition 86. Race is likely to be accepted as a criterion of social differentiation by detribalized autochthones in (former) exploitation colonies for the purpose of self-identification and of activating solidarity in nation-building.

C. NATION-BUILDING AND TRIBALISM

Nation-building generally proceeded by the expansion of centralized state power over preexisting societal units. A nation tends to be preformed by the efforts of a modern state to promote the demotic integration of the state population (cf. II D).

In a colony the modern state is represented by the metropolitan government exercising political control over the autochthonous societies and/or the emerging settler society through the colonial administration. A postcolonial nation tends to be preformed by the colonial policies of the metropolis.

Proposition 87. The demotic integration of autochthones into the colonial society intitiated by the colonial administration tends to be counteracted by the racial differentiation between metropolitans and autochthones.

Definition 55. *"Nation-building" in colonial/postcolonial situations refers to the processes of social change by which the population of a (former) colony (or sections thereof) is integrated into an emerging national society of the demotic type* (cf. *Definition 10*).

Proposition 88. In settlement colonies the colonial society tends to be transformed into a modern nation in accordance with II D, b.

Proposition 89. When settlers become alienated from the metropolitan society, they tend to secede; the colonial society dominated by them is transformed into a new nation.

Proposition 90. During the colonial and postcolonial periods the autochthones tend to be integrated into the colonial (national) society in accordance with III.

Proposition 91. In former exploitation colonies the emerging national society is likely to be formed by detribalized autochthones to the exclusion of the metropolitans.

Definition 56. *"Detribalization" refers to the alienation of autochthones from their parent society and their transfer to the colonial (national) society.*

Definition 57. *"Tribalism" refers to the divisive force of ethnicity in postcolonial nation-building* (cf. **Proposition 17**), *as well as to the resistance of autochthonous societies against nationalization in former exploitation colonies.*

Proposition 92. In the process of decolonization the colonial society tends to become the nucleus of the emerging national society.

Proposition 93. In a former exploitation colony nationalization requires the economic and cultural modernization of the autochthonous societies in order to break down traditional tribal structures and to incorporate mobilized individual tribesmen directly into the emerging national society.

Proposition 94. In the postcolonial period the resistance of autochthonous societies in former exploitation colonies against nationalization tends to be expressed in ethnic terms.

Proposition 95. In former exploitation colonies the national core tends to be identified with one ethnic unit in accordance with **Propositions 30, 31.**

> If there is no one sufficiently dominant ethnic unit, a power struggle between several ethnic units is likely to ensue, causing typical national problems.

Proposition 96. In former exploitation colonies national problems are likely to arise, unless the homogenization and demotic integration of the autochthones has been accomplished by the colonial administration before the ideas of modern nationalism have captured the public mind (cf. *Definition 22* and **Propositions 31, 35**).

Proposition 97. Regional differences or shifts in the distribution of political power and/or economic prosperity in a former exploitation colony are likely to activate latent conflicts between ethnic units; at the same time, economic and political problems are likely to be expressed in ethnic terms.

a. Autochthonous Elites in (Former) Exploitation Colonies

The role of autochthonous elites in nation-building differs according to their type, the principal distinction being that between traditional and modern elites.

Definition 58. By *"traditional elite"* we understand the rulers of autochthonous societies, their kinsfolk and staff.

Definition 59. By *"modern elite"* we understand the autochthones who, on account of their advanced schooling according to metropolitan standards, have attained high positions particularly in politics, administration, education, and business.

Proposition 98. Traditional elites, having a stake in the preservation of the status quo, are likely to uphold ethnic values and to legitimize their own authority in ethnic terms when challenged by a modern elite and/or by the demotic institutions of the nation-state.

Proposition 99. Modern elites are likely to split over the issue of ethnicity under the following conditions.

1. If a modern elite identifies with the postcolonial nation-state and seeks to maintain control over it, the elite is likely to adopt demotic nationalism.
2. If a modern elite identifies with a particular autochthonous society, and if they are entrusted by the traditional elite with key positions in the regional institutions dominated by the autochthonous society, the modern elite is likely to promote modernization within the framework of the autochthonous society, to legitimize their own authority in ethnic terms, to oppose the centralizing and homogenizing tendencies of the modern elite that is identified with the nation-state, and to adopt ethnic nationalism.

D. FORMATION OF ETHNIC GROUPS

In colonial/postcolonial situations autochthones migrating from traditional rural to modern urban areas tend to form ethnic groups in accordance with III.

Proposition 100. When autochthones are transferred from their parent society to the colonial society and/or to the postcolonial society, they tend to form secondary ethnic groups in accordance with **Propositions 43, 50, 53a, 60, 64.**

Proposition 101. The parent society of autochthones who form an ethnic group in the colonial/national society, need not be coextensive with one particular autochthonous society, but it may also be either a subunit of such a society or a combination of several autochthonous societies that are ethnically related.

Proposition 102. Autochthones who have migrated across international boundary lines are likely to form ethnic groups on the basis of their country of origin.

Proposition 103. An autochthonous society that has become modernized and collectively integrated into a postcolonial national society but is not identified with its national core tends to be transformed into a primary ethnic group (cf. **Proposition 68**).

Selected Bibliography

In addition to the References of individual chapters, supplementary readings, which either are of major theoretical significance or contain pertinent information on parallel cases not explicitly treated in this volume, are listed below for further consultation. With a few exceptions only books published since 1960 are included. More extended lists of pertinent literature will be found in Banton, 1967; Berry, 1958; Blalock, 1967; Deutsch and Merritt, 1970; Kuper and Smith, 1969; Lemberg, 1964; Schermerhorn, 1970; Simpson and Yinger, 1965; Smith, 1971; Synder, 1954; van den Berghe, 1967, as cited below.

Agyeman, Dominic Kofi, *Erziehung und Nationwerdung in Ghana: Eine Untersuchung der Beziehung zwischen europäischem Erziehungswesen und nationaler Integration in einem ehemaligen Kolonialgebiet*. Munich doctoral dissertation, 1973.

Alba, Victor, *Nationalists Without Nations: The Oligarchy Versus the People in Latin America*. New York: Frederick A. Praeger, 1968.

Almond, Gabriel A., and James S. Coleman (eds.), *The Politics of the Developing Areas*. Princeton, N.J.: Princeton University Press, 1960.

Allsworth, Edward (ed.), *Soviet Nationality Problems*. New York: Columbia University Press, 1971.

———, *The Nationality Question in Soviet Central Asia*. New York: Frederick A. Praeger, 1973.

Apter, David Ernest, *Some Conceptual Approaches to the Study of Modernization*. Englewood Cliffs, N.J.: Prentice-Hall, Inc., 1968.

Aumüller, Ingeborg, *Zum Problem der "Nationwerdung" in Sansibar*. Munich doctoral dissertation, 1972.

Balandier, Georges, *Sociologie actuelle de l'Afrique Noire: Dynamique sociale en Afrique centrale*. (2me éd., mise à jour et augm.). Paris: Presses Universitaires de France, 1963.

———, *Anthropologie Politique*. Paris: Presses Universitaires de France, 1967.

Banton, Michael, *White and Coloured: The Behaviour of British People Towards Coloured Immigrants*. London: Jonathan Cape, 1959.

———, *Race Relations*. London: Tavistock Publications Ltd., 1967.

Barth, Fredrik (ed.), *Ethnic Groups and Boundaries: The Social Organization of Cultural Difference*. Boston: Little, Brown & Co., 1969.

Bastide, Roger, *Formes élémentaires de la Stratification Sociale*. Paris: Centre de documentation universitaire, 1965.

Beckers, Gerhard, *Religiöse Faktoren in der Entwicklung der südafrikanischen Rassen-frage: Ein Beitrag zur Rolle des Kalvinismus in kolonialen Situationen.* Munich doctoral dissertation. München: Wilhelm Fink Verlag, 1969.

Behrendt, Richard F., "Der Nationalstaat: Universales Entwicklungsorgan?," in *Soziale Strategie für Entwicklungsländer,* ed. Richard F. Behrendt. Frankfurt: S. Fischer Verlag, 1965, pp. 331–450.

Beltrán, Gonzalo Aguirre, *El Proceso de Aculturacion.* Problemas Cientificos y Filosoficos 3. Mexico: Universidad Nacional Autonoma de Mexico, 1957.

Bendix, R., *Nation-Building and Citizenship: Studies of Our Changing Social Order.* New York: John Wiley & Sons, 1964.

Benedict, Burton, *Mauritius: Problems of a Plural Society.* London: Pall Mall, 1965.

Berry, Brewton, *Race and Ethnic Relations* (2nd ed.). Boston: Houghton Mifflin Company, 1958.

Bettelheim, Bruno, and Morris Janowitz, *Social Change and Prejudice.* New York: The Free Press of Glencoe, 1964.

Black, C. E., *The Dynamics of Modernization: A Study in Comparative History.* New York: Harper & Row, 1966.

Blalock, Hubert M., Jr., *Toward a Theory of Minority-Group Relations.* New York: John Wiley & Sons, 1967.

Blumer, Herbert, "Industrialization and Race Relations," in: *Industrialization and Race Relations, a Symposium,* ed. Guy Hunter, New York: Oxford University Press, 1965, pp. 220–253.

———, "Race Prejudice as a Sense of Group Position," in: *Race Relations, Problems and Theory,* eds. J. Masuoka and P. Valien. Chapel Hill: University of North Carolina Press, 1961.

Borrie, W. D., et al., *The Cultural Integration of Immigrants,* A Survey based upon the Papers and Proceedings of the Unesco Conference held in Havana, April 1959. Paris: UNESCO, 1959.

Bromley, Yu. (ed.), *Soviet Ethnology and Anthropology Today.* The Hague: Mouton & Co., 1974.

———, "The Term *Ethnos* and its Definition," in Yu. Bromley (ed.), *Soviet Ethnology and Anthropology Today.* The Hague: Mouton & Co., 1974.

Bühl, Walter L., *Evolution und Revolution: Konstruktionsprinzipien einer Theorie des Gesellschaftswandels angesichts der Dritten Welt: Eine wissenssoziologische und wissenshaftstheoretische Kritik der symmetrischen Soziologie.* München: Wilhelm Goldmann Verlag, 1970.

Camerjan, I., and S. L. Bonin, *Equality of Rights between Races and Nationalities in the USSR.* Paris: UNESCO, 1962.

Carter, Gwendolen Margaret (ed.), *National Unity and Regionalism in Eight African States: Nigeria, Niger, the Congo, Gabon, Central African Republic, Chad, Uganda, Ethiopia.* Ithaca, N.Y.: Cornell University Press, 1966.

Choi, Dharom P. (ed.), *Portraits of a Minority: Asians in East Africa.* New York: Oxford University Press, 1966.

Cohen, Roland, and John Middleton, *From Tribe to Nation:* Scranton: Chandler, 1970.

Coleman, James S., and Carl G. Rosberg, Jr. (eds.), *Political Parties and National Integration in Tropical Africa.* Berkeley: University of California Press, 1964.

Cox, Oliver Cromwell, *Caste, Clan and Race: A Study in Social Dynamics.* New York: Doubleday and Co., 1948.

de Reuck, Anthony, and Julie Knight (eds.), *Caste and Race: Comparative Approaches.* London: S. and A. Churchill Ltd., 1967.

Depres, Leo (ed.), *Ethnicity and Resource Competition in Plural Societies*. The Hague: Mouton & Co., 1975.

Deutsch, Karl W., and W. J. Foltz (eds.), *Nation-Building*. New York: The Atherton Press, 1963.

——, *Nationalism and Social Communication: An Inquiry into the Foundation of Nationality* (2nd and revised ed.). Cambridge, Mass.: M.I.T. Press, 1969.

——, and Richard L. Merritt, *Nationalism and National Development: An Interdisciplinary Bibliography*. Cambridge, Mass.: M.I.T. Press, 1970.

Doob, Leonhard W., *Communication in Africa: A Search for Boundaries*. New Haven, Conn.: Yale University Press, 1961.

——, *Patriotism and Nationalism: Their Psychological Foundations*. New Haven, Conn.: Yale University Press, 1964.

Eisenstadt, Shmuel, *The Political Systems of Empires: The Rise and Fall of the Historical Bureaucratic Societies*. New York: The Free Press of Glencoe, 1963.

——, "Political Modernization: Some Comparative Notes," *International Journal of Comparative Sociology*, V (1964), pp. 3–24.

——, *Modernization: Protest and Change*. Englewood Cliffs, N.J.: Prentice-Hall, 1966.

Emerson, Rupert, "Nationalism and Political Development," *Journal of Politics*, XXII (1960), pp. 3–28.

——, *From Empire to Nation. The Rise of Self-Assertion of Asian and African Peoples*. Cambridge, Mass.: Harvard University Press, 1960.

Fishman, Joshua A., et al. (eds.), *Language Loyalty in the United States: The Maintenance and Perpetuation of Non-English Mother Tongues by American Ethnic and Religious Groups*. The Hague: Mouton & Co., 1966.

——, *Language Problems of Developing Nations*. New York: John Wiley & Sons, 1968.

Foot, Paul, *Immigration and Race in British Politics*. Baltimore, Md.: Penguin Books Ltd., 1965.

Francis, Emerich K., *Ethnos und Demos: Soziologische Beiträge zur Volkstheorie*. Berlin: Duncker & Humblot, 1965.

Franck, Thomas M., *Race and Nationalism: The Struggle for Power in Rhodesia-Nyasaland*. New York: Fordham University Press, 1960.

Freyre, Gilberto, *The Masters and the Slaves: A Study in the Development of Brazilian Civilization*. New York: Alfred A. Knopf, 1946.

——, *The Mansions and the Shanties: The Making of Modern Brazil*. New York: Alfred A. Knopf, 1963.

Fröhlich, Dieter, *Nationalismus und Nationalstaat in Entwicklungsländern: Probleme und Integration ethnischer Gruppen in Afghanistan* (Afghanische Studien, vol. 3). Meisenheim am Glan: Verlag Anton Hain, 1970.

Geertz, Clifford (ed.), *Old Societies and New States: The Quest for Modernity in Asia and Africa*. New York: The Free Press of Glencoe, 1963.

Girard, Alain, and Jean Stoetzel, *Français et Immigrés: L'attitude française: L'adaption des Italiens et des Polonais*. Paris: Presses Universitaires de France, 1953.

Glass, Ruth, *Newcomers: The West Indians in London*. London: Centre for Urban Studies, and George Allen and Unwin Ltd., 1960.

Glazer, Nathan, and Daniel Patrick Moynihan, *Beyond the Melting Pot: The Negroes, Puerto Ricans, Jews, Italians and Irish of New York City*. Cambridge, Mass.: Harvard University Press, 1963.

Goldhagen, Erich (ed.), *Ethnic Minorities in the Soviet Union*. New York: Frederick A. Praeger, 1968.

Gordon, Milton U., *Assimilation in American Life: The Role of Race, Religion and National Origins*. New York: Oxford University Press, 1964.

Gossett, Thomas F., *Race: The History of an Idea in America*. Dallas, Texas: Southern Methodist University Press, 1963.

Gray, Richard, *The Two Nations: Aspects of the Development of Race Relations in the Rhodesias and Nyasaland*. London: Oxford University Press, 1960.

Greely, Andrew M., *Why Can't They Be Like Us? America's White Ethnic Groups*. New York: Dutton, 1971.

Grunebaum, Gustave E. von, *Modern Islam: The Search for Cultural Identity*. Berkeley: California University Press, 1962 (esp. Chap. 9: "Problems of Muslim Nationalism"; Chap. 10: "Nationalism and Cultural Trends").

Guetzkow, Harald, *Multiple Loyalties: Theoretical Approach to a Problem in International Organization*. Princeton, N.J.: Princeton University Press, 1955.

Gulliver, P. H., *Tradition and Transition in East Africa: Studies of the Tribal Element in the Modern Era*. London: Routledge and Kegan Paul, Ltd., 1969.

Harris, Marvin, *Patterns of Race in the Americas*. New York: Walker & Company, 1964.

Hartz, Louis, et al., *The Founding of New Societies: Studies in the History of the United States, Latin America, South Africa, Canada and Australia*. New York: Harcourt, Brace & World, 1964.

Haug, Marie, "Social and Cultural Pluralism as a Concept of Social System Analysis," *American Journal of Sociology,* LXXIII (1967), pp. 294–304.

Haugen, Einar, "Dialect, Language, Nation," *American Anthropologist,* LXVIII (1966), pp. 922–935.

Heard, Kenneth, *Political Systems in Multi-Racial Societies*. Johannesburg: South African Institute of Race Relations, 1961.

Heller, Hermann, *Staatslehre*. Leiden: A. W. Sigthoff's Uitgeversmaatschappij N. V., 1934.

Hertz, Frederick O., *Nationality in History and Politics: A Psychology and Sociology of Nationalism*. London: Routledge & Kegan Paul Ltd., 1957.

Hobson, John Λ., *Imperialism, a Study*. London: George Allen and Unwin, 1902.

Hodgkin, Thomas, *Nationalism in Colonial Africa*. New York: New York University Press, 1957.

Hunt, Chester, and Lewis Walker, *Ethnic Dynamics*. New York: Dorsey Press, 1974.

Hunter, Guy, *Southeast Asia, Race, Culture and Nation*. New York: Oxford University Press, 1966.

Johnson, Chalmers A., *Peasant Nationalism and Communist Power: The Emergence of Revolutionary China 1937–1945*. Stanford, Calif.: Stanford University Press, 1962.

Johnston, Ruth, *Immigrant Assimilation: A Study of Polish People in Western Australia*. Perth: Peterson Brohenska, 1965.

Koch, Hans, "Die Sowjetunion und das Nationalitätenproblem," in *Der Bolschewismus: Eine Ringvorlesung im Rahmen des "Studium Universale,"* München: Studentenwerk, 1956, pp. 147–195.

Kozlov, V., "On the Concept of Ethnic Community," in Yu. Bromley (ed.), *Soviet Ethnology and Anthropology Today*. The Hague: Mouton and Co., 1974.

Kraus, Michael, *Immigration, The American Mosaic: From Pilgrims to Modern Refugees*. New York: D. van Nostrand Company, 1966.

Kuper, Leo, and M. G. Smith (eds.), *Pluralism in Africa*. Berkeley: University of California Press, 1969.

Kurz, Ursula, "Partielle Anpassung und Kulturkonflikt: Gruppenstruktur und Anpassungsdispositionen in einem italienischen Gastarbeiterlager." Munich doctoral dissertation. *Kölner Zeitschrift für Soziologie und Sozialpsychologie,* XVII (1965), pp. 814–855.

Lemberg, Eugen, *Nationalismus* (2 vols.). Reinbek bei Hamburg: Rowohlt Taschenbuch Verlag, GmbH, 1964.

Le Page, R. B., *The National Language Question: Linguistic Problems of Newly Independent States.* London: Oxford University Press, 1964.

Levy, Marion J., Jr., *Modernization and the Structure of Societies: A Setting for International Affairs.* Princeton, N.J.: Princeton University Press, 1966.

Lewytzkyi, Boris, *Die sowjetische Nationalitätenpolitik nach Stalins Tod (1953–1970).* München: Ukrainische Freie Universität, 1970.

Lieberson, Stanley, "A Societal Theory of Race and Ethnic Relations," *American Sociological Review,* XXVI (1961), pp. 902–910.

Liess, Otto Rudolf, *Sowjetische Nationalitäten-Strategie als Weltpolitisches Konzept* (=Ethnos, vol. 12). Vienna: Wilhelm Braumüller, 1972.

Liu, Shao-ch'i, *Internationalism and Nationalism* (3d ed.). Peking: Foreign Language Press, 1952.

Mair, Lucy, *New Nations.* Chicago: University of Chicago Press, 1963.

Mannoni, O., *Psychologie de la Colonisation.* Paris: Editions du Seuil, 1950. Engl. transl.: *Prospero und Caliban: The Psychology of Colonization* (2nd ed.). New York: Frederick A. Praeger, 1964.

Markov, Walter (ed.), *Lateinamerika zwischen Emanzipation und Imperialismus, 1810–1960.* Berlin: Akademie-Verlag, 1961.

Mason, Philip, *The Birth of a Dilemma: The Conquest and Settlement of Rhodesia.* London: Oxford University Press, 1958.

———, *Prospero's Magic: Some Thoughts on Class and Race.* London: Oxford University Press, 1962.

———, *Patterns of Dominance.* London: Oxford University Press, 1970.

Mayer, Philip, *Townsmen or Tribesmen: Conservativism and the Process of Urbanization.* Cape Town: Oxford University Press, 1961.

Mazrui, Ali A., *Towards a Pax Africana: A Study of Ideology and Ambition.* Chicago, Ill.: Chicago University Press, 1967.

Mehden, Fred R. von der, *Religion and Nationalism in Southeast Asia.* Madison: University of Wisconsin Press, 1963.

———, *Politics of the Developing Nations* (2nd ed.). Englewood Cliffs, N.J.: Prentice-Hall, 1969.

Minogue, K. R., *Nationalism.* London: B. T. Batsford Ltd., 1967.

Mitchell, J. C., *Tribalism and the Plural Society.* London: Oxford University Press, 1960.

Montague, Joel B., Jr., *Class and Nationality: English and American Studies.* New Haven, Conn.: College & University Press, 1963.

Mühlmann, Wilhelm, *Rassen, Ethnien, Kulturen: Moderne Ethnologie.* Neuwied: Hermann Luchterhand Verlag GmbH, 1964.

Nettl, J. P., and Roland Robertson, *International Systems and Modernization of Societies: The Formation of National Goals and Attitudes.* New York: Basic Books, Inc., 1968.

Newman, William M., *American Pluralism: A Study of Minority Groups and Social Theory.* New York: Harper & Row, 1973.

Niebuhr, R., *The Structure of Nations and Empires.* New York: Charles Scribner's Sons, 1959.

Nin, Andrés, *Els Moviments d'emancipació national: l'aspecte teòric i la solucio pràctica de la questió*. Paris: Edicions Catalanes, 1970.

Nuseibeh, Hazem Zaki, *The Ideas of Arab Nationalism* (2nd ed.). Ithaca, N.Y.: Cornell University Press, 1959.

Park, Robert E., *Race and Culture*. Glencoe, Ill.: The Free Press, 1950.

Patterson, Sheila, *Dark Strangers: A Sociological Study of the Absorption of a Recent West Indian Migrant Group in Brixton, South London*. London: Tavistock Publications Ltd., 1963.

Pierson, Donald, *Negroes in Brazil* (new ed.). Carbondale, Ill.: Southern Illinois University Press, 1967.

Price, Charles, *Southern Europeans in Australia*. Melbourne: Oxford University Press, 1963.

Pujana, Luis, *Kapitalistische Industrialisierung und Baskischer Nationalismus: Eine Untersuchung über die wirtschaftlichen Bedingungen der Baskischen Nationalistischen Partei in Bizcaya, 1893–1937*. Munich doctoral dissertation, 1976.

Pye, Lucian W., *Politics, Personality and Nation Building: Burma's Search for Identity*. New Haven, Conn.: Yale University Press, 1962.

Renier, Gustaaf Johannes, *The Dutch Nation: An Historical Study*. London: George Allen and Unwin Ltd., 1944.

Rex, John, "The Plural Society in Sociological Theory," *British Journal of Sociology*, X (1959), pp. 114–124.

————, and Robert Moore, *Race, Community and Conflict: A Study of Sparkbrook*. London: Oxford University Press, 1967.

Richardson, Alan, "The Assimilation of British Immigrants in Australia," *Human Relations*, X (1957), pp. 157–166.

Richmond, Antony H., *The Colour Problem: A Study of Racial Relations* (rev. ed.). Harmondsworth: Penguin Books Ltd., 1961.

Rogers, Cyril A., and Charles Grantz, *Racial Themes in Southern Rhodesia: The Attitudes and Behavior of the White Population*. New Haven, Conn.: Yale University Press, 1962.

Rose, Arnold M., and Caroline B. Rose (eds.), *Minority Problems: A Textbook on Intergroup Relations*. New York: Harper & Row, 1965.

Rose, Peter Isaak, *The Subject is Race*. New York: Oxford University Press, 1968.

Rotberg, Robert I., *The Rise of Nationalism in Central Africa. The Making of Malawi and Zambia. 1873–1964*. Cambridge, Mass.: Harvard University Press, 1967.

Royal Commission on Bilingualism and Biculturalism, *A Preliminary Report*. Ottawa: Queen's Printer, 1965.

Russell, Peter (ed.), *Nationalism in Canada*. Toronto: McGraw-Hill Company of Canada, 1966.

Rustow, Dankwart A., *A World of Nations: Problems of Political Modernization*. Washington, D.C.: The Brookings Institution, 1967.

Sharabi, Hisham B., *Nationalism and Revolution in the Arab World*. Princeton: D. van Nostrand Company, 1966.

Shibutani, Tamotsu, and Kian M. Kwan, *Ethnic Stratification: A Comparative Approach*. New York: Macmillan, 1965.

Silvert, K. H. (ed.), *Expectant Peoples: Nationalism and Development*. New York: Random House, 1963.

Simpson, George E., and J. Milton Yinger, *Racial and Cultural Minorities: An Analysis of Prejudice and Discrimination*. (3rd ed.). New York: Harper & Row, 1965.

Sithole, Ndabaningi, *African Nationalism*. Cape Town: Oxford University Press, 1959.

Smal'-Stockyi, Roman, *The Captive Nations: Nationalism of the Non-Russian Nations in the Soviet Union*. New York: Bookman Associates, 1960.

Smiley, Donald V., *The Canadian Political Nationality*. London: Methuen Publications, 1967.

Smith, Anthony D., *Theories of Nationalism*. London: Gerald Duckworth & Co. Ltd., 1971.

Snyder, Louis L., *The New Nationalism*. Ithaca, N.Y.: Cornell University Press, 1968.

————, *The Meaning of Nationalism*. New York: Greenwood Press, 1954 (reprinted: 1968).

Sulzbach, Walter, *Imperialismus and Nationalbewußtsein*. Frankfurt: Europäische Verlagsanstalt, 1959.

————, "Zur Definition und Psychologie von "Nation" und "Nationalbewußtsein," *Politische Vierteljahresschrift*, III (1962), pp. 139–158.

Symmons-Symonolewicz, K., "Nationalist Movements: An Attempt at a Comparative Typology," *Comparative Studies in Society and History*, VII, (1965), pp. 221–300.

Schapera, Isaak, *Government and Politics in Tribal Societies*. London: C. A. Watts and Co. Ltd., 1956.

Schechtmann, Joseph B., *The Refugee in the World: Displacement and Integration*. New York: A. S. Barnes, 1963.

Schermerhorn, R. A., *These Our People: Minorities in American Culture*. Boston, Mass.: D. C. Heath, 1949.

————, *Comparative Ethnic Relations: A Framework for Theory and Research*. New York: Random House, 1970.

Taft, Ronald, *From Stranger to Citizen: A Survey of Studies of Immigrant Assimilation in Western Australia*. London: Tavistock Publications Ltd., (1966).

Tannenbaum, Frank, *Slave and Citizen: The Negroes in the Americas*. New York: Alfred A. Knopf, 1947.

Thompson, Edgar T., and Everett C. Hughes (eds.), *Race: Individual and Collective Behavior*. Glencoe, Ill.: The Free Press, 1958.

Tömmel, Sieglinde, *Nationwerdung und Nationalliteratur: Politische und Literarische Entwicklung in Belgien, 1830–1890*. Munich doctoral dissertation, 1972.

Tumin, Melvin M., *Caste in a Peasant Society: A Case Study in the Dynamics of Caste*. Princeton, J.J.: Princeton University Press, 1952.

Veiter, Theodor, *Das Recht der Volksgruppen und Sprachminderheiten in Österreich*. Part I: Volk, Volksgruppe, Nation: Theoretische Grundlegung. Wien: Wilhelm Braumüller, Universitäts-Verlagsbuchhandlung GmbH, 1966.

Verweg-Janker, H., and P. O. M. Brackel, *The Assimilation and Integration of Pre- and Postwar Refugees in the Netherlands*. The Hague: Martinus Nijhoff, 1957.

Wagley, Charles, and Marvin Harris, *Minorities in the New World: Six Case Studies*. New York: Columbia University Press, 1958.

Wallerstein, Immanuel (ed.), *Social Change: The Colonial Situation*. New York: John Wiley & Sons, 1966.

Walter, Paul A. F., Jr., *Race and Culture Relations*. New York: McGraw-Hill, 1952.

Wenskus, Reinhard, *Stammesbildung und Verfassung: Das Werden der frühmittelalterlichen Gentes*. Köln: Hermann Böhlau Verlag, 1961.

Wertheim, W. F., *Het Rassenproblem: De Ondergang van sen Mythe*. Den Haag: Albani, 1949.

————, *Indonesian Society in Transition: A Study of Social Change* (2nd ed.). The Hague: W. von Hoeve Ltd., 1959.

Westie, Frank R., "Race and Ethnic Relations," in *Handbook of Modern Sociology,* ed. Robert E. L. Faris. Chicago: Rand McNally, 1964, pp. 576–618.

Whitaker, Arthur Preston, *Nationalism in Latin America, Past and Present.* Gainesville, Fla.: University of Florida Press, 1962.

———, and David C. Jordan, *Nationalism in Contemporary Latin America.* New York: The Free Press of Glencoe, 1966.

Williams, Robin M., "Racial and Cultural Relations," in *Review of Sociology, Analysis of a Decade,* ed. Joseph B. Gittler. New York: John Wiley & Sons, 1957, pp. 423–464.

Worsley, Peter, *The Third World.* London: Weisenfeld and Nicolson, 1964.

Van den Berghe, Pierre Louis, *Race and Racism: A Comparative Perspective.* New York: John Wiley & Sons, 1967.

———, *Race and Ethnicity: Essays in Comparative Sociology.* New York: Basic Books, 1970.

Van der Zanden, James W., *American Minority Relations: The Sociology of Race and Ethnic Groups.* New York: The Ronald Press, 1963.

Yin, Robert K. (ed.), *Race, Creed, Color, or National Origin: A Reader on Racial and Ethnic Indentities in American Society.* Itasca, Ill.: F. E. Peacock Publ., 1973.

Yetman, Norman R., and C. Hoy Steele, *Majority and Minority: The Dynamics of Racial and Ethnic Relations.* Boston, Mass.: Allyn & Bacon, 1971.

Ziegler, Heinz O., *Die moderne Nation: Ein Beitrag zur politischen Soziologie.* Tübingen: J. C. B. Mohr (Paul Siebeck), 1931.

Znaniecki, Florian, *Modern Nationalities.* Urbana: University of Illinois Press, 1952.

Zubaida, Sami (ed.), *Race and Racialism.* London: Tavistock Publications Ltd., 1970.

Zubrzycki, Jerzy, *Settlers of Latrobe Valley: A Sociological Study of Immigrants in the Brown Coal Industry in Australia.* Canberra: Australian National University Press, 1965.

Index

Names of authors listed in the Selected Bibliography have not been indexed

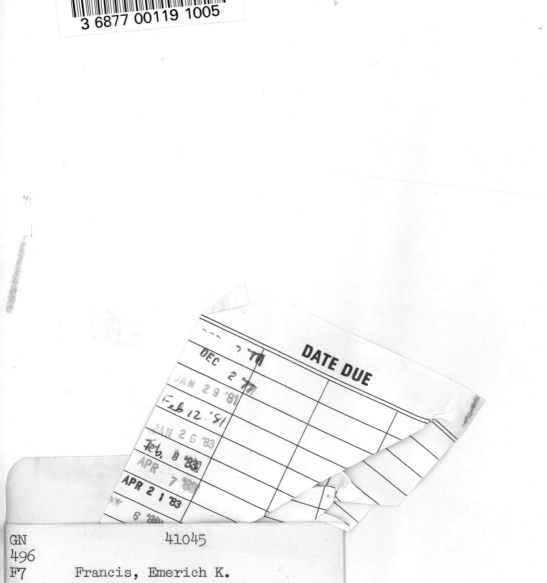